INTRODUCING
The Old Testament

JOHN DRANE

LION

Published by
Lion Publishing plc
Sandy Lane West, Oxford, England
ISBN 0 7459 1349 0

First edition 1987
10 9 8 7 6

A catalogue record for this book is available
from the British Library

Printed and bound in Slovenia

INTRODUCING
THE OLD TESTAMENT

John Drane's introductions to both Old and New Testaments have received wide acclaim: half a million copies have been printed around the world in over fifteen languages. The Old Testament material has now been revised for this new volume: with its awareness of current scholarship, faithfulness to the text and to historical detail, this book will be stimulating and informative for both the individual reader and schools and colleges.

To David and Pat Alexander

Contents

Chapter 1. Introducing the Old Testament

Section One: The Old Testament Story

Chapter 2. The founding of the nation

Chapter 3. A land flowing with milk and honey

Chapter 4. A king like the other nations

Chapter 5. The two kingdoms

Chapter 6. Judah and Jerusalem

Chapter 7. Dashed hopes and new horizons

Chapter 8. The challenge of a new age

Section Two: The Old Testament Faith

Chapter 9. The living God

Chapter 10. God and the world

Chapter 11. God and his people

Chapter 12. Worshipping God

Chapter 13. The Old and the New

Foreword

Of all the literature that has come to us from the world's ancient civilizations, none is as fascinating – or as provocative – as the Hebrew Bible. It is highly esteemed by three of the world's great religions – Islam, Judaism, and Christianity – and yet to many people it seems perplexing to read, and difficult to understand.

So how can we make sense of its contents in a way that says something to people living at the end of the twentieth century? Ever since the Enlightenment, generations of experts have tried to answer that question in relation to the needs of their own day. A hundred years ago, scientific study of the Old Testament was in its infancy, and pioneering thinkers then produced many theories that have not stood the test of time. But they also emphasized that, if we are to understand the books of the Hebrew Bible at all, then we must begin by asking what they meant when they were originally written.

How did they relate to the needs and aspirations of their authors and their original readers? And what can an understanding of other cultures of the time tell us about the ancient nation of Israel? With the passage of time, many new discoveries have come to light which have helped to give more precise answers to some of these questions. Thanks to the work of archaeologists, and to insights from soci logical analysis, we now have a more complete picture than ever before of the world in which the Old Testament books took shape. We can understand more comprehensively the hopes and fears of people in that ancient world, and as a result it is easier to see how their books were related to the ongoing concerns of everyday life.

This introductory guide to the Old Testament takes full account of all these developments. In order to set out the issues as clearly as possible, the book is divided into two main sections. The first deals with the historical context of the Old Testament, and also investigates the origins and literary connections of its various parts. This is an indispensable first stage for understanding the religious message of the Old Testament – and that is what forms the subject of the second part of the book. These two sections began life as two separate books, *The Old Testament Story*, and *Old Testament Faith*. But they naturally belong together, and have been revised at several points for this new combined edition.

This book will provide a reliable guide to some of the present concerns of Old Testament scholars. As such, university and seminary faculty and students will find it a helpful and comprehensive introduction to serious study of the subject. Schools and colleges will also find it contains invaluable resource materials – generally printed in special boxes, so as not to distract the reader from the clarity of the main text.

Ordinary readers will also want to use it in their own homes. Along with its companion volume, *Introducing the New Testament*, it is an invaluable aid to discovering what the Bible says, and what it might mean for life in our own generation.

ROMANIA

ITALY

Ø Rome

YUGOSLAVIA

BULGARIA

△ Mt Vesuvius

ALBANIA

Istanbul ⊙

Thessalonica ●   Philippi ●

GREECE

△
Mt
Olympus

SICILY

TURK

Izmir ⊙

Corinth ⊙   Athens ⊙

● Ephesus

● Colossa

MALTA

GREEKS
Height of power: 3rd and
2nd centuries BC. Alexander
the Great brought the
Eastern Mediterranean
under Greek rule

Aegean Sea

RHODES

Mediterranean Sea

CRETE

Alexandria ⊙

EGYPT

Cairo

EGYPTIANS
Height of power: 3000-100
BC. Egypt was the great
southern power in the time
of the Old Testament,
although it suffered periods
of weakness

Memphis ●

■ Fertile Crescent

● Ancient city names

○ Modern city names

⊙ Bible names still in use today

| 0 | 100 | 200 | 300 | 400 | 500 miles |

| 0 | 200 | 400 | 600 | 800 kilometres |

River Nile

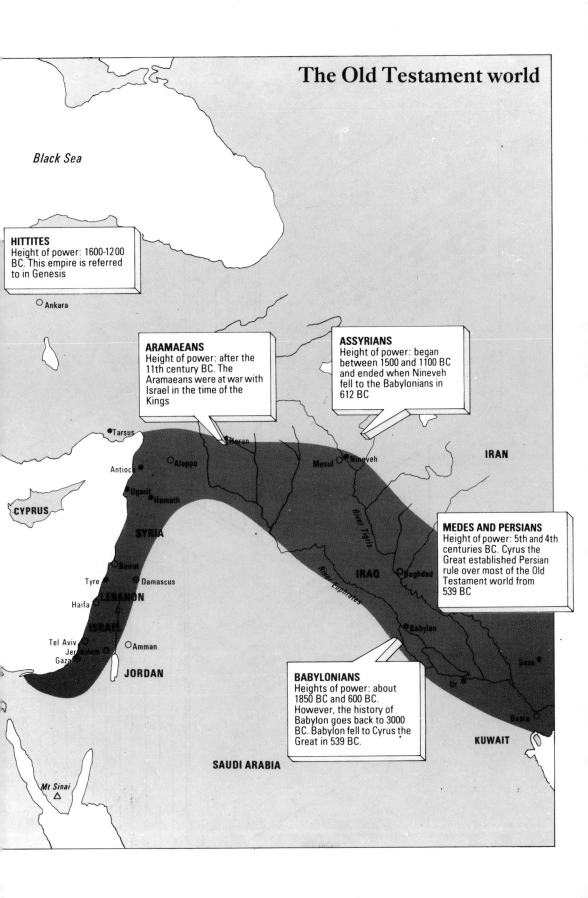

The Old Testament world

Black Sea

HITTITES
Height of power: 1600-1200 BC. This empire is referred to in Genesis

○ Ankara

ARAMAEANS
Height of power: after the 11th century BC. The Aramaeans were at war with Israel in the time of the Kings

ASSYRIANS
Height of power: began between 1500 and 1100 BC and ended when Nineveh fell to the Babylonians in 612 BC

●Tarsus

Haran

Mesul ●Nineveh

IRAN

Antioch ●

○Aleppo

●Ugarit
●Hamath

CYPRUS

SYRIA

MEDES AND PERSIANS
Height of power: 5th and 4th centuries BC. Cyrus the Great established Persian rule over most of the Old Testament world from 539 BC

River Tigris

●Beirut

Tyre ● ○Damascus

Haifa ● **LEBANON**

IRAQ ○Baghdad

River Euphrates

●Babylon

Tel Aviv ● **ISRAEL**

Jerusalem ● ○Amman

Gaza ●

Susa ●

Ur ●

JORDAN

BABYLONIANS
Heights of power: about 1850 BC and 600 BC. However, the history of Babylon goes back to 3000 BC. Babylon fell to Cyrus the Great in 539 BC.

Basra ●

KUWAIT

SAUDI ARABIA

Mt Sinai
△

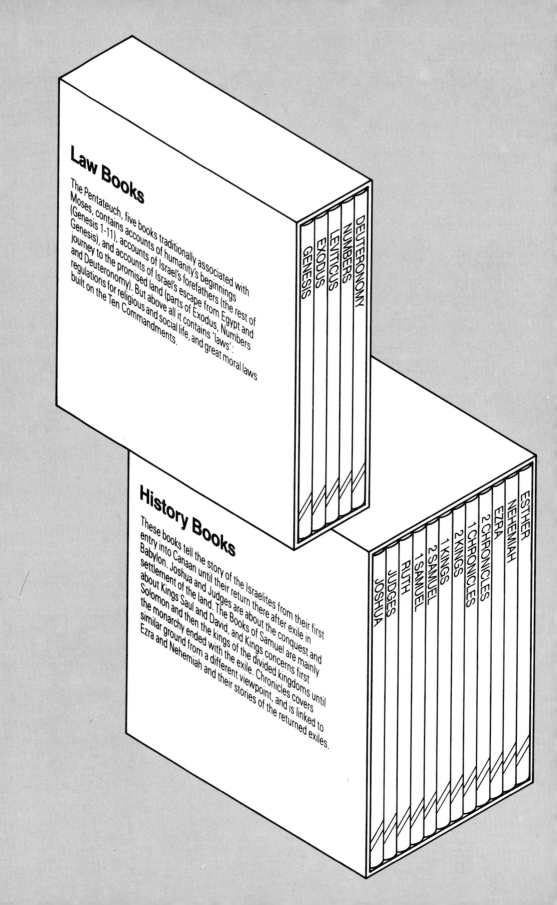

Law Books

The Pentateuch, five books traditionally associated with Moses, contains accounts of humanity's beginnings (Genesis 1-11), accounts of Israel's forefathers (the rest of Genesis), and accounts of Israel's escape from Egypt and journey to the promised land (parts of Exodus, Numbers and Deuteronomy). But above all it contains 'laws': regulations for religious and social life, and great moral laws built on the Ten Commandments.

GENESIS
EXODUS
LEVITICUS
NUMBERS
DEUTERONOMY

History Books

These books tell the story of the Israelites from their first entry into Canaan until their return there after exile in Babylon. Joshua and Judges are about the conquest and settlement of the land. The Books of Samuel are mainly about Kings Saul and David, and Kings concerns first Solomon and then the kings of the divided kingdoms until the monarchy ended with the exile. Chronicles covers similar ground from a different viewpoint, and is linked to Ezra and Nehemiah and their stories of the returned exiles.

JOSHUA
JUDGES
RUTH
1 SAMUEL
2 SAMUEL
1 KINGS
2 KINGS
1 CHRONICLES
2 CHRONICLES
EZRA
NEHEMIAH
ESTHER

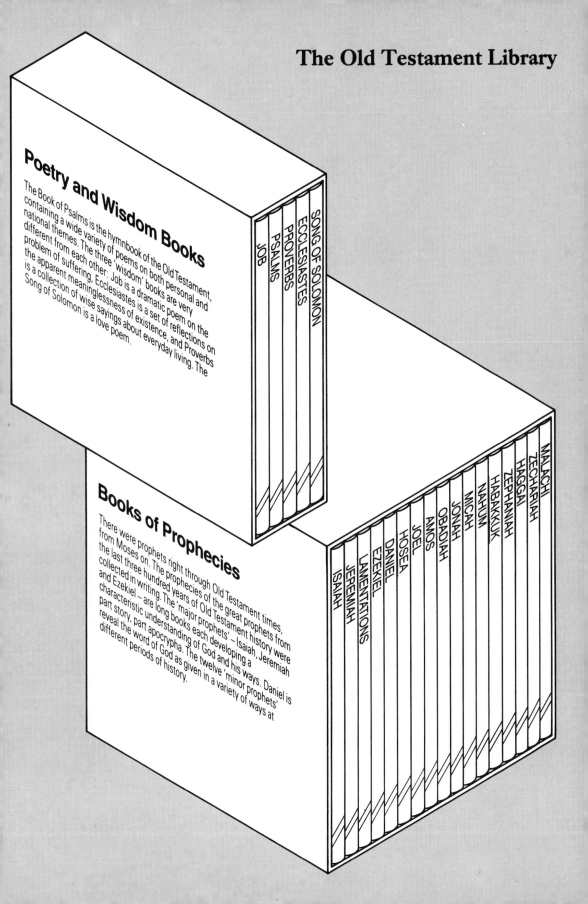

The Old Testament Library

Poetry and Wisdom Books

The Book of Psalms is the hymnbook of the Old Testament, containing a wide variety of poems on both personal and national themes. The three 'wisdom' books are very different from each other: Job is a dramatic poem on the problem of suffering, Ecclesiastes is a set of reflections on the apparent meaninglessness of existence, and Proverbs is a collection of wise sayings about everyday living. The Song of Solomon is a love poem.

JOB
PSALMS
PROVERBS
ECCLESIASTES
SONG OF SOLOMON

Books of Prophecies

There were prophets right through Old Testament times, from Moses on. The prophecies of the great prophets from the last three hundred years of Old Testament history were collected in writing. The 'major prophets' – Isaiah, Jeremiah and Ezekiel – are long books each developing a characteristic understanding of God and his ways. Daniel is part story, part apocrypha. The twelve 'minor prophets' reveal the word of God as given in a variety of ways at different periods of history.

ISAIAH
JEREMIAH
LAMENTATIONS
EZEKIEL
DANIEL
HOSEA
JOEL
AMOS
OBADIAH
JONAH
MICAH
NAHUM
HABAKKUK
ZEPHANIAH
HAGGAI
ZECHARIAH
MALACHI

1 Introducing the Old Testament

THE OLD Testament is one of the great classics of world literature. There can be few other books that are so old and yet still read by so many people. Though its stories happened long ago and in unfamiliar places, we are still fascinated by them today. For in its pages we have the rich literary treasures of a whole nation: the ancient people of Israel. Its story begins in the Stone Age and ends in the world of the first Christians. The most recent parts are over 2,000 years old, while the origins of its earliest works are lost forever in the mists of antiquity. But its unique combination of epic stories, history, reflective philosophy, poetry, and political commentary is held together with all the elements of adventure, excitement and suspense that we might expect from a modern thriller. The Old Testament has survived the ravages of time to become in our day the raw material for Hollywood movies on the grand scale, as well as a book to which many people still turn for personal inspiration.

It is, of course, more than just one book. It is a whole library of books – and therein lies its appeal. From the great epic stories of heroes such as Abraham, Moses, Joshua, or David, to the more reflective books such as Job or Ecclesiastes, there is something here for everyone. Enchanting stories of human intrigue and passion stand side by side with philosophical enquiries into the meaning of human life.

Unlikely materials, you may think, from which to construct a coherent collection of literature. But they are perfectly joined together by the fact that they are part of a common story. For the Old Testament writers were convinced that both their books and their nation came into being not just through social, economic, or political pressures, but because of God and his activity. Beyond all the interest of its individual stories, the Old Testament is a deeply religious book. It asserts that this world and all its affairs are not just a haphazard sequence of coincidences: they are in the control of a supreme God. Not a God who is a remote, unknowable divine force, but one with whom men and women can – and do – have personal dealings. This message is set out in the first few pages of the book of Genesis, and it is explained and emphasized many times in what follows.

The story

Genesis 1:1—2:4
Isaiah 44:1—50:11

Genesis 11:31—12:5
Deuteronomy 6:3

The framework of the Old Testament as we know it today makes it clear that this God is the God of the whole world. But as the story unfolds, it also narrows down to tell us how he became a living reality in the life of a particular group of people. What God did for them was conceived on a grand, international scale. In its earliest episodes, it is a story that spans most of the ancient world, beginning with a childless couple – Abraham and Sarah – in the Mesopotamian city of Ur and leading on to a nation in a 'land flowing with milk and honey'.

In between, we have the immortal stories of Isaac, the son of

Genesis 21—27
Genesis 25—35
Genesis 37—50

Abraham and Sarah, of Jacob, and of how his family unwittingly ended up as slaves in Egypt. This was one of the great low points of Israel's early history. But under Moses, a dynamic leader trained in the court of the Egyptian kings, it was to become the central focus of Israel's national consciousness. Generations of later Old Testament writers had no doubt that even this was a part of God's plan for his people. With great insight and sensitivity the prophet Hosea pictures God as a loving father, and Israel as his child: 'When Israel was a child, I loved him and called him out of Egypt as my son . . . I was the one who taught Israel to walk. I took my people up in my arms . . . I drew them to me with affection and love. I picked them up and held them to my cheek; I bent down to

Hosea 11:1—4

them and fed them.' Almost 200 years later, and after many calamities, this conviction was still of central importance: 'When I chose Israel, I made them a promise. I revealed myself to them in Egypt and told them: I am the Lord your God. It was then that I promised to take them out of Egypt and . . . lead them to a land I

Ezekiel 20:5—6

had chosen for them, a rich and fertile land, the finest land of all.'

Escape from Egypt

With their dramatic escape from slavery in Egypt – the event we call the 'exodus' – Israel's destiny began to take shape. But between the exodus and their entry to the land of Canaan, we find the story of God's Law given to Moses at Mt Sinai. As the Old Testament writers thought out the meaning of their nation's experience of God, they always gave his Law a central place. The occasion when the Law was given was a fearful and serious moment: 'the whole of Mount Sinai was covered with smoke, because the Lord had come down on it in fire. The smoke went up like the smoke of a furnace, and all the people trembled

The Old Testament is an exciting book, full of battle and adventure. But it is more than just a story-book. Through it all builds the great theme of the relationship between a people and their God.

Exodus 19:18–19 · violently . . . Moses spoke, and God answered him with thunder.'

As we read the laws of the Old Testament today (contained mostly in the books of Exodus, Leviticus and Numbers), we can easily identify with the fear of ancient Israel. What we find more difficult to understand is the great joy that went with it. For when we read these laws from our own modern perspective, they may seem harsh and unreasonable. But the people of the Old Testament never thought like that. They never regarded the Law as a heavy burden, for they looked back beyond the smoke and fire of Sinai to the events that went before it – and they knew that God's law was very firmly based on his love. Their obedience was the free and loving obedience of those who are grateful for undeserved benefits. It is no coincidence that the Ten Commandments begin not with an instruction, but with a reminder of God's love and goodness: 'I am the Lord your God who brought you out of Egypt, Exodus 20:2 where you were slaves . . . '

In due course, the nomadic way of life that went right back to Abraham himself was replaced by a settled farming life in a new

When they settled in the 'promised land', the Israelites moved from a nomadic life to a settled, agricultural existence.

land. Here, Israel began to ask new questions about their faith in God. So far, they had known the God Yahweh ('the Lord') whom Moses served as a God of the desert. But new questions began to bother them. Did he know how to grow crops? What was his experience in rearing sheep to have many lambs? These may seem rather naive questions, but for these people they were the most important questions of all. Life itself depended on the answers, and the struggle to find those answers dominates the rest of the Old Testament story in one way or another.

For when Israel settled in her new land, other gods and goddesses were already worshipped there – and they had long and apparently successful experience in agricultural matters. So there began a long battle of loyalties between Yahweh, the God of the desert, and the new gods and goddesses of the land of Canaan: Baal, Asherah, Anat, and their accomplices. Israel was tempted to forsake her own God in preference for these others. From the earliest times, there were local heroes like the so-called 'judges' who were prepared to resist such spiritual treason. But as time passed, things went from bad to worse, and the great prophets of the Old Testament protested over and over again that the people of Israel had left their own true God for the worship of false gods.

Decline of the nation   Israel's national fortunes reached their high point in the days of David and Solomon (about 1010-930 BC). But then they began to decline. The great kingdom was partitioned. Then first the northern part collapsed, to be followed in due course by the southern part. Prophets, from the courageous Elijah to the introspective Jeremiah, spoke out in both north and south against the social and political corruption which signalled the decline of the entire nation. Though they spoke in different circumstances, to the people of their own time, they were united in their belief that the people of Israel had come to ruination because of their increasing neglect of the Law of God, and their increasing fondness for the false gods and goddesses of Palestine.

Israel's demise was complete by the year 586 BC, when the capital city of Jerusalem, together with its magnificent buildings, was captured and partly destroyed by the Babylonian king Nebuchadnezzar II. This was a disaster of immense proportions. But once more, out of the ashes of defeat there arose new life. The new leaders of Israel had an even greater vision than their predecessors. For they were convinced that even this new disaster was all a part of God's plan for his people. They set out to re-assess the lessons of the past, and they were quite sure that God would not forget his earlier promises. There would be a new creation and a new exodus on an even greater scale than before. For the whole world would now be the scene of God's renewed activity. Israel would be 'a light

Isaiah 49:6   to the nations – so that all the world may be saved'.

With this, the story has come full circle. It began with Abraham and the promise that through him God would bless many nations – a promise that was challenged from many different directions. Politically and economically, it was always under threat – whether from the Egyptians, the Canaanites, the Assyrians, or the Babylonians. Religiously, it was undermined from within as the people of Israel were tempted to forget the God of their ancestors and turn to the worship of other, more convenient religions – religions which allowed their moral and spiritual responsibility to be left behind in the shrine instead of forming the basis of everyday life in home and market place. But God's intention for his world never failed: 'the holy God of Israel keeps his promises . . . I, the Lord, was there at the beginning, and I, the

Isaiah 49:7; 41:4   Lord, will be there at the end.'

This figure is a Canaanite Baal, or storm god. The struggle against idolatry recurs throughout the Old Testament. Was Israel's Lord just one god among many, or was he the only God?

Understanding the story

It is easy to get a general impression of the Old Testament story. But for many people, this most fascinating of books is also the most puzzling. So how can we make sense of it for ourselves? That is a big question. But for the moment, let us just make a few comments on some of the most distinctive features of the Old Testament and its contents. By doing so, we can suggest a few general principles, which we can then apply in later chapters to the understanding of specific problems.

● Most of us are familiar with the Old Testament as the first half of the Christian Bible. The fact that we call it 'the Old Testament' only serves to emphasize that. For it is 'old' not because it is ancient, but by contrast to the records of the early church which we call 'the New Testament'. Christians believe that these two quite separate writings properly belong together. They have always felt that the events surrounding the origins of the Christian faith were part and parcel of God's dealings with men and women through the ancient nation of Israel, recorded in the Old Testament. But we must never assume that the Old Testament was actually written by Christians, nor that its message is primarily a Christian message. Christians are not the only people who have a special interest in the Old Testament. These books are the sacred writings of the Jewish faith (Judaism), and if we are to make sense of them then we must read them in their own terms. Though Christians may feel that the Old Testament is incomplete without its Christian sequel, we shall never fully understand it if we look at it through exclusively Christian spectacles. This is why many people today prefer not to speak of 'the Old Testament' at all, but rather of 'the Hebrew scriptures' or 'the Hebrew Bible'.

● We must also bear in mind that the Old Testament is quite different in character from a modern book. It is even different from the books that make up the New Testament. All the New Testament books had their origin in the same social and religious context, and on the whole we can be tolerably sure of the identity of their authors, and of the reasons why they wrote. But in the case of the Old Testament, there are very few books for which we can positively identify a particular author or date. The Old Testament is essentially an edited anthology – a collection of writings by different people, and from different ages. Nobody ever sat down to gather the New Testament into one unified collection: it just arose spontaneously from the reading habits of the early church. But somebody *did* set out to edit and organize the books of the Old Testament, to form a coherent account of the life of the nation of Israel. In fact, more than one person did so. The earliest editions of Old Testament materials were probably gathered together during the reigns of David and Solomon. Like any other prosperous nation, the people of Israel began at this time to take a keen interest in the past. By now they had a settled way of life in their own land – a stark contrast with the experiences of their earliest ancestors. They no doubt had their own tribal histories which they preserved and handed on by word of mouth from one generation to another. But they had not written them down. They were more concerned with the problems of daily survival than with creating literary masterpieces. That was left to scribes working in the more leisurely atmosphere of the later royal courts of Israel.

Of course, they could only bring the story up to their own time. What comes later was the work of yet further writers. Much of the Old Testament is associated with the names of the prophets, and many of its books contain their sermons and speeches dealing with various aspects of national life and policy. Parts of the Old

The Old Testament is the Bible of the Jew as well as the Christian. In it he sees the growth of his nation, and all the promises God made to Israel. The difference lies in the two understandings of how these promises are being fulfilled.

Testament history books were doubtless written by those whose outlook was deeply influenced by these prophets. But the final stage in the Old Testament story was reached only after the destruction of the state, which the prophets had so clearly foreseen. As Israel's new leaders began to pick up the scattered pieces of a great legacy, they consciously set out to apply the lessons of the past to their own hopes for the future. And to help do that, they began to collect the whole of Israel's national literature, as well as writing their own assessment of the nation's achievements.

● A further distinguishing mark of the Old Testament is the enormous time span that it covers. Whereas the whole of the New Testament was written in the space of something like sixty or seventy years, the Old Testament story covers many centuries. Even if the story proper only begins with the exodus, that still takes us back 1,200 years before the Christian era – and the Old Testament also contains accounts of things that pre-date even that.

The very earliest parts of the Old Testament take us to a world very different from our own – a world where civilization itself was a relatively recent arrival. Its story begins in modern Iraq, in what the ancients called 'the Fertile Crescent'. This part of the world had witnessed many remarkable developments long before the story of

Facing page: The Old Testament is a structure, put together by a people as its life developed. Our understanding of it is helped enormously if we know how it is made: what the different materials are in which it is built, and what the foundations are.

Israel's history began. Great empires had come and gone, and as early as 3000 BC the Sumerian people living in ancient Mesopotamia had written down their traditional stories and beliefs for the generations that would follow them. One of their great successors was the Babylonian king Hammurabi, whose law code written on clay tablets some 1,700 years BC still survives as a lasting monument to the culture of those ancient times. Many other texts from this ancient world have come to light in recent years – from Nuzi in Iraq, from Ebla·in northern Syria, and from Ras Shamra further south. Then there are the many records and monuments of that other great and ancient civilization centred on the River Nile in Egypt.

By comparison with these empires, the people who wrote the Old Testament were latecomers. The shape of their world was already formed by other nations – and to understand their story fully we need to know something of the story of these other peoples too. For the fortunes of Israel were always inextricably bound up with the manoeuverings of the two super-powers of the day: the one based on the Nile, and the other based on the rivers Tigris and Euphrates. But then the Old Testament takes us beyond even the last of these great empires, for Israel survived longer than them all, and her national literature also documents the period that prepared for the

The nation of Israel came into being in a world where other civilizations were already old. The culture and literature of Babylon, on the River Euphrates, has some points of contact with the Old Testament.

arrival of the next great super-power of world history: the Roman Empire.

It is hardly surprising if we find the Old Testament slightly confusing at times. For its pages cover almost half the history of civilization. The circumstances of the early parts of the story are quite different from the situation we meet in the later parts – and neither bears too much resemblance to the world we know today.

● We can also appreciate something of the Old Testament's distinctive character when we look at its books purely as literature. As we have already seen, it is above all a religious book. It does not set out to give what we might regard as an impartial, independent account of the events it describes. The Old Testament story has

been written for a purpose, and its different parts were used by men and women living at different times to speak to the people of their own generation.

Some have taken this to mean that the Old Testament story is essentially fictional: a kind of moralizing tale that is valuable for whatever lessons it teaches, but which is out of touch with what actually happened. But this attitude is unrealistic. It takes no account of the fact that many events and people mentioned in the Old Testament are also mentioned in the records of other nations of the time. It is also based on a false confidence in our ability to gain access to the 'bare facts' of history. Even today, our knowledge of an event which we did not witness depends very heavily on the perspective of those who did. When we watch a news report on television, the impression we receive depends entirely on the perspective of the camera and the reporter. If the camera had taken its pictures from a different angle, or if the reporter had interviewed different people – still more if we had been there ourselves – our overall assessment of what was taking place may well have been significantly different. Even a documentary programme which tries to see all sides of an issue must eventually reflect the perspective of its writer.

We do not normally regard this as a barrier to understanding. We may wish to make a different judgment ourselves on this or that matter, but we simply take it for granted that to understand any situation fully we need to take account not only of the facts but of

The scrolls of the Law in an Israel synagogue remind us of the high place the Old Testament writings have always held in Judaism. For Jews and Christians see these books as the record of how God revealed himself to humanity.

the outlook of our sources of information. It is the same with the Old Testament. The more clearly we can understand the intentions of those who wrote and handed on these books, the more likely are we to arrive at a useful appreciation of their significance and meaning.

We must remember that these writings are not just one person's assessment of the history of a nation: they are a national archive. The people who wrote and edited these books were themselves a part of that nation and its history. It is not easy for the detached observer to grasp exactly what this means. But we can find a useful analogy in the pictures that medieval artists painted of the life and times of Jesus. The crucifixion was a favourite theme, and there are many great works showing Jesus hanging on a cross between two thieves. But when we look more closely, the people around the crosses often seem somewhat out of place. Instead of Roman soldiers, we see soldiers of the sixteenth century. The people too belong to that age – and the city where the scene takes place is not Jerusalem in AD 33, but Venice or Rome in AD 1500.

When we look at such a picture we do not usually feel that it casts doubt on the reality of the crucifixion of Jesus. Indeed, we may unconsciously follow the artist's example, and pencil in an image of ourselves and our own society. In a way, this is what the writers of the Old Testament story were doing as they depicted their national past. From generation to generation, they knew that the story of Abraham, Moses, and the rest was their own story. They were a

The Old Testament world was different from ours in many ways, and we need to be aware of the differences. But this does not prevent us from applying its teachings to the world of today. We share a common humanity with the people of whom we read.

part of it, because they saw in it the continuing story of God and his dealings with their nation. As a result, they could recognize in the failures and triumphs of the past the realities and the potential of their own age.

The story and the faith

But what of the distinctively religious aspects of the Old Testament books? It is, of course, possible to read the Old Testament and never discover its faith. If we think of religious faith as a collection of carefully articulated systematic beliefs about God and how he relates to every conceivable circumstance of human life and thinking, then we are likely to be disappointed by the Old Testament. It certainly contains nothing comparable to a modern book of systematic theology.

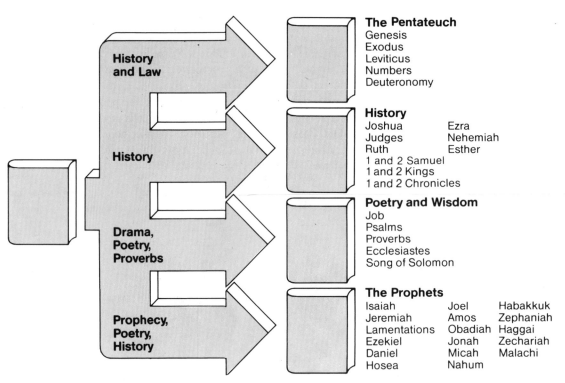

History and Law

History

Drama, Poetry, Proverbs

Prophecy, Poetry, History

The Pentateuch
Genesis
Exodus
Leviticus
Numbers
Deuteronomy

History
Joshua	Ezra
Judges	Nehemiah
Ruth	Esther
1 and 2 Samuel	
1 and 2 Kings	
1 and 2 Chronicles	

Poetry and Wisdom
Job
Psalms
Proverbs
Ecclesiastes
Song of Solomon

The Prophets
Isaiah	Joel	Habakkuk
Jeremiah	Amos	Zephaniah
Lamentations	Obadiah	Haggai
Ezekiel	Jonah	Zechariah
Daniel	Micah	Malachi
Hosea	Nahum	

The library of Old Testament books

So how can we begin to understand the specifically religious dimension of the Old Testament? Where and what is the Old Testament faith? This is one of the more difficult issues for Old Testament scholars today, for a variety of reasons:

● We have already seen that the Old Testament is not a single, unified book. It contains many different types of literature – and together they cover the greater part of 1,000 years in the history of ancient Israel. Because of this it is a good deal easier to identify the faith of various Old Testament authors than it is to discover a comprehensive 'Old Testament faith'. Indeed, many scholars believe that the best we can hope for is to speak of 'the faith of the prophets', or 'the faith of the psalmists', and so on.

● Is the Old Testament a guide to what people should believe, or is it a record of what people in Israel did as a matter of fact believe? As a book of history, it is both of course. But depending on which one we call 'the Old Testament faith', we will obviously reach rather different conclusions. For example, the prophets declared that true worship of God included the way a person behaves in everyday life, not just ritual actions at a shrine. But both prophets and historians make it perfectly clear that this understanding of worship was not shared by the majority of people in ancient Israel. Similar diversity of opinion can be found on many other issues. So from the outset we need to clarify what we are looking for when we talk of the Old Testament faith. Is it the sort of religious beliefs that were generally held in Israel, or are we trying to extract some system of ideal beliefs out of the Old Testament records?

Amos 5:21–24; Micah 6:6–8; Isaiah 1:10–17

● Just to complicate things a little more, we also need to remember that both actual practice and the ideals of people such as the prophets changed from one period of Israel's history to another. Take the question of marriage. By the time of Ezra, towards the end of the Old Testament period, it was assumed that one man would marry one woman. But in earlier times it was the common practice for a man to have several wives, and this practice is never explicitly forbidden anywhere in the Old Testament. The same is true of laws governing things such as food, keeping the sabbath day, or circumcision, all of which were a good deal more important after the time of exile in Babylon than they had been before.

Faith, religion and theology

In view of this complexity, some would say there is no such thing as a comprehensive Old Testament faith. On this view, the best we could hope for would be a carefully researched description of the history of Israelite religion, tracing the ways it developed over many generations. This kind of historical understanding is certainly a vital part of any assessment of the relevance of the Old Testament, and much of this book is taken up with the discussion of questions that will help us to see how the Old Testament faith related to the world in which it developed.

We need to compare it with the religious beliefs and aspirations of other nations of the time, in order to be able to appreciate what made its message distinctive. Moreover, many of those features of the Old Testament that seem strange and unfamiliar to twentieth-century readers were part and parcel of everyday life in the ancient Middle East. Things like sacrifice, and much of the structure of Israelite worship, were common to many different cultural contexts in Old Testament times – and by understanding this context we can often gain invaluable insights into religious themes in the Old Testament itself. Even the language that it uses is at times very similar, if not identical to terms used in other religions of the day – and this, too, can often help us to grasp the full meaning of apparently obscure Old Testament passages.

But, of course, the Old Testament has another context than just the world of ancient Israel. Today, we know it as a part of the Christian Bible – and to understand it as such we need to ask more searching questions that will take us further than just viewing it as part of the religious history of the ancient world. When we approach the Old Testament from a Christian standpoint, we need to move beyond purely historical and literary matters, and ask theological questions too.

How do the religious ideas of the Old Testament relate to the Christian faith as it is explained in the teaching of Jesus and the rest of the New Testament? Is it possible to square the Old Testament's ideas with Christian beliefs? Even many Christians find it hard to think that the description of God in the Old Testament can be reconciled with the message of the New – while in some quarters it is taken for granted that there is an unbridgeable chasm between the ethical perspectives of both parts of the Christian Bible. And what about things like sacrificial worship? To most western Christians today this is frankly offensive. But is it saying something fundamental about God's nature and about true religious belief and practice – or is it a peripheral part of the culture of the day?

These are all big questions. Perhaps too big for us to answer fully in the scope of a book like this. But they are key questions for every Christian reader of the Old Testament. We shall keep coming back to them, especially in the second part of this book. But most of our attention must be focussed on setting the Old Testament faith in its proper social and historical context. Once we have understood it in its own world we have a better chance of applying it sensibly to ours.

Organizing the Old Testament

The Old Testament is a complete library of literature, containing books of many different types. If we were to take them all separately to a modern library, it is certain that they would not all be placed on the same shelf. Some books we instantly recognize as history: Genesis, Joshua, Judges, 1-2 Samuel, 1-2 Kings, 1-2 Chronicles, Ezra and Nehemiah. Others, like Exodus, Leviticus, Numbers and Deuteronomy, are law books, though not the kind a modern lawyer would use. For they contain a mixture of civil and religious laws, as well as some stories that we might more reasonably regard as history. Then there are books of poetry: religious poetry in Psalms and Lamentations, and love poetry in the Song of Solomon. Other Old Testament books contain what we might regard as philosophy. Job, Ecclesiastes and Proverbs deal with some of life's deepest questions – the existence of God or the problem of unjust suffering – as well as offering guidelines for contented living. On top of this there is a wide range of what seem like social and political pamphlets – the books of the prophets – though even these are always written from a religious standpoint. And finally there are a number of books which appeal to different readers in different ways. For some, Ruth, Esther and Jonah look like novels, presenting a distinctive message by means of a fictional story. Others would rather classify them as history – though nevertheless, history with a meaning.

But this is not how the Jews arranged these books. They looked at them in a different way. The order of the books in the Christian Old Testament comes not from the manuscripts of the Hebrew Bible, but from the Greek translation that was made in Egypt sometime before the beginning of the Christian era (the Septuagint). A Hebrew Bible is usually arranged in three separate sections:

● **The Law** This consists of the first five books, from Genesis to Deuteronomy. Genesis, of course, contains nothing at all that we would recognize as 'law'. It is a collection of stories, and at first sight we would expect it to be regarded as some sort of history. But the Old Testament notion of 'law' was much more comprehensive and far-ranging than ours. For us, 'the law' is a set of rules and regulations – a legal code that can be interpreted by lawyers with special training, and applied in a court of law by a judge. It would certainly be unusual for a modern person to agree with one of the poets of ancient Israel who wrote, 'your law is my delight'. But the Hebrew word for 'law' *(Torah)* had a much broader reference than just rules and regulations. It really meant 'guidance' or 'instruction', and in the Old Testament the Law was the place to discover what men and women should believe about God, and what duties he required of them in return. This is why the Torah is closely bound up with the stories of Israel's early history. For it is a basic assumption in the Old Testament that knowing and obeying God is not just a matter of blind obedience to a few religious and moral rules: it is rather a question of experiencing God's concern and love in a personal and social context.

Psalm 119:77

● **The Prophets** The Jews included here books that we would be more likely to call history: Joshua, Judges, 1-2 Samuel, and 1-2 Kings. These they called 'the former prophets', while the rest ('the latter prophets') consisted of those books associated with the names of Isaiah, Jeremiah and Ezekiel ('the major prophets') together with the writings of the twelve other so-called 'minor prophets', Hosea to Malachi. We might find this combination of history and sermons rather unusual. But by calling the history writers 'prophets', the Jews drew attention to the fact that these books were not just simple records of fact. They were interpretations and applications of the meaning of history. All the prophetic works – former and latter – are accounts of how God had spoken to his people Israel. Sometimes he spoke through the events of history. At other times through the words of people. But it was the same God and the same message.

● **The Writings** This is where we find the remaining books. These include the poetry of Psalms, Proverbs and Job, as well as 'the five scrolls' (the Megilloth): Ruth, Song of Solomon, Ecclesiastes, Lamentations, and Esther. These five are different from one another in a literary sense. But they were grouped together because each of them was used at one or other of the Jewish religious festivals: Ruth at Pentecost, Song of Solomon at Passover, Ecclesiastes at Tabernacles, Lamentations to celebrate the destruction of Jerusalem, and Esther at Purim. Finally, the Hebrew Old Testament is completed by the books of Daniel, Ezra, Nehemiah, and Chronicles.

The reason for this unusual arrangement of the books was historical. For the three sections roughly represent the three stages in which the Old Testament was put together. The first part of it to be permanently recorded was the Law, followed by the prophets,

There is more than just history in the books of the Old Testament. They also bear record to a people of creativity, who expressed their joy and their worship in songs and poems of great beauty.

and then much later by the Writings. This is why the books of Ezra, Nehemiah, and Chronicles were included in the final section. We would tend to think of them as history books, and list them alongside the 'former prophets'. But they were written later than that, from the perspective of the age that survived the destruction of Jerusalem in the sixth century BC. The books of Chronicles contain many of the same stories as the books of Samuel and Kings. But they are an analysis of the meaning of those stories, and an application of their lessons to the people of a later generation. By then, both the Law and the Prophets were widely accepted as sacred and important books, and it would not have been possible to make any further additions to their number.

Archaeology and the Old Testament

The Rosetta Stone, found by scholars who accompanied Napoleon's army when he occupied Egypt, is in Greek, in demotic and in ancient Egyptian hieroglyphics. It provided the first clues for understanding ancient Egyptian; the first hieroglyphs were deciphered through distinguishing the name 'Ptolemy' in all three scripts.

If we compare a book on the Old Testament written 100 years ago with one written today, the thing that is most obvious is the radical change that has taken place in our knowledge of the world of the Bible. Last century, study of the Old Testament was largely a literary affair: the text itself was studied in minute detail, and dissected in much the same way as an anatomist might deal with a corpse. But today, Old Testament study is vibrant and living, and is dominated by social and cultural considerations that would have been quite foreign to earlier generations of scholars. One of our major concerns is to see how the Old Testament fits into the world of its day – to analyse its contents not just ideologically, but historically and sociologically. This has all been made possible by the recent explosion of our knowledge of the ancient world. Thanks to the consistent efforts of archaeologists, we now have a better idea than ever before of what it was actually like to live in the world of

the Old Testament. We can appreciate the social and political realities of life in ancient Israel in a new way that has shed untold light on many difficult passages of the Old Testament.

Explorers have always had an interest in the materials left over from earlier civilizations. In the seventeenth century many ancient objects of interest and beauty were taken by such people to their wealthy patrons all over Europe. But it was not until the eighteenth century that anyone took a scientific interest in the subject. The archaeological exploration of Bible lands began when Napoleon's armies invaded Egypt in 1798, taking with them a team of scholars to study the ancient monuments. They made many significant discoveries – not least the Rosetta Stone. This had an inscription in both Greek and Egyptian hieroglyphs, and it enabled scholars to decipher ancient Egyptian for the first time. But it was only at the end of the nineteenth century that truly scientific procedures began to be applied to sites in the Middle East on a widespread scale.

A typical site in Palestine will take the form of a large mound, or *tell*. Many of these sites look just like large hills. perhaps as high as thirty or forty metres, and covered with trees or grass. But under the surface is to be found the ruin of an ancient city. Sometimes cities were built on a natural hill, for that was an easy site to defend. But many of these tells began at ground level, and have been raised to their present height by the normal processes of building over many years. For in the ancient world most buildings were made of mud and wood. When a settlement was either destroyed by an enemy, or just fell into decay, the inhabitants would gather together any available materials that could be re-used, and set to work to build their own town on the ruins of the old. The new level could be as much as two or three metres higher than the one that preceded it. So over many years, the ground level was gradually raised, and the whole mound took on the appearance of a giant cake with many different layers superimposed one on top of the other.

Archaeologists have used a number of basic rules to guide their investigations at sites like this:

● Digging must be done in such a way as to keep separate and distinct the successive strata, or layers, of occupation. The ideal way to do this, of course, would be to start at the top and slice off each layer in turn. But this

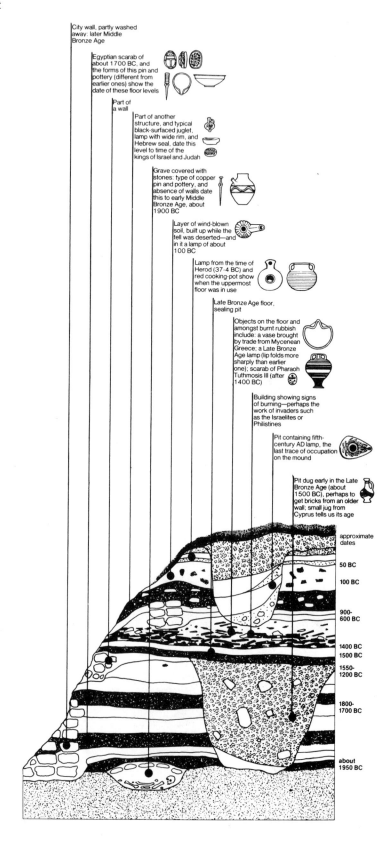

City wall, partly washed away: later Middle Bronze Age

Egyptian scarab of about 1700 BC, and the forms of this pin and pottery (different from earlier ones) show the date of these floor levels

Part of a wall

Part of another structure, and typical black-surfaced juglet, lamp with wide rim, and Hebrew seal, date this level to time of the kings of Israel and Judah

Grave covered with stones: type of copper pin and pottery, and absence of walls date this to early Middle Bronze Age, about 1900 BC

Layer of wind-blown soil, built up while the tell was deserted—and in it a lamp of about 100 BC

Lamp from the time of Herod (37-4 BC) and red cooking-pot show when the uppermost floor was in use

Late Bronze Age floor, sealing pit

Objects on the floor and amongst burnt rubbish include: a vase brought by trade from Mycenean Greece; a Late Bronze Age lamp (lip folds more sharply than earlier one); scarab of Pharaoh Tuthmosis III (after 1400 BC)

Building showing signs of burning—perhaps the work of invaders such as the Israelites or Philistines

Pit containing fifth-century AD lamp, the last trace of occupation on the mound

Pit dug early in the Late Bronze Age (about 1500 BC), perhaps to get bricks from an older wall; small jug from Cyprus tells us its age

approximate dates

50 BC

100 BC

900-600 BC

1400 BC
1500 BC

1550-1200 BC

1800-1700 BC

about 1950 BC

Excavation of a tell

The mound seen here is a 'tell' – the site of ancient Lachish. As archaeologists excavate a section of the tell, they find evidence of the different stages of the town's history.

Great care is required as an archaeological dig progresses. Each fragment of pottery or other artefact has to be catalogued and the level at which it is found must be carefully noted.

would be impractical. It would be too time-consuming, and impossibly expensive. Instead, the archaeologist usually cuts into the mound as we would cut a slice from a cake. This gives access to a cross-section of the mound's contents, and the whole process is called 'stratigraphic excavation'. Its one disadvantage is that the archaeologist may cut his slice at the wrong place in the mound. For instance, the site of the city of Hazor in northern Israel was excavated in 1928 by the famous archaeologist John Garstang. He

concluded that the city was deserted between 1400 and 1200 BC. But thirty years later, the Israeli archaeologist Yigael Yadin dug a trench at a different point on the same mound, and found extensive evidence of people living there at just that period!

● It is vital to have an accurate recording of every level that is excavated, and of every object that is found. Plans must be drawn and photographs taken, because once a layer of the mound is removed, no one can put it back together again. If objects are taken away indiscriminately it is impossible to assess their significance. They must be studied in relation to the precise spot where they are uncovered, and in relation to other things that are found with them.

● Archaeologists must also compare what they find with what others have found in other places. Pottery provides a good example of the importance of this. For every bucketful of significant objects, dozens of bucketsful of pottery are discovered. This is because pottery was always in common use, and it was very easily broken – but it was virtually impossible to destroy completely. Fashions in pottery changed in the ancient world. The size, shape, texture, and decoration varied from time to time, and though some styles were in use for a

A pottery jar, found at the Qumran monastery by the Dead Sea, shows how the pieces were reassembled after excavation.

long time, others were limited to a specific period. So when the archaeologist finds the same types at several different situations it is reasonable to conclude that the layers in which they are found were occupied at about the same time. In fact, pottery is one of the most important clues to the dating of a particular find. It was Sir Flinders Petrie who, at the beginning of the twentieth century, first realized this. By comparing pottery from different sites, and noting its various styles, he evolved what he called a 'Ceramic Index' – a collection of pottery types which could be accurately dated, and which proved an invaluable aid to the work of all subsequent excavators.

But what use is all this to students of the Old Testament?

● It is not very often that archaeologists discover things that have a direct reference to events and people mentioned in the Bible – though there are many examples of this, especially in the records of the Assyrian and Babylonian kings, where we find accounts of some of the events recorded in the Old Testament.

● More often, archaeology helps us to set the Old Testament story in its true context. It is, for example, highly unlikely that any archaeologist will ever find a reference to the story of Abraham. But archaeology has shown that migrations like that of Abraham were taking place all over the Fertile Crescent during the second millenium BC, and that some of the customs mentioned in Genesis were practised at the time.

● Occasionally, the findings of archaeologists can illuminate specific passages in the Old Testament. In 1 Samuel 4, we have the story of how the Philistines captured the ark of the Covenant from Israel in a fierce battle near the town of Shiloh, where the ark was kept. Readers of the Bible had often surmised that Shiloh itself must have

been destroyed at the same time, for when Israel recovered the ark it was not returned there. Now, excavation has shown that Shiloh was indeed destroyed at the time of this incident in the eleventh century BC.

● Archaeology is also often a help in interpreting difficult parts of the Old Testament. For example, Ezekiel mentions three people as examples of great goodness: Daniel, Noah, and Job (Ezekiel 14:14). But it is curious that the prophet should place Daniel, believed to be one of his own contemporaries, in the same class as two ancient figures. Archaeology has shown that he was probably not talking of the hero of the Old Testament book of Daniel at all, but of an ancient king renowned for his religion and justice, who is mentioned in religious poems from Assyria to Canaan, some of which are nearly 1,000 years older than Ezekiel.

● Sometimes the findings of archaeology seem as if they cannot be reconciled with what we read in the Old Testament. For example, according to Joshua 7:1 — 8:29 a great battle was fought at a place called Ai during the conquest of Canaan. But according to the archaeologists, the town was destroyed about 2400 BC. It was not rebuilt, and so there was no town there in the days of Joshua. Of course, there could be many reasons for this apparent discrepancy. It may be that archaeologists have wrongly identified the site. It would not be the first time such a mistake had been made, but it seems unlikely in this instance. It is also possible that other discoveries could be made in the future which would resolve the problem. Or it could be, as many think, that we should look for the meaning of the Old Testament story elsewhere – perhaps in the fact that the word Ai in Hebrew means just 'the ruin'. Whatever the full explanation may be, we must take seriously both the Old Testament picture and the evidence of archaeology.

Section One
The Old Testament Story

2 The founding of the nation

Genesis 11:27—50:26
Exodus 1:1—20:21

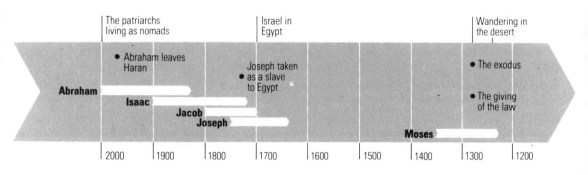

As FAR back as we can see, the people of ancient Israel had a well developed sense of their own history. They were especially conscious of the fact that their own way of life and religion was different from that of their neighbours. The main concern of the average Canaanite farmer was with agriculture. His religious worship was designed to ensure that nothing would interrupt the cycle of the seasons from one year to another. But for Israel the key to understanding life's mysteries was not to be found in the world of nature, but in the unique and unrepeatable facts of history.

Like other farmers, the people of ancient Israel celebrated the annual gathering of the harvest in a religious ceremony. But as they

The annual harvest celebration was a time when the Israelites remembered their indebtedness to God. They gave the 'firstfruits' of the harvest as an offering to maintain the worship of the Lord.

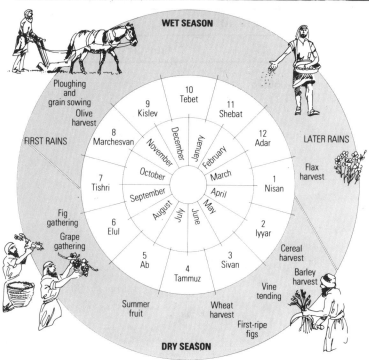

Israel's agricultural year

did so, their thoughts centred not on ploughing, sowing, and reaping, but on the history of their nation. When they presented a part of the harvest to God, they affirmed their deepest convictions about life in words that are still central to the faith of Jewish people, even today:

'My ancestor was a wandering Aramean . . . who took his family to Egypt to live. They were few in number when they went there, but they became a large and powerful nation. The Egyptians treated us harshly and forced us to work as slaves. Then we cried out for help to the Lord, the God of our ancestors. He heard us and saw our suffering, hardship, and misery. By his great power and strength he rescued us from Egypt. He worked miracles and wonders, and caused terrifying things to happen. He brought us here and gave us this rich and fertile land. So now I bring to the Lord the first part of the harvest that he has given me.'

Deuteronomy 26:5–10

No other statement sums up so eloquently what the Old Testament is all about. In just a few words, this ancient creed recalls the most important elements in the Old Testament story. It tells how God had rescued a disorganized group of slaves from Egypt and made them a nation in their own right; and how in response to his undeserved goodness, the people had given him their worship and obedience.

The early Old Testament stories are of people on the move, owning no land, taking with them their flocks and all they possessed.

Beginnings

Genesis 32:28

The 'wandering Aramean' is occasionally given the name 'Israel', but he is more often referred to in the Old Testament as Jacob. It is not clear why he should have been referred to as an Aramean. The Arameans became prominent in the Old Testament world only after about the eleventh century BC, when they established a small empire based in Syria. But like the Israelites, who also emerged as a nation at about the same time, their origins must go further back than that. Throughout the third millenium BC (3000-2000 BC) large numbers of wandering nomads were constantly moving from the deserts of Arabia into the territories controlled by the great civilization centred on Mesopotamia. The reasons for these movements are complex and uncertain. In about 2000 BC, groups of people whom the Babylonians called 'Ammuru' ('westerners'), and who are perhaps to be associated with the Amorites of the Old Testament, moved in and established their own culture in Babylon itself, at Mari, and elsewhere. Many scholars believe that some of these people were the ancestors not only of the Arameans and the Canaanites, but also of Israel itself. The Old Testament certainly suggests there was some close ethnic connection between all these groups, and its earliest stories of Jacob's ancestors are set in this kind of context.

The founding fathers

Genesis 11:27–30

Joshua 24:2

Genesis 15:7;
Isaiah 29:22

Exodus 20:2;
Deuteronomy 5:6

Genesis 24:4

The story begins with Abraham – or, rather, with his father Terah – in the city of Ur, at the very heart of the ancient Mesopotamian civilization. For some undisclosed reason, they left their home city and the whole family moved some 560 miles/900km north-west to the city of Haran. Both these towns had important shrines for the worship of the moon god Sin, and some Old Testament scholars have supposed that this could explain their move. There is certainly plenty of evidence to suggest that Abraham and his family were originally pagans. In a later account of the same events, a much later leader of Israel began his story of Israel's history with the words, 'Long ago your ancestors lived on the other side of the River Euphrates and worshipped other gods.' Some have discerned traces of some sort of religious argument, which involved Abraham's family in physical danger. For in a rather obscure passage, Abraham is said to have been 'rescued' from Ur in just the same way as the escaping slaves were later 'rescued' (the same Hebrew word) from Egypt.

On the other hand, it is only in the Hebrew manuscripts of Genesis 11 that the city of Ur is mentioned at all. The Greek (Septuagint) version places Abraham's original home 'in the land of the Chaldeans', and this could have been a place much nearer to Haran in North Syria than to Ur near the Persian Gulf. Other stories certainly suggest that Abraham's roots were much stronger in Haran than in Ur, for when he later sent for a wife for his son Isaac, he told his servant to go to 'the country where I was born', and this turns out to be not Ur, but the area around Haran.

Despite this close connection with the town of Haran and its

Haran, in modern Syria. From here Abraham, the 'wandering Aramean', moved south into Canaan.

Genesis 12:10–20

surrounding countryside, Abraham did not make his permanent home there. The book of Genesis tells how he moved on to a different part of the Fertile Crescent – this time travelling another 450 miles/700km south-west, into the land of Palestine. There he lived a wandering life, moving about from place to place to find enough grazing for his flocks and food for his family. This was the only way newcomers could settle, for the best parts of the land were already occupied by both farmers and city dwellers. This explains why Abraham moved mostly in the south of the country, just to the north and west of the Dead Sea. This was not the best land, but it had many areas suitable for grazing, and only a small resident population. When the grass was exhausted there, nomadic tribes could move either to an oasis like Beersheba or into the fields adjoining towns like Shechem and Hebron. No doubt this land was farmed by the Canaanites, but they probably allowed nomads like Abraham to put their animals onto it after the crops had been gathered. But even this source of supply was uncertain, and like many other nomadic peoples of the period, Abraham was forced to move as far afield as Egypt at a time of severe famine.

Were the patriarchs real people?

The nomadic existence described in Genesis fits in well with the picture archaeologists have built up of the life of the region in the early part of the second millennium BC.

One of the major preoccupations of Old Testament scholars for the greater part of the twentieth century has been the question of how the patriarchs Abraham, Isaac, and Jacob can be related to the history of Old Testament times. A hundred years ago, the stories were commonly regarded either as fiction, or as the vaguely remembered exploits of tribes – even at times of ancient gods or goddesses – personified to become the story of just a few individuals. On this view, the patriarchs could not be regarded as real people, but as representations of various social and religious movements in the millennium before Israel became a nation in the true sense.

As the twentieth century has progressed, however, there has been a marked change of opinion on the subject, largely due to the discoveries of archaeologists. In particular, ancient documents found at the sites of Mari and Nuzi had a far-reaching impact on the study of these stories, and in recent times it has been taken for granted that

the stories of the Hebrew patriarchs not only reflect the existence of real individuals, but their exploits and way of life accurately reflect the conditions of the Middle Bronze Age period (2000–1500 BC). Professor John Bright's judgment is typical: 'We can assert with full confidence that Abraham, Isaac, and Jacob were actual historical individuals ... a part of that migration of seminomadic clans which brought a new population to Palestine the early centuries of the second millennium BC.' A number of pieces of evidence seem to support this claim:

● **The patriarchal names**
Names like Abraham, Isaac, and Jacob have been found in many ancient documents. They seem to have been especially popular among the Amorite peoples living in various parts of northern Mesopotamia about 2000 BC Other names familiar from Genesis – Terah, Nahor, Serug, Benjamin, Levi, Ishmael – were also widely used, though not always relating to people. Sometimes they appear as the names of places. Of course none of the

These Bedouin, bargaining for sheep, have plenty in common with Abraham and Lot, whose shepherds are described as quarrelling over pasture nearly 4,000 years earlier.

some kings (Genesis 14). But it is impossible to identify the kings mentioned in the Old Testament with any known rulers, though their names are typical of the time. There is, however, plenty of evidence to show that the general wandering existence portrayed in Genesis reflects many aspects of what is known of life in the early part of the second millennium BC. Evidence from both Mari and Egypt shows that many tribes were moving about freely at this time, and the excavation of Canaanite cities has suggested that the details of the patriarchs' journeyings could be authentic. They roam about in the places which could have been available to them at this period – and these were generally not the places where nomads could have found a temporary home in later times.

occurrences of these names outside the Bible actually refers to the people mentioned in the Old Testament. But they show that names of this type were commonly used during the second millennium BC.

● **The patriarchal life-style**
The Tale of Sinuhe shows a nomad chief living in much the same way as Abraham, in about 1900 BC. Like Abraham, this chieftain also took part in a war with

● **The patriarchal customs**
The social and legal customs of the patriarchs are often different from those of later Israel. For example, in Leviticus 18:18 a man is forbidden to be married to two sisters at once – but Jacob was (Genesis 29:15–30). Abraham himself married his half-sister Sarah (Genesis

20:12), though this was also prohibited later (Leviticus 18:9, 11; 20:17; Deuteronomy 27:22). The fact that these anomalies have been preserved in the stories of the patriarchs suggests that the people who wrote them down did not try to assimilate them to the practices of their own day, but handed on authentic traditions as they had received them.

This impression may be confirmed by certain legal documents discovered at Nuzi. For some of the customs described here seem to explain and illuminate otherwise obscure parts of the Old Testament stories. For instance, there is the story of how Abraham's childless wife Sarah presented him with a slave girl by whom to have a child (Genesis 16:1–14). A text from Nuzi explains how in certain marriage contracts a childless wife could be required to provide her husband just such a substitute. Furthermore, if a child was subsequently born to the slave, Nuzi law forbade the expulsion of the slave wife – and perhaps this could explain why Abraham was so reluctant to send away Hagar and Ishmael (Genesis 21:9–13). Another way in which childless couples at Nuzi could ensure the continuation of their family line was by adopting a slave who would take the place of a son. He would then inherit their property – though if a natural son was eventually born, the slave-son would lose his rights. When Abraham expressed a fear that his slave Eliezer would succeed him (Genesis 15:1–4), some such custom could have been in his mind. Other customs associated with the stories of Jacob have also been documented at Nuzi.

Until recently, these have been considered compelling arguments for placing the stories of the patriarchs in the early part of the second millenium BC. There have always been elements of the stories that are difficult to fit into such a context – things like the mention of Philistines (Genesis 21:34; 26:6–22), Chaldeans (Genesis 11:31; 15:7), and camels (Genesis 12:16; 24:35; 30:43; 32:7,15), which were apparently not in widespread use before the twelfth century BC. Scholars like Bright have explained these references as incidental anachronisms introduced unconsciously when the stories were first written down. But this view is now being challenged. It is argued by some that the alleged anachronisms are more basic to the stories than was once thought, and also that the relevance of the 'parallels' from Mari and Nuzi has

been greatly exaggerated. Writing of the story of Abraham, John Van Seters says: 'one cannot use any part of it in an attempt to reconstruct the primitive period of Israelite history'. Instead, he traces the origin of these stories to the time when they were written down, and concludes that they must be essentially a work of fiction. There is much of importance in what he claims, but these two issues are not of equal weight.

The nature of tradition

If a story about events taking place sometime between 2000 and 1200 BC was written down between 1000 and 900 BC, that does not necessarily mean that it is going to be worthless as history. This is especially the case with stories that have been handed on by word of mouth for many generations before being committed to writing. There are many examples of this in more recent times. For instance, when the American Alex Haley set out to trace his ancestors who had been seized from Africa by slave traders, his only sources of information were oral family history. As his book *Roots* shows, not only did he find that this was confirmed again and again by written records: he also discovered that at the appropriate points the oral history of his family in America – and even written documents, where they existed – corresponded in a remarkable way with tribal histories going back for many generations in Africa itself. The existence of so-called anachronisms in the Old Testament does not undermine this general consideration. We have already compared the early Old Testament histories to classical medieval paintings which depict contemporary Europeans in scenes from the Bible, and the fact that a story has been recorded for the benefit of a later age does not make it historically worthless.

The use of parallels

The strongest positive support for the essentially historical character of these stories has been the evidence of Nuzi and Mari. This too has been challenged at a number of points:

● It is rightly pointed out that for such parallels to mean anything, they must come from a time and place with which the Hebrew patriarchs could reasonably be associated. The place is no problem: both Mari and Nuzi are located in areas that play an important part in the Genesis stories. But the date is another question. For it has usually been claimed that these parallels date the patriarchs somewhere between 2000 and 1800 BC. But the Nuzi texts only go back to about 1500–1400 BC. Against this, it has been argued that customs of the sort described do not come from nowhere, and they must have existed long before they were written down. That is probably true, but it does not really take us very far. For they were also in existence long *after* they were written down, and most of the practices to which attention has been drawn were probably carried on throughout the whole period from 2000 to 1200 BC.

● Then there is the fact that the Nuzi materials have often been used very selectively. For example, the childless wife who gave her husband a slave girl was not typical of Nuzi practice in general. The more normal rule would have been to allow the man to find another wife. Some of the other parallels cited by Bright are not entirely representative: indeed, out of more than 300 Nuzi texts dealing with family affairs, less than a half dozen are regularly used to reconstruct a background for the Genesis stories!

● Some Nuzi texts have actually been misinterpreted in the enthusiastic rush to find parallels to the Old Testament. It was at one time claimed that a Nuzi text could explain Rachel's theft of Laban's household gods (Genesis 31:17–21). It was supposed that the possession of them would give her certain rights of inheritance. But it is now clear that the Nuzi 'parallel' does not suggest this at all. Of course, one mistaken parallel does not discount the others, but it does remind us of the difficulties involved in making such comparisons accurately. Part of the difficulty is that the Nuzi texts are legal documents, whereas in Genesis social and legal practices are described only incidentally. In such circumstances, it is all too easy to try to fill in what we perceive as gaps by stretching the external evidence to fit – even when it could be quite irrelevant.

It is clear from all this that some scholars have in the past tried to claim too much, in particular on the question of precise dates for the patriarchs. But it is equally clear that the way of life depicted in these stories in Genesis is quite different from the practices of later Israel, and has some significant similarities to what we know of life in the second millenium BC. Any understanding of the historical setting of Abraham, Isaac and Jacob must account for these features, and for that reason many continue to believe that they preserve for us a broadly accurate account of the activities of those characters whom they describe.

Abraham's journeys

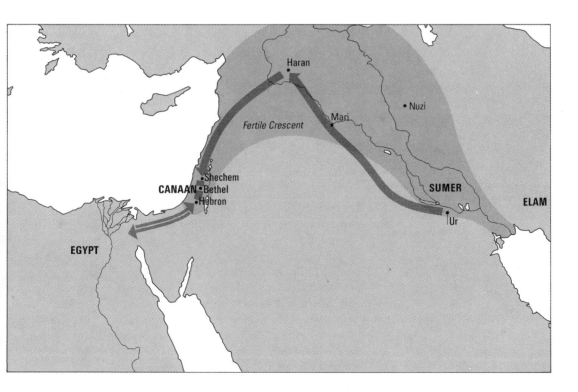

Perhaps the most we can certainly say about the stories of Abraham is that his journeys correspond to population movements that were taking place in the Fertile Crescent throughout the Middle and Late Bronze Ages (roughly 2000–1200 BC). Desert tribes were constantly moving into the Fertile Crescent from outside, and within this green belt individual tribes were always moving from one place to another in search of food and water for themselves and their flocks.

The patriarchs and their God

Genesis 12:1–2

To us, it seems natural to want to relate Abraham to the social world of his day. But the central interest in the book of Genesis is not in the movements of nomads and refugees in the ancient world: it is in Abraham's experience of God. His move from Haran was not determined by political and social issues; it was the result of a challenge and a promise made to him by God. Nor was this an experience unique to Abraham. It was also the common experience of his successors, Isaac and Jacob – not to mention the conviction of the rest of the Old Testament, that a personal experience of God was vital for the very survival of the whole nation of Israel. One of the reasons for our difficulty in placing the patriarchs historically is just the fact that the stories told about them are of a personal nature, telling how they met God in every circumstance of life.

For them, God was not a remote, impersonal force. Nor was he someone who must be approached only through the complex paraphernalia of religious rituals carried out in especially holy places. He was with them in the problems of everyday life, helping them to find wives and to have children, as well as meeting their deepest personal and emotional needs. It is no coincidence that for these people, the most natural way to describe God was to call him

Genesis 26:24; 31:5,29,42,53; 32:9; 46:1,3; 48:15; 49:25; 50:17

'the God of my father'. For he was as close to them as their own family. Indeed, in an important sense, he was a part of their family: he was their leader, and they were his children. Unlike those who had a more settled existence, these wandering tribes were never tempted to think of their faith in God as something that was to be locked up in a temple or some other sacred place. It was something that went with them, and affected their everyday life wherever they happened to be.

This is why many later writers came to regard Abraham as supremely 'a man of faith'. This was the great legacy of the patriarchal generation to the history of Israel. They were deeply committed to the belief that religion was of no value if it could do no more than produce a theology. It must be relevant and meaningful in the normal experiences of human life. In later ages, Israel was often tempted to forget this ideal, and to suppose that their God, like the gods of other nations, would be satisfied with the perfunctory performance of religious rituals. But there were always those who were ready to call the nation back to the ideals that had been held by their ancestors, as they embarked on a new life and a new destiny with only God's promise to guide them.

Down into Egypt

This same theme found its greatest expression in the one event in their early history that Israel was to remember most fondly: the deliverance of a group of their ancestors from slavery in Egypt.

We have now moved beyond the story of Abraham's visit to Egypt, and into the family life of Jacob. As a result of feuding and jealousy among Jacob's family, one of his sons found himself being *Genesis 37* carted off to Egypt as a slave. But after many hardships and misadventures, the unfortunate Joseph was unexpectedly elevated to an important position in Egyptian society. In the face of a great famine, the Egyptian king appointed this foreigner to supervise the rationing of food, and especially to control its distribution to those wandering tribesmen who would inevitably make their way over the *Genesis 39—41* Sinai peninsula to the more prosperous land of Egypt. It was while engaged in this work that, unknown to them, Joseph's brothers (who had sold him into slavery years before) came before him to *Genesis 42* ask for food. After much suspense and heart-searching, Joseph revealed his true identity, and the brothers, along with their aged *Genesis 43—47* father, were reunited and went to live in Egypt.

Their new-found prosperity was, however, only temporary. Jacob, Joseph, and the rest all died in old age, but their descendants were not to have a happy life. A new Egyptian ruler came to power, *Exodus 1:9* and he did not like what he saw: 'These Israelites are so numerous and strong that they are a threat to us'. And so the family of Jacob was gradually reduced to slavery, poverty and despair.

It is tempting to set the story of Joseph in the times of the Hyksos Empire in Egypt. These rulers were themselves non-Egyptians, and

Brick-making in Egypt has not changed all that much from the days of Israel's slavery. But they were reduced to making bricks without straw.

for that reason may have been more likely to appoint an outsider like Joseph to a position of some authority. Much of the detail of the Old Testament story seems to reflect what we know of the life of Egypt at this time – and the 'new king, who knew nothing about Joseph' would perhaps be an appropriate way to describe a native Egyptian king who came to power after the Hyksos had been removed from office.

Exodus 1:8

The Old Testament is not concerned with such details, however. For though this period of slavery was a real evil, it was also the source of great triumph. As the oppression of the slaves grew worse, so the need for deliverance grew stronger – deliverance that was an impossible dream, but that finally became a reality through the dynamic leadership of a man called Moses. Though he had an Egyptian name, and was brought up as an Egyptian, Moses had been born into an Israelite family.

Exodus 2:1–10

No doubt he was familiar with Egyptian life and culture. Some have suggested that he was also deeply influenced by the religion of Egypt. For the Pharaoh Akhen-aten (1369-1353 BC) had been a fanatical worshipper of just one god – the sun god (Aten). Moses too was devoted to the service of just one God. Certainly there are resemblances between Atenism and the religion of Moses. Like the God of Moses, Aten was described as 'the god beside whom there is none other'. The worshippers of Aten also laid heavy emphasis on their god's teaching, just as Moses later emphasized the importance of the Torah. Then again, parts of an ancient psalm in praise of the wonders of creation use similar language to an Egyptian hymn to the sun which was attributed to Akhen-aten. But this use of similar language and imagery in worship is a common thing throughout the ancient world, and in any case many scholars think that the hymn of Akhen-aten was itself based on another piece of religious poetry that originated in Canaan.

Psalm 104

What Moses taught the slaves from Egypt had many distinctive features that are not found in Egyptian religion. Like the patriarchs, Moses knew a God who was not just a manifestation of the world of nature, but the God who controlled the world and who could be known in a personal way. The origin of Moses' faith was found not in Egypt, but in the deserts of the Sinai Peninsula. After dropping out of Egyptian society, Moses had come to this region where he met the leader of a nomadic tribe, a man called Jethro. He married Jethro's daughter, and looked after his sheep. And it was while doing so that he met God. Standing by a bush that was on fire yet seemed as if it would not burn away, Moses was commissioned by 'the God of Abraham, Isaac, and Jacob' to rescue the slaves from Egypt. Moses wanted to see neither the Egyptians nor the slaves. Finally, he agreed to return to Egypt to try to persuade the king to release the slaves. But he also had a message for the slaves themselves. In their affliction, they had not always remembered God. But now they would experience him for themselves in a new and dynamic way. For Moses took with him a fresh and deeper understanding of the nature of God. He was to tell the slaves in

Exodus 3:1–10

Moses married into a nomadic tribe from the Sinai peninsula. In Sinai Moses met the Lord at the 'burning bush', and there he brought the Israelites after the exodus.

Exodus 3:14 Egypt: 'The one who is called I AM has sent me to you'.

The precise meaning of this personal name of God is discussed more fully in Chapter 9. There are many problems about it, and even its pronunciation is not absolutely certain. The word translated 'I am' in our English versions is the Hebrew YHWH, and most scholars think this was probably pronounced as 'Yahweh'.

Yet in spite of much uncertainty, the general significance of this personal name of God is clear: it is a declaration that God is the Lord of the whole world and its history. What he had done in the past, he was doing in the present – and would continue to do in the future.

The great escape

What God did for Israel's ancestors enslaved in Egypt was never in any doubt. It is a central part of Judaism even today. At the annual Passover festival, the Jewish child asks about its meaning, and is given the answer:

'We were Pharaoh's slaves in Egypt, and the Lord our God brought us forth with a mighty hand and an outstretched arm. And if the Holy One, Blessed be He, had not brought our forefathers forth from Egypt, then we, our children, and our children's children would still be slaves in Egypt. So, even though all of us were wise, all of us full of understanding ... we should still be under the commandment to tell the story of the departure from Egypt. And the more one tells the story of the departure from Egypt, the more praiseworthy he is.'

As far back as we can see, we find the deeply held conviction that in these events God himself had been at work on his people's behalf. They had not escaped by their own effort – nor even because they had a specially deserving cause – but simply because the God of whom Moses spoke had, for some inexplicable reason, chosen to deliver them.

The account of that momentous deliverance has all the ingredients of a great epic story. The slaves leave secretly in the middle of the night, only to be pursued by the Egyptian armies. Just as they are about to be caught, trapped by a stretch of water, a way miraculously opens before them and the slaves get to the other side,

The exodus

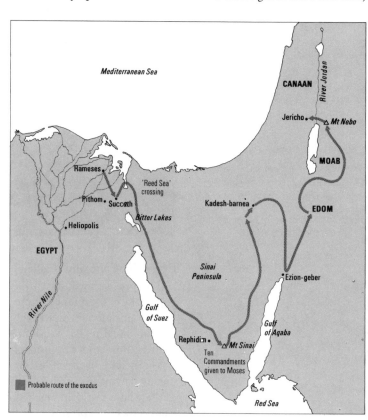

Exodus 12;13:17–22;14—15

Exodus 16—18

while the pursuing army perishes beneath the waves. Guided by Moses, they head out into the Sinai desert, and their first and greatest destination: Mt Sinai.

It is difficult to be clear about the actual location of these events. For example, the crossing of the water has traditionally been located at some point on the Red Sea. But the Old Testament does not make this identification. The Hebrew words speak of a 'sea of reeds', which would be an unlikely name for the Red Sea. In any case, the area of Goshen where the slaves had lived was much further north than the Red Sea, probably near the city of Avaris. It is therefore likely that the water that divided to allow them to cross was somewhere in the region of what is now the Suez Canal.

The location of Mt Sinai is also questionable. Traditionally, it has been located in the south of the Sinai Peninsula, at the site now called Jebel Musa. But since Moses' father-in-law Jethro, who was

Exodus 3:1;18:1–12

Exodus 17:8–16

a Midianite, is clearly associated with this mountain, some have suggested that it should be located much further east, across the Gulf of Aqaba, which was the land of the Midianites. Others have suggested that Sinai should be located at Jebel Hilal, just to the south of Palestine itself, since the escaping slaves had an encounter with Amalekites, who also lived much further north than the traditional site. But it is difficult to locate the mountain by this means. For both these other tribes were nomads themselves, and could have been found almost anywhere. It is certainly not unlikely that a group such as the Old Testament describes would have headed south on their escape from Egypt, rather than going directly east. For the main roads between Egypt and Canaan were patrolled by many Egyptian garrisons, whereas the only activity in the south centred around a number of isolated copper mines.

There need be no reasonable doubt about the facts of the story. The conviction that in this event Israel had her true beginning is deeply embedded in the very oldest parts of the Old Testament – and it is hardly the sort of story that a proud nation would invent to explain their origin, if it had no basis in fact. Like most other nations, Israel later assimilated and accepted people from other racial and cultural backgrounds. But it was to this event – the exodus – and to this group of ancestors, that Israel traced their unique relationship with God.

The covenant

The exodus was just the beginning of the story. For it was not until the escaping slaves reached Mt Sinai that the full impact and meaning of all this became clear to them. Just as the escape from Egypt formed the core of later Israel's national consciousness, so the events at Mt Sinai became the crucial factor in her religious outlook. For here in a solemn convocation, the escaping slaves recognized their debt to Yahweh and to his servant Moses, and

Exodus 19—24

pledged themselves to serve and worship him. The reality of the experience is not to be found in the dramatic descriptions of the presence of God on the holy mountain. The central feature of this awesome occasion was the commitment that God made to Israel, and the obligations that Israel accepted in return.

God's care and concern for his enslaved people had been active even before they were aware of it. The escape from Egypt was the culmination of God's purposes for them. And from this point onwards, the memory of that momentous event and the people's response to it was to dominate the national life of Israel.

This is what the Old Testament means by 'the covenant': an agreement in which the freed slaves were reminded of what God had done for them, and they were called in return to promise to fulfil his commands and to be loyal to him. These commands were essentially moral requirements. Honesty, truth and justice were far more important to Yahweh than the mechanical performance of religious rites. They are summarized in the Ten Commandments and, as we shall suggest in Chapter 11, they formed the basic foundation for the whole of later Israelite society.

Exodus 20:1–17

How old is the covenant?

Readers of the Old Testament have often supposed that the high moral ideals recorded in the book of Exodus and elsewhere are too sophisticated to have originated in the primitive age of Moses. The great German Old Testament scholar of the nineteenth century, Julius Wellhausen, argued that the whole idea of the covenant as it is portrayed here was a reading-back into Israelite history of the circumstances and beliefs of a much later age – the age of the great prophets.

Some still approach the Old Testament with this assumption, but it has been seriously challenged in a number of ways, especially through the findings of archaeology. Wellhausen was studying the Old Testament at a time when archaeology scarcely existed as a scientific enterprise, and it was all too easy for him to regard the history of ideas as an evolutionary progression from very primitive notions to very sophisticated ones. Since he saw the pinnacle of Old Testament thinking in the later prophets, it was taken for granted

An Egyptian frieze depicts ploughing and sowing. The Israelites were leaving the cultivated regions round the Nile for a wilderness where water was scarce and crop non-existent.

This figure of a goat was excavated from the Royal Graves at the site of Ur. It has been dated to approximately 2500 BC. The site of this ancient city, associated with Abraham, gives evidence of a civilization that reached back to the fifth millennium BC.

that the earlier generations had a much cruder outlook. But more recent discoveries have demonstrated quite categorically that this was not the case. The ancient civilizations of the Akkadians, the Sumerians, the Egyptians and others were of a high order, and much of the civil (case) law of the Old Testament bears a close resemblance to concepts of justice going back at least as far as the law code of King Hammurabi of Babylon (about 1700 BC).

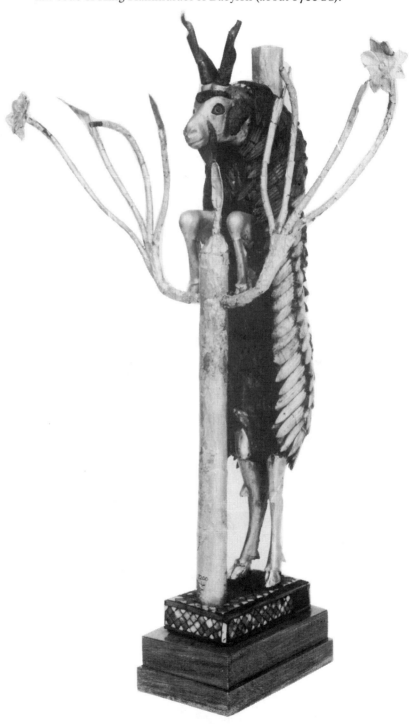

The researches of others into the religious life of later Israel have also suggested that the distinctively religious and moral requirements of the Old Testament law (the apodictic law) can be traced to a very early period. Following the findings of the Scandinavian scholar Sigmund Mowinckel and the German Albrecht Alt, many scholars believe that an important aspect of the religious life of Israel was a festival held every autumn, in which the covenant between God and his people was both commemorated and renewed. On this occasion, the people were reminded of what God had done for them, and of his requirements of them – to which they in turn reaffirmed their allegiance. It is argued that the Ten Commandments, and other laws associated with them in the book of Exodus, were recited on such occasions. And since our evidence for such a covenant renewal ceremony comes very early in Israel's history, there is every reason to suppose that the high ideals found there, and the covenant basis on which they exist, go back to the earliest period of Israel's experience of God.

Joshua 24

The ark of the covenant

According to the Old Testament, the spiritual realities of this covenant relationship were expressed in Israel's worship of God, even in the desert. Worship was conducted in a special tent-shrine, often called the 'tabernacle'. But the central focus was a wooden box called 'the ark of the

This carrying chest belonged to Egyptian Pharaoh Tutankhamun. The ark of the covenant may have been made along similar lines.

covenant'. Like similar 'holy boxes' in Egypt, it was decorated with religious symbols, and overlaid with gold. Naturally, it needed to be portable, and was equipped with rings so it could be carried shoulder-high on poles.

According to one of the most ancient pieces of poetry in the Old Testament, this portable ark represented in symbol the fact that God was with the escaping slaves (Numbers 10:35-36). Yahweh was not a God who could be depicted as an idol. But the ark was a kind of visible throne for the invisible Yahweh. It was a symbolic reminder of the central events of Mt Sinai: God was with his people, and he alone was to be their guide. Indeed, the connection with the covenant-making events may have been quite a literal one, for according to some Old Testament passages, the ark itself contained the actual tablets on which the covenant agreement had been set out (1 Kings 8:21).

As time passed, the ark assumed even greater importance in the life of the people. The fates of Israel's earliest kings – Saul and David – hinged on their treatment of the ark. Saul despised it – and was rejected. David respected it – and was politically successful. It also came to play an important part in the worship of the temple at Jerusalem. The religious poetry of Psalm 132 suggests that in a covenant renewal ceremony there the ark would be paraded through the streets of the city, returning to the temple as a sign of God's renewed and lasting presence with his people. Other psalms also reflect its important position in the ritual of worship at the temple, though they do not always mention it by name. Many scholars believe that when the Old Testament uses the title 'the Lord of hosts', this is really a reference to God's presence as symbolized in the ark. Other terms, such as 'glory' also seem to be used regularly in reference to it (e.g. 1 Samuel 4:21–22).

The Old Testament gives no hint of the ark's ultimate fate. No doubt it was one of the religious objects that later kings of Judah moved in and out of the temple as their religious allegiances changed (see chapter six). But all trace of it disappears after the invasion of Nebuchadnezzar in 586 BC.

The form of the covenant

The general idea of a 'covenant' was not unique to ancient Israel. Covenants regulated all sorts of behaviour in the ancient world, notably international relations. When we look closely at the legal framework of the covenant drawn up between Israel and her God at Mt Sinai, we can see a number of similarities with other legal documents from the late Bronze Age period (1400–1200 BC). One of the clearest examples of this legal form is to be found in a series of treaties relating to the Hittite Empire. These treaties clearly define the duties of smaller states which had been annexed by the more powerful Hittites. Naturally, the subject matter of such treaties was generally of a political nature. These legal forms were also used by other nations than the Hittites. But the interesting thing about them for us is their similarity to the Old Testament arrangement. The secular covenant agreements usually have a number of elements, many of which are also found in the Old Testament:

● **Introduction of the Speaker** In a political treaty, the king would introduce himself by name, just as God does in the introduction to the Ten Commandments (Exodus 20:1).

● **Historical Background** The king then reminded the other party of what he had done on their behalf – usually military intervention of some kind. In the Old Testament, God reminds his people of their deliverance from Egypt (Exodus 20:2).

● **Requirements** Then follow the obligations which are placed by the king on the other party. In a political treaty these would normally be military obligations; in the Old Testament, the requirements of the Law.

● **The Document** Arrangements were then made for the treaty to be written down, and deposited in a suitable place to be read at specified times. There is no such provision closely linked with the Ten Commandments in the book of Exodus, but there are similar instructions in Deuteronomy 27:1–8.

● **Witnesses** were called to seal the covenant – usually, the gods of both states. In the Old Testament we find a number of examples of witnesses to the covenant. In Exodus 24, twelve pillars were set up, probably for this purpose – and in the covenant ceremony recorded in Joshua 24, a large stone was erected to be a witness (Joshua 24:25–28).

● **Curses and Blessings** were then invoked for those who broke or kept the treaty. In the Old Testament, there is a long series of such curses and blessings in the book of Deuteronomy (Deuteronomy 27:11 — 28:68).

It is not suggested that Moses actually used a legal document of this kind – still less that he got it from the Hittites, though Israel did later make such a treaty with the Gibeonites (Joshua 9). There are many problems involved in tracing the exact relationship between the covenant made at Mt Sinai and these covenant forms used in the political sphere. It is not at all difficult to locate all the elements of the secular treaty form somewhere in the Old Testament, but there is no one single context which contains them all. We must also remember that Israel was in covenant with God, not with a military ruler, and this must have added a distinctive element to the understanding of the covenant.

Nevertheless, the fact that the events at Mt Sinai were articulated and preserved in a form of words that had such a widespread use in the time of Moses gives us no reason to look to a much later date for the origin of Israel's distinctive faith.

To the promised land

Mt Sinai was not the final destination of the escaping slaves. But it was an essential first step, for in this encounter at the holy mountain, we can see how this motley collection of refugees was beginning to be moulded into the nucleus of a nation. Informed by a new understanding of God, and fired with a new consciousness of their own part in his plans, they pressed on eastwards to the borders of Canaan, the land which eventually would see their embryonic faith achieve its full maturity. Many years were to pass before that would happen. For the land was no more theirs than it had been Abraham's, or Isaac's, or Jacob's. It belonged to other people – people with long experience of living in sophisticated urban communities, and with far greater material resources at their disposal.

Even the journey through the desert was to prove hazardous. For the refugees had to work out for themselves the full implications that the events of Mt Sinai should have in their everyday living. In addition to that, they came into conflict with many other groups of wandering nomads who, like them, were wanting to establish a

The mountains of Sinai, where Israel's covenant relationship with the Lord was formed.

permanent homeland for themselves. But Moses' faith and determination never wavered. Though he himself did not live to set foot in the land that was to become his people's national home, he had no doubt of the final outcome of their struggle. For like Abraham before him, he was convinced that the direction of his own life, and the future of the escaped slaves and their descendants, was not at the mercy of impersonal social and political forces. It was in the control of a loving and all-powerful God: 'People of Israel, no god is like your God . . . There is no one like you, a nation saved by the Lord. The Lord himself is your shield and your sword, to defend you and give you victory.'

Deuteronomy 33:26,29

Dating the exodus and conquest of Canaan

Twenty years ago it would have been difficult to find any reputable scholar who would not have dated the exodus and Israel's entry into Canaan somewhere between about 1280 and 1240 BC. But today an increasing number are inclined to give more weight to an older view that dated these events about 1440 BC. Many complex arguments are involved, and there is much uncertainty about basic issues, such as the nature of the 'conquest' itself. Some of them are discussed in the next chapter. Here we shall confine ourselves to the specifically chronological issues.

Old Testament dates

According to 1 Kings 6:1, Solomon began to build the temple in Jerusalem in the fourth year of his reign, which is said to be 'Four hundred and eighty years after the people of Israel left Egypt'. Working back from Solomon's time, that brings us to a date of almost exactly 1440 BC for the exodus. At first, this may seem to be clear-cut and decisive. But other facts need to be taken into consideration:

● If we add together the successive periods of rule of the various judges, the time between the exodus and Solomon works out at a minimum of 554 years. Of course, we do not know for certain that the judges followed one another in chronological succession. Since they were mainly local leaders, there was probably a good deal of overlap between them, in which case this period of time could in reality be much less than it first seems to be. In addition, the period of forty years often figures in these stories, and that span of time was used conventionally in the Old Testament to indicate one generation. So perhaps it was never intended to be a very precise measurement of time.

● At the end of the book of Ruth, the genealogy of Solomon separates him from Nahshon, his ancestor who lived at the time of the exodus (Numbers 1:7) by only six generations. That would normally be about 200 years – though here, as in other biblical ancestor lists, some generations may have been left out.

● According to Exodus 12:40, the Israelite tribes left Egypt after they had lived there for 430 years. If we assume that the exodus took place in about 1250 BC, that would mean that Joseph went to Egypt in the time of the Hyksos rulers. They were themselves not Egyptians, and would therefore have been more likely than native rulers to favour a

person like Joseph. But if we date the exodus in 1440 BC, and then add 430 years to that for Israel's stay in Egypt, we would arrive at a date for Joseph much earlier than most scholars would assign to Abraham! But here again there is an element of doubt. For the Septuagint makes the 430 years include both the time the Israelites were in Egypt, and the time they were in Canaan before this.

So the most we can conclude on the basis of the dates in the Old Testament is that it is very difficult to take the statement of 1 Kings 6:1 at its face value. Indeed it may well be that it was never intended to be taken as a strict chronological statement. For 480 years is twelve times forty, which could therefore indicate a dozen generations, or simply a very long time. If we understand this figure in this way, then most of the other Biblical dates seem to favour an exodus sometime in the thirteenth, and not the fifteenth century.

The Tell-el-Amarna Letters

We have already mentioned these documents briefly. They consist of a series of pillar-shaped tablets written in cuneiform script, mostly in a form of Akkadian, which was the diplomatic language of the time. They date from the early fourteenth century, and were written by various rulers in Canaan and Syria to Pharaoh Akhen-aten (1369–1353 BC) and his predecessor Amenhotep III (1398–1361 BC). In particular, they complain of the activities of groups of people called 'Aperru', whose warlike activities were creating tensions and disturbance throughout the area. At one time scholars were inclined to identify the Aperru with the Old Testament Hebrews, and the invasions into southern Canaan mentioned in the Amarna Letters were thereby identified with the invasion of Joshua. If this could be shown to be true, it would of course suggest that the exodus from Egypt had taken place earlier than the date of these letters – which in turn could plausibly take us back to 1440 BC again. But we now know that it is simplistic and improbable just to identify Aperru and Hebrews. And in any case, the stories of the book of Joshua concern armed infiltration into Canaan from the east rather than from the south. But it is possible that the general movements of which these texts speak may be reflected in other parts of the Old Testament story.

The Amarna Letters, tablets written in cuneiform script, give evidence of a period of instability in the relationships between Egypt and her neighbours in the years before Israel setted in Egypt.

Pithom and Rameses

We are on much firmer ground with a statement in Exodus 1:11, that 'The Israelites built the cities of Pithom and Rameses to serve as supply centres for the king of Egypt'. Pithom was actually an old town, but the finest structure in it was a temple built by Rameses II (1290–1224 BC), and there is no evidence for any earlier pharaoh building there. Rameses is certainly to be identified with the capital city of Rameses II, built by him on the site of the ancient capital Tanis. This may have been the capital of the Hyksos

kings in the century preceding their expulsion in 1540 BC, but the pharaohs of the succeeding dynasty had their capital at Thebes (except for Akhenaten, who moved even further from Tanis). All this would appear to date the exodus sometime after 1290 BC. And evidence from the reign of a later pharaoh, Merneptah, suggests that it could not have been later than about 1240 BC. For in about 1220 BC, he recorded an attack on various peoples in Canaan, in the course of which he mentions 'Israel' as part of the settled population of the land.

Archaeology in Canaan

The storm centre of this whole debate is found in the evidence for destruction at various sites in Canaan itself.

● At one time, the strongest argument for dating the exodus towards the end of the fifteenth century BC was the conclusion of the English archaeologist John Garstang that Jericho had been taken by Joshua not later than 1400 BC. Indeed, he excavated the remains of walls and other buildings which he believed proved the historical truth of the Old Testament story even down to its details. But his interpretation of the evidence does not square with the facts (see chapter 3).

● The same is true for most other sites that have been excavated. For while there is much evidence of destruction throughout Canaan in the thirteenth century BC, there is very little that can positively be connected with the Old Testament story. Many sites do provide evidence of a destruction in which the sophisticated culture of the Canaanite city-states was replaced by a much more primitive lifestyle, and some scholars have taken this as evidence of the Israelite invasion. But in reality, it is not quite so simple. For we have no real evidence to inform us of the nature of a typically Israelite culture at this period, other than by the circular assumption that this less sophisticated style was Israelite! In any case, with only a few exceptions the cities that have yielded most evidence for such a thirteenth-century destruction are not those that feature most prominently in the Old Testament record.

● Those who favour a fifteenth-century date for the exodus have recently argued that the evidence of decay and collapse in thirteenth century Canaanite society had nothing to do with the Israelite conquest. Instead, they argue, it reflects the events depicted in the book of Judges. But this view is itself problematical, for there is no absolutely clear-cut archaeological evidence to support a fifteenth-century invasion either, unless we are prepared to indulge in a wholesale modification of the dating that archaeologists have given to events throughout this entire period.

If we restrict our attention to these detailed points, there is no doubt that the argument is very finely balanced, and probably the only safe conclusion to draw is that we cannot certainly date the exodus and conquest. But the very uncertainty of this evidence has led a number of scholars to wonder whether we are asking the right question here. Instead of searching for evidence of a once-for-all conquest of Canaan by the Israelite tribes, perhaps we should understand their arrival in the land from a different perspective – either by supposing that only one particular group was involved in the exodus events, or by seeing the emergence of Israel as a nation more in terms of the internal development and change of Canaanite society. These alternatives are considered in the next chapter.

The 'round tower', excavated at Jericho, dated to the Neolithic period (7000 BC). The archaeological remains show that Jericho had many different periods of occupation. So to extract from the archaeological evidence a definite date for Israel's 'conquest' is virtually impossible.

3 A land flowing with milk and honey

Joshua
Judges

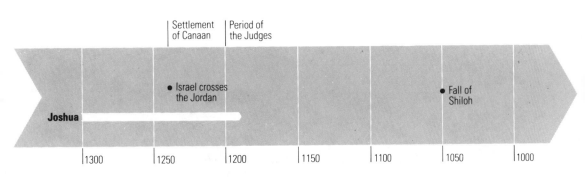

Settlement of Canaan | Period of the Judges

Israel crosses the Jordan

Fall of Shiloh

Joshua

1300   1250   1200   1150   1100   1050   1000

Canaan before Israel

THE LAND of Canaan had a long and illustrious history of its own. Documents discovered at Ebla in north Syria testify to the existence of many important towns there as early as 2300 BC, and the city of Jericho is believed to be the oldest city in the world, going back perhaps as far as 9000 BC.

So the land to which Moses led his people was a well organized country. Throughout most of the second millennium BC it was controlled by the Egyptians. But they worked through local rulers, of whom there were a great many. Egyptian records and archaeological findings paint a picture of intensely populated city-states, especially in the central, most fertile parts of the country. Each city was independent, with its own land – just enough to provide for its needs – and its own rulers. The next city might be as little as 3 miles/5km away, but every local king considered himself directly responsible to Egypt, rather than to his neighbours. This was an important part of Egyptian policy. For the land of Canaan was of strategic importance to Egypt's own political security. The great trade routes linking Egypt with the other power centres in the ancient world ran through Canaan, and it is no coincidence that the greatest concentration of small city-states was to be found along the road from Egypt to Syria and Mesopotamia. In the hill country, things were not so well organized. Fewer people wanted to live there anyway, and in addition, a city in the hills needed much more land to be self-sufficient. For this reason, it had always been easier for nomadic peoples to move about in these more remote areas of the country.

By the end of the Late Bronze Age, however, Egypt's power was diminishing and at about this time (1220 BC) we find the first

The Philistines occupied a coastal strip; this picture is of one of their warships. In the time of the judges and the early kings they were a highly aggressive enemy.

This stone monument (or 'stele') was erected by King Merneptah of Egypt after a military expedition into Canaan. Its text includes the earliest known reference to 'Israel' outside the Bible.

reference outside the Bible to 'Israel' as the name of a nation. After a military expedition into Canaan, King Merneptah of Egypt erected a stone monument as a record of his exploits. In its inscription, he triumphantly declared that 'Israel is laid waste'. Subsequent events showed this optimism to be unjustified. For Egypt's power in the area soon collapsed, and the strong alliance of Egyptian-backed Canaanite city-states began to lose its grip. Within a short time, the whole land had fallen into the hands of only four or five separate rulers, all of whom were newcomers. Israel was certainly one such group. The Philistines were another. They had originally come from Crete, and they settled mainly along the sea coast. Here, they adopted the political organization of their predecessors, and established five city-states of their own: Gaza, Ashkelon, Ashdod, Ekron, and Gath. They also eventually gave their name to the whole country (Palestine).

Israel's new state was quite different. Under the old regime in Canaan, political power went hand in hand with possession of a city. This meant that real power must always be kept in the hands of just a few privileged people. But the covenant at Mt Sinai had given Israel a different understanding of human society, in which class

Facing page: Settling Canaan.

structure had no part to play. No one had any right to claim a position of superiority, for they had all been slaves together, and the only thing that made them a nation was the undeserved generosity of God himself. The Israelites' national identity was always firmly based on their understanding of the nature of God, and this was to have far-reaching consequences not only during the early period of their history, but throughout their entire existence as a nation. It meant that all elements of their population (the tribes) were of equal importance, and their ultimate responsibility was not to some centralized power structure, but to God alone.

Israel moves in

These changes in Canaanite political life are all well documented from Egyptian records, as well as by archaeological evidence from various sites throughout the land. Between about 1400 and 1200 BC radical changes came about. The power of Egypt declined, and the relatively advanced culture of the Canaanite city-states was replaced by a less sophisticated way of life – and at the end of it, Israel had emerged as a force to be reckoned with. So much is clear. But when we try to discover exactly how these changes took place, we are soon involved in one of the most complex issues in the study of the Old Testament. For there is no generally agreed understanding of the course of Israel's development at this period. Different scholars have formed their own theories. All of them can claim some support in the Old Testament itself, but none of them is free from problems. At least three main explanations have been proposed in recent years:

● **Armed struggle** A quick reading of the stories in the Old Testament book of Joshua can give the impression that the land of Canaan became the land of Israel almost overnight, as a result of a series of spectacular battles and conquests. But in fact Joshua records the capture of only a few Canaanite city-states, and makes it clear that even at the end of Joshua's successful military exploits much of the land remained unconquered. Nevertheless, the successes of Joshua's armies form the core of the Old Testament story, and many scholars believe that the successful settlement of the Israelite tribes in Canaan owed more to this than to any other cause.

Joshua 13:1–7

The evidence of archaeology has often been claimed to support this belief. In the 1930s, the English archaeologist John Garstang carried out extensive excavations at the site of Jericho, and he discovered what he took to be incontrovertible evidence of Joshua's capture of the city: walls that had literally fallen flat, and much evidence of destruction by fire. According to Professor Garstang, this had happened not long after 1400 BC, and on his reckoning this was almost exactly the time when the Israelite armies were invading the land. Investigations by later archaeologists, however, have shown this picture to be totally false. Following the usual procedure, Garstang dated his finds by reference to the layer of the mound at Jericho in which he found them. But what he did not

Joshua 6

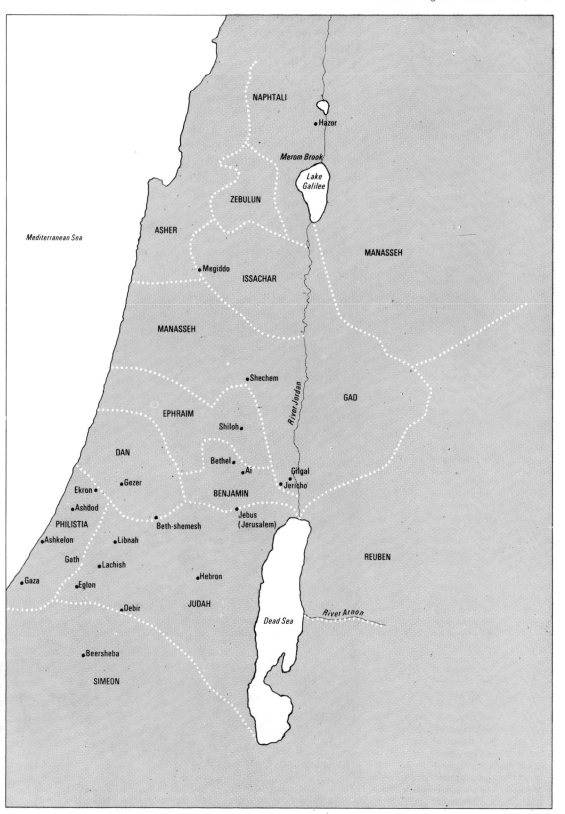

NAPHTALI

• Hazor

Merom Brook

Lake Galilee

ZEBULUN

ASHER

MANASSEH

• Megiddo

ISSACHAR

MANASSEH

Mediterranean Sea

• Shechem

River Jordan

GAD

EPHRAIM

Shiloh •

DAN

Bethel •
• Ai

Gilgal •
• Jericho

Ekron •
• Gezer

BENJAMIN

• Ashdod

PHILISTIA

• Jebus
(Jerusalem)

• Beth-shemesh

• Ashkelon

• Libnah

Gath

• Lachish

REUBEN

• Gaza

• Eglon

• Hebron

• Debir

JUDAH

Dead Sea

River Arnon

• Beersheba

SIMEON

know was that over the centuries much of the top of the mound had been worn away at this point – and for that reason, the remains he found were actually from a much lower level than they appeared to be. In fact, they were from a city that had existed on the site a full thousand years earlier than the time of Joshua. Unless other finds come to light (and archaeologists have not yet worked over the whole mound of Jericho), it seems that nothing substantial is left of the city that stood there at the end of the Late Bronze Age.

Evidence from other sites is more specific, and shows that there was a violent and widespread destruction of Canaanite cities during the thirteenth century BC. The fact that this destruction was followed by a much more primitive culture than the one it replaced

The time of Joshua and the judges is often called the period of 'the conquest'. Certainly many battles were involved, not only as Israel moved in to Canaan but also as they struggled to take full possession. In a sense, these conflicts still continue.

has been taken to prove that it was the work of the Israelite tribes: coming in from the desert, their way of life would be much less sophisticated than that of the Canaanite cities. That is no doubt true, but it does not in itself prove that the destruction uncovered by archaeologists was the work of Israel's armies. Others have argued that this collapse of Canaanite culture came about because of internal feuding among the city-states, which in turn was encouraged by the decline of the Egyptian power that had so successfully united the land. In addition, some also argue that the exodus and conquest of Canaan took place earlier than this, perhaps in the fifteenth century BC. If that is true, then the thirteenth-century evidence would be irrelevant anyway, though it

could be related to the general social unrest that seems to be depicted in the Old Testament book of Judges. In any case, we need to remember that the Israelites were not the only ones who were staking their claim at this time. Philistines, Ammonites, and others were all pressing in from various quarters, and much of this destruction could be their work.

In the present state of our knowledge, archaeology has little truly useful information to give us about the Israelite conquest of the land. This has led some to doubt whether there ever was a 'conquest' in any real sense. They point out that the military strength of the Canaanite city-states would easily have repelled wandering tribes with no real experience of warfare – especially since the Canaanites possessed relatively sophisticated equipment, such as chariots. But this argument carries little weight. For one thing, Canaanite culture was declining anyway. And in addition, the history of guerilla warfare readily demonstrates how minority groups inspired by a vision of what they believe to be right can often

Although the book of Joshua suggests that the Canaanites were easily defeated by Israel, this may only have been because the separate city-states failed to unite. Their weaponry, from war chariots down to such swords and daggers as these, was fairly sophisticated.

overthrow highly organized and well-equipped armies that in theory should have quelled their opposition effortlessly. The whole picture of Israel's early history is so dominated by the stories of military success that to ignore it would require a wholesale rejection of the Old Testament account – and there is no reason why we should do that. But equally, the Old Testament gives us no reason to include only this one element in our portrayal of Israel's life in these early days. According to the book of Joshua, the military campaigns secured for Israel a foothold in the central hill country, which was to be the heart of their territory. But the flatter and more fertile areas like the Plain of Jezreel were not taken over at this time – and in addition, many fortified towns such as Jerusalem and Gezer also stayed firmly in Canaanite hands.

● **Infiltration** The apparently incomplete nature of the initial conquest of the country has led other scholars to suggest that much – or even all – of the land was taken over in a different way, as the Israelite tribes gradually infiltrated Canaanite society until eventually they became the dominant group. This understanding of the situation has been especially articulated by the German scholar Albrecht Alt.

He began by analysing the social structure of the land both before and after the period when Israel was emerging as a nation.

He noted that the structure of Israelite society was quite different from the closely controlled hierarchy that had been established by the Canaanite city-states. But he also drew attention to the fact that those invaders like the Philistines, who settled where the city-states had been strongest, were forced by social and economic pressures to take over this form of government themselves. Since this did not happen in Israel, he argued that the Israelites must have established their rule first in those parts of the land where the power of the city-states was minimal. That is, in the hill country. Instead of a violent conquest, Alt believed that the Israelite tribes had settled in a gradual way. Rather than wandering about as nomads with their flocks from season to season, they began to stay for longer periods in particular places. Then they eventually penetrated the structure of the few power centres that were to be found in the hill country, until they became a significant element of the settled population.

This is an unconvincing view of the matter if we take it to be the only way in which Israel settled the land. The kind of patient, self-conscious process of infiltration that Alt described is more plausible to modern theorists than it would be to homeless refugees, especially those who were convinced that their destiny was not a matter of chance but was all part of the design of their loving and powerful God. In addition, the political system developed by Israel at this early stage had nothing to do with the kind of social tensions that Alt described: instead, it was a conscious projection into the political sphere of the religious experience of the slaves from Egypt. It is also doubtful whether Israel's earliest nomadic life followed the kind of pattern that Alt suggested. For these and other reasons, only a minority of others have accepted his interpretation of Israel's settlement in the land.

But despite this, the theory in a broader sense does seem to explain some of the facts that emerge from the Old Testament story. For it seems likely that some cities came into Israelite hands by other means than conquest. Shechem is a good example of this. There is no record of a military conquest here by Joshua, and yet even before his death it was a major centre of Israelite activity, and
Joshua 24 seems to have served as a sort of capital town. The evidence of archaeology is consistent with this, for Shechem did not share in the general wave of destruction and decline that was going on elsewhere in the thirteenth century BC. Of course, it is possible to explain the archaeological evidence differently in order to support an earlier date for the conquest of Canaan. We know that the Egyptians destroyed the city sometime between 1545 and 1525 BC, and if the Israelite tribes arrived shortly after that, they would have found Shechem unoccupied, and so they could have settled the area without the need for conquest. On the other hand, there are many difficulties involved in dating the exodus and conquest quite so early. Others have pointed out that an earlier story tells how
Genesis 34;48:22 Shechem was conquered by Jacob and his sons, and they suggest that when the invading tribes arrived several centuries later they found the city was occupied by people who were, literally, their

Joshua 6:22–25
Judges 1:22–26

A figurine of a Canaanite goddess, found at Ugarit. Much of the religious mythology of the Canaanites was concerned with sex and fertility.

relatives – and this is why they did not need to overthrow it. It is not possible to be certain how and why Shechem came to be so important to Israel, but it does seem to be an example of a city that was taken over in a more or less peaceful way.

● **Conversion and revolution** Another interesting possibility is that some inhabitants of Canaan could have been won over to Israel's side by a process of religious conversion. The family of the prostitute Rahab at Jericho may be an example of this, as also may be another group associated with the city of Bethel. Then there is the rather odd position of the Gibeonites, who came and asked to be incorporated into the nation of Israel, and who were accepted by Joshua on the basis of a covenant treaty.

Incidents like these have been taken as evidence that Israel's 'conquest' of Canaan was far more dependent on moral victories than on military might. Indeed some have asserted that there was no 'conquest' in any physical sense at all, but that what changed the population from 'Canaanites' into 'Israelites' was the result of some sort of social revolution, a 'peasant's revolt', led not by political considerations but by moral and religious convictions. They point out that the new understanding of God's character derived from the covenant at Mt Sinai was quite different from the religion of Canaan. Moses had declared that God was interested in people on a personal level, and that he was active in the events of everyday life for their benefit. This was in stark contrast to Canaanite religion, where the gods existed to preserve the existing order both in the world of nature and in the world of politics. They were powerful supporters of the ruling classes, whereas the God of Israel was committed to support the oppressed and downtrodden – and he had proved it in the events of the exodus. It is therefore not surprising that many Canaanite peasants should have been attracted by this new assessment of the human situation. As a result, they overthrew their local city rulers and allied themselves with Israel's dynamic concept of God as the true ruler and guide of his people. And in the process, 'Canaan' became 'Israel'.

This view has not found a great deal of favour among Old Testament scholars. Some have argued that it owes more to the modern Marxist view of history than it does to the Old Testament. No doubt it has been influenced by modern concerns, but that in itself does not make it untrue, for one of the most fruitful ways of understanding the past can often be by use of a theoretical model of this kind to provide a framework within which to assess the event. A much stronger argument against this view is that there is no positive Old Testament evidence in its favour. Indeed, the opposite is true. For on this view, the term 'Israel' does not denote a racial or national entity. Instead, it becomes a descriptive term for people sharing the same ideology. 'Israel' becomes not so much a nation as a kind of political party. But of course the Old Testament accounts of the conquest of Canaan are united in portraying Israel as a national group that is quite separate from the Canaanites.

To be sure, others could be accepted as a part of the nation of

Israel. Indeed, the solemn assembly at Shechem was almost certainly an important occasion when such converts to faith in the God of Israel were formally incorporated into the nation. But there is no support in the Old Testament for the view that such racial outsiders comprised the majority of the nation. If this had been the case, we would surely have expected to find some trace of it, however slight, in the relevant Old Testament passages.

Joshua 24

The story of how Israel settled in the land is obviously very complex. Great political and social movements leading to the formation of a new nation can hardly be simple and straightforward. Modern thinkers are often tempted to try to understand the past from just one perspective, and Old Testament scholars are no exception. They have tried to depict the early history of Israel in black and white terms, usually rejecting the diversity of the Old Testament story in favour of just one of its strands. But history seldom develops in such a simple way, and it is not at all unlikely that the people of Israel became a nation in their own land by adopting different tactics at different times and places.

Israel settles down

In some ways, the real struggle for the land only began after Joshua was dead. Israel was fortunate in managing to avoid confrontation with the various great world powers of the time. The Egyptians and the Hittites were both in decline, while the new power of Assyria was not yet ready to expand into Canaan. The real challenge was in Canaan itself, where the Israelite tribes held control of only a few areas of the country. To make matters worse, the Israelite settlements were isolated from each other by two powerful groups of Canaanite city-states: one group, just to the north of Shechem, centred on towns like Megiddo, Dothan, and Beth-Shan; and another, to the south of Shechem, extended westwards from the northern end of the Dead Sea right across to the Mediterranean coast. On top of that, the Israelite tribes were not always able to subdue the Canaanite population even in those areas where they had achieved some sort of dominance. The tribes of Manasseh, Ephraim, Zebulun, Asher and Naphtali were all forced to come to some mutual agreement with the native population of the land. When we add to this the fact that other invaders were also trying to carve out their own territories, it is hardly surprising that the situation was so volatile.

Judges 1:27–36

All this is described in the Old Testament book of Judges. The book takes its name from the fact that its heroes are called 'judges'. To us, this suggests they were concerned with the administration of law, and the Hebrew word for 'judge' is in fact very similar to titles given to government officials elsewhere in the ancient world – at Mari, Ebla, and Ugarit. Some of the people mentioned in Judges may well have had some administrative function. But it can be misleading to compare the 'judges' of early Israel with figures in other cultures. For without exception, they all had a monarchy, and a much more sophisticated political apparatus than Israel had at this time. The great judges of the Old Testament stories were not anonymous officials. Nor did they owe their position to a bureaucratic or hereditary appointment. It was something that stemmed naturally from their remarkable gifts of great wisdom, bravery, and leadership – qualities that were demonstrated not in legal arguments about justice, but in the actual work of getting justice for their people. They were men and women of great political vision and religious devotion. They were determined that the promises of God and the commitment of his people, expressed in the covenant made at Mt Sinai, should be enshrined in the very fabric of their new society.

The Old Testament names twelve judges, but records details about only six of them. Of these, only one, Othniel, is linked with the tribes that settled in the south. All the others are associated with northern tribes. This perhaps reflects the relative strength of Israel in different parts of the country at the time. But it could also suggest that the stories themselves were first handed down, and later written down, in the northern part of the country. The meaning that the editor of the book of Judges found in these stories is certainly similar to the message of the prophets who later flourished in that part of the country. Like many other Old Testament writers, he suggests that the true meaning of Israel's experience can only be understood from a religious viewpoint. He tells us plainly at the beginning of the book that all the stories follow the same pattern, and teach the same lesson:

Judges 1:11–15; 3:7–11; Joshua 15:13–19

Judges 2:11–23

- When Israel was faithful to God, she prospered.
- When she deserted her God, Yahweh, for other gods, she was unable to resist her enemies.
- Finding herself in great distress, Israel turned again to God, and he provided a deliverer (the judges).
- After the death of a judge, the same pattern of events was repeated again.

Every one of the stories about the judges is used to illustrate and give substance to this theological understanding of Israel's fortunes. For this reason, it has often been suggested that the narrative is less than accurate as history. Given the personal nature of much of the story, it is obviously impossible either to prove or disprove that. But the overall picture that emerges appears to be true to life.

Judges 4—5

Judges 3:12–30
Judges 6:1—8:35
Judges 10:6—12:7
Judges 13:1—16:31

Deborah and Barak fight with the Canaanites, the native inhabitants of the land, while the others deal with various groups who, like Israel, were trying to gain access to the land for themselves: the Moabites (Ehud); the Midianites (Gideon); the Ammonites (Jephthah); and the Philistines (Samson). Most of these people were local heroes, fighting local battles. The story of Samson is almost a personal crusade against the Philistines. The fact that he was able to marry a Philistine woman suggests that, though the Philistines soon became Israel's greatest enemy, relationships with them at this stage were still more or less friendly.

The story of Deborah and Barak gives us more insight into the

Judges 4:23–24

After the dreariness of the barren wilderness, the country into which the Israelites were moving must have seemed startlingly beautiful and fertile. They described it as 'a land flowing with milk and honey'.

nature of Israelite society at this period. Their exploits against the Canaanites, led by Sisera, the army commander of Jabin, king of the city of Hazor, are vividly described in the great poem which was almost certainly written by an eye witness of the events which it describes. It was certainly written sometime in the twelfth century BC, and that takes us right back to the time of the judges themselves. Deborah and Barak were probably trying to break through the line of Canaanite city-states that isolated the northern area of Galilee from the Israelite settlements around Shechem. For though Jabin's city, Hazor, lay to the north of Galilee, the battle itself took place just to the south-west of the Plain of Jezreel, and involved a coalition of Canaanite city-states. Possession of this great plain was of vital importance. All of the trade routes had to go this way, and whoever controlled this area effectively controlled most of the land. The outcome of the battle was victory for Israel. The Canaanite kings were not entirely routed, but their power was broken, and it was only a matter of time before Israel was able to overthrow Jabin and his influence.

The Canaanite kings had many sophisticated weapons, including chariots, and the Israelites were successful only because they were able to form an effective alliance. Deborah managed to unite six of the Israelite tribes – Zebulun, Naphtali, Ephraim, Benjamin, Manasseh, and Issachar – and the one thing that brought them together was their common faith in God. The editor of the book of Judges was not exaggerating when he claimed that obedience to God led to success, while disobedience led to failure. When the tribes were united by their common heritage derived from the covenant at Mt Sinai, they were an effective coalition. But when they began to drift away from the worship of the God of whom Moses had spoken, purely sectional and selfish interests came to be all-important, and they were powerless against their enemies.

Life in the days of the judges

What was life really like in those early years when the character and identity of the nation of Israel were being established? Like any other emerging nation, Israel certainly had her troubles. Looking back from his own more settled times, the editor of the book of Judges felt that at times it verged on anarchy: 'Every man did what was right in his own eyes' (Judges 21:25).

It is not hard to see why he felt like that. The gruesome story of how a woman traveller was sexually assaulted and murdered in the town of Gibeah is no doubt a typical example (Judges 19). But what happened as a result of this incident is of great significance in understanding the nature of Israelite society at this time. For the woman's male companion sent a message to all the other tribes, telling them what had happened. They were all outraged, and formed a large army to punish the tribe of Benjamin for allowing such a thing to happen in their territory. In the struggle that followed, the tribe of Benjamin was all but exterminated (Judges 20). Under normal conditions, the different tribes of Israel were primarily concerned with their own affairs. But when the need arose, they obviously had a strong sense of national solidarity, and could unite to confront a common threat – whether it came from outside enemies, or from internal subversion. But what was it that held them together like this? We may find a clue in the deep remorse that was felt after the Benjaminites had been subdued. For there was great concern that Benjamin should not be wiped out altogether: 'Israel must not lose one of its twelve tribes. We must find a way for the tribe of Benjamin to survive . . . ' (Judges 21:17). The alliance of twelve tribes – and no less – was clearly of some importance to them.

As long ago as the middle of the nineteenth century, German scholars were suggesting that this incident gives us an important insight into the social and political organization of early Israel. But it was not until the 1930s, with the work of Martin Noth, that the full implications of this became clear. He observed that many ancient communities were divided into a regular number of groups, or tribes. In the Old Testament itself we find twelve Ishmaelite tribes (Genesis 25:13–16) and twelve Edomite tribes (Genesis 36:10–14). Unfortunately, nothing else is known about these near-neighbours of Israel. But we do have more specific information about associations of tribes in ancient Greece and Italy, especially a group that was associated with the shrine of the god Apollo at Delphi. These groups came to be known as 'amphictyonies', from two Greek words which mean 'to live around'. In this case, they lived around a particular religious centre, and their common allegiance to the worship of their god was the thing that bound them together and gave them mutual obligations to one another.

Professor Noth identified a number of distinctive features of the life of such an amphictyony, which he believed can also be found in the Old Testament:

● A fixed membership The Greek amphictyonies always had either six or twelve members. The reason for this was perhaps a practical one, for with twelve months in a year it meant that each tribe could take it in turn to look after the central sanctuary. Whatever the origin of Israel's twelve tribes, it is certainly interesting that, though the actual names given to the tribes could vary, the number twelve is always preserved in the Old Testament.

● A central shrine The main focus of the Greek amphictyonies was the

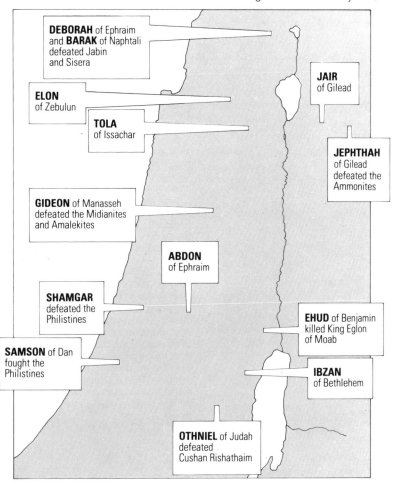

DEBORAH of Ephraim and BARAK of Naphtali defeated Jabin and Sisera

JAIR of Gilead

ELON of Zebulun

TOLA of Issachar

JEPHTHAH of Gilead defeated the Ammonites

GIDEON of Manasseh defeated the Midianites and Amalekites

ABDON of Ephraim

SHAMGAR defeated the Philistines

EHUD of Benjamin killed King Eglon of Moab

SAMSON of Dan fought the Philistines

IBZAN of Bethlehem

OTHNIEL of Judah defeated Cushan Rishathaim

shrine of their god, and this also became a centre for the administration of laws that were common to all the member states. By definition, an amphictyony must have such a central place of worship. But was there such a place in ancient Israel? The story in Joshua 24 seems to suggest that Shechem could have been a kind of central sanctuary. But later, when the tribes united against Benjamin, they went not to Shechem, but to Bethel (Judges 20:18) – and not long after, in the time of Samuel, Shiloh appears as the most important place of worship (1 Samuel 1–4). The apparent absence of just one shrine could be due to the fact that, unlike other gods, the God of Israel could not be contained in just one place. He was present with his people everywhere, and this presence was symbolized by the portable ark of the covenant. Perhaps therefore this sign of God's presence that could be moved about from place to place was itself the central focus for all the tribes.

But if so, could it also have been a kind of administrative centre, served by its own officials? Martin Noth believed that it could, and he argued that the officials of the Israelite amphictyony were to be identified with the so-called 'minor judges' – that is, those of whom we know nothing more than their names (Judges 10:1–5, 12:8–15). He further suggested that the law which they administered is found in Exodus 21-23, the 'Book of the Covenant'.

● An annual festival In the Greek amphictyonies, each member state sent official delegates to an annual convention, which took place at the central shrine. This was partly a religious occasion, and partly an administrative council. The evidence for such an annual pilgrimage in the Old Testament is limited. But there is the story of how Joshua gathered the tribes together at Shechem, to remind them of their obligations under the covenant (Joshua 24), and the later story of Samuel's parents tells how they went to the sanctuary in Shiloh once a year – though there is nothing to suggest they were any sort of official delegates (1 Samuel 1:1–8). It is in fact very difficult to find evidence of such delegates in early Israel, though Noth believed that passages like Numbers 1:1–15 could have been lists of such people. But this is very uncertain.

● **A common purpose** The job of an alliance like this was to defend the central shrine and to uphold the common interests and laws of the constituent states. There are two striking illustrations of such a common concern in the book of Judges. On the one hand, we have the story of how six tribes united under Deborah to oppose a common threat from the Canaanites (Judges 4—5). And on the other, we have the story of how eleven tribes acted against a gross violation of covenant law by the tribe of Benjamin (Judges 19—20). According to Noth, these two incidents document the development of the amphictyony, with an alliance of twelve tribes arising out of the six-tribe group headed by Deborah. But other interpretations are possible, especially if one is prepared to imagine that the stories have been rewritten in the light of social conditions in later Israel.

Martin Noth's reconstruction of life in the time of the judges has been very influential in Old Testament study for the past fifty years. It has always been difficult to match every detail of the Old Testament with the evidence from Greece and Italy, and for that reason some have not accepted it. They point out that the Greek amphictyonies flourished in a time and place far removed from Israel in the period of the judges – and in any case, they suggest, the Greek evidence is not as clear-cut as Noth liked to think.

Certainly, his idea must always remain just a theory. But it does shed light on some aspects of Israel's national consciousness. It is certain that a shared faith in God was the main strength of the alliance between the Israelite tribes. Though that faith may not have been expressed in just one central place, its power was none the less real for that. Though the tribes had their own leaders from time to time – the judges – they realized that God himself was the real 'judge' of his people (Judges 11:27), and their devotion was to be given not to human leaders, but to him alone (Judges 8:23; 9:1–57). It would be surprising if such a devotion did not have a tangible form in the social and political institutions of Israel's national life.

Israel and the religion of Canaan

A clay tablet, one of many found at Ugarit (Ras esh-Shamra) with 'cuneiform' writing.

Politically, the Canaanite city-states were eventually displaced by the Israelite tribes. But ideologically, the Canaanites exerted an enormous influence on Israel for many centuries. The editor of the book of Judges makes it quite plain that the religion of Canaan was a more formidable force than its armies, and when Israel was tempted to adopt it, disaster was the inevitable outcome: 'Then the people of Israel sinned against the Lord and began to serve the Baals. They stopped worshipping the Lord, the God of their ancestors, the God who had brought them out of Egypt, and they . . . served the Baals and the Astartes. And so the Lord became furious with Israel and let raiders attack them and rob them . . . and the Israelites could no longer protect themselves . . . They were in great distress' (Judges 2:11–15).

This message was never irrelevant to the life of Israel. Centuries later, the great Old Testament prophets, from Elijah to Jeremiah, were saying the same thing: that the people of Israel were going to ruin because of their love for

the gods and goddesses of Palestine.

So who were these gods and goddesses – 'the Baals and the Astartes'? Some of the answers to that question have been unearthed by archaeologists at the tell of Ras esh-Shamra, on the coast of modern Syria, just opposite Cyprus. This was the site of the ancient Canaanite citadel of Ugarit. Its heyday was in the fifteenth and fourteenth centuries BC, something like 200 years before the time of the exodus. But we have every reason to believe that the religion practised in southern Palestine at the time of the Israelite conquest was very similar to the religion of these people who lived further north. In an annexe to the temple at Ugarit, archaeologists have made one of the most exciting discoveries of all time. For in a large collection of clay tablets, we find the story of Baal and the other Canaanite gods and goddesses who are mentioned in the Old Testament. These tablets date from about the thirteenth century BC, and are written in a language that has come to be known as Ugaritic. It is

On the coast of modern Syria, at the tell of Ras esh-Shamra, was once the Canaanite city of Ugarit. This picture is of an entrance to the great palace there. Archaeologists have unearthed at Ugarit a great deal of evidence about Canaanite religion and civilization in the centuries leading up to the exodus.

An altar to the god Moloch (or Molech), with a receptacle for collecting the blood. Moloch was the god of the Ammonites, and was associated with child sacrifice. Some of the religious practices of the region were cruel and depraved, which helps to explain why the Israelites were warned off them so strongly. But later in the Old Testament child sacrifice appeared in Israel too.

similar to Hebrew, and is one of the earliest known scripts to use an alphabet. The tablets contain much valuable and important information not only about the gods of ancient Ugarit, but also about religious practices. And the many religious objects also found here – altars, statues, etc. – help us to understand how these gods were worshipped.

A number of gods and göddesses play a part in these stories. There is El, the chief of the gods, and his female companion Asherah. But they take a back seat to Baal, the weather god, and his lover Anat, the goddess of love and war. One story tells how Baal was attacked by Mut, the god of barrenness and sterility. As in many ancient fertility myths, he overcomes Baal and his powers of life and fertility, and scatters his body to the four corners of the earth. While El, the father-god, leads the heavenly mourning for his lost son, Anat, the goddess of fertility, goes out to take her revenge:

She seizes Mut, the son of El,
with the knife she cuts him,
with the shovel she winnows him,
with fire she burns him,
with millstones she grinds him,
on the field she throws him.
The birds eat his remains,
the feathered ones make an end to
    what is left over.

Baal's power is brought back as he renews his sexual relationship with Anat – and that in turn ensures the fertility of the earth and its inhabitants for another season. This was the main point of Canaanite religion. Without the rains that fall from October to April, agriculture would have been impossible. And so when the rains stopped in May, it seemed as if Baal was dead, and needed to be revived. Some experts believe that the story of Baal's revival by Anat was the central feature of an annual New Year Festival in ancient Canaan. On this occasion, held every autumn, the king and a temple prostitute would act out the story of Baal and Anat, to make sure that all would be well for another year. No doubt the same kind of rites went on in every local shrine throughout the land. Temple prostitutes feature prominently in the Old Testament descriptions of Canaanite worship, and sexual intercourse with them was considered to be as much a part of the job of a farmer as were the actual operations of agriculture.

This is why the challenge of Canaanite religion often proved irresistable to the Israelites. For though they knew their God Yahweh was all-powerful in the desert, and in war, they doubted his ability to control the weather and the fertility of fields and flocks. This led to all sorts of compromises. Some gave up the worship of Yahweh altogether, and

In occupying Canaan, the Israelites were moving from a nomadic to a more settled existence. The life of agriculture and of towns would have required them to develop laws and traditions not needed in the nomadic life.

of belief and worship. After all, the Canaanite city-states were successful in getting the best from the land, and if they claimed this was due to their religion, then at least it would seem to be worth consideration. But in reality, the worship of Yahweh and the worship of Baal could not be mixed, for there were fundamental differences between the two:

● Yahweh, the God of Israel, was a God who acted in history. He was not a god of nature who was revealed only in the yearly cycles of summer and winter. He was a personal God, who had disclosed his character in personal ways, through his encounters with Abraham and Moses.

● The Canaanite rituals were first and foremost magical rites. They were designed to bully the gods into making the earth fertile year by year. This was the whole reasoning behind the sexual intercourse which a farmer would have with a temple prostitute. For it was hoped that the farmer's activities would induce the gods to do the same, and thus produce more fruitful crops. By contrast, the God of Israel could not be bullied by magic. He had not been forced to call Abraham, or to deliver the slaves from Egypt: all that he did arose from his own spontaneous love and care for his people.

● The Canaanite view encouraged the assumption that religion had nothing to do with behaviour in normal life, but only with the special ritual that was performed in the shrines. This notion is still widely held today. But it runs completely contrary to the Old Testament's understanding of God. The God of Israel was not most concerned with the empty performance of hollow rituals, but with the way people behave in everyday life. This lesson was hammered home over and over again by the prophets, as they declared that Israel's religious duty was not something that took place in a shrine, but in the market-place: 'to do what is just, to show constant love, and to live in humble fellowship with our God' (Micah 6:8).

● In view of this, it is not surprising that Israel's God demanded exclusive worship. The gods and goddesses of Canaan were always tolerant of other gods – they were, in a sense, their own relatives! But the God of Israel had demanded the exclusive obedience of his people (Exodus 20:1–3). And now that we can understand the nature of Baal worship, it is not difficult to see why the writers of the Old Testament were so adamant in emphasizing this.

worshipped the Canaanite deities instead. Others tried to amalgamate the two, while yet others worshipped mainly Yahweh, but felt obliged to use Canaanite shrines and Canaanite rituals in doing so. The texts from Ugarit have shown that the denunciations of Israel by the great prophets were far from exaggerated. But the extent of the compromise that was made is clear from the Old Testament itself. Even the leading Israelite families could give their children Canaanite names. One of the sons of Saul was Jonathan ('Gift of Yahweh'), but another was Ish-Baal ('Man of Baal') – while the names of Baal and Anat were attached to many Israelite towns and villages.

It is not surprising that the Israelites were tempted to adopt Canaanite ways

4 A king like the other nations

1 and 2 Samuel
1 Kings 1:1—12:20
Psalms
Song of Solomon

Proverbs
Ecclesiastes
Job

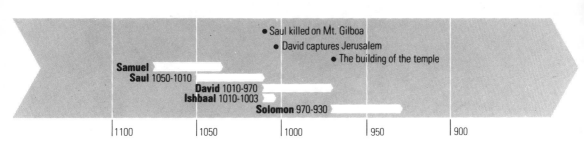

- Saul killed on Mt. Gilboa
- David captures Jerusalem
- The building of the temple

Samuel
Saul 1050-1010
David 1010-970
Ishbaal 1010-1003
Solomon 970-930

| 1100 | 1050 | 1000 | 950 | 900 |

'YOU HAVE been our king from the beginning, O God; you have saved us many times.' The words were written centuries later, but they sum up well enough the ideals of the early days of Israel's history. Though the tribes may from time to time have their human leaders, in the end God himself was their only true sovereign. Even the great judges were not important in themselves. They were just men and women whom God had inspired to lead their people in times of special need.

Psalm 74:12

The judges themselves recognized this. When some of the tribes suggested to Gideon that his bravery and courage deserved the reward of a permanent position of power, he would have nothing to do with it. It was, he declared, impossible for his people to be ruled both by God himself and by a human king. His son Abimelech did not have the same scruples, and he managed to persuade the people of the city of Shechem to make him their king. But his success was short-lived. The tribes were determined that the monarchies of the Canaanite city-states would not form a model for Israelite society. The belief that God was their ruler was not just a pious fiction, but something that would be applied in everyday life.

Judges 8:22–23

Judges 9

The tribes were held together not by the institutions of a shared government, but by the experiences of a shared faith, symbolized by the ark of the covenant. But it was perhaps inevitable that eventually

The histories of the kings often concentrate on warfare, on great events, the life of the towns. But Israelite society was still mainly rural, and normal life was lived in the village and the countryside.

the symbol should be mistaken for the reality. The priests concerned with the common worship of the tribes now saw the opportunity to carve out a comfortable niche for themselves. They began to think of their own position and their ritual operations as the true focus of Israel's faith.

Samuel and the ark

1 Samuel 1—3

We can see from the stories about Samuel's early life that the ordinary people did not go along with this. But life at the time was so insecure that they could do little about it. For an apparently greater threat was looming: the Philistines.

While the Philistines had been establishing their position, they were held in check by neighbouring tribes or local heroes like Samson. But now they were out for the total domination of the country. They were a strong and powerful force. They had adapted the government of the Canaanite city-states to their own advantage. But they had one thing their Canaanite predecessors never had: a strong sense of national unity. Though they were independent, the Philistine cities could act in a concerted and unified way. This made them a formidable enemy. For they were also technically more advanced than Israel, and knew how to use chariots and iron weapons in war.

1 Samuel 4:1—11
1 Samuel 5:1—7:1

Both politically and militarily, Israel was less well organized than the Philistines, and could offer no effective resistance to the advancing armies. After a devastating defeat near Aphek, the leaders of the Israelite tribes realized that they were powerless. Where were the inspiring leaders and the brave exploits of previous generations? Why was their God no longer with them, as he had been with the great judges? They decided they must make certain that God went with them into battle: 'Let's go and bring the Lord's Covenant Ark from Shiloh, so that he will go with us and save us from our enemies.' Unfortunately, their plan did not work out. The ark of the covenant was captured, its shrine at Shiloh destroyed, and the Israelite army was decimated.

Their religious mistake was clear enough. Following the lead of the sons of Eli the priest (who were themselves killed in the battle), they had forgotten the close personal nature of Israel's relationship to God – preferring instead to suppose that he could be contained in a box. But now the box was gone, and they were effectively the vassals of the Philistines. It seems unlikely that the Philistines wanted the whole land for themselves. More probably they were trying to take over the position once occupied by the Egyptians: they would be the rulers, and the Israelites and Canaanites would be their subjects. That did not make it any less painful for Israel. But what could they do to get rid of them? Samuel seemed powerless, yet he was the only surviving representative of the old order. And although the ark of the covenant took its own revenge on the Philistines and was eventually returned to Israel, the old fervour and enthusiasm did not return with it. It seemed as if the old tribal alliance and its simple trust in God had failed.

Saul

Moreover, the Philistines were not the only challenge that the Israelite tribes had to face. Other groups, many of them racially related to Israel, were pressing in from the east side of the River Jordan. Among them were the Ammonites. They attacked the people of Jabesh Gilead, and made it a condition of peace that the right eye of every citizen should be put out. It was not long before this news had travelled far and wide – and a powerful army was raised from among the tribes of Israel to deal with this new threat.

The man who put new life into the Israelites was Saul. He was on his way home from the fields when he heard what was happening in Jabesh Gilead. Like the judges before him, he was moved to fury by 'the spirit of God'. He cut up the oxen he was driving, and sent the pieces throughout the whole district, with the gruesome message: 'Whoever does not follow Saul and Samuel into battle will have this done to his oxen!' So Saul rallied his army, and Jabesh Gilead was set free.

1 Samuel 11:6

1 Samuel 11:7

Up to this point, the story is quite similar to the tales told about the judges. But a new departure was made after Saul's great victory, for the people gathered at the shrine in Gilgal, and acclaimed him as their king. According to the stories in 1 Samuel, this was not a spontaneous action but the culmination of much debate among the Israelite leaders. For the appointment of a king was not something to be taken lightly. After all, if it was wrong for Gideon to be king, how could it now be right for Saul? The Old Testament reports this argument in some detail. Indeed, the two sides were put with such vigour that scholars commonly reckon they can trace two distinctive accounts of Samuel and his role in the affair:

1 Samuel 11:13–15

● In one Samuel seems to be a relatively unknown local figure, who appoints Saul as king under God's direct guidance. The monarchy will save Israel from her enemies, and for this reason is generally looked on with favour in these sections of the story.

1 Samuel 9:1—10:16; 11:1–15

● In another account Samuel seems to be a national figure, and a man who disapproves of the appointment of a king, because this would mean a rejection of God himself as the true king of Israel

1 Samuel 8:1–22; 10:17–27

We need not doubt that the editors of the book of Samuel have taken material from many different sources and incorporated it into their own story. Nor need we be surprised that they should have included what some modern readers might regard as contradictory stories. They are only contradictory if we look at them from a purely literary viewpoint. But they represent a tension that must have existed at the time, and which was never really satisfactorily resolved. On the one hand, a strong leader was needed to unite the tribes into an alliance powerful enough to fight the Philistines; but on the other, the existence of such a leader would inevitably weaken the conviction that God was Israel's only true king. This tension is clearly reflected in the stories about Saul.

In some respects, he was not so much a king as a kind of perpetual judge. It was certainly important that he should be seen to have the same popular appeal and military prowess that the judges had possessed. But in practical terms, Saul had his difficulties. Up to

For his campaigns against the Philistines, Saul did not conscript a people's army for particular battles. Rather he recruited a fairly small professional army, paid for by taxation.

this point, the main military force in Israel had been the large army of volunteers from the tribes. It was with such a spontaneously recruited force that Saul had been able to avenge the people of Jabesh Gilead. But this sort of arrangement was only for great emergencies. It was not the way for a king to operate. Nor was it altogether practical to get rid of the Philistines in this way. Guerilla warfare would be far more effective than large pitched battles – and for that, a small body of professional soldiers would be much more suitable than a large force of untrained volunteers. So, like the Philistine and Canaanite kings, Saul formed his own personal army.

1 Samuel 13:2;14:52

By all accounts it was a successful move, for he was able to drive the Philistines at least from the hill country, which gave him greater freedom of movement. But this military efficiency was bought at a price. For though Saul lacked most of the trappings of the oriental monarch, and even his headquarters at Gibeah was by no means a palace, he was separating himself from his people. His professional army owed its allegiance not to the tribes in general, but to Saul himself as its commander in chief. Since Saul appears to have had no resources of his own, he must have needed someone else to pay for the army – and that meant the tribes. Though there is no direct evidence for it in the Old Testament, he was probably forced to

1 Samuel 13—14

1 Samuel 15:1–35

raise some kind of taxation from his people. It could well have been financial stringency that forced Saul to disregard Samuel's instructions about the goods of the defeated Amalekites. But as a result of this, Saul came to be regarded as a headstrong, selfish man who put his own will and wisdom before the will of God, and who was too ready to jettison the old religious ideals when they interfered with his own military strategy.

If Saul's army had been successful against the Philistines, his life might well have turned out differently. But he made very little headway against the well-organized Philistine armies, and in terms

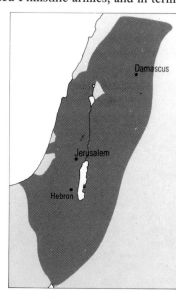

Right: The kingdom of Saul

Far right: The kingdom of David

Trade in Solomon's time

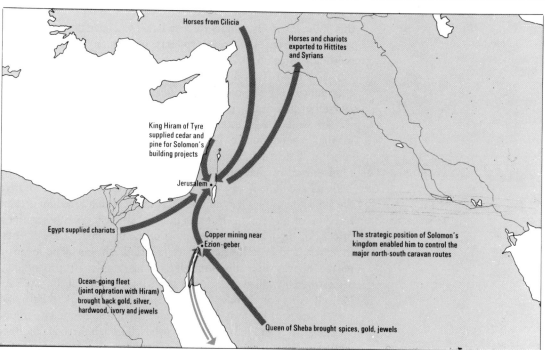

of territory, Saul was very much a king without a kingdom. The three Canaanite cities of Jerusalem, Aijalon and Gezer still separated the centre of the country from the south, and to the north the strategic Plain of Jezreel was still controlled by the Philistines.

In order to survive, Saul needed to be a king over people rather than territory. But he had lost much of his popular support by choosing to enlist his own personal army. No doubt he could have regained his initial popularity if he had not been overtaken by jealousy and suspicion of one of his young subjects, a shepherd *1 Samuel 16 – 28* called David. The deep depression to which this led suggests that by the end of his life Saul was mentally deranged. He died a lonely and forlorn figure by his own sword after a crushing defeat at the hands of the Philistines on Mt Gilboa. The complexity of Saul's personality eludes us, but he emerges as a tragic figure. He had great potential as the recognized successor to the judges, but the *1 Samuel 31* nature of the conflict in which he was involved more or less forced him to go against the old tribal ideals of his people – and led to his downfall.

'Has even Saul become a prophet?'

The question arises out of an incident recorded in 1 Samuel 10:5–13. After being anointed by Samuel, Saul went up to worship at the sanctuary of Gibeah, and as he was on his way he encountered a group of prophets who were shouting and dancing to frenzied music, in some sort of religious ecstasy. Quite unexpectedly, Saul himself was caught up in the same excitement, and he too joined in their dancing and singing. This was such an unexpected turn of events that bystanders spoke of Saul becoming 'a different person' under the influence of this religious enthusiasm, and many expressed their surprise that a reputable person like him should become mixed up with it all.

The fact that this could happen to Saul will probably surprise no one today. We all know of religious groups whose fervour and excitement leads them into wild and uncontrollable behaviour of this sort – often stimulated by music, as was the case here.

Many readers of the Old Testament, however, are surprised to see people like this described as 'prophets'. For the typical prophet of the Old Testament is not a person who indulges in religious excitement: he is a person with a message from God to his people, who expresses that message in clear language, appealing not to the emotions of his hearers but to their reason and sense of religious commitment.

A number of observations can be made on this issue:

● Some have drawn attention to the statement in 1 Samuel 9:9, that 'At that time a prophet was called a seer . . . ' A seer would be someone who tried to discover God's will by semi-magical means – much like a modern fortune-teller. Perhaps then, it is argued, the confusion is just a matter of terminology, and the great classical prophets with their incisive comments on social and political affairs simply evolved over a period of time out of such unsophisticated practitioners. There are certainly some statements in the Old Testament that could be taken to support this view. Amos, for example, seems to distinguish himself from a 'prophet' who would give messages for money (Amos 7:14), while Micah 3:6–7 seems to refer to the same sort of people.

● At the same time, some passages do seem to refer to ecstatic experiences in the lives of the great prophets. Even Jeremiah was described as a 'madman' (admittedly, by his enemies, Jeremiah 29:26–27). Hosea was accused in much the same way (Hosea 9:7) – and some of the experiences of these later prophets (especially people like Ezekiel) were certainly most unusual. We also know of at least one occasion when the prophet Elisha gave his message to the accompaniment of music (2 Kings 3:15–19), while the behaviour of one of his fellow prophets provoked a king of Israel to call him 'that crazy fellow' (2 Kings 9:11).

● There are parallels to all this in other cultures of the time. From the Old Testament itself we have a description of the behaviour of the prophets of Baal, who sought to invoke the power of their god by a self-induced religious ecstasy (1 Kings 18:20–29). Unfortunately we know very little about such people in Canaan itself. But we do have some evidence from Mari in the form of a series of letters dating from the eighteenth century BC. They concern a wide variety of prophetic functions, one of the most important of which was the encouragement of a king in times of particular difficulty – especially the giving of advice in times of war. It is perhaps significant here that we find mention of prophets advising kings elsewhere in the Old Testament, though their advice (as at Mari) was not always what their masters wanted (2 Samuel 12:1–15; 1 Kings 22:1–28).

What then are we to make of all this? One possibility is that these bands of ecstatic enthusiasts arose spontaneously as a means of inspiring the people of Israel in times of great difficulty. And no time was more difficult for them than the time of Saul, with the threat of the Philistines hanging over them. This function of these ecstatics may later have been continued and refined in those prophets who were attached to the royal courts of Israel and Judah. Their precise relationship with the great preaching prophets of the Old Testament is still uncertain. But both types of prophet obviously thought of themselves as the communicators of a message from God to his people.

David

David was made of different stuff from Saul. He was a charismatic figure in every sense of the word, and would overcome tribal suspicions and resistance to the idea of a king, to unite the whole of Israel into a remarkably powerful alliance.

When the Old Testament stories were first written down, David was already Israel's greatest national hero. He was the traditional composer of Israel's best-loved songs (the Psalms), and the man about whom many of the most popular stories were told. We can see this in the way the writer of the book of Samuel introduces him to his narrative. In contrast to the stories of Saul, the accounts of David's life have been composed with great artistry and literary

1 Samuel 19—20
1 Samuel 17

skill. The stories of his friendship with Saul's son Jonathan, and of his unexpected defeat of the Philistine giant Goliath have become favourites even with modern readers.

David's rise to power

David was obviously a striking character. Not many shepherds become kings, and he must have had some extraordinary talent to rise so quickly to a position of such eminence in Saul's court. The features that impressed Saul also impressed his people, and it was not long before they were singing David's praises in the streets:

1 Samuel 18:7

'Saul has killed thousands, but David tens of thousands'. This kind of popularity aroused Saul to intense jealousy, and so he dismissed David from the court, giving him instead the command of a thousand soldiers in his private army. But David could not be held back. His military exploits were amazing, and 'everyone in Israel

1 Samuel 18:16

and Judah loved David because he was such a successful leader'. His admirers even included Saul's daughter Michal, who fell in

1 Samuel 18:17–27

love with David and married him. But Saul became more and more envious, and set out deliberately to kill him. As a result, David was

1 Samuel 19—22

forced to go into exile, in the south of the country.

There he was secure from Saul, for between them lay a number of fortified Canaanite city-states, including Jerusalem. In the south, David probably forged some sort of alliance with the Philistines, for

1 Samuel 22:1–2

he was able to organize a kind of court at Adullam and to protect

At Ein Gedi by the Dead Sea, a stream flows down a gorge to the shore. The whole area abounds in caves, and this is the region where David hid from Saul and his soldiers during the years of his exile from court.

1 Samuel 25

1 Samuel 27

1 Samuel 29

1 Samuel 30

1 Samuel 31

himself and his troops by running a protection racket. He also strengthened his position here by marriage alliances, and obviously became closely involved with Achish, the Philistine king of Gath. Achish wanted to take David with him to the battle of Gilboa, where Saul met his death. But he was left behind when his loyalty was questioned by the other Philistine chiefs. They were right to do so, for David had been playing a double game with Achish. But it turned out to David's advantage. For while the Philistines had been arguing about David, Amalekite raiders had attacked the town of Ziklag. On his return, David went out to avenge his people. He took back all that the Amalekites had taken, and more besides – and then tactfully distributed it among the people of the towns where he was best known.

Saul was finished. He died in disgrace, and for all practical purposes, his kingdom fell into the hands of the Philistines. But David's position was assured. He had already established himself among the southern tribes, and he was now recognized as their leader – the king of Judah, reigning at Hebron. The southern tribes of Judah had always been isolated from the northern tribes, and they had probably never been a full part of Saul's kingdom. So they had no qualms about accepting David. He had already shown his prowess in battle, and he continued to protect the people for a further seven-and-a-half years.

2 Samuel 2:10–11

But David was not satisfied with this. He knew that Israel would never be truly great until northern and southern tribes were fully united. In the north, Saul's son Ishbaal (Ishbosheth) had taken his father's place. But he had no popular support. In his fury against David, Saul had gone so far as to kill the priests who looked after the tribal sanctuary at Nob. That in itself was enough to ensure that no son of his would ever be acclaimed by the tribes. Ishbaal's only real supporter was Abner, the commander of Saul's personal army. And when even he defected to David's side, Ishbaal was finished. David agreed to become king of all the Israelite tribes, and the northern group gave their allegiance to him. The Philistines could see what was coming. They did not like the idea of a united kingdom of Israel, and they moved in to try to cut the links between north and south. But they were defeated many times, and from then onwards the kingdom of David was the dominant political force in Palestine.

1 Samuel 22

2 Samuel 2:8 — 4:12

2 Samuel 5:1–5

2 Samuel 5:17–25

A new king and new ways

Jerusalem was captured by David, who moved his capital there from Hebron. Known ever since as 'the city of David', Jerusalem became and has remained the focus of devotion for the people of Israel.

A new kingdom needed a new capital. Hebron was too far in the south, and the north had no organization to speak of since the defeat at Gilboa and the murder of Ishbaal. So David found a new capital in Jerusalem. It was a masterly stroke. This city had belonged to neither northern nor southern tribes, and so it would not engender new jealousies. It had been one of the last remaining bastions of Canaanite sovereignty that had effectively isolated north

from south during the time of Saul. So its brilliant capture by David's troops, climbing up a water shaft into the city, also removed one of the last physical barriers to the unity of the new kingdom.

2 Samuel 5:6–10

It was therefore 'the city of David' in a distinctive way. He built new fortifications, and a palace for himself. He employed foreign craftsmen for the work, and established a relationship with the Phoenicians that was to last for some considerable time. Unfortunately, very little remains now of the Jerusalem of David's time. But there can be no doubt that he and his successor Solomon transformed it into a major administrative centre, probably aided by the considerable bureaucratic expertise of its original Jebusite inhabitants, who were now incorporated into the kingdom of Israel. This was just a small section of a fairly large foreign population that became a part of David's kingdom. For as he extended his influence in all directions, he defeated Edomites, Moabites, Ammonites, and Syrians, as well as Philistines – and their towns and people gave their allegiance to David.

2 Samuel 5:11–12

The spoils captured in these military expeditions, and the taxes paid to him by conquered peoples, financed the erection of many fine buildings in Jerusalem. It also enabled David to increase the number of mercenaries in his personal army, and to establish a full royal court at his new palace. But he was always careful to preserve those all-important links with his people's past. One of his earliest acts was to bring the ark of the covenant to Jerusalem. To the tribes, this had always been the central symbol of their whole existence. It reminded them of their escape from Egypt, of their covenant with God at Mt Sinai, and of the common worship of Yahweh their God that held them together.

2 Samuel 6

We need not doubt that David's religious commitment played an important part in all this. But the arrival of the ark of the covenant in Jerusalem also had social consequences. It gave David's own position a special seal of approval. More than that, for in a sense, the ark installed in David's city now became David's personal possession. It certainly removed the power centre from the tribes themselves, and vested it in a state authority that was separate from the old tribal loyalties. In other words, David achieved what Saul had failed to do: he established his own position independently of the continued acclamation of the people. The nation was controlled by his own army, with his own city – even, perhaps, his own national shrine at the centre of things.

David was undoubtedly a great leader: a military strategist who overcame Israel's enemies, and a politician who brought the people of the whole of Palestine to a unity never known before – and certainly never since – under a ruler of their own race. Admittedly, this was made easier by the relative weakness of Egypt and Assyria at the time. But David's achievement was still remarkable.

The old ways and new ideas

2 Samuel 11

David was, however, vulnerable. One of the most significant stories told about him in the Old Testament is of his adultery with Bathsheba and the murder of her husband Uriah. It was not

2 Samuel 12:1–15

unusual for an oriental king to behave like this. But it is surprising to find the bold denunciation of David's behaviour by the prophet Nathan, and the deep sincerity of David's subsequent repentance. Even David was to be subject to a greater power than himself. But his position itself was not threatened. For on a previous occasion, Nathan had declared that God would make a specially close

2 Samuel 7:1–17

personal relationship with David's family. Not only would David's son succeed him, but God himself would be 'his father, and he will

2 Samuel 7:14
2 Samuel 7:16

be my son'. And David was assured that God would 'make your kingdom last for ever. Your dynasty will never end'.

Many kings in the ancient world, especially in Mesopotamia, thought of themselves as sons of the gods. But whereas for them, this idea often became a crude legitimation of everything they did, in the Old Testament it established a moral framework within which the kings were to operate. The king in Jersualem was now firmly linked to the covenant relationship between God and his people established at Mt Sinai. The king was incorporated into that, and this gave him special privileges. But he was also faced with the moral requirements of the Sinai covenant, and his position as God's 'son' meant he could be punished by God, just as any other

2 Samuel 7:14

parent would punish his children for wrongdoing.

Inevitably, the kings of David's dynasty did not live up to these high aspirations. They were, after all, only human – and the tragedy, as Samuel had foreseen, was that the kings of Israel were to become like the kings of other nations, more often concerned for themselves than for their covenant obligations to God and to their

1 Samuel 8:10–18

people. But this promise to David and his family was to assume great importance at a later stage in Israel's history, as frustrated political ambitions came to be transferred to a future hope for an ideal descendant of David, the Messiah.

Solomon

2 Samuel 13—19
2 Samuel 20:1–22

Towards the end of David's reign, the prospective heirs began to jockey for position. Revolts led by David's son Absalom and by Sheba, a man from the tribe of Benjamin, were crushed, and by the time of David's death his son Adonijah was the most obvious successor. He had the support of Abiathar the priest and Joab, who

1 Kings 1:5–10

was commander of the popular army drawn from the Israelite tribes. But another son, Solomon, had more powerful friends. His mother Bathsheba had been David's favourite wife, and she was supported by Nathan, the priest Zadok, and Benaiah, the commander of David's personal army. In the end, Solomon won. With the exception of Abiathar the priest, who was sent off into exile,

1 Kings 1:11—2:46

Adonijah and all his supporters were killed. Right from the start, Solomon's position as king was founded on court intrigues and military strength. Unlike his father David, and Saul before him, he did not seek popular acceptance by the tribes, and in Solomon Israel certainly got a king like the kings of the other nations around them. Unlike Saul and the Judges (and, to a lesser extent, David), Solomon was not a leader among equals, but the figurehead of a new ruling class that was determined to maintain its position of superiority by whatever means were necessary. For the first time, Israel was a state, rather than a nation, and this led to far-reaching changes in Israelite society.

The empire

1 Kings 11:14–25

1 Kings 4:26;10:26

Solomon did not continue the military conquests of David. Indeed, there is evidence to suggest that both the Edomites and the Syrians recovered some territory from Israel during Solomon's reign. Solomon was more concerned with the defence of his own position than the defence of his people. So he poured vast resources into the development of the private army that his father had left to him. What had probably been in David's day little more than a personal bodyguard for the king now developed into a sophisticated fighting force, with 1,400 chariots and 12,000 men and horses. Chariots had once been the monopoly of the Canaanite city-states, and it was this more than anything else that had prevented the tribes in the days of the Judges from penetrating to the plains in the centre of the country. Solomon probably utilized Canaanite expertise in such weapons, for his own chariots were stationed exclusively in the old Canaanite cities.

Alliances

1 Kings 9:16–17

1 Kings 9:26–28;10:22

1 Kings 10:28–29

This perhaps opened the door for Canaanite influences in Israel. But foreign influence was to be felt more particularly in Solomon's trading activities. He traded with Phoenicia, with Arabia, with Syria and Cilicia, and probably with north and east Africa too. He allied himself with Egypt by marrying an Egyptian princess. This must have been an important alliance, for he had a special palace built for his Egyptian wife. The pharaoh of the time also took it seriously, for he captured the city of Gezer and gave it to Solomon as a wedding gift. This is the latest occasion we know of when Israel acquired a Canaanite city, and the archaeological evidence from Gezer shows clearly enough how the Egyptians destroyed it, and how Solomon rebuilt it in a distinctive style.

Another of Solomon's close allies was Hiram, king of Tyre. The Phoenicians had widespread trading links throughout the Mediterranean Sea, and they gave Solomon assistance to develop his own sea trade in the Red Sea and the Indian Ocean. They also probably helped him with the expertise necessary to build and operate his own copper refineries on the Gulf of Aqabah. Solomon was also a horse dealer on a grand scale, trading with the Egyptians in the south and the Hittites in the north.

The temple

2 Samuel 7:1–17

2 Samuel 24:18–25; 2 Chronicles 3:1

The profits from all this activity helped to finance the erection of many buildings in Jerusalem – Solomon's own palace, a palace for his Egyptian wife, a hall of audience for state occasions, a smaller judgement hall. And, of course, the temple.

David had originally wanted to build a permanent temple to house the ark of the covenant. He had been unable to do so, but that did not stop him securing a site and gathering together items to go into a temple. Solomon was remembered by later generations of

Israelites largely because of his completion of this project. Like everything else that he attempted, the work was carried out on a lavish scale. The best materials were imported at great cost, and skilled craftsmen were brought in from Phoenicia. Naturally, they used their own art forms in its construction, and the general design of the temple they produced was thoroughly Canaanite. Though it was to contain the ark of the covenant, which symbolized the presence of Israel's God Yahweh, the actual plan of the temple was identical to temples of Baal that have been discovered elsewhere in Palestine.

1 Kings 5—7

Some have also suggested that Solomon adopted the same attitude to the temple as the rulers of Ugarit took to their own temple of Baal. They point out that the Jerusalem temple was consecrated at exactly the same time in the year as the Baal temple at Ugarit, just before the beginning of the all-important autumn rains. And it is beyond doubt that Solomon took upon himself some of the most important religious functions. He offered sacrifices and he blessed the people. Yet Saul and David had been expressly forbidden to do both these things – and Saul's attempt to do so had led directly to his downfall. Because of the central importance later attached to Jerusalem and its temple, the writer of the book of Kings makes no comment on these particular features of Solomon's kingship. But he does criticize what many saw as Solomon's active promotion of the interests of 'foreign gods'. His careless disregard for the faith of the tribes must have been a major factor in his eventual downfall. Solomon may have been renowned for his wisdom, but it was not the kind of practical wisdom that led to a sympathetic understanding of his own people, or to an appreciation of the kind of king that Israel's faith would tolerate.

1 Kings 6:1, 37–38;8:2
1 Kings 3:15; 8:62–66
1 Kings 8:14–61
1 Samuel 15:10–35

1 Kings 11:1–13

Arts and sciences

The 'wisdom' attributed to Solomon was in fact not just common sense and insight. It was rather part and parcel of a great international intellectual movement of the day that is often simply referred to as the 'wisdom movement'. The writer of 1 Kings explicitly compares Solomon's 'wisdom' with that of other ancient rulers: 'Solomon was wiser than the wise men of the East or the wise men of Egypt. He was the wisest of all men . . .' And the nature of this intellectual endeavour becomes clearer when we learn that 'He composed three thousand parables and more than a thousand songs. He spoke of trees and plants . . . he talked about animals, birds, reptiles, and fish'. This is comparable with the intellectual pursuits of kings and philosophers in ancient Egypt and Mesopotamia, who compiled encyclopedic descriptions of the world and all its affairs – from astrology to politics and zoology. The knowledge thus gained was sometimes distilled into pithy sayings, such as we find in the Old Testament book of Proverbs, parts of which are said to have been composed by Solomon himself. In a later period, professional 'wise men' could be found as religious advisers whose position was comparable to that of a priest. But at this stage the pursuit of 'wisdom' was probably a secular interest.

1 Kings 4:30–31

1 Kings 4:32–33

Proverbs 10:1; 25:1

Jeremiah 18:18

Solomon's temple

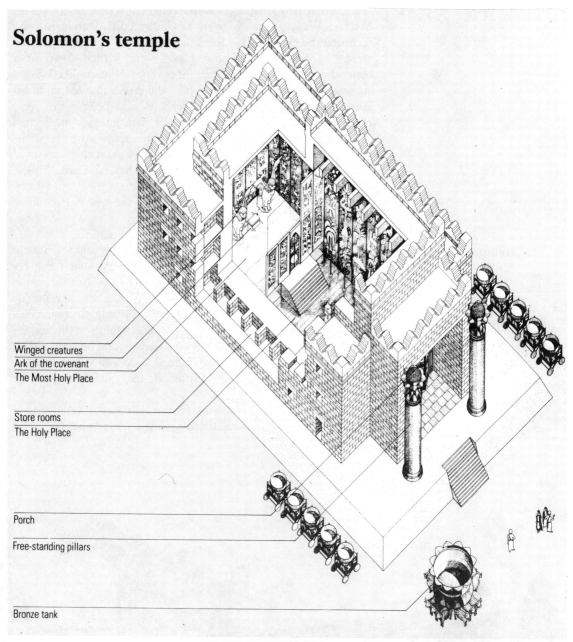

Winged creatures
Ark of the covenant
The Most Holy Place

Store rooms
The Holy Place

Porch

Free-standing pillars

Bronze tank

In building the temple, Solomon used the best and costliest materials. He bought timber from Hiram, King of Tyre, who supplied the famous Lebanon cedarwood, used also for temple building in Egypt and Assyria.

All.this activity stimulated the development of other literary skills in Israel. We know that Solomon had his own official archivists who recorded the events of his reign. It is also widely believed that the stories of Samuel, Saul and David were written down in a continuous narrative at this time. It is certainly not unlikely that a successful king would want to record the events that led up to his accession to the throne. Many scholars also believe that as a reaction against all this self-centred artistic and intellectual endeavour, other writers during Solomon's reign wove the traditional stories handed down by the tribes into a great epic account of Israel's earliest history – to emphasize again how Abraham, Moses, and the early tribes had prospered not because of their own efforts, but because of their humble dependence on the love and goodness of God in choosing them to be his own people.

1 Kings 11:41

Balancing the books

There was certainly a strong build-up of ill feeling and resentment against the style of Solomon's rule. It was bad enough that his actions should violate so many of the old tribal ways. But the people saw no reason why in addition they should actually pay for his extravagance through taxation. Yet it was inevitable, for Solomon's trading activities could not generate sufficient funds to finance the life of his court. On occasion, he could try to pay off his creditors by offering them land. This is what he tried to do with Hiram of Tyre, but the towns he offered were refused. So the people had to pay for their king.

1 Kings 9:10–14

The administrative framework for the collection of taxes already existed, for David had inaugurated a modest system whereby twelve

The wealth of Solomon's kingdom and his extended alliances made Israel into a major trading nation.

different districts of his territory would support his court with provisions for one month each year. Solomon extends this to provide the means for collecting taxes, and each district was placed in the charge of a single officer. The idea did not appeal to the people. It was not just that they were reluctant to pay their dues. To them, the very idea of a privileged elite being served and paid for by the ordinary citizens was a fundamental denial of the traditions of their people. At Mt Sinai, their ancestors had stood as equals before God. They had all been slaves. And the development of Israelite tribal society in the days of the judges had sought to express that. But now the old ways were being eroded: instead of twelve tribes serving God, there were twelve districts serving the king. And the fact that the worshippers of Baal at Ugarit had a very similar way of supporting their own royal house can only have served to emphasize the essentially pagan nature of the idea.

1 Kings 4:7–19

But there was worse to come. The taxation raised in the districts was still not enough to balance Solomon's books. So he introduced what the Old Testament euphemistically calls 'forced labour' – in other words, slavery. This was the last straw, and a coup was planned by one of the officers in charge of the taxation districts – a man called Jeroboam. His plot was uncovered, and he fled into exile in Egypt for a while. But the movement that he started could not be stopped. The tribes in the northern part of Solomon's kingdom – the original tribes who had chosen Saul as their leader – had had enough. Not only did they regard Solomon's demands as excessive, but they believed them to be unfair, for the southern tribes – who first made David their king – appear to have been excluded from the taxation districts altogether.

1 Kings 5:13; 11:28

1 Kings 11:26–40

1 Kings 4:7–19

So the seeds of Solomon's destruction were sown. Judged by the standards of world powers, Solomon was outstandingly successful, the greatest of all Israel's rulers. But judged by the moral and spiritual standards of the covenant, he was a miserable failure.

The stories about David and Solomon

The books of Samuel and Kings belong together. They are a compilation of different stories, brought together by an editor or editors to make one great account of Israel's history, that probably included the books of Joshua and Judges as well. Quite often, the editors refer to their sources of information (e.g. 1 Kings 11:41). At other points, modern scholars have tried to uncover the origins of their stories. This can often be an unprofitable exercise, but in the case of the stories of David and Solomon many people believe that such 'source analysis' can show that we are actually reading a kind of 'court history' that was written down more or less at the same time as the events themselves happened.

The stories in 2 Samuel 9 — 20 and 1 Kings 1 — 2 are undoubtedly among the most vivid narratives in the whole Old Testament. They are well written and excitingly presented, with the kind of psychological appreciation of human relationships that gives an added plausibility to what they say. In this respect they are quite different from what precedes or follows them – and even from the final chapters of 2 Samuel itself (21 — 24).

In 1926, the German scholar Leonhard Rost suggested that this section of Samuel and Kings was originally a self-contained story, and that it was originally written to prove that Solomon was the legitimate heir to David's throne. There is no doubt that the accession of Solomon is surprising, for he was a relatively minor son, and apart from a short notice of his birth in 2 Samuel 12:24–25 there is no mention of him before he became king. He also came to power through a court intrigue, and by murdering his opponents – and, Rost suggested, many loyal Israelites must have been asking awkward questions about the morality of all this. So a supporter of Solomon set out to justify his position – and, in the nature of things, he must have done so at an early date in Solomon's reign.

There was a well established tradition of such political apologetic among other nations at the time, especially the Hittites. So, encouraged by international contacts, and the new opportunities for artistic endeavour provided by Solomon's court, Solomon's friend took the older traditional stories about David's reign, and showed how the elder sons Amnon, Absalom, and Adonijah, had all disqualified themselves by their disregard for the covenant traditions (2 Samuel 13:8–14; 16:22; 1 Kings 2:13–17). This was why Solomon emerged as David's successor – and the brutal events which brought him to power were a regrettable but necessary evil.

Rost hailed this narrative as the beginning of real history writing in the ancient world. But more recent scholars have qualified his judgment. They point out, for example, that these stories contain much that is unfavourable to David and Solomon – and therefore, perhaps what we now have is a kind of expurgated version of a series of stories that originally disapproved of the Davidic dynasty. But this carries no weight if the original intention was apologetic: in such a situation, unfortunate facts have to be faced, and explained away in some way or another. But it has also been suggested that much of the material is more like a novel than real history. It certainly includes some surprising details – like the conversation that Amnon had with Tamar when he raped her (2 Samuel 13:1–21). But this does not call into question the general veracity of the narrative. It simply shows that it was written in the first instance by a journalist rather than an annalist. This in turn perhaps suggests that it was not really the official court record of David, but a popular account of Solomon's origins, designed to win the support of the average person in the street for the new king.

After Solomon

When Solomon died he was succeeded by his son, Rehoboam. But by then an irreversible change of mood had come over the northern tribal grouping. They had had enough of dynastic kingship, and they were looking for a return to the old ideal in which the people, and not an elite ruling class, would decide their own fate.

So when Rehoboam went north from Jerusalem to Shechem to secure the allegiance of the northern tribes, their local leaders announced the terms on which they would be prepared to acknowledge him as their king. Rehoboam's oldest and most experienced advisers told him to listen sympathetically. But he rejected their advice, and told the northern leaders that worse was to come: 'My father placed heavy burdens on you; I will make them even heavier. He beat you with a whip; I'll flog you with a horsewhip!' He regarded them as rebellious subjects, and got ready to force them back into line. But it was too late. Jeroboam had already returned from Egypt, and the people had accepted him as their king.

1 Kings 12:1–7

1 Kings 12:14

1 Kings 12:21–24

It was an irreversible change. From this point onwards, the northern tribes had their own king and their own kingdom – Israel. And the descendants of David in Jerusalem ruled over a much smaller kingdom in the south – Judah. Israel's golden age was past. She had asked for 'a king like the other nations' without fully appreciating the distinctive nature of the society that God had established in the covenant at Mt Sinai. And in a choice between king and covenant, the covenant must come first.

Society and religion

The years between Saul and Solomon saw the establishment of a distinctively Israelite society for the first time. Despite the problems that it caused, the idea of a monarchy was accepted, and even when the ten tribes broke away under Jeroboam they did little to change the outward forms of the society established by Solomon: they simply explained them in a different way.

So it is to be expected that the events of these difficult years should have set the pattern for Israel's life for many years to come. As we read the Old Testament books, that is precisely what we find. Perhaps nowhere is this more obvious than in the case of the Psalms and the 'wisdom literature' of the Old Testament. For though the editors of Israel's history books could see much to be ashamed of in the activities of David and Solomon, both of them soon came to be revered in the religious tradition of their people. David was credited with the authorship of much of the Old Testament book of Psalms, while Solomon was thought of as the founder of the 'wisdom movement' in ancient Israel. Not many scholars today would accept such traditions at their face value. But it is obvious that these kings and their successors in Jerusalem exerted a considerable influence on the religious and cultural life of their people.

The important religious message of these Old Testament books is dealt with in some detail in Chapters 11 and 12 below. But it is appropriate here to notice some aspects of the picture they provide of religious life and culture in ancient Israel.

The divided kingdom

The Psalms

The Old Testament book of Psalms consists of 150 separate pieces of religious poetry or songs, arranged in five separate sections, or 'books'. As a collection, they were probably brought together for use in the worship of the restored temple that was built in Jerusalem about 520 BC, after the Jewish exile in Babylon (see chapter seven).

Psalm 137

Naturally, some of the psalms were written at that time. But the majority were not, and it is widely agreed that they originated in the worship of God by ancient Israel during the period from about 1000 BC to 586 BC. Many of the psalms have titles, but these were not a part of the original compositions, and are rightly relegated to footnotes in modern versions such as the *Good News Bible* . Some of these titles contain musical directions, indicating the tune to which particular compositions were to be sung, or the musical instruments used to accompany them. Others indicate that a particular psalm was connected with David, the sons of Korah, Sons of Asaph, and others. The precise meaning of such ascriptions is often unclear. Even the term 'A psalm of David' could just as easily mean 'A psalm for David', and may not necessarily have been intended as a claim that he was its author. Such a title could also indicate that the psalm in question originally belonged to a collection of songs issued by the Davidic royal house in Jerusalem, or that it was written for the king there, who was of course always David's descendant. Most scholars today would not rule out the possibility that some of these psalms could go back to David himself. But we really have no way of being sure.

Life is always a kaleidoscope of conflicting experiences and emotions – and we find this variety reflected in the contents of the Old Testament psalms. Not all psalms are the same. Some of them are majestic hymns of praise to God, reflecting the joy of the jubilant worshipper who is at peace with God and with the world.

Psalms 145—150

By contrast, others reflect the darker moments of human experience. Sometimes the worshipper recognized his or her own guilt as

Psalms 51;130

the cause of the trouble. But on other occasions the worshipper protests that he is truly innocent, and ought not to be suffering in

Psalms 13;71

the first place. Such emotions are familiar to us all, for they are part and parcel of life in every place and at every time.

In other psalms, we can see how the whole nation might react in a

Psalms 44; 74; 80; 83

time of national disaster or uncertainty. We can also share in the great ceremonial events of national life, like the coronation or

Psalm 45

wedding of a king – while yet other psalms give us a glimpse into the heartfelt gratitude to God felt by an individual worshipper who

Psalms 30; 92; 116

had been delivered from some personal trial.

In the early years of this century, the psalms were classified along these lines by a German scholar, Hermann Gunkel. These psalms, he suggested, fall into five main categories: Hymns of Praise, Individual Songs of Lament, Community Laments, Individual Songs of Thanks, and Royal Psalms. His classification has stood the test of time, though it is in some respects unsatisfactory. For example, Gunkel tended to make too sharp a distinction between individual and community psalms. A number of psalms that begin as the words of a single person go on to speak not just of an individual, but of the whole nation of Israel. The category of 'Royal Psalms' can also be questioned. For all the Royal Psalms could easily be fitted into other categories, and the only thing that binds them together is their apparent reference to the king.

Psalms 51; 102; 130

The psalms must have been used in a number of different ways. Gunkel, for example, assumed that they were mostly personal expressions of piety – the sort of poetry that any worshipper would use to express his or her deepest feelings about life and about God. Others have argued that the psalms do not reflect individual experiences, but the experiences of the whole nation of Israel over a long period of time. It has even been suggested that they are a kind of spiritual temperature chart of Israel's history from the earliest days up to the time after the exile. Both these elements are no doubt present. But what is fundamental to the varied thoughts of the psalms is a deep religious experience that their authors knew to be relevant to the whole of life. For the sense of God's reality can come as readily from nature as from Israel's history or from the writer's own private experiences.

Psalms 8; 104
Psalms 78; 105
Psalms 31; 130

The Psalms and Israel's worship

Some scholars have suggested that the psalms were more fundamental to Israelite worship than we have suggested here, and that in them we have a detailed account of the religious activites at the Jerusalem temple in the period before the exile to Babylon. Two points in particular have contributed much to our understanding of this subject:

● Many of the psalms can be understood not just as hymns, but as more comprehensive liturgies. Not only do they reflect the praise and penitence of the worshippers – they also contain God's response to that worship (e.g.Psalms 2, 12, 20, 21, 45, 50, 81, 89, 91, 95, 108, 110, 132). These responses are often similar in both style and substance to the messages of the Old Testament prophets. And so it has been suggested that there was in the temple at Jerusalem a group of prophets whose job it was, alongside the priests, to lead the people in worship. When it was first made, this claim was a surprise to many Old Testament scholars. In the nineteenth century it had often been taken for granted that in Old Testament times the prophets and the priests were firmly opposed to each other, with the priests being concerned with the mechanical performance of rites of 'religion', while the prophets concerned themselves with true revelation – bringing a living word from God to their people. It is certainly true that most of the prophets had hard things to say about the meaningless performance of empty religious rituals. But this sharp division between priest and prophet often owed more to the intense anti-Catholic views of the scholars who made it than it did to the evidence of the Old Testament. Even Amos, who is often thought to be one of those most fiercely opposed to religious rituals, apparently delivered his messages in the course of organized worship at Bethel. And the book of Jeremiah not only lists prophets and priests together as leaders of the community (Jeremiah 18:18), but also gives other indications of the association of prophets with the Jerusalem temple (e.g. Jeremiah 5:30–31; 23:11; 26:7,16; 27:16; 29:26). These prophets are often called 'cult prophets' to distinguish them from people like Amos or Jeremiah. In Jeremiah's time, most of them were giving false reassurance to the people, and as a result their office disappeared after the Babylonian exile. But the book of Psalms gives some indication that at an earlier period they had a full and perfectly legitimate part to play in the worship of God at the temple.

● A number of scholars have also claimed on the basis of the psalms that the king played a significant role in the worship at the temple. They observe that elsewhere in the ancient world, kings were often thought of as divine or semi-divine beings, whose well-being was crucial to the continued prosperity of their people. His involvement in religious ritual was often connected with the cycle of the seasons – as, for example, in Babylon where the king appeared in the annual New Year Festival as the personification of a god, whose ritual death and resurrection symbolized the death and renewed vitality of nature. We have already noticed a number of occasions when David and Solomon played an important part in Israelite worship – and no doubt their successors continued to do so. Of course, neither they nor their people ever thought they were divine, though they did have a special position as a result of God's blessing upon them (Psalm 2:7). Yet some still insist that there was an annual festival in Israel at which the king underwent a ritual humiliation and restoration along the lines of the Babylonian festival. The Scandinavian scholar Sigmund Mowinckel is on safer ground when he argues that the annual celebration of the New Year in Israel centred more on the enthronement of God himself, and the celebration of his continued lordship over the forces of chaos and disorder. Others however have denied this, preferring instead to see the New Year festival in Israel (the Feast of Tabernacles) as an occasion for solemn renewal of the covenant made at Mt Sinai – or even as an annual celebration of the establishment of the royal family of David. Certainly it is difficult to accept that the king in ancient Israel was exclusively, or even mainly, a religious functionary. There is no evidence to show that the Babylonian idea of kingship was widely held in the ancient world. And in addition, much of the theory relies on intelligent guesswork that lays too much emphasis on the psalms and not enough on the rest of the Old Testament. Admittedly, there is everywhere an insistence that the king of Judah has been appointed and chosen by God himself. But much of this is a theological comment on a simple fact of life, and the overall impression the Old Testament gives of the kings is of men whose activities (naturally and inevitably) had some interaction with religious worship, but whose main sphere of operation was elsewhere, in the judicial and diplomatic functions of the ancient monarch.

Wisdom

Just as David was traditionally associated with the types of religious poetry we find in the book of Psalms, so Solomon was often linked with the so-called 'Wisdom' books of the Old Testament in Jewish tradition. One such book (now contained in the Apocrypha) is actually called The Wisdom of Solomon.

Paradoxically, there is only one book in the Old Testament proper that mentions Solomon in its title – and that is not a wisdom book at all! This is the Song of Solomon. It probably has no direct connection with Solomon, other than the fact that his name occurs in it a number of times. Indeed, the way he is mentioned in these passages suggests very strongly that he was not the author of it. Its exact origins are uncertain. It contains at least one Persian word and one word that may be Greek, which would suggest it was written some time after the rise of the Persian empire in 539 BC. But it also has features that suggest a much earlier origin, while there is some evidence of similar poetry from the nations surrounding Israel, dating from long before the time of Solomon himself. It is quite likely therefore that it is really an anthology of poetry, rather than a continuous composition written at one particular point in time.

Song of Solomon 1:1,5; 3:7–11; 8:11–12

Song of Solomon 4:13

Song of Solomon 3:9

Its subject is certainly timeless – human love. It is a collection of erotic love poems, in which a woman and her lover encourage one another in their sexual relationship. Many readers of the book, both Jewish and Christian, have been alarmed by its frankness, and they have often given it a symbolic meaning – asserting that it represents the relationship between God and his people Israel, or between Christ and the church. But such ideas were certainly not in the

The Song of Solomon is a collection of love poems, in which a young bride and groom celebrate their love with great beauty and frankness.

mind of those who first included it in the Old Testament. For them, God was the creator of all things, including sexual relationships – and a collection of love poems was no more out of place than the story of God's dealings with his people in the great events of their history.

Solomon's name and influence has more often been connected with two other Old Testament books: Proverbs and Ecclesiastes. Along with the book of Job, and two other Jewish works, Ecclesiasticus and Wisdom of Solomon, these are usually classed together as 'wisdom' books. Their message is explored in detail in Chapters 9 and 11 below. But knowing a little of their origins will help us here to understand the nature of Israelite culture.

What is wisdom?

There is no short, simple answer to this question. When Solomon is described as a 'wise man', the description seems to include many different characteristics. To be wise was 'to know the difference between good and evil'. But it also included political skills to deal with his own people and diplomacy in international relations, as well as the possession of the sort of knowledge we would associate

1 Kings 3:9
1 Kings 3:9
1 Kings 5:7,12

1 Kings 4:33
1 Kings 4:32
1 Kings 3:16–28

with a botanist or zoologist. In addition to all that, Solomon's wisdom also included the ability to write poetry and sensitivity in resolving legal disputes.

From this, it seems that when the ancients spoke of 'wisdom' they included all those elements in a person's character and upbringing that enable them to be a mature and successful member of society. In order to find a meaningful place alongside our fellow human beings, there are certain things we need to know. Nowadays, we often place most emphasis on educational achievements. We spend much time and effort in becoming proficient at particular skills, which will fit us to carry out a particular job. No doubt vocational training had its place in the life of the ancient world. But being fully equipped for life involves much more than that – and it is this that forms the substance of the wisdom literature of the Old Testament. These wisdom books reflect a broad cross-section of moral and intellectual thinking in the ancient world, and we can trace the influence of several specific life situations in their pages:

● **The Family** Many modern Western people feel that it is the job of the state to prepare their children for life, both in terms of vocational training and in moral and religious teaching. But for most people elsewhere, it is in the context of the family that children can learn by both precept and example the distilled wisdom of previous generations. Here, they learn how best to relate to other people, and what not to do if they want to have a happy and fulfilled existence. All of this is based on the experience of their parents, and before them of the grandparents, who in turn learned much from their own forebears. And it was always the same in ancient Israel. Many of the sayings in the book of Proverbs certainly originated in this context and have the form of advice given by a parent to a child, such as: 'Listen to what your father teaches you, my sons . . . When I was only a little boy, my parents' only son, my father would teach me . . . Pay attention to what I say, my son. Listen to my words . . . they will give life and health to anyone who understands them. Be careful how you think; your life is shaped by your thoughts.'

Proverbs 4:1, 3–4, 20, 22–23

● **The Village** As well as being a part of a family, we are all part of a larger community in the place where we live, and much of the 'wisdom' that equips us for life is derived from our relationships in that context. Again, this is something that is becoming increasingly alien to many Western people, who live in isolation from others, often relying on the television to provide them with a sense of 'community'. But even in the West, there are still many places which have the sense of community that is widespread elsewhere in the world. In my own village in Scotland, I know where to go if I want to meet the local worthies and get their advice and opinions on the issues of the day. And this is precisely what happened in ancient Israel. Everything happened at the city or village gate. Justice was dispensed there – and it was also the forum where the great issues of life were debated. It was the place where people went to exchange views and ideas – and some of this 'wisdom' is undoubtedly con-

The books of Proverbs and Ecclesiastes are concerned, in their very different ways, with how to find wisdom in everyday life. Though centred on life in God, much of their teaching is rooted in the practicalities of daily affairs.

tained in the wisdom books of the Old Testament. Job says in one of his speeches that he himself had regularly taken his place at the city gate with those who went to debate and ponder on life's great mysteries – and we can be quite sure that much of the argument contained in that book had been well rehearsed in that setting in many an Israelite settlement. Proverbs also refers to the discussions at the city gate, and no doubt much of the advice of that book came from the same context.

● **The Royal Court** The sort of advice that was given in the family and at the city gate would not be unique to Israel. People of all cultures have their equivalents, and the ancient world was no different from ours in that respect. One of the results of Solomon's great expansion of trade and international diplomacy was that the people of Israel became familiar with the 'wisdom' traditions of the surrounding nations. Just as the Queen of Sheba came to Jerusalem to find out about Israelite wisdom, Israelites were no doubt busy discovering the wisdom of other races. There was a good deal of such wisdom literature available elsewhere, especially in Egypt. One Egyptian text has many striking similarities with parts of the Old Testament book of Proverbs. It was probably in such international circles that the knowledge of 'trees and plants . . . animals, birds,

Job 29:7

Proverbs 24:7; 31:23, 31

1 Kings 10:1–13

Proverbs 22:17—23:11

1 Kings 4:33

reptiles, and fish' was handed on. Solomon specialized in such 'wisdom', and it must have been a more intellectual pursuit than the moral advice that was evolved in the family and the village community. The more intellectual nature of such knowledge has led to the suggestion that from the time of Solomon onwards there may have been in Israel a group of professional 'wise men', whose job it was to study and teach such subjects in specialized schools. We certainly know of the existence of such people at a very much later date (about 180 BC), though their main subject of study then was the

Ecclesiasticus 38:24; 39:1–4

Old Testament itself. But at a slightly earlier date, Jeremiah mentions 'wise men' alongside priests and prophets as leaders of the

Jeremiah 18:18

nation – and of course in the time of Solomon there were many professional diplomats, who must have been taught reading, writing and other intellectual skills by someone. So there may have been schools in ancient Israel in which knowledge was pursued for its own sake, though we cannot be certain.

The wisdom books

Like the Psalms and most of the messages of the prophets, the wisdom books are written in poetry. In Hebrew poetry the most important feature is not its metrical form, but a device known as 'parallelism', in which the ideas that are communicated are the most important thing. In the simplest form of poetry ('synonymous parallelism'), the second line of a typical couplet simply repeats in different words the thought of the first line:

> Who has the right to go up the
>   Lord's hill?
> Who may enter his holy Temple?
> Psalm 24:3

'Antithetic parallelism' can make the same point by placing one part of the couplet in a positive form, and the other expressed negatively:

> Good people will be remembered
>   as a blessing,
> but the wicked will soon be
>   forgotten.
> Proverbs 10:7

There are many other more subtle and intricate forms of verse, and sometimes there is a parallelism just of form, and not of meaning.

Many other literary devices are used in the wisdom books. Riddles and parables, autobiographical advice, as well as dialogue (as in Job). The acrostic is also occasionally used. This is a poetic composition in which each couplet or section begins with a different letter of the alphabet, starting with the first letter and working through to the end. Psalm 119 is the most striking example in the

Old Testament, but Proverbs 31:10–31 also uses the same device.

Proverbs

This book is a collection or anthology of practical wisdom. The title (1:1) attributes the book to Solomon, though it is only in one section (10:1—22:16) that Solomon is explicitly connected with its teaching. Other sections are attributed to Agur (30:1–33) and Lemuel (31:1–9), both characters of whom we know nothing. And yet other sections are presented as anonymous compositions, which is what we would expect in view of the likely origins of the kind of practical advice that the book contains.

Many of the wisdom sayings in Proverbs go back a long way into Israel's history, and were obviously composed long before the book itself was edited in its present form. The earliest date we could possibly give to this final editing would be the sixth century BC, since Hezekiah, king of Judah from 715 to 687 BC, is mentioned (25:1). But it is more likely that the final editing of Proverbs was not completed until around the third century BC.

The book is mostly concerned with advice about relationships in different areas of life. As such, it is the kind of advice about good manners and sensible behaviour that could have originated in any society. But the editor has gone out of his way to emphasize that the true meaning of such wisdom could only be found in a living relationship with God himself: 'To have knowledge, you must first have reverence for the Lord' (1:7).

Ecclesiastes

This is a very different kind of book from Proverbs. Whereas Proverbs takes an optimistic view of life, and makes a positive assessment of its potential, Ecclesiastes is essentially negative and sceptical. This need not surprise us if the wisdom books are indeed based on the distilled experiences of real people. For there can be few of us who have not stood alongside the author of Ecclesiastes and asked whether life has any real meaning, or whether instead it is not 'all useless' (1:2). The author vacillates between these two. Though he believes in God, he finds that his faith seems to give little meaning to the details of everyday life. There is no mention of Israel's history here, nor of the nation's experiences in events like the exodus, which could well have provided some sort of answer to the writer's questions. Instead, like many a modern believer in his position, he felt that the mere reiteration of traditional religious dogmas would not solve his immediate problems. But he was prepared to accept that the meaning of life could be known to God, even if it was not possible for the human mind to comprehend it all. In practical terms, 'all we can do is to be happy and do the best we can while we are still alive. All of us should eat and drink and enjoy what we have worked for. It is God's gift' (3:12–13).

The apparent unbelief of Ecclesiastes has often caused problems for Jewish and Christian readers of the book. But it does bear witness to two facts that are of fundamental importance. For it reminds us that there is a dimension of human life which we cannot understand by the exercise of our own reasoning. And it testifies to the reality of doubt and uncertainty about God and his ways, even in the midst of a community of believing people.

Ecclesiastes identifies its author as 'David's son, who was king in Jerusalem' (1:1). This was probably meant to indicate Solomon. But there are compelling reasons against supposing that he had any connection with it:
● The writer often writes from the point of view of an oppressed subject rather than that of an absolute monarch like Solomon (4:1).
● He also seems to have lived in a province of a great empire like that of the Persians, for he gives a warning against the spies of the rulers (5:8).
● Political upheavals are mentioned, but of a kind that were not experienced in Solomon's time (4:13–16).
● The Hebrew of Ecclesiastes shows clear Aramaic influences. Aramaic was the language of the Persian Empire, which suggests a date in the third or second century BC. A date in this period seems the most likely.

Job

The book of Job falls into two parts, with a prologue and epilogue written in prose (1—2, 42:7–17) and the rest in poetry. The prologue and epilogue contains an old story about Job. He was an upright and God-fearing man, who was also 'the richest man in the East' (1:3). But then in a series of inexplicable calamities he lost all that he had and was himself afflicted with a dreadful disease. This part of the story depicts God as the president of a heavenly court, and explains Job's sufferings by reference to an accusation brought against Job by the prosecutor, Satan. The charge was that Job was pious only because he found that piety paid. So he was put to the test to verify his faith – and, at the end of the story (42:7–17), Job's proverbial patience was rewarded by renewed prosperity and happiness. Some features of this story (such as the part played by Satan) suggest a fairly late date in Jewish history. But other features seem to set it in a very early historical context. Perhaps it was an ancient story that was adapted by a later wisdom writer, to provide an opportunity for the exploration of the place of suffering and evil which forms the major part of the book.

Job is clearly not a wisdom book in the same sense as Proverbs. Indeed, it seriously questions the easy-going optimism found in much of that book, with its assumption that doing good will lead to success and prosperity. For Job it had led to just the opposite, and though his friends tried to convince him of the truth of the conventional view, he would have none of it. But this was not the only problem with which Job contended. For in the midst of his suffering, he was also wrestling with the same problems as the writer of Ecclesiastes. Far from finding God in these adversities, Job felt abandoned by the very God whom he had so diligently served. Where was God, he asked – indeed, what sort of a God was he to leave his servant apparently at the mercy of a meaningless and evil universe?

Job's friends had no answer to that question. Nor is any answer given to it. For when the writer records God's answer to Job, there is no question of his

The book of Job deals in dramatic form with the universal problem of sorrow and suffering. How can the just God allow us to experience so much pain?

giving an explanation either of Job's suffering or of the apparent meaninglessness of life. Instead he emphasizes in majestic poetry the grandeur and greatness of both God and the world – and in doing so he turns Job's thoughts away from himself and directs them to the majesty of God and his creation (38—41). And in the face of this self-revelation of God's character and personality, Job recognizes that the only response to make is one of trust and worship. The 'why' of human suffering was not answered as an intellectual question. It is never answered in that way anywhere in the Bible. Job's friends held a common view. They believed that a person whose life was full of suffering

must be a great sinner. But the writer of the book of Job had no time for such easy assumptions. No one could *explain* the presence of evil in God's world. But they could face up to it in the strength that God gives. For the book of Job does have a message to those who suffer undeservedly. As Job realized he could never resolve his own predicament, and was forced to rely on God alone, he found his broken heart was healed as God burst into his life and assured him again of his constant care and love.

Other wisdom passages

In recent years a number of scholars have suggested that writings originating from wisdom schools can be traced elsewhere in the Old Testament. They point to some of the oracles of the prophets, especially in Amos and Isaiah, which seem to propound similar views. We have already noted the theory that the 'Succession Narrative' (2 Samuel 9—20; 1 Kings 1—2) could have been a moralistic 'wisdom' writing, and the same idea has been put forward regarding the stories of Joseph (Genesis 37, 39—50). Here again it is suggested that Joseph is portrayed as an ideal example of a person who lived his life according to the kind of rules we find in the book of Proverbs. It has also been suggested that the portrayal of the heroine of the book of Esther may owe something to such motives. There is nothing to prove any of these speculations, and it is unlikely that any of these stories came into existence purely as a means of demonstrating the value of practical wisdom. At the same time, the book of Job gives us one example of an older story that was taken up and reinterpreted in this way, and if the concerns of the wisdom books were, as we have suggested, deeply embedded in the very fabric of Israelite society, then it would be surprising if the same lessons were not hammered home in other types of Old Testament literature.

5 The two kingdoms

1 Kings 12:21—22:53
2 Kings 1:1—18:12
Amos
Hosea

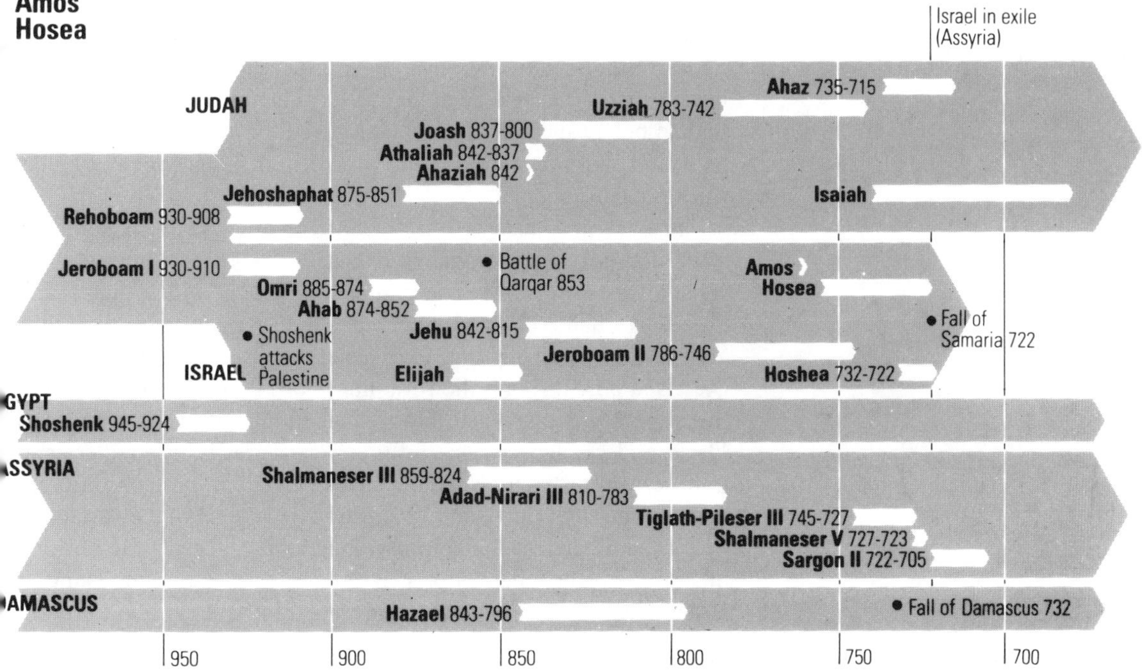

Israel in exile
(Assyria)

JUDAH

Ahaz 735-715

Uzziah 783-742

Joash 837-800
Athaliah 842-837
Ahaziah 842

Jehoshaphat 875-851

Isaiah

Rehoboam 930-908

Jeroboam I 930-910

• Battle of
Qarqar 853

Amos
Hosea

Omri 885-874
Ahab 874-852

Jehu 842-815

• Fall of
Samaria 722

• Shoshenk
attacks
Palestine

Jeroboam II 786-746

ISRAEL

Elijah

Hoshea 732-722

EGYPT
Shoshenk 945-924

ASSYRIA

Shalmaneser III 859-824
Adad-Nirari III 810-783

Tiglath-Pileser III 745-727
Shalmaneser V 727-723
Sargon II 722-705

DAMASCUS

Hazael 843-796

• Fall of Damascus 732

| 950 | 900 | 850 | 800 | 750 | 700 |

A kingdom divided

WHAT HAPPENED after Solomon's death is often referred to as 'the division of the kingdom'. As a statement of fact, that is what happened: the extensive empire ruled over by Solomon was split into two. But in reality, this split was nothing more than the concrete political expression of an ideological division that had existed for much longer. The northern tribes, led by Ephraim, and the southern tribes led by Judah, had only ever been truly united by their common allegiance to David. Both groups looked on him as a leader following in the footsteps of the judges. His position was assured only because God had chosen and equipped him, and his continued rule was valid only in so far as he lived up to the responsibility that involved. But Solomon's reign was different. He had been part of an established dynasty, and that in itself raised new questions about his relationship to the old order of things. The fact that Solomon had violated so many of the ancient traditions, together with the fact that he was not a northerner, helped considerably to revive the old rivalries and suspicions between the two groups of tribes.

Back to the old ways

So when the tribes in the north saw their chance to opt out of the vast bureaucratic state centred on Jerusalem, they lost no time in doing so. They were not motivated just by political expediency, nor even primarily by a feeling of outrage at the injustices which Rehoboam promised to impose on them. Over and above all this, they had a deep desire to get back to the old ways, to retrace their national footsteps and go back to their roots. They wanted to recapture the spontaneity of belief and action that characterized the generation that escaped from Egypt. Of course, they saw clearly enough that they could not return precisely to those early days. Then, the judges had been leaders of their own tribes, and it was exceptional for them to unite all the tribes. In the new political climate, that was impractical. The new leader must be a national figure. But equally, he must never succeed to the throne just because his father had been king. Every king must demonstrate that he had been called and equipped by God for the job at hand – and he would stay as king only if he was seen to be carrying out God's will among his people.

This view was accepted in theory by the people of the southern state of Judah: they too believed that God should be the ultimate ruler of his people. But the political context in which they found themselves had led to the emergence of a permanent royal family, and they were firmly convinced that God's rule would now be exercised only through the royal house of David. The old ideals of the days of the judges had found their fulfilment in the promise to David and his successors, and therefore it was both pointless and unnecessary to try to ascertain God's direct will in each different generation. This view doubtless owed a great deal to the social and political situation of the southern kingdom, especially the position of its capital Jerusalem. For it is striking that once Omri, king of Israel, had founded his own royal capital in Samaria, the northern state too came to accept the concept of a royal family – first in Omri's own family, and later in Jehu and his successors.

Political changes   A casual reading of the Old Testament books of Kings may suggest that Judah was by far the more important of the two kingdoms – and, in its lasting religious influence, it has certainly proved to be. But in the two centuries following the death of Solomon, the northern kingdom of Israel had more territory, a larger population, and was in every way the more wealthy, more civilized, and even at times the more religious of the two. Israel was therefore a greater force in the international politics of the time. But by the same token, it was also less secure than Judah. Judah's capital, Jerusalem, was well away from all the main trade routes, and the kingdom's strategic importance was consequently less. So, despite its greater prosperity, the kingdom of Israel had a shorter and more troubled history than the kingdom of Judah, and almost exactly 200 years after Jeroboam was first acclaimed as king of Israel, the whole of his kingdom was wiped out, and its subjects taken away to Assyria to become the so-called 'ten lost tribes'.

In the shorter term, too, the decision of the northern tribes to go their own way led to considerable social and economic changes in the life of the people of the two kingdoms.

● **Lost territory**   The people of Israel and Judah were no longer able to hold separately the large empire that they had held together under David and Solomon. The province of Aram (Syria) in north-east Palestine had already been lost in part during the reign of Solomon, and it soon became a powerful nation in its own right, based on the city-state of Damascus. It was a serious rival to the Israelite kingdoms, and frequently invaded the Israelite territory to the east of the River Jordan. All but one of the Philistine city-states regained their freedom from Judah in the south, though they were no longer a military threat. The Ammonites also took this chance to throw off Israelite rule, and the Moabites probably did

The cobbles of an ancient street in Dan, town of the most northerly of Israel's twelve tribes. Israel was said to extend 'from Dan to Beersheba'. But from the time when the kingdom was divided, and the northern tribes separated from Judah and Benjamin in the south, Israel never refound its unity as one territory.

the same. Judah fared slightly better than Israel, and still retained some kind of control over the trade routes through the Gulf of Aqaba in the south. And Rehoboam built new fortifications in many of his cities.

2 Chronicles 11:5–12

But the loss of all this territory left both Israel and Judah as very second-rate powers. In the time of David and Solomon, the united kingdom had been the major power centre in the whole area. From now on, the two kingdoms were little more than pawns in the political games of the superpowers based in Egypt and Mesopotamia. The strength of both kingdoms was considerably weakened by the invasion of Shoshenk I, king of Egypt (called Shishak in the Old Testament). He moved in about five years after the separation of the two states, eager to re-establish the authority that Egypt had enjoyed in Canaan before the arrival of the Israelite tribes. The Old Testament only mentions this campaign in relation to Judah, and relates how Rehoboam was forced to give him treasure from both the temple and palace, to stop Shoshenk actually attacking Jerusalem.

1 Kings 14:25–28

This seems to have worked, for in an inscription in the temple of Amun at Thebes, Shoshenk makes no mention of towns in Judah being taken. He does however mention a number of towns in Israel, and an Egyptian inscription found at Megiddo suggests he must have overrun most of Palestine. In an interesting detail of his temple-list, he mentions a place called 'the Field of Abram', which is the only reference outside the Bible to connect a person of that name with Palestine. Of course, Shoshenk did not want to occupy the country, though no doubt he left troops at strategic places. A later king of Judah, Asa, faced an attack from the same quarter led by a man called Zerah. He is described as a Sudanese, but was probably an Egyptian officer left in charge of troops in south Palestine at the time of Shoshenk's invasion.

2 Chronicles 14:9–15

● **Petty squabbles** The two kingdoms were incapable of keeping all their territory partly because they were also fighting each other. They were at war for something like fifty years, fighting over the border territory that was just to the north of Jerusalem. This was perhaps inevitable. Jerusalem's original appeal to David had been its unique position midway between the two groups of tribes. But now what had been a tactical advantage became a strategic liability. Judah's capital was too near the border with the northern kingdom, and that made it especially vulnerable to attack. Rehoboam, Abijam, and Asa, kings of Judah, and Jeroboam, Nadab, and Baasha, kings of Israel, were squabbling over the land in this area for a considerable time. Baasha, king of Israel, managed to move in as close as five miles to the city of Jerusalem and when it looked as if he would advance further, Asa of Judah appealed for help to Benhadad, king of Damascus. This king already had a treaty with Baasha. But Asa must have made him a very attractive proposition, for he sent an army to attack the towns in the north of Israel. This forced Baasha to withdraw his army from the frontier with Judah. It was not the last time that Judah adopted such tactics,

1 Kings 14:30; 15:16–22

but they eventually discovered to their cost that it was a very short-sighted policy.

● **Social unrest** The northern kingdom of Israel also turned out to be politically unstable. In theory, they thought it was right to go back to the old idea that every leader of the people should be chosen and equipped directly by God. But as a political and social institution, this was simply unworkable. At best, it meant that Israel was 'a kingdom based on revolution by the will of God' (A.Alt). In practice, it often meant that the nation was torn apart over the issue of the kingship. For one thing, it was open to any military adventurer to try to seize the throne, whether or not he had any religious support. And in addition, it was only natural that those kings whose reigns had been properly accredited should in due course want their own sons to succeed them. So Israel was in constant turmoil. In the first fifty years, the throne was seized three times by a usurper who assassinated his predecessor. Jeroboam reigned for twenty-one years, but only one of the eight kings who followed him reigned for more than ten years (Baasha), and some lasted only a matter of months.

There were many problems. But this was also a constructive period. The evidence of archaeology shows that at this time the Hebrew people really were the settled, permanent occupiers of their land, and the Canaanites were quite definitely their subjects.

Religious problems

It was all very well for Jeroboam to come to power in the north on a wave of popular enthusiasm, but he soon needed to get down to the business of running his kingdom. In doing so, he had many formidable obstacles. Not least of them was that in the north, there was no obvious capital city that could form the centre of his government. The Old Testament mentions three capitals where he

1 Kings 12:25; 14:17

operated in turn: Shechem, Penuel, and Tirzah. Various reasons have been suggested for this. Possibly he was forced to retreat from one to the other in the face of Shoshenk's invading armies. More likely, there was a popular resistance to the idea of having a capital, on religious grounds. For it had been through the possession of his own personal city that Solomon had been able to behave with such disregard for the tribal traditions. At least if Jeroboam had no fixed capital, there was less chance that he would build up a state apparatus to work for his own personal benefit.

But it was essential that at least one of the functions of the city of Jerusalem should be located at a permanent site in the north. For the temple built at Jerusalem to house the ark of the covenant was an important link with the people's past. It was natural that the tribes in the north, with their fierce devotion to all that the Ark symbolized, should want to go on pilgrimages there. Yet politically, it was essential that Jeroboam should stop them from doing so. To allow this would have been tantamount to an acknowledgement that Jerusalem still had some sort of power over the northern tribes – and the free passage of pilgrims from one state to the other would only increase the risk of subversive action to undermine

1 Kings 12:26–27

Jeroboam's position as king.

On top of that, Jeroboam had a considerable Canaanite element in the population of his territory, and he needed to try in some way to unite them with the native Israelites. He hit on an idea that he believed would solve both problems at once. He would displace the old loyalties to the temple in Jerusalem by building his own new religious centres. The sites he chose were at Dan in the extreme north, and Bethel in the south near to the border with Judah. These had been old centres of Canaanite worship, yet both of them also

Genesis 12:8; 31:13; Judges 18:30; 20:18–28; 1 Samuel 7:16

had important connections with events in the earlier history of the people of Israel.

But Jeroboam's actions in setting up these places of worship were to earn him the lasting condemnation of the Old Testament writers.

1 Kings 12:28–33

For at these two shrines, Jeroboam placed golden bulls. This was a bold effort to bind the different elements of the population together, and to reconcile Canaanite beliefs with the distinctive faith of Israel. The Canaanite elements of the population would have no difficulty in associating these bulls with their own fertility god Baal, who was often represented as a bull. And, in theory, the Israelites could regard the bulls as thrones for their own invisible God Yahweh, just as the ark of the covenant in Jerusalem represented his invisible presence. In the event, it was a foolish move. Jeroboam's people regarded these bulls as their god, and worshipped them just as the Canaanites did. Like Saul before him, Jeroboam had overstepped his authority. He had moved against the very convictions that had brought him to power in the first place. And the prophet who announced his accession now pronounced his

A golden bull from ancient Egypt. Jeroboam placed golden bulls at the shrines of Dan and Bethel.

doom. Though he had been God's choice, Jeroboam had lost God's approval, and he would have to go, to be replaced by a king who would obey God.

1 Kings 14:1–16

New alliances

1 Kings 15:25–32

1 Kings 15:34

1 Kings 16:1–7

1 Kings 16:8–14

1 Kings 16:15–20

Jeroboam's immediate successor was his son Nadab. But he was not accepted by the people, and had the approval of no religious leaders. He lasted for just a few months, and then Baasha came to power. The people recognized him as the right man, and he had a relatively long reign of twenty-four years. But he too followed in Jeroboam's footsteps, and 'led Israel into sin'. Like Jeroboam, he was rejected by a prophet speaking in the name of God. When he died, his son Elah tried to succeed him. He reigned for less than two years, but had no popular backing and Zimri assassinated him in a military coup and seized the throne for himself. He was not the right man either, and he lasted for only seven days.

This kind of chaos naturally weakened the position of Israel. But the man who got rid of Zimri was to be one of Israel's greatest kings. Not only did he re-establish much of the nation's prestige, but he did it so successfully that when he died his son was recognized as the most appropriate person to follow him. The father was Omri, and the son was Ahab.

Prosperity again

1 Kings 16:21–28

1 Kings 16:29—22:40

The Old Testament says very little about Omri for, in the view of the writer of 1 Kings, he was even more wicked and irreligious than any of his predecessors. As in so many cases, his social and political achievements are mentioned only briefly, and we are told that 'Everything else that Omri did and all his accomplishments are recorded in *The History of the Kings of Israel*' – which, of course, is a book we do not possess. By contrast, his son Ahab features very prominently in the Old Testament story. But even there, we are told far more about his religious outlook than about political affairs during his reign.

Yet there can be no doubt about the greatness of Omri and his son. For under their rule, Israel once again became a force to be reckoned with.

● **Internationally,** Omri and Ahab strengthened the kingdom's position with a number of new alliances and fresh conquests. They put an end to the long-standing but stupid warfare with Judah, and this led to a new period of prosperity and peace in the southern state also. Jehoshaphat, king of Judah, took control of many trading routes in the south, and the new friendship between the two states was eventually sealed by the marriage of Ahab's

1 Kings 22:41–50; 2 Kings 8:25–27

1 Kings 16:31

daughter, Athaliah, to Jehoshaphat's son, Jehoram. Israel made peace in the same way with the Phoenicians of Tyre. This alliance was also sealed with a marriage: this time, Ahab himself married a Phoenician princess called Jezebel. Omri also managed to gain control over Moab again. The Old Testament tells us nothing of this, but we know of it from a large black stone inscription erected by king Mesha of Moab after he had finally managed to release his

2 Kings 3

kingdom from Israel's grasp following the death of Ahab. Naturally, much of this inscription dwells on Mesha's victory rather than on his previous submission to Omri. But it says quite plainly that 'Omri, king of Israel, humbled Moab for many years'.

● **Internally,** Omri secured his own position by building a new capital. This is what David had done by capturing Jerusalem. Omri went one better, and chose an entirely new site, with no previous settlement on it. It is almost certain that he was trying to imitate David's success. For just as Jerusalem had been chosen because of its central position between the northern and southern tribes, so Samaria was roughly midway between the mainly Canaanite cities nearer the coast, and the predominantly Israelite towns further inland. This was to be Omri's own city, just as Jerusalem had been David's own city. Under Omri and Ahab it was built up into a fine place, well fortified and with many elegant

1 Kings 16:32; 2 Kings 10:18–27

buildings. Like Jerusalem, it also had a temple – for Baal. This came to be seen as Ahab's greatest mistake: 'He sinned against the Lord more than any of his predecessors. It was not enough for him

1 Kings 16:30–31

to sin like King Jeroboam; he went further . . . and worshipped Baal'. But Ahab's religious observance was probably more concerned with politics than religion as such. Like Jeroboam before him, he had the problem of uniting the Canaanite and Israelite elements of his population. What went on in Samaria was mainly, if not exclusively, for the benefit of the Canaanites. It was, after all, organized like a Canaanite city-state. But the city of Jezreel was still

Below: The Moabite Stone, put up by King Mesha of Moab in Omri's day. Its inscription contains information not included in the Old Testament account.

Below right: The ruins of Ahab's palace look down from the hill on which once stood the city of Samaria, capital of the northern kingdom of Israel.

of great importance, and it could well be that Ahab had in effect two capitals: Samaria for the Canaanites, with a temple for Baal, and Jezreel for the Israelites, with a temple for their God, Yahweh. It is certainly significant that both Ahab's sons had distinctively Israelite names (Ahaziah and Joram) – and that is more than could be said even for a great hero like David!

Decay and collapse

The tensions that Omri and Ahab created between their state and the covenant faith of their people soon became overpowering. In the normal course of affairs, Ahab would have discovered, like Solomon, that it was impossible to accept the worship of foreign gods and still keep the loyalty of the tribes. But matters were brought to a head even sooner by Jezebel. For she was not content with the easy-going tolerance of Ahab. She wanted Baal to become the god of Israel. There may have been a political reason for this – to show that Israel was subject to her own kingdom of Tyre. But more likely it was in the honest conviction that hers was a religion of a more civilized people. In addition, she was devoted to

The city of Megiddo was one of Ahab's chariot cities. Ahab's water tunnel and a pagan altar have been excavated. Built to guard the pass through the Carmel range on the main north-south coastal highway, Megiddo reflects layer after layer of Bible history.

The kings of Israel and Judah

Solomon's kingdom divides ●

Shoshenk attacks Palestine ●

ISRAEL

JUDAH

920

910

900

890

880

870

860

THE HOUSE OF DAVID

REHOBOAM 930-908
was the son of Solomon.
At the beginning of his reign
the northern tribes broke away
from the south to form their
own kingdom

ABIJAH 908-906

ASA 906-875

Elijah

JEHOSHAPHAT 875-851
Judah was prosperous again
during his reign, and there was
peace between Israel and Judah

Battle of ●
Qarqar 853

JEHORAM 851-842

AHAZIAH 842
was assassinated
by Jehu of Israel

ATHALIAH 842-837
seized power when her
son Ahaziah was killed

JOASH 837-800
was the son of Ahaziah.
He came to power when
Athaliah was deposed
in a palace coup

Jerusalem, capital of the southern
kingdom of Judah.

AMAZIAH 800-783

JEROBOAM I 930-910
became king of the northern tribes
after Solomon's kingdom was divided

THE HOUSE OF JEROBOAM

NADAB 910-909

BAASHA 909-886
assassinated Nadab and
usurped the throne

THE HOUSE OF BAASHA

ELAH 886

ZIMRI 886

OMRI 885-874
was one of Israel's greatest kings.
He strengthened the kingdom through alliance and
conquest, and built Samaria as Israel's capital

THE HOUSE OF OMRI

AHAB 874-852
attempted to unite the Israelite and
Canaanite elements of the population, and
compromised Israel's covenant faith

AHAZIAH 852-850

JORAM 850-842

Samaria, capital of the northern
kingdom of Israel.

JEHU 842-815
originally an army officer,
he assassinated Joram and purged
Baal worship from Israel

THE HOUSE OF JEHU

JEHOAHAZ 815-801

JEHOASH 801-786

JEROBOAM II 786-746
under his rule Israel
enjoyed prosperity

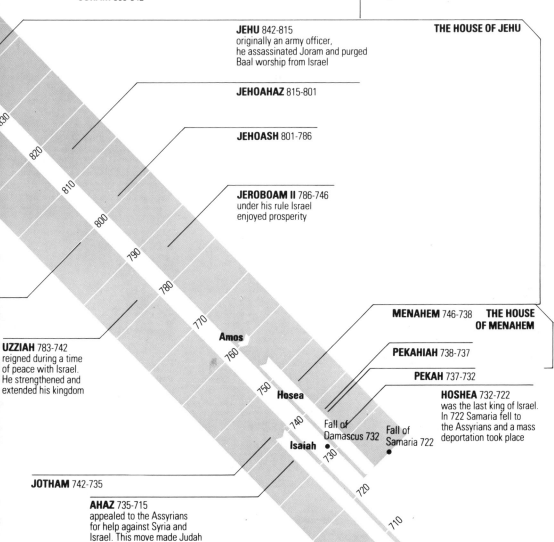

830
820
810
800
790
780
770
760
750
740
730
720
710
700

MENAHEM 746-738 **THE HOUSE OF MENAHEM**

PEKAHIAH 738-737

PEKAH 737-732

UZZIAH 783-742
reigned during a time
of peace with Israel.
He strengthened and
extended his kingdom

Amos

Hosea

Isaiah ●

Fall of
Damascus 732

Fall of
Samaria 722 ●

HOSHEA 732-722
was the last king of Israel.
In 722 Samaria fell to
the Assyrians and a mass
deportation took place

JOTHAM 742-735

AHAZ 735-715
appealed to the Assyrians
for help against Syria and
Israel. This move made Judah
dependent on Assyria

her husband – and the worship of Baal gave far more power to the king than did the covenant religion of Yahweh, God of Israel.

It was at this point that things were disrupted by the emergence of a man called Elijah. He was a fierce spokesman for the covenant traditions of his people, and he realized that this institutionalized worship of Baal was something very different from the local and casual worship of Baal that still went on in village shrines throughout the land. It was a direct threat to the very fabric of the nation.

Elijah and the religion of Baal

On Mount Carmel, overlooking the plain of Jezreel, Elijah had his great confrontation with the prophets of Baal.

Elijah is a significant character in the Old Testament. In some ways, he is a member of that line of ecstatics whose influence can be traced in the early stories of Saul. He certainly had some connection with a group of prophets like those whom Saul encountered (1 Kings 18:4,13) and his movements could at times be unpredictable and beyond human apprehension (1 Kings 18:12). But these are not the most distinctive marks of his personality. For he was first and foremost a man with a message. He believed that the God whom he knew and worshipped was not just a God who had lived and worked in the past: he was a God who was present with his people here and now, and who had his own understanding of the important issues in their national life. In this respect, Elijah was the forerunner of the great prophets whose messages are preserved in the books of the Old Testament that bear their names – men like Amos, Isaiah, Jeremiah, and others.

The precise nature of the conflict between Baal worship and the ancestral faith of Israel is made clear in three stories from the life of Elijah:

● Elijah came from Gilead, from the very edge of the desert in the east of the country (1 Kings 17:1–7). His lifestyle was spartan, and his clothes were rough. He was immediately recognizable as a devotee of the style of life followed by the tribes with Moses in the desert. He was a miracle worker (1 Kings 17:8–24), but his miracles were mostly concerned with the fertility of the land, especially the holding back or sending of rain. This, of course, was supposed to be the special function of the Canaanite Baal. But Elijah was determined to prove that it was really his own God, Yahweh, who controlled the rain. So he challenged 450 prophets of Baal and 400 prophets of Asherah to a contest on Mt Carmel. This was a high ridge near the territory of the Phoenicians. It had originally belonged to Israel during the

days of David and Solomon. But the altar to Yahweh erected there then had now been displaced by an altar to Baal. Elijah was determined to sort out once and for all the religious priorities of his people. He challenged the prophets of Baal and Asherah to bring fire from heaven – presumably he meant the lightning that would normally come before a rain storm. After much religious ecstasy, they were exhausted – and unsuccessful. But where they failed, Elijah succeeded – not by following their bizarre ecstatic practices, but by a simple prayer to his own God. As a result, the long period of drought ended with deluges of rain (1 Kings 18:1–46). It was Yahweh, not Baal, who controlled the weather!

● In spite of that, Jezebel still held the power, and she was all the more determined to track down the elusive Elijah. He felt (mistakenly) that he alone was left as a faithful spokesman for the God of Israel. In fear of his life he ran away from Jezebel right to the south of Judah, then south again from Beersheba to Mt Sinai. This was the place where Moses had taken the escaping slaves. It was the very centre of his people's faith, where the covenant had been made, and where God's people could still gain fresh inspiration. And that was what Elijah found. In an experience of deep emotion, he was reminded that though God indeed had power over nature, his supreme activity was to be seen in the events of everyday life. He had delivered the slaves from Egypt, and was still active in his people's lives. Elijah was sent back to stir up a political ferment in both Syria and Israel, that would lead to the overthrow of the house of Omri and its allies (1 Kings 19:1–18). Commitment to the covenant faith did not make him a mere reactionary: it transformed him into a political activist, reminding his people by his social

involvement that the God of Mt Sinai was still their only true king.

● The story of Naboth's vineyard brings out the meaning of all this in social terms (1 Kings 21:1–29). When Ahab wanted to have this piece of land to extend his own garden, he knew it was impossible. For the land of Israel belonged not to individuals, but to God – and particular people only held it in trust because God had given it to them. This was quite different from the Canaanite notion, as Ahab well knew. After all, his father Omri had been able to buy the site of Samaria outright from a Canaanite. But Ahab was still too much of an Israelite to accept that land could be seized by the king just to suit his own inclinations. So he sulked for what he knew he could never rightly possess. His wife, Jezebel, on the other hand, took a different view. She regarded the life and property of every subject as belonging to the king, and so she had no hesitation in having Naboth killed, and confiscating his property for her husband's use. It was Elijah who so boldly denounced the queen's action – just as Nathan had done when David acted on the same principles (2 Samuel 12:1–15). For Elijah, religious belief was concerned with common life and politics, and even the queen was not above the law of the covenant from Mt Sinai. For in the covenant community, every man and woman stood equal. This meant that economic and social justice were a concern of God and his representatives just as much as ritual and worship. This theme was taken up by all the great prophets of the Old Testament. But it first emerges in the testimony of Elijah, who pronounced the death sentence on Jezebel and the whole house of Omri, and declared that God would ultimately intervene to restore justice and freedom to his people.

1 Kings 22:51–53; 2 Kings 3:1–27

Ahab managed to survive, and he was succeeded in turn by his two sons Ahaziah and Joram. But there was nothing they could do to prevent the disintegration and eventual collapse of the royal house of Omri. It was not long before a revolution was instigated by devotees of the covenant faith of Israel. They had chosen an army officer by the name of Jehu to be the next king of Israel, and he was anointed in the aftermath of a great battle between Israel and Syria,

2 Kings 9:1–13

at Ramoth-Gilead. Joram had been wounded in the battle and had returned to Jezreel to recuperate. Jehu therefore left the battlefield, and with a band of his own men headed straight for Jezreel. When he got there he found that by a stroke of luck Ahaziah, the king of

2 Kings 9:14-37

2 Kings 10:1-11

2 Kings 10:18-31

2 Kings 13:6

Hosea 1:4-5

2 Kings 10:23-24

Jeremiah 35:6-10

Judah, was also there visiting Joram. Since he was a relative of Ahab too, Jehu had no hesitation in assassinating both of them, along with Jezebel the queen mother. He followed up this bloodbath with an appeal to the city rulers of Samaria to come over to his side – which they did, and signified their allegiance to him by presenting him with the heads of seventy members of Ahab's family who were left there. Not content with that, Jehu managed to trick all the priests of Baal into coming to the temple in Samaria, and there had them all butchered on the spot.

But Jehu's purge cannot have been all that extensive, for by the time his son Jehoahaz became king all the paraphernalia of the Baal worship had been reinstated in Samaria. Jehu was not as loyal to the covenant faith as his supporters had hoped – and 100 years later the prophet Hosea declared that the violence that accompanied his rise to power was quite incompatible with the faith that Jehu professed to uphold.

Yet it is not difficult to see why Jehu's revolution succeeded. For though Omri's dynasty had been so successful, it was suffering from so many tensions that its collapse was inevitable:

● The strongest opposition had been evoked by the Baal worship at Samaria, instigated by Jezebel and encouraged by Ahab. The fact that Jehu joined forces with a fanatical religious movement led by Jehonadab, son of Rechab, shows just how strong the reaction was. For these Rechabites were trying to opt out of civilized, settled life altogether. They neither built houses, nor cultivated the soil, nor drank wine. All these things were typical of the life of Canaan, but they wanted to get back to the kind of life the escaping slaves had with Moses in the desert. They were convinced that the settled life of farming could never be reconciled with Israel's ancestral faith, and so it must be abandoned.

● There was also a certain amount of social unrest and injustice in the land, much as there had been towards the end of Solomon's reign. This time it had been caused partly by a great famine during the time of Ahab. This had increased the number of poor people, and led to a radical division in society between the rich merchants and the poor peasants. The story of how Ahab took over Naboth's vineyard was by no means unique, and many small farmers found themselves being displaced by rich and powerful princes at this time.

● Externally too; Israel was under pressure. New enemies were making their presence felt, especially Assyria (based in Mesopotamia) and Syria (based in Damascus). The Assyrians had pressed as far west as the Mediterranean Sea during Ahab's reign. A casual alliance against them was formed by the king of Damascus, along with Ahab and the king of Hamath. They met Assyria at the Battle of Qarqar, just north of Hamath in 853 BC, and managed to repel the Assyrians. Ahab's military strength can be judged from the fact that though he could provide only half as many troops as Syria (but the same as Hamath), he had 2,000 chariots, which was more than Syria and Hamath put together. Israel obviously had fewer people than Damascus, but far greater material resources. But Benhadad, the king of Damascus, was not interested in a lasting peace with Ahab, and according to the Old Testament Ahab was killed in battle with the Syrians at Ramoth-Gilead. His sons were powerless to regain this lost territory, and no doubt lost the support of the army for that reason. This is perhaps why the military Jehu, fast driving and ready for desperate action, was readily accepted as the new king of Israel.

2 Kings 20:1–34; 22:29–40

Growing insecurity

As things turned out, Jehu himself was relatively powerless in political terms. He naturally lost the support of the powerful alliance with Phoenicia – and he also lost the support of Judah, whose king he had killed. Power was seized in Judah by Athaliah, the queen mother, who was Ahab's sister. She murdered all the other possible claimants to the throne, except for one child, Joash, who was rescued by the priest Jehoiada. Athaliah reigned in Jerusalem for six years, and encouraged Baal worship. But she was deposed in a palace coup led by Jehoiada, and Joash was installed as king.

2 Kings 11:1–21

During this period of uncertainty and weakness, Israel could easily have been overcome by the Syrians of Damascus, had they not been fully occupied resisting the armies of the Assyrian king Shalmaneser III. He had a deliberate plan for extending his own empire, and he made annual military expeditions, of which he kept detailed records. Some territories he conquered altogether, but

Countries in conflict

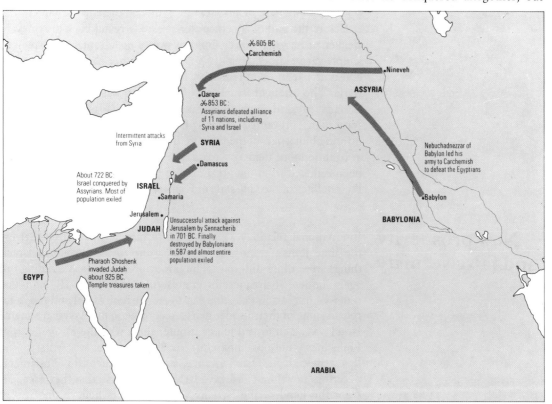

from most he simply took tribute. This was the king who had been successfully repelled by the coalition of which Ahab had been a part. But shortly after Jehu came to power, he was back with a vengeance. In 841 BC he moved through the whole area. Damascus was besieged, and much of the Syrian kingdom was invaded. Both Phoenicia and Israel had to pay tribute to keep the Assyrians at bay. Shalmaneser describes all this in great detail. Not only does he mention that he took tribute from Jehu of Israel; he also lists what he was given, and depicts Jehu himself bowing down low to present these gifts. This is a most interesting record, for the picture of Jehu

This Assyrian obelisk, the famous 'Black Obelisk' from the time of Emperor Shalmaneser, depicts King Jehu of Israel paying tribute as leader of a vassal state. It is the only known portrait of an Old Testament figure.

preserved on Shalmaneser's Black Obelisk is the only contemporary portrait we have of any Israelite named in the Old Testament.

Before the end of Shalmaneser's reign, a revolt back in Nineveh weakened Assyrian power. But this was of no advantage to Israel. It simply gave Hazael, king of Damascus, another chance to get even, and under Jehu's son Jehoahaz, Israel became almost a province of

2 Kings 13:1–9, 22–23

Syria. The whole of Israel east of the Jordan was occupied, and the Syrians pressed into Judah in the south. Joash, the king in Jerusalem, prevented Hazael from attacking the city only by

2 Kings 12:17–18

offering him a part of the treasure from the temple.

In little more than 100 years, the states of Israel and Judah had been reduced from the great empire that Solomon held to become the satellites of the city-state of Damascus.

New prosperity and false security

International relations were in such turmoil at this period that by the time Jehu's grandson, Jehoash, came to the throne in Israel things were quite different. The power of Assyria was building up again under Shalmaneser's grandson, Adad-Nirari III, and his renewed interest in Palestine was to enable both Israel and Judah to regain some of their former glory. According to the Assyrian annals, Israel was again forced to pay tribute, along with the Edomites and Philistines – but not, apparently, Judah. Damascus was worst hit by this renewed Assyrian advance, and when the Old Testament describes how 'the Lord gave Israel a saviour, so that they escaped

2 Kings 13:5

from the hand of the Syrians', some scholars believe that it was referring to the Assyrian king Adad-Nirari III.

In any event, the Assyrian attack on Damascus gave Jehoash the chance he was looking for, and he soon began to recover Israel's lost territory to the east of the River Jordan. Amaziah, the king of Judah, also recovered lost territory from Edom at this time. But then, he foolishly declared war on Israel, and as a result Judah was so decisively defeated that Jehoash of Israel actually raided Jerusalem itself. With this, Amaziah lost the confidence of his own people and was soon assassinated. But, as had always been the case in Judah, his place was taken by his son Uzziah.

2 Kings 14:1–16
2 Kings 14:17–22

National revival

2 Kings 14:23—15:7

2 Chronicles 26:1–15

There followed then two of the longest and most prosperous reigns in all Israelite history: Jeroboam II of Israel, and Uzziah of Judah. They reigned for over forty years each, and though the Old Testament gives no specific details of their military activities, the two kings between them extended their borders almost to the original extent of Solomon's united kingdom.

Uzziah repaired the fortifications of Jerusalem, reorganized his army, and equipped it with new types of armoury. He introduced new agricultural practices to the land, and was even able to reopen part of Solomon's copper refineries on the Gulf of Aqaba. This led to a revival of trade through the Red Sea, and since the two kings of Judah and Israel were at peace with one another, between them they must have controlled all the major trade routes of the area.

The splendid buildings erected by Jeroboam II in Samaria demonstrate well enough the prosperity of the northern state. Many people became very rich as a result of the increased opportunities for international trade. They also became very religious, for they concluded that their new-found wealth must be a sign of God's favour upon them. They came to believe that their position was assured, and their kingdom was impregnable, and began to look forward with eager anticipation to the coming of a great 'day of the Lord', when Israel would finally be victorious over all enemies.

But not everyone thought like that. For during the reign of Jeroboam II many people once again began to ask if all this high living was compatible with the covenant faith of Israel. Some scholars believe that in reaction against all this, a new edition of Israel's early history was written, reflecting the memories that had been handed down in the northern tribes. They believe that many of these stories, which emphasized the work of Moses, later came to form a part of the Old Testament, especially in the books of Genesis and Exodus. But whether it took that precise form, there can be no doubt that there was strong disapproval of Israel's style of life at this time. For it was towards the end of Jeroboam II's reign that the prophet Amos delivered his striking messages, in which he declared that Israelite society was rotten to the core. Though many were rich and prosperous, others were penniless and oppressed. The great shrines like Bethel were full of worshippers, but it was all just empty ritual – and for people like that 'the day of the Lord', when it came, would not be a time of triumph but a day of doom.

Amos 8:4–6

Amos 5:18–27

The book of Amos

Nowadays we commonly think of a prophet as a person who predicts the future. But this was not the way the great Old Testament prophets saw themselves. They were essentially God's messengers sent to remind their people of the covenant made at Sinai, and to apply it to the everyday life of their towns and villages. They were not fortune tellers, but politicians and preachers.

They did occasionally write some parts of their message down (e.g. Jeremiah 30:2; 36:1–2). But it is unlikely that any prophet actually wrote the books now found in the Old Testament. Indeed, these writings are not really 'books' in the sense of having a connected argument from start to finish. They are much more like an anthology of a great person's thoughts. That is why modern translations of the Bible make a clear division between the various sections, for the messages of these prophets were gathered together by editors, and they often did not place them in any sort of chronological order. The same people occasionally added historical and biographical passages, explaining the prophet's situation, together with stories of incidents in his life. The book of Amos contains all these types of material.

The man and his message

Amos himself came for the town of Tekoa, which was just south of Jerusalem in Judah (1:1). But his message was for the people of the northern kingdom and he delivered it in one of the religious sanctuaries set up by the first Jeroboam, at Bethel (7:10–17), and possibly also in Samaria itself (3:9–4:3). While he was in Bethel, Amaziah, the priest of the sanctuary, tried to send him back to Judah, telling him that his own people should pay for his services. He obviously thought Amos was some kind of professional prophet, who was looking for a full-time job attached to a permanent place of worship. We know that there were such full-time prophets in both Israel and Judah. Some of them seem to have had an official position alongside the priests (Jeremiah 35:4–5), while others were court officials who would say anything the king wanted to hear (1 Kings 22:1–28).

But Amos was not this kind of man. He had been a simple shepherd and he was not delivering his challenging messages to tickle the ears of his political masters, but because God had shown him the rotten state of Israelite society – and he was impelled to do something about it (7:10–17; 3:3–8). Amos saw a complete breakdown of morality and covenant faith, not only in

The prophet Amos, the earliest whose words are systematically recorded in the Old Testament, was a shepherd. His message to Israel was an uncompromising warning that God's judgment would come unless they brought back justice into their society.

Israel but also in the nations with whom it was most closely associated: Syria, the Philistines, Tyre, Edom, Ammon, (1:3–2:5). Of course, all but Judah had never been a part of the covenant faith. But Amos condemned them in God's name. They had refused to treat each other as people. They had disregarded the elementary principles of human dignity: acting with great cruelty, taking whole communities into slavery, breaking treaties, and exacting merciless revenge on neighbouring states.

All this was just a prelude to God's judgment of Israel. Israel might not have done any of these things, but she had broken the covenant relationship with her God in very fundamental ways. Though the northern state had ostensibly been founded on a conviction that all members of the community were of equal worth and value, this had never become a social reality. Instead, some had become rich on the back of others – and they were increasing their wealth at the expense of the rest. People were selling themselves into slavery because they could not repay trival debts (2:6–8). The rich were feasting themselves and playing in idle luxury, while others were homeless (3:9–4:1; 5:10–13).

Judgment – and hope

Paradoxically, in the middle of all this there was great religious fervour. The shrines were full of worshippers, all carrying out their ritual observances with meticulous care. They would make sure they did not violate the weekly day of rest – but as soon as it was over, they could hardly wait to get back to the legalized robbery that went on in every market-place. This false religious confidence incensed Amos more than anything. The rich believed they were prospering because they were very religious. But if only they had the eyes to see it, they would have realized they were wealthy because they had disregarded the basic requirements of their covenant faith.

So Amos declared God's total lack of interest in this kind of empty ritual: 'Go to the holy place of Bethel and sin, if you must! Go to Gilgal and sin with all your might! Go ahead and bring animals to be sacrificed . . . offer your bread in thanksgiving to God . . . this is the kind of thing you love to do' (4:4–5). But God had other ideas: 'The Lord says, "I hate your religious festivals, I cannot stand them! . . . I will not accept the animals you have fattened to bring me offerings . . ."' (5:21–22). These had not been the things that characterized Israel's experience of God in the desert. The covenant relationship forged at Sinai was concerned not with religious ritual, but with a personal relationship between God and his people — a relationship of love and concern that should have created a new society marked by the same qualities. So Amos pleaded in God's name: 'Stop your noisy songs; I do not want to listen to your harps. Instead, let justice flow like a stream, and righteousness like a river that never goes dry' (5:23–24).

Not that Amos expected to be heard. For the real trouble was that the worship at Bethel and Gilgal was not the worship of Israel's covenant God at all: it was the worship of Canaanite gods and goddesses, with their rather different view of society (2:7–8; 5:26–27; 8:14). Israel had gone too far. Her leaders were unable to tell the difference between truth and lies. But it would all come to an end – and soon. Just as God had intervened in Israel's history before, he would do so again – and Israel would be totally destroyed, her people taken away into exile, and her cities devastated (5:1 – 9:10). The prosperity of the day

of Jeroboam would indeed culminate in 'the day of the Lord'. But instead of a day of great blessing, it would be a day of judgment and despair (5:18–20).

The last paragraph of Amos (9:11–15) gives just a slight ray of hope, and because of this some scholars believe it was added later by the book's editor, to alleviate the blackness of Amos's message. But it does not really contradict what he says. Amos knew that the nation was heading for a great disaster. But he also knew that events were in God's control: 'I will give the command and shake the people of Israel like corn in a sieve. I will shake them among the nations to remove all who are worthless' (9:9). Because of that, an element of mercy and love would always be found even in judgment. For Amos's God was the one who had rescued his people from Egypt, and who had shown his overpowering love for them in so many ways throughout their history. It was inevitable, therefore, that though the present looked bleak, beyond the storm clouds of God's anger Amos could still dimly see the clear rays of God's love.

Assyria on the move

It was not long before Amos's dire predictions were to become a dreadful reality. The moral disintegration that began in Jeroboam II's reign led to social and political disintegration in the years after his death, with a rapid succession of weak kings, assassinations and revolts. At the same time, the power of Assyria was increasing again with the accesssion to the throne of Tiglath-Pileser III. He had a new expansionist policy that he hoped would avoid the failures of his predecessors. Instead of merely taking tribute from defeated nations, he would incorporate conquered states into the Assyrian empire. To ensure that they did not revolt, the leading elements of the population would be moved away to other parts of the empire, and replaced with settlers similarly displaced from elsewhere.

2 Kings 15:17–22

The first mention of an Assyrian invasion of Israel occurs in the account of Menahem's reign. He tried to keep the kingship within his own family by paying tribute to Tiglath-Pileser, but his son Pekahiah reigned for only two years before he was removed by an anti-Assyrian revolt led by Pekah. He went on to form a new alliance against the Assyrians with Rezin, king of Syria. They tried

Isaiah 7:1–17

to persuade Jotham, king of Judah, to join them. He refused, and when a new king came to power in Jerusalem, they declared war on Judah.

This move struck terror into the people of Jerusalem, and brought into prominence one of the Old Testament's greatest prophets: Isaiah. He advised the new king, Ahaz, that this threat to his security would come to nothing – and before the new born child Immanuel could tell the difference between good and bad, both

Isaiah 7:10–25 Syria and Israel would collapse. As it turned out, Isaiah was right. But Ahaz did not believe him. It was perhaps on this occasion that in desperation he offered his son as a sacrifice to try to change the 2 Kings 16:3–4 course of events. He certainly went out to get the Assyrians on his side – and in response to his appeal, they attacked Damascus, 2 Kings 16:5–9 killed Rezin, and took away his people.

But it was a foolish move, for by doing this Ahaz had given up his own independence. He went to Damascus to pay homage to Tiglath-Pileser, and brought back from there the plan for an altar that was erected in the temple at Jerusalem, as a sign of submission 2 Kings 16:10–18 to the Assyrian Empire and its gods. As Isaiah had warned, it was a short-sighted policy to go to the Assyrians for help.

Meanwhile in Israel, things were going from bad to worse. Pekah's position was weakened because the Assyrians took over yet 2 Kings 15:29 more of his territory, and he was assassinated by Hoshea. Hoshea realized that the kingdom was in grave danger of disappearing entirely, and so he surrendered – unwillingly – to the Assyrians. But once the immediate danger was past, he soon began plotting against them again. He saw his chance when Shalmaneser V replaced 2 Kings 17:1–4 Tiglath-Pileser III, and appealed for support to the king of Egypt.

But Egypt was powerless to help, and when Shalmaneser moved his armies against Israel no one could stop him. Samaria fell after a 2 Kings 17:5–6 siege lasting two years, and in his annals Sargon II (Shalmaneser's successor) tells how he deported 27,290 people from Israel and replaced them with others from elsewhere in his empire. An Assyrian officer was put in charge of the land, and Israel was finished.

The Assyrians

The Assyrian Empire was based in northern Mesopotamia, chiefly around the cities of Nineveh, Asshur and Kalah. The people of this area had exerted a strong influence in that region for a long time, and we can trace their existence back to a time long before the Israelites emerged as a nation. But it was not until the early days of the Hebrew monarchy that the Assyrians began to take an interest in the lands that lay to the west of their home.

Tiglath-Pileser I (1115–1077 BC) was the first king to try to move westwards. But he had not thought out his strategy with sufficient care, and though he got as far as the northern part of Syria he was unable to establish a firm power base there. In the next few centuries, the Assyrians concentrated on setting up a strong administrative structure, into which conquered territories could easily be incorporated. They also developed a well trained and highly disciplined army, ready to move at a moment's notice. The description of them in Isaiah 5:26–29 clearly reflects the impression that these troops made on those who saw them: ' . . . here they come, swiftly, quickly! None of them grows tired; none of them stumbles. They never doze or sleep. Not a belt is loose; not a sandal strap is broken. Their arrows are sharp, and their bows are ready to shoot. Their horses' hooves are as hard as flint, and their chariot-wheels turn like a whirlwind. The soldiers roar like lions that have killed an animal and are carrying it off where no one can take it away from them.'

Ashurnasirpal II (883–859 BC) renovated the Assyrian capital at Kalah, and established a firm control over his Mesopotamian territories, and this new security gave his son Shalmaneser III (858–824 BC) the chance to expand his empire to the west. He was the emperor whose forces met Ahab and his Syrian allies at the battle of Qarqar in 853 BC. But it was almost another 100 years before the toughest emperor of them all came to the throne: Tiglath-Pileser III (745–727 BC). He was also acclaimed as king of Babylon in southern Mesopotamia, and he was an expert military strategist. He saw that the key to imperial expansion was the establishment of a clearly defined policy. Though many of the records from his reign are confused and uncertain, he obviously had a clear strategy for annexing other states.

First of all, he would try to make a treaty with other rulers, persuading them to acknowledge his sovereignty in exchange for certain limited privileges. But any hint of revolt by such vassals would be dealt with at once – usually by direct invasion, followed by the taking over of a good deal of their territory, and the installation of a new king to rule over what was left in accordance with Assyrian instructions. Any more revolts would lead to the whole state being taken over and turned into an Assyrian

province – with its native leaders being deported to other parts of the empire.

We can see how this happened in stages in the case of Israel – though it was not an unchangeable procedure, for neither Judah nor the Philistine city-states were ever dealt with in precisely this way.

Tiglath-Pileser III represented the zenith of Assyrian power. Some of his successors still had expansionist ideas. Indeed, Esarhaddon (681–669 BC) actually annexed Egypt itself. But by the end of his reign, Assyria's imperial power was spent. The reign of his successor, Ashurbanipal (669–627 BC) saw the establishment of a remarkable library of cuneiform texts at Nineveh. But it also witnessed an extended civil war in Babylon, and revolts in other parts of the empire. By the end of his reign, the empire was beginning to disintegrate and its collapse was inevitable.

Hosea and the fall of Samaria

The indecision and opportunism of the last few kings of Israel is all reflected in the book of Hosea. Hosea began his work as a prophet after Amos, but probably before the end of Jeroboam II's reign, and he continued until after the Assyrians had captured Samaria.

The disorders and constant revolts of the people against their kings are all vividly described here: 'In the heat of their anger they murdered their rulers. Their kings have been assassinated one after another, but no one prays to me for help.' (7:7). Israel thought she could do without God, and so she 'flits about like a silly pigeon; first her people call on Egypt for help and then they run to Assyria! But I will spread out a net and catch them like birds as they go by. I will punish them for the evil they have done.' (7:11–12). Yet in spite of her impending doom, Israel seemed to be quite unaware of what was happening: 'The Lord says, "The people of Israel are like a half-baked loaf of bread. They rely on the nations around them and do not realize that this reliance on foreigners has robbed them of their strength. Their days are numbered, but they don't even know it."' (7:8–9).

The man and his message

We know very little about Hosea himself. But he was obviously a countryman. He refers with the knowledge of experience to the morning mist and the dew (13:3), to the fragrance of the cedar trees of Lebanon

(14:6), to corn and wine and olive oil (2:8), and to the work of ploughing and harvesting (10:11–13). Along with all this, Hosea has a strong nostalgia for the life of the desert. For he loved not only his own countryside, but also its history, and he could look back with excitement to the old stories of Jacob and Moses and the Exodus (11 — 13). Amos was logical and impartial. He saw God's dealings with Israel as just one example of his dealings with other nations. But Hosea could never be like that. He was too deeply attached to his own homeland. He loved the land, he loved his people, and he was sure that God loved them too.

Hosea received his message for the nation from God through a personal tragedy in his own life. The story begins with Hosea's marriage to a woman called Gomer. Some interpreters believe that this woman was a temple prostitute whom Hosea tried to win over to his own understanding of God's relationship with his people. But it is just as likely that her sexual promiscuity was quite unexpected. In any event, Hosea and Gomer had three children, each of them given symbolic names that would convey a message about the fate of the nation. The first was called Jezreel, as a reminder that God would still avenge Jehu's massacre there; the second was called Unloved, to declare that Israel seemed to have gone beyond God's love and forgiveness; and the other was called Not-my-people. Gomer subsequently left Hosea to live

Hosea was as concerned for social justice as his predecessor Amos. In the true prophetic tradition, he saw the oppression and inequality of his day as an offence against God.

Amos had been. Amos denounced the great public evils of the people – but Hosea saw behind them the breakdown of morality in homes throughout the land, all of which sprang ultimately from unfaithfulness to the God of the covenant.

God and Israel

The people of Israel believed they would get prosperity and good harvests by observing the fertility rites of Baal worship. But these rituals involved the very same sexual indulgence that had ruined Hosea's own home life. Just like Gomer, Israel was saying, 'I will go to my lovers – they give me food and water, wool and linen, olive-oil and wine' (2:5). This was the typical thinking of the worshippers of Baal. They worshipped him for what they could get out of him, like prostitutes making love for money. But in fact, Hosea knew that it was Israel's own God Yahweh who provided all these things: 'She would never acknowledge that I am the one who gave her the corn, the wine, the olive-oil, and all the silver and gold that she used in the worship of Baal' (2:8).

This was not how Israel should love her God. She must love him for what he is and in gratitude for what he has done. So Hosea returns over and over again to what God had done for his people Israel. Sometimes he uses the picture of his own relationship to Gomer. At other times, he thinks in terms of God as the father of his people: ' . . . the more I called to him, the more he turned away from me. My people sacrificed to Baal; they burnt incense to idols. Yet I was the one who taught Israel to walk. I took my people up in my arms, but they did not acknowledge that I took care of them. I drew them to me with affection and love. I picked them up and held them to my cheek; I bent down to them and fed them.' (11:2–4).

Amos had little hope in his message. For him, the 'day of the Lord' was almost entirely a day of punishment. But Hosea speaks of God making 'Trouble Valley' into 'a door of hope' (2:15). God still loved his people, and in due course Israel would come back to him: 'She will respond to me . . . as she did when she was young, when she came from Egypt. Then once again she will call me her husband – she will no longer call me her Baal.' (2:15–16). To be sure, Gomer had suffered the consequences of her action – and so would Israel: 'Samaria must be punished for rebelling against me. Her people will die in war; babies will be dashed to the ground, and

with another man (1:2—2:5).

In the next recorded event from Hosea's life, he goes to the market place and sees a prostitute who has fallen into some sort of slavery from which she can be released for a small payment. And he is so moved by her plight that he buys her and takes her to live with him (3:1–5). Some interpreters believe this was a different woman altogether from Gomer. But if we compare the details of the story with the message that Hosea brought about God's relationship to his people Israel, it makes more sense to assume that this prostitute was in fact Gomer, who had presumably therefore been abandoned by the man she was living with.

Certainly this personal tragedy was the key to Hosea's message for the nation. Just as his love for Gomer had been rejected and despised, so had God's love for Israel. And if a man like Hosea felt so deeply grieved when his wife left him, how must God feel over the unfaithfulness of Israel? Because of his personal involvement in this way, Hosea was able to see deeper into the nature of Israel's wrongdoing than pregnant women will be ripped open' (13:16). But God would never give up Israel, any more than Hosea could give up his own wife: 'How can I give you up, Israel? How can I abandon you? . . . My heart will not let me do it! My love for you is too strong . . . ' (11:8).

In return, God was looking for the unreserved commitment of his people. Unlike Baal, he was not primarily interested in religious rituals. Instead, he was seeking a personal relationship between his people and himself: 'What I want from you is plain and clear: I want your constant love, not your animal sacrifices. I would rather have my people know me than burn offerings to me.' (6:5–6). What was required was a return to the old simplicity that had characterized the life of the slaves who escaped from Egypt. They knew how much God had done for them, and because of his faithfulness and love they knew they could unreservedly commit themselves to his care. Israel had come a long way since those days, but God's love was unchanging – and that message was to become increasingly important to the Bible writers as time went by.

Dating the Old Testament story

At first glimpse, it might seem easy to give dates to the events recorded in the Old Testament. There are certainly many lists of ancestors and descendants of prominent people, as well as complicated comparative datings at a number of points in the narratives. But it is extraordinarily difficult to condense all this material into one consistent chronological system. There are a number of significant problems:

● Different ancient versions of the Old Testament actually have different figures at many points. The Hebrew version (the Massoretic Text) is not always the same as the Greek version (the Septuagint).

● We do not fully understand the basis on which the Old Testament's dating system operates. For instance, it usually refers to numbers of years within a given king's reign. But do these years include the year in which he became king – or is 'the first year' of a reign actually the first full year after the king's accession? Lack of certainty on this point can lead to considerable differences in dating, even over a short period of time.

● In the earlier Old Testament books, people are often credited with amazingly long life spans, regularly running into hundreds of years. There are similarly extravagant claims in many records from ancient Mesopotamia, but we do not know precisely how to understand them in relation to our own calendar. It seems likely that such calculations were based on a shorter year than our twelve month period, but in the absence of certain knowledge we can deduce very little from them.

● Many scholars feel that the figures given in the Old Testament are stylized, and perhaps even symbolic. For example, the whole time scheme of the Hebrew Old Testament seems to be designed so as to give special prominence to four important events in Israel's history: the exodus, Solomon's building of the temple, the end of the Babylonian exile, and the Maccabean reconsecration of the temple. We also find the frequent use of the number forty, which perhaps suggests that it stands for something – maybe just indicating a long time, or a generation (though a literal generation would be much shorter than that). This figure occurs frequently in the stories of the judges, and if we add all the time indications up there, we have a period in excess of three hundred years. Yet we know from other evidence that the time between Moses and Samuel can hardly have been more than half that length.

There are obviously many uncertainties in trying to assign accurate dates to events in the Old Testament. But from the time of the great empires founded by the Assyrians and the Babylonians, we have detailed records written by their own annalists, and these often mention people and events also described in the Old Testament. Moreover, the Assyrian and Babylonian records can be easily dated in absolute terms. This means that it has been possible to work out a general chronological framework for the Old Testament, by using these other materials and combining them with the dating methods found in the Bible story.

Naturally, different scholars make their own judgments on such complex issues. But the dates given in this book are widely recognized as being accurate to within about ten years or less for the earlier Old Testament stories – while the dates given for events and people during the Assyrian and Babylonian periods (and later) are much more accurate than that.

Some incidental details in the Old Testament have been strikingly confirmed by recent discoveries. The note in 1 Kings 6:7 that 'no hammer, chisel or any other tool was heard at the temple while it was being built' is explained by the fact that 'Solomon's quarry' is deep under old Jerusalem, where the stone for the building was quarried and dressed. Though so near to the temple, no sound of the underground quarrying would carry to the construction site above.

6 Judah and Jerusalem

2 Kings 18:13—25:21   Nahum
Isaiah 1—39   Habakkuk
Micah   Jeremiah 1:1—39:10
Zephaniah

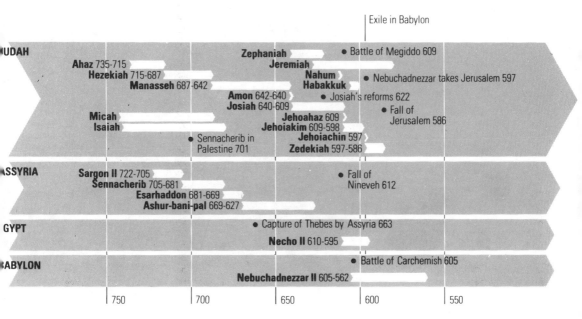

Danger and uncertainty

WITH ISRAEL gone, and Samaria reduced to a heap of ashes, life in Judah changed dramatically. Jerusalem was no longer protected from Assyria by its remote location. The border of the Assyrian Empire was now less than twenty miles away, and Judah's security was threatened. Ahaz had only made things worse by actually offering to subject himself to the Assyrians, in exchange for protection against the kings of Damascus and Israel. Isaiah had been unable to prevent this, but he had no doubt of the likely outcome of such political madness. In a characteristically picturesque message, he declared that the people of Jerusalem 'have rejected the quiet waters from the brook of Shiloah' (near Jerusalem), in exchange for 'the flood waters of the River Euphrates, overflowing all its banks. They will sweep through Judah in a flood, rising shoulder high and covering everything'. Instead of trusting in God, Ahaz and his people had deliberately courted disaster by their cowardly submission to the Assyrians.

Isaiah 8:5–8

Ahaz himself was too cautious to allow that to happen during his reign. But he was sowing the seeds of eventual collapse.

● **Politically,** Ahaz's acceptance of Assyrian rule was inept. But it also had immediate and serious social repercussions for his people. The halcyon days of Uzziah were gone for ever. Much of Judah's territory had been lost – and along with it, a large slice of the royal income. That in itself would have been bad enough to lead to a major economic recession for Ahaz. But his problems were increased by considerable numbers of refugees from the northern kingdom of Israel. He was forced to extend Jerusalem, building new houses and defences to settle these people. It was perhaps inevitable that people should be tempted to get whatever they could for themselves, with no thought of the wider social and moral consequences.

● **Religiously,** Ahaz was encouraging this. Not only was he officially promoting the worship of Assyrian gods – even in the

Isaiah warned King Ahaz that his servility towards the Assyrians would lead to Judah's downfall.

temple itself – but he also allowed many other forms of native Canaanite religions to prosper. The arrival of northern refugees probably just made this worse. But it meant that the distinctive message of Israel's own faith was once again in danger of being lost.

Isaiah was deeply concerned about all this. He knew that the social and political collapse of the northern kingdom had been caused by its failure to pay due attention to the demands of the law from Mt Sinai. And he could see the same things happening in Judah. There was plenty of religious activity, but little evidence of its impact in everyday life. Isaiah's messages at this period bear a remarkable resemblance to the dire warnings that Amos had given: 'Listen to what the Lord is saying to you . . . He says, "Do you think I want all these sacrifices you keep offering to me? . . . I am tired of the blood of bulls and sheep and goats . . . I am disgusted with the smell of the incense you burn . . . I hate your New Moon Festivals and holy days; they are a burden that I am tired of bearing . . . Stop all this evil that I see you doing . . . and learn to

The prophet Micah asked: 'Shall I acquit the man with wicked scales, and with a bag of deceitful weights?' The prophets were concerned with the ordinary dealings of society, and with the honesty without which social and commercial life begins to break down.

do right. See that justice is done – help those who are oppressed, give orphans their rights, and defend widows.'"

Isaiah 1:10–17

The same message was emphasized by the prophet Micah. But whereas Isaiah belonged to the upper classes, Micah was a farm worker. He saw even more clearly what was wrong with society, because he had experienced its injustice for himself. Judah, he said, was rotten from top to bottom. Even her leaders 'hate justice and turn right into wrong . . . building God's city, Jerusalem, on a foundation of murder and injustice'. They might manage to persuade their own prophets to promise that 'wine and liquor will flow' for them, but messages like that were just 'lies and deceit'. People had got their standards mixed up. They believed that God's approval and support could be secured by religious observances. But Micah knew that the real basis of the covenant society was not empty ritual, but justice and equality: 'What shall I bring to the Lord, the God of heaven, when I come to worship him? Shall I bring the best calves to burn as offerings to him? Will the Lord be pleased if I bring him thousands of sheep or endless streams of olive-oil? Shall I offer him my first-born child to pay for my sins? No, the Lord has told us what is good. What he requires of us is this: to do what is just, to show constant love, and to live in humble fellowship with our God.'

Micah 3:9–10

Micah 2:11

Micah 6:6–8

Like Amos before him, Micah saw little hope for people whose view of God's nature was so twisted. 'Twist and groan, people of Jerusalem, like a woman giving birth, for now you will have to leave the city and live in the open country. You will have to go to

Isaiah described Judah as God's vineyard. He expected a good harvest, but the grapes it bore were sour.

Babylon ... Zion will be ploughed like a field, Jerusalem will become a pile of ruins, and the Temple hill will become a forest.'

Micah 4:10; 3:12

There were times when even Isaiah felt the same. In a dramatic picture, he describes Judah and Jerusalem as God's vineyard – a vineyard from which he had great expectations. Instead, all he got was sour grapes. So the vineyard must be destroyed: 'I will take away the hedge round it, break down the wall that protects it, and let wild animals eat it and trample it down.'

Isaiah 5:5

But Ahaz was not disposed to listen to messages like these. He believed he had already secured a measure of prosperity for his people. But in reality, he was undermining the foundations of society. Instead of trusting in God, he was terrified of the Assyrians, and insisted on trusting his own political judgment. Judah had lost her independence to Assyria, and Isaiah could see no hope as long as Ahaz was king. So he withdrew from public life, and until the death of Ahaz he gave his teaching only to a small group of his own personal friends.

False confidence

Ahaz was succeeded by his son, Hezekiah. By the time he came to power, the Assyrian emperor Sargon had become preoccupied with other problems in the east and north of his empire. This meant the states in Palestine had a little more freedom, and they lost no time trying to turn that freedom to real political advantage. Egypt's power was also increasing at this time, and the Philistine city-states were soon plotting with the Egyptians to get rid of Assyrian domination once and for all.

Naturally, they tried to get the support of Judah. No sooner was Hezekiah enthroned in Jerusalem than Philistine ambassadors came to ask for his help. But Isaiah warned them that Assyria's power was far from broken: 'Howl and cry for help, all you Philistine cities! Be terrified, all of you! A cloud of dust is coming

Isaiah 14:31

from the north – it is an army with no cowards in its ranks.' Undaunted, the Egyptians tried to persuade Hezekiah to join their revolt – and Isaiah repeated his message. In a dramatic anticipation of what would happen to the rebels, the prophet took off all his clothes and walked naked round the streets of Jerusalem. This, he said, was 'a sign of what will happen to Egypt and Sudan. The emperor of Assyria will lead away naked the prisoners he captures from those two countries. Young and old, they will walk barefoot

Isaiah 20:3–4

and naked, with their buttocks exposed, bringing shame on Egypt.' Hezekiah had more sense than his father, and listened carefully to Isaiah's advice. It was just as well he did, for in a short time the Assyrian army had moved in strength against the Philistines and the Egyptians. They were unable to defend themselves, let alone Judah, and their power collapsed just as Isaiah had predicted.

Reform in Jerusalem

Hezekiah was still tempted to make his own bid for freedom. But he now realized that he would need to move carefully. So he began

2 Kings 18:1–8

surreptitiously by reforming the religious practices of his people.

Isaiah and Micah had both complained that the worship of their own God Yahweh was being mixed up with the worship of other gods. Some of these gods were certainly the local Canaanite Baals that had caused such havoc in the northern kingdom of Israel. But in addition, Ahaz had erected an altar to the Assyrian gods in Jerusalem as a sign of his political allegiance. Hezekiah soon saw that if he got rid of these things, he could please religious fanatics like Isaiah, but he could also make a start on establishing his own independence from Assyria. A number of features of Hezekiah's reforms indicate the clear political intention behind it:

● As well as clearing the Jerusalem temple of all the paraphernalia of alien worship, he also tried to close down even legitimate places of worship elsewhere in the country. That would ensure the temple in Jerusalem would be the only place where the people could worship God. Of course, this temple had always been Judah's national shrine. But when Solomon first built it, it also became an instant symbol of the king's own power. Hezekiah knew that if he could persuade his people to worship only in his own temple, that was bound to strengthen their loyalty to him and to his successors.

● Hezekiah's own people were not the only ones who were invited to worship in Jerusalem. He also sent a message to those who were left in what had been the territory of northern Israel. This

2 Chronicles 30:1–12

King Hezekiah faced a constant military threat from Assyria. As part of his preparation for a possible siege, he had a water tunnel dug to bring water from outside the Jerusalem city well to the Pool of Siloam inside the city. This constant water supply stood the city in good stead when Sennacherib's army invaded.

state was now part of the Assyrian Empire, and therefore had no official ties with Israel's national faith. But Hezekiah knew that many of its inhabitants were still descended from the old Israelite tribes – and if they could be tempted to come south and worship in Jerusalem, that may begin to undermine the Assyrian power on his doorstep. Hezekiah certainly made strenuous efforts to link his reign with the corporate memory of the old kingdom in the north, even calling his son Manasseh, which was the original name of one of the ten northern tribes.

● As well as reorganizing religious worship, Hezekiah also made military preparations for the inevitable Assyrian backlash. He built new defences in Jerusalem and many other cities. He reorganized

2 Chronicles 32:5; Isaiah 22:9–11

2 Chronicles 32:5–8
2 Chronicles 32:27–29

2 Kings 20:20;
2 Chronicles 32:30;
Isaiah 22:9–11

the army, built new store cities, and rationalized his civil service. In Jerusalem itself he built the Siloam Tunnel, to make sure the city would have plenty of water in the event of a siege. Hezekiah was determined that, when the right opportunity presented itself, he would have a good chance of seizing a real and lasting independence from the Assyrians.

His chance came with the death of Sargon. Soon afterwards, both the king of Babylon and a new Egyptian king sent a message asking Hezekiah to help overthrow the Assyrians. Isaiah warned

Isaiah 30:1–7; 31:1–3

against this, but his warnings feel on deaf ears. The only ruler in Palestine who was opposed to this plan was the Philistine king of Ekron. But Hezekiah soon overcame his opposition, by arranging some sort of revolt among his own officials. The Assyrian king Sennacherib describes how 'the officials, the politicians, and the people of Ekron, had thrown Padi, their king, into fetters . . . and handed him over to Hezekiah the Jew'. After this, all the Philistine city-states seem to have fallen in with this new anti-Assyrian alliance.

The Assyrians move in

The inevitable happened. The Assyrian king Sennacherib could not allow this kind of revolt, even on the edge of his empire. He marched south through Palestine, and Egypt and the Philistines

'Sennacherib's prism', an Assyrian document inscribed on stone, describes the siege of Jerusalem from the invaders' point of view. Sennacherib speaks of shutting Hezekiah in Jerusalem 'like a bird in a cage'.

collapsed at once. Then he moved against Judah, using the same tactics as his predecessor Shalmaneser had adopted against the northern kingdom of Israel. First, he would weaken Hezekiah's position by taking over much of his territory. Instead of making the towns and villages of Judah a part of his own empire, he handed them over to various Philistine kings. But the result was the same: Hezekiah had no supporters to whom he could appeal for help. And so Sennacherib moved in the direction of Jerusalem. In his own vivid account, he describes how he had Hezekiah shut up in his own capital city 'like a bird in a cage'.

Hezekiah could see there was no chance of escape. The best he could hope for was to save the city itself by paying Sennacherib a huge tribute. The Assyrian king was prepared to accept this, and so Hezekiah sent large quantities of gold and silver treasures to the town of Lachish, where Sennacherib was encamped with his army.

2 Kings 18:13–16

It is not altogether clear what happened next. The Old Testament continues with the story of a siege of Jerusalem which ended in complete failure. The Assyrian army apparently camped outside the city in force, in the hope that the people would depose Hezekiah and so save themselves from the hardship of a siege. Then, just as the fall of the city seemed imminent, the Assyrian army suddenly withdrew, after many of its soldiers had died in some mysterious way.

2 Kings 18:17—19:37

The Assyrian records have a detailed account of Sennacherib's activities in Judah, but they do not mention this event. That in itself is not too surprising, for their official annals often ignored defeats. Most scholars believe that the Old Testament story is authentic enough, but they differ about when it actually happened. Some think it must have been a part of Sennacherib's campaign in 701 BC. But he is hardly likely to have besieged Jerusalem immediately after receiving such a large payment of tribute. Others have noted that the story mentions 'King Tirhakah of Sudan'. A king of that name ruled in Egypt from about 689 BC, and it is therefore possible that this incident took place later, perhaps as a result of another attempted revolt by Hezekiah. On the other hand, we have no knowledge from Assyrian sources of a second expedition by Sennacherib into Palestine.

2 Kings 19:9

Assyria's final fling

2 Kings 19:37;
Isaiah 37:38

We know comparatively little of what was going on in Judah in the years immediately following Sennacherib's invasion. Sennacherib himself was murdered, and his successor was Esarhaddon, who was to be one of Assyria's most powerful rulers. When he died, his empire was divided between his two sons. Ashur-bani-pal reigned at Nineveh, and Shamash-Shanakin at Babylon.

During this period, Assyria eventually achieved her greatest ambition. Ashur-bani-pal finally managed to crush Egypt, and captured its capital city, Thebes. Assyria now dominated the whole of the Fertile Crescent, including the rival superpower of Egypt. But Ashur-bani-pal was not primarily a great warrior. He had no

Ashurbanipal, depicted on this relief killing a lion, was emperor of Assyria in the time of Manasseh's reign in Jerusalem. He collected a library of historical documents at his capital, Nineveh, mostly in the form of clay tablets written on in cuneiform script. A great many of these documents have been pieced together and give a remarkably full record of Assyrian civilization.

need to be: his predecessors had already established the empire on a firm foundation.

He was able to turn his attention instead to the enrichment of Assyrian culture, and his palace at Nineveh became a great centre of both the literary and the visual arts. His artists produced some of the most striking work of the ancient world, and his scribes gathered an amazing library of literature. Not only did they catalogue the events of recent history with great precision, but they also collected the ancient traditions of Mesopotamia, which went back right to the very dawn of civilization. Their writing methods may seem primitive to us today, for they used the material that lay ready to hand: river mud. First they formed the mud into conveniently-sized blocks, then they wrote on them with wedge-shaped sticks while the mud was still wet. Once this 'cuneiform' writing was complete, the blocks could be baked solid in the heat of the sun. This meant their books were bulky, but they were also virtually indestructible, and even today it is still possible to piece together mud blocks that have been broken for centuries. It is due to this royal library at Nineveh that we have so much detailed knowledge of the ancient civilizations of the area and of their national traditions.

There was little to say about life in Jerusalem and Judah at such a time as this. Hezekiah's successor, Manasseh, had no room to flex his nationalistic muscles. He was no match for Assyria's power, and was in complete subjection to it. The Assyrian records mention him only as a source of building materials and troops, and confirm that he continued to pay regular taxes. The Old Testament makes no direct mention of Assyrian power during Manasseh's long reign, but it shows quite clearly the reality of it in its description of events

2 Kings 21:1–18 in the Jerusalem temple. Judah's own national faith was once more neglected, and all sorts of pagan ceremonies were promoted, including star worship. Like Ahaz before him, Manasseh was forced to express his subservience to the Assyrians by worshipping their gods. But this time he made sure there would be no protests from people like Isaiah: those who disagreed with his policies were

2 Kings 21:16 put to death. Because of all this, the Old Testament writers regarded him as the most wicked of all the kings. And his son Amon

2 Kings 21:19–26 continued the same unhappy policies.

Reform and renewal

Then came an unexpected opportunity for change. Things suddenly began to move on the fringes of the Assyrian Empire. The Egyptians regained their independence. The kingdom of Lydia in the north-west, and the Medes in the east, began to harrass the Assyrians. At the same time, hordes of Asian raiders (Scythians) swept down from the north. All of this had an unsettling effect on the empire. Indeed, its internal stability had already been shaken by feuding between Ashur-bani-pal and his brother. And within a few years of Ashur-bani-pal's death, the Assyrians were fighting for survival against the Babylonians and the Medes.

As before, the weakening of Assyrian power led to the revival of national hopes in Judah. This time, they centred around Amon's son, Josiah, who became king in Judah while he was still only a boy.

2 Kings 22:1–2 As soon as he grew up, Josiah set about re-asserting his country's independence. Assyria's problems now looked serious, and he saw a real chance of restoring the kingdom to something like the glory of the days of David and Solomon. He did not quite manage that, but nevertheless Josiah had considerable success in extending his territory. Archaeological evidence shows that he controlled land as far north as Galilee, and his influence extended east of the River Jordan into Gilead. He also had some power over the Philistine states in the west – and all this was consolidated with at least two

2 Kings 23:31, 36 marriages.

This territorial expansion went hand in hand with a thorough-going religious reformation. This was only to be expected, for the terms of Assyrian rule had closely integrated religion with politics. Ahaz and Manasseh had both demonstrated their allegiance to Assyria by worshipping Assyrian gods in Jerusalem. Hezekiah's move for independence had started with the removal of the paraphernalia of Assyrian religion, and Josiah had to do the same. In the event, he was far more successful than Hezekiah had ever been: he even managed to ban the symbols of Assyrian domination in the territories of the former northern kingdom of Israel. The sanctuary established at Bethel by Jeroboam I was destroyed, along with many local shrines and their priests.

2 Kings 23:15–20

But the central feature of Josiah's reform was the discovery of a long-forgotten book in the temple at Jerusalem. This book was not the cause of the reform, for it only came to light after the workmen had started to renovate the temple. But once discovered, it played a significant part in the subsequent course of events. The Old Testament story does not directly identify this book. But three main ideas seem to have dominated it:

2 Kings 22:3–20

● Israel was a united people, and therefore the political division between Judah and Israel was meaningless.

● The central plank of Israel's faith must be belief in only one God.

● Israel's one God must be worshipped in only one place.

A lost book

Up to this point, Josiah's reform had probably been more concerned with getting rid of Assyrian objects than with promoting the worship of Israel's God Yahweh for his own sake. But this book provided a new, positive impetus. At times of political crisis and uncertainty, people often try to go back to the old ways, even today. And in Josiah's time, many nations in the ancient world were taking a new look at their own national heritage for the same reasons. So when an ancient book was discovered in Jerusalem, it was naturally treated with special reverence. As it happened, this book also played right into Josiah's hands, for its main ideas seemed to give a

The Assyrian Empire

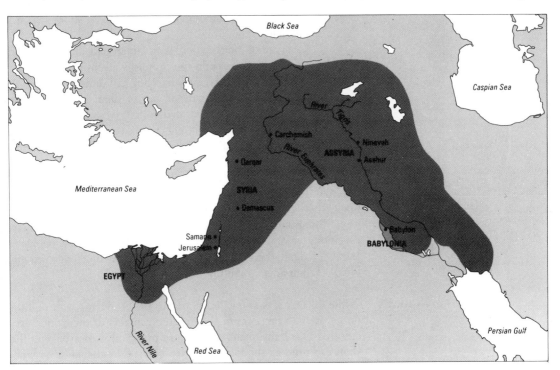

religious backing to the political moves he was already making. He was trying to restore Judah's control over the former territory of the whole of the united nation of Israel. He was getting rid of Assyrian gods. And he needed to strengthen his personal position by insisting that the religious allegiance of the people should be given to his own royal temple in Jerusalem.

There can be no doubt that this book was the Old Testament book of Deuteronomy. Some scholars have occasionally suggested that, far from being an ancient book, Josiah had actually arranged to have it written for precisely the reasons just mentioned. But this is highly unlikely. If Deuteronomy had been written in Josiah's time, it would have reflected his own situation much more clearly. In particular, it would have identified the one place where God should be worshipped as the temple in Jerusalem. But in fact, Deuteronomy does not do this – and in any case, Josiah was not the first king of Judah to try to strengthen his position by this stratagem: Hezekiah had already tried it before him.

Deuteronomy does not in itself support the centralization of worship in Jerusalem, and it actually has many close links with the dynamic view of kingship that had been followed more self-consciously in the northern kingdom of Israel. For this reason, many scholars believe that the 'one sanctuary' mentioned in Deuteronomy was not Jerusalem, but the place where the ark of the covenant had been kept during the earliest period of Israel's settlement in the land. The whole book clearly emphasizes the lessons that had been forcefully presented by northern prophets like Amos and Hosea: that the nation's prosperity could only be assured if they were willing to return to the old ways, and recognize the demands for justice and equality that had been so important in the covenant made at Mt Sinai.

This is something that the people of Judah had forgotten. They were laying more emphasis on the promises given to David and to his successors. Instead of asking what they had done to deserve the punishment that was being handed out to them by Assyria, they reassured themselves with the belief that Jerusalem was God's chosen city – Zion – and so nothing could ever happen to it. It was impregnable, and would always be that way. Even Isaiah had agreed with this point of view. Though he saw Assyria's iron hand as the agent of God's punishment, he still could not believe that Judah's day was finished. But now, as Josiah and his people read this old book, they could see very clearly that unless they changed their ways, Judah and its people were indeed finished. So in a solemn ceremony reminiscent of the events of Mt Sinai, the people of Judah pledged their allegiance once again to the long-forgotten ideals of their ancient faith.

The Babylonians While all this was going on in Judah, the Assyrians were fighting desperately to hang on to the tattered remains of their once great empire. The Babylonians were more powerful than ever, and they soon captured all the main Assyrian cities. The defeated Assyrians

Deuteronomy 12:5

Isaiah 1:10–20; 2:6–21; 5:26–30
Isaiah 9:1–7; 11:1–16; 14:1–2

2 Kings 23:1–3

tried to re-establish themselves at Haran, but they were soon ejected from there as well. Some thirteen years after Josiah's reformation in Judah, the Assyrians made a last-ditch effort to regain this town. This time, their old enemies the Egyptians came to help them. Necho II, now king of Egypt, could see that his real rival was no longer the king of Assyria but Nabopolasser, king of Babylon. Judah had no reason to be involved in all this. But for some inexplicable reason Josiah decided that he would try to stop the Egyptians from

A representation of a demon from Babylon. Unlike Israel to the north, Judah survived the years of Assyrian dominance. But the Babylonian Empire took over control of the region, and none of the Judean kings after Josiah could resist their influence.

reaching the beleaguered Assyrian army. He was unable to do so, and died in the attempt at Megiddo. As a result, Judah came under Egyptian domination for a while.

But nothing could stop the advance of the Babylonians now. Four years after the final collapse of Assyria the Babylonian army met the Egyptians in battle at Carchemish, and decisively defeated them. At this Jehoiakim, a king of Judah who had been put in power by the Egyptians, was forced to transfer his allegiance to the Babylonian Nebuchadnezzar. But like his predecessors, he was

2 Kings 24:1

always searching for a suitable opportunity to reassert his own independence.

When Babylon was defeated by the Egyptians some four years later, he decided to take his chance. But he had seriously misjudged the situation. The Babylonian Nebuchadnezzar moved in strength through the whole of Palestine, and besieged Jerusalem with his army. He was determined to replace Jehoiakim with a king who could be trusted. As it happened, the job was done for him, for Jehoiakim died during the course of the siege, and was replaced by his son Jehoiachin. He could see that resistance was futile, and surrendered to Nebuchadnezzar. But the Babylonian did not trust him. Instead, he took him off into exile in Babylon, along with many of the leading citizens and a large quantity of the treasures from both palace and temple.

Three prophets

Three of the shorter Old Testament books seem to have originated during the reigns of Josiah and Jehoiakim: Zephaniah, Nahum, and Habakkuk. We know virtually nothing of the prophets whose messages they contain, but they were all concerned with one subject: the way that God was using nations like Assyria and Babylon to achieve his own ends.

● **Zephaniah** is identified as a descendant of Hezekiah (1:1), and he probably delivered his messages in the earliest days of the reign of Josiah. Judah and Jerusalem, he declared, were being brought to ruination by the worship of Canaanite gods like Baal, as well as the astral deities of the Assyrians (1:4–6). But Zephaniah did not blame Josiah himself for this state of affairs. Instead, he singles out his court officials (1:8–9), which suggests that Josiah was still a boy and his great religious reforms were a thing of the future. Probably therefore Zephaniah delivered his messages some time between 640 and 622 BC, and this date would also fit in well with the theme of the poem which ends the book (3:14–20). For this is a celebration hymn, following the deliverance of Judah and Jerusalem from some particular enemy – possibly the Scythians, who were advancing south towards Egypt at about this period. But the jubilation with which the book closes is not reflected in the rest of the prophet's messages.

Zephaniah warned his people against a false confidence in the security of Jerusalem just because of God's promises to David. The 'day of the Lord' would be coming soon enough – and it would not be a day of rejoicing for the people of Judah, any more than it had been for the people of

Samaria (1:7–18). They would experience God's anger, just as other nations would. Even Assyria, which God had used to punish his own people, would in turn be destroyed themselves because of their pride and self-satisfaction (2:13–15). But like Isaiah before him, Zephaniah saw that God could both punish his people, and yet still show his love for them. Though Jerusalem was doomed, 'a humble and lowly people' would survive (3:12), and through them God's promises would come true.

● **Nahum** belongs to a period nearer the end of Josiah's reign, either just before or just after the collapse of the Assyrian capital Nineveh in 612 BC. Nahum too saw that, though Assyria had been the instrument of God's punishment for his people, they had over-reached themselves – and they would be punished in their turn. The collapse of Nineveh (Nahum 2—3) is described in such vivid language that some scholars have argued that the prophet must actually have witnessed the scene. But others believe that his apparent realism is a purely imaginary – though remarkably accurate – description of the city's fall, and was probably written even before the Babylonians finally moved in. Either way, the message of the book is the conviction that God himself, and not the Assyrians, is the Lord of history. He can use nations to achieve his own ends, but he is the one who is in control. This was obviously an important issue for the people of Judah, who had suffered so much at the hands of Assyria. Because of the poetic form of the book, and the dramatic content of it, some have suggested that Nahum's messages were put together in this form to be used as a

Habakkuk's prophecies were given at a time when Babylonian military power was dominant and no other army would resist them. This time of warfare brought great suffering and humiliation on the people, and Habakkuk tried to understand how God could be found at such a time.

part of the worship in the temple at Jerusalem, to celebrate Nineveh's downfall, and to remind the worshippers of God's great power.

● **Habakkuk** tackled the same problem, but this time from a more reflective perspective. He lived slightly later than Nahum, in the reign of Jehoiakim. By the time he delivered his messages, Egypt had been defeated at the battle of Carchemish (605 BC), and Habakkuk now had a chance to reflect on the Babylonian style of government. He was not impressed with what he saw. Things in Judah were bad enough, and society was collapsing in moral and political anarchy (1:2–4). God was rightly using superpowers like Babylon to discipline his people. But were the Babylonians any better? They 'catch people with hooks, as though they were fish. They drag them off in nets and shout for joy over their catch! They even worship their nets and offer sacrifices to them, because their nets provide them with the best of everything.' (1:15–16). So, asked Habakkuk, how could God tolerate this kind of inhuman wickedness, while dealing so sternly with the lesser evil that was going on in Jerusalem?

He found the answer to that in the conviction that the Babylonians would themselves be punished by God. Like Nahum, he could see that God himself was in charge of history. And though he could use even evil nations to accomplish his intentions, he would never allow them to get away with their wrongdoing: 'You are doomed! You founded a city on crime and built it up by murder. The nations you conquered wore themselves out in useless labour,

and all they have built goes up in flames. The Lord Almighty has done this. But the earth will be as full of the knowledge of the Lord's glory as the seas are full of water . . . The Lord will make you drink your own cup of punishment, and your honour will be turned to disgrace.' (2:12–14, 16).

Of course, Habakkuk realized that this kind of answer to the problem of evil in the world is not much direct use to those who are actually suffering. But he also included some practical advice for his people: 'Those who are evil will not survive, but those who are righteous will live because they are faithful to God' (2:4). There is some debate as to the precise meaning of these words, but almost certainly we should translate the Hebrew to refer to the faithfulness of God himself, first experienced by his people in the events of the exodus, and repeated many times since then. It was in these words that Paul and Luther found the heart of Christianity, and of course the commitment of which they spoke is essentially a human response to the faithfulness of God himself. This confidence in God was eloquently expressed by Habakkuk in the closing verses of his book – and it was to be needed in the dark days that were ahead for Judah: 'Even though the fig-trees have no fruit and no grapes grow on the vines, even though the olive-crop fails and the fields produce no corn, even though the sheep all die and the cattle-stalls are empty, I will still be joyful and glad, because the Lord God is my saviour. The Sovereign Lord gives me strength. He makes me sure-footed as a deer, and keeps me safe on the mountains' (3:17–19).

Jeremiah and the fall of Jerusalem

Jeremiah 1:4

Jerusalem finally fell to the Babylonians, and most of its people either became refugees or were taken into exile. It seemed that the history of Judah had come to an end

Jeremiah 1:11–12

Even before Josiah's reformation in 622 BC, another young prophet called Jeremiah had already begun his work. He belonged to a family of priests from Anathoth, a village about four miles north-east of Jerusalem. Like the other prophets, he was convinced that God himself had spoken to him, and given him a message for his people. He was to be 'a prophet to the nations', communicating the will of God in the midst of much international turmoil. This was certainly an appropriate time for the emergence of such a person. For by the year of his call, 627 BC, Assyria's power was crumbling and independence for Judah once more seemed a real possibility.

But Jeremiah could not share in the mood of national optimism. He saw many things wrong in his nation. They had ignored the covenant laws of God, and would have to pay the price for their disobedience. One day he saw an almond tree in blossom. Now the Hebrew word for 'almond' sounded rather like another Hebrew word that meant 'watching' – and Jeremiah saw this tree as a sign that God was watching over his people, looking for the appropriate time to carry out his sentence of destruction. When he saw a pot of boiling

water on a fire that was fanned by a wind from the north, he realized that this too had a message in it. God's anger was about to boil over against Judah: 'Destruction will boil over from the north on all who live in this land, because I am calling all the nations in the north to come. Their kings will set up their thrones at the gates of Jerusalem and round its walls, and also round the other cities of Judah. I will punish my people. . .'.

Jeremiah 1:13–16

Of course, things soon began to change with the religious reforms instituted by Josiah. And Jeremiah was almost certainly in favour of all this. He certainly wanted to get rid of foreign religious influences, and some of his messages may well have been delivered in support of Josiah, for they angered his relatives in Anathoth, who decided to try to kill him. Their reaction would make sense if Jeremiah was supporting Josiah's closure of all the sanctuaries except the temple in Jerusalem, for as priests they would presumably be in danger of losing their jobs.

Jeremiah 11:1–23

False confidence

Jeremiah's picture of an almond tree in blossom was not a comforting one. The Hebrew word for 'almond' sounds like 'watching'. Jeremiah was convinced that the Lord was watching over his people, against the time when he should bring on them the judgement due for generations of disobedience to the covenant.

But Jeremiah soon saw that Josiah's reform was not going to have much lasting effect on the way of life of the people. By the time of Jehoiakim things were as bad as they had ever been. But he also believed that Josiah's emphasis on the Jerusalem temple had actually undermined the faith that was emphasized in the ancient book found there. For instead of facing up to their responsibilities under the covenant law, his people developed a pathetic and misguided confidence in their religious institutions. They came to believe that as long as they performed all the religious rituals in the temple, God would actually preserve them from their enemies and all would be well.

In the end, events proved Jeremiah was right. But in the short term, he was disappointed and depressed. The people refused to listen to his message. And he was puzzled himself, because it was not coming true. Instead of the doom that Jeremiah had predicted, Judah was enjoying a period of great prosperity. Under Josiah her territory was enlarged and there never seemed any shortage of money for grand new building projects. Under the circumstances, people like Jeremiah were unlikely to be taken seriously. When Nineveh was destroyed in 612 BC, his message seemed to be quite discredited.

The end is coming

But the picture soon changed. Three years later, Josiah was dead and the Egyptians had taken over the land of Judah. The prosperity that had gone before had been attributed to the fact that things had been set right in the temple at Jerusalem. So what had gone wrong now? Why had God not saved his apparently faithful people from the power of Egypt? In this situation, Jeremiah's messages did not look so unrealistic. And when under Jehoiakim the reforms of Josiah virtually disappeared, the stage looked set for the scenario of disaster that Jeremiah had so vividly described. Even Jehoiakim himself could see that, and he made a concerted effort to get rid of opponents like Jeremiah. At least one prophet, Uriah, was killed, and Jeremiah himself was brought to trial. He escaped death, but he still

Jeremiah 26:20–23
Jeremiah 26:7–24

Jeremiah 20:1–2

continued his messages of doom and destruction, and was beaten up and put into the stocks for a night.

Even that did not stop him. God had spoken to him, and he could not refuse to communicate the message: 'When I say, "I will forget the Lord and no longer speak in his name", then your message is like a fire burning deep within me. I try my best to hold it in, but can no Jeremiah 20:9 longer keep it back'. But he was banned from delivering his messages in public at the temple. So he withdrew from public life for

The people of Jerusalem were deported to Babylon in stages. At first only the leaders were taken in the days of King Jehoiachin, while Zedekiah was put on the throne as a puppet ruler. Only after his revolt was the city fully crushed. Jeremiah characterized this intervening time as being like a basket of figs, of which the good ones stood for those already in exile, and the bad ones for the leaders who remained.

the rest of Jehoiakim's reign, and sent out his messages in a new way. This time he got his friend Baruch to write them down, and then he took them into the streets and read them out.

In the reign of Jehoiakim, Jeremiah's messages were no longer general declarations of disaster, but definite predictions of the impending end of Jerusalem, and especially of the destruction of its temple. Jeremiah was sure that the idea that God was bound to protect his own temple and city was false.

But Jeremiah's challenge came not just from his enemies. He had his own problems with the message God had given him. If it was so correct, why did no one else accept it? After all, Jeremiah had not refused God's call, even though he wanted to do so. He had laid himself open to disbelief and ridicule, and had become involved in Jeremiah 15:10–21 endless arguments. He had given up the ordinary human joys of

Jeremiah 20:7–18

home and family to be a spokesman for God – and he felt that God had deceived him. He had to learn some hard lessons, and some of the most striking parts of his book are taken up with this kind of self-examination. But he was also learning an important new lesson, for out of the crisis of his own life he discovered what it meant to trust God in a personal and living way.

Dark days in Jerusalem

When Nebuchadnezzar captured Jerusalem in 597 BC, he placed a new king, Zedekiah, on the throne there. But things did not change. Instead of learning their lesson, the people of Jerusalem concluded that they were specially favoured by God, because they had not been carried off into exile. The prophet Jeremiah had no time for all this. He knew that what had happened was a just punishment for the people's wrongdoing – and worse was to come. He pointed to two baskets of figs in the market. One contained good figs, the other was full of rotten figs. The good ones, said Jeremiah, were the exiles in Babylon. The bad ones were the people left in Judah, and

Jeremiah 24

they would suffer the same fate as figs that were too bad to eat.

Zedekiah did not know which way to turn. Jeremiah told him the only sensible thing to do was to accept Babylonian domination, and he wanted to listen. But he was a weak man. When the Egyptians tried to persuade him to join a revolt against Babylon, many prophets advised Zedekiah to do so. But Jeremiah would not change his mind. He appeared with a wooden yoke on his

Jeremiah 27

shoulders. He was confronted in the temple by a prophet called Hananiah. This prophet poured scorn on Jeremiah's message, and to prove his point he smashed Jeremiah's yoke. Jeremiah knew this was a false message, and he quickly replaced the wooden yoke with

Jeremiah 28

an iron one.

In the event, Jeremiah was right. The Babylonian army moved up to crush the rebellion masterminded by Egypt, and Judah was finished. After a siege of eighteen months Jerusalem fell to Nebuchadnezzar. Zedekiah tried to escape, but he was captured. His family was killed before his eyes, and then he was blinded and carried off to Babylon along with most of the leading people of the land. This time the Babylonians made sure of their victory. They systematically destroyed all the main buildings in Jerusalem, including the temple. A palace official named Gedaliah was made

2 Kings 25:1–26

governor of Judah. There would never be a king again.

Jeremiah's dreadful predictions had come true. The temple was gone. But he knew that God's promises could not be overthrown so easily. Like Habakkuk, Jeremiah knew that God could be trusted to keep his word, and there would be a future for his people. Even while Jerusalem was under attack, Jeremiah had bought a piece of land in his native village, as an expression of his confidence for the

Jeremiah 32:1–25
Jeremiah 37:11—38:13

future. The action nearly cost him his life, for he was arrested as a traitor while leaving the city to go and view the property.

Yet his trust in God was not founded on a crudely materialistic expectation. He had already made it plain that his people's future and the real meaning of the faith from Mt Sinai was not to be found in the temple. All the institutions connected with that were only of limited value. God was not truly to be found in the ritual of sacrifice, but in a personal and living relationship of trust and commitment. The exiles in Babylon were to learn that soon enough. But it was an insight that had already been given to Jeremiah. For he saw beyond and through the disaster and destruction, to a new relationship that God would establish with his people. God himself had remained faithful to the covenant made at Mt Sinai, but his people had been unable to respond to his love. They had not managed to live up to the high ideals. What they needed now was a 'new covenant', that would repair the omission of the old – a covenant that would not just ask them to be obedient to God, but that would actually give them the moral power to be so.

'The new covenant that I will make with the people of Israel will be this: I will put my law within them and write it on their hearts. I will be their God, and they will be my people . . . all will know me, from the least to the greatest. I will forgive their sins, and I will no longer remember their wrongs. I the Lord have spoken.'

Jeremiah 31:31–34

The Lachish Letters

The last days of Judah are depicted vividly in the book of Jeremiah, where the prophet's message reflects the disarray and confusion of the people. They could see the Babylonians coming, and were powerless to do anything about it. The picture we get from Jeremiah has been supplemented by one of the most remarkable finds ever made by archaeologists in a Bible city: the Lachish Letters.

The city of Lachish lay to the south-west of Jerusalem, and its history began long before the Israelite tribes ever came into the land. It was an important city from the time of Joshua onwards, and has been more thoroughly excavated than most Israelite towns. The material found there by archaeologists has been of great importance for our understanding of the development of the Hebrew language, and the discovery of Canaanite altars and other religious objects has added to our knowledge of the kind of practices so often denounced by the prophets in the Old Testament. The city was destroyed by Sennacherib in 701 BC, and then later Nebuchadnezzar captured it in about 587 BC, just before the final collapse of Zedekiah's Jerusalem. The Lachish Letters relate to this sequence of events.

They are actually what archaeologists call 'ostraca', that is, scraps of broken pottery with messages written on them. A total of twenty-one of these ostraca were found, mostly in what appears to have been the guardroom of the city gate. Not all of them are now legible,

but the majority of them that are were addressed to a man named Yaush, who was probably the military commander of Lachish at the time. Many of the messages were written by a man called Hoshayahu, who seems to have been the officer in charge of a military outpost to the north of Lachish. The same name is found in Jeremiah (42:1; 43:2), but there is no reason to think they were the same person. Yet the letters do give us a fascinating insight into the same situations as were described by Jeremiah:

● Jeremiah 34:1–7 reports a message given by Jeremiah to Zedekiah while Nebuchadnezzar's army was moving against Jerusalem. At the same time, 'the army was also attacking Lachish and Azekah, the only other fortified cities left in Judah' (Jeremiah 34:7). Azekah was almost half-way between Lachish and Jerusalem, and in one of the Lachish ostraca Hoshayahu writes 'we are watching for the signals of Lachish . . . for we cannot see Azekah'. Azekah was perhaps midway between Hoshayahu's post and Lachish, and was therefore used as a signalling station . But at the time of writing, it had apparently fallen to the Babylonians.

● The name Jeremiah is found in two of the letters, though there is no reason to identify this person with the Old Testament prophet in either case. But there is a clear reference to 'the prophet' in at least two of these letters, and the term may be found in a further two. Some have suggested that the person referred to so clearly as 'the

Fragments of a letter, written on pottery by a military commander at an outpost near Lachish, bear witness to a desperate state of affairs as the Babylonian army advanced.

prophet' must have been Jeremiah himself. Others argue that it could be Uriah, since the same letter also refers to 'Coniah, son of Elnathan' going to Egypt – and according to Jeremiah 26:22, Jehoiakim sent a man called Elnathan to bring Uriah from Egypt to face death in Jerusalem. This identification is highly questionable, for the letters did not originate in Jehoiakim's reign, but later in the time of Zedekiah. Nevertheless, even these uncertain references do indicate that such prophets as Jeremiah were performing an important role in national affairs at this period in Judah's history.

The first scholar actually to decipher these letters thought that the story behind them was closely linked with the prophetic movement in Jerusalem. Hoshayahu was apparently trying to justify his actions in some matter connected with confidential letters. According to Professor Torczyner, Yaush, the commander, was a supporter of the prophets, and Hoshayahu had been responsible for betraying Uriah when he fled to Egypt. This explains why Yaush was storing the letters in his guardhouse, so they could be used as evidence in Hoshayahu's trial later.

But this is only a conjecture (and perhaps not a very likely one). The greatest value of these letters is the insight that they give us into the people of Jeremiah's day, and their reactions as they faced the inevitable end of their nation at the hands of the Babylonian army.

The prophets

In the course of our study of the Old Testament story, we have met many people who are described as 'prophets'. They clearly played a crucial role in the history of the two nations, Israel and Judah – and their messages dominate the Old Testament as we have it today. They are among the greatest religious teachers of all time, and had a profound impact on the life of those who knew them.

But how did they fit into the social structures of their day? And how would ordinary people understand what they were doing?

At one time it was fashionable to suppose that it was through their activity that a primitive and superstitious popular religiosity was transformed into the high ideals of morality that we find in the Old Testament today. But we now know that Old Testament prophecy as a whole is much more complex than that simplistic explanation suggests.

We are alerted to this complexity as soon as we appreciate that the Old Testament uses four different Hebrew expressions for 'prophet'. Some passages seem to suggest that the terminology changed with the passage of time (1 Samuel 9:11), but in reality we cannot now tell the technical difference between these terms. The fact that the terminology is so diverse, however, clearly suggests that prophets differed from each other, and that prophecy was not just a single social and religious phenomenon. We find people called prophets operating in many different social contexts: as diviners (1 Samuel 9:1–25); as ecstatics, often in groups who are distinguished by special marks and clothing (1 Samuel 10:5–8; 19:18–24; 1 Kings 20:35–43; 2 Kings 1:8; 2:23–24; 4:38; 6:12); as royal court prophets (1 Samuel 22:5; 2 Samuel 12:1–15; 24:11; 1 Kings 20:35–43); as war prophets (Judges 4:4–9; 1 Kings 20; 22:1–28); as cultic prophets (1 Samuel 10:5–8; 2 Kings 4:18–25); as 'false' prophets (1 Kings 22; Micah 3:5–6; Isaiah 9:15; Ezekiel 13:2; Jeremiah 6:14).

Prophecy was a very diverse phenomenon. Some prophets seem to have operated in more than one way. For instance, Samuel is at one time a seer, when he tells Saul about his lost asses (1 Samuel 9:11), but he then goes on to give specific messages about the

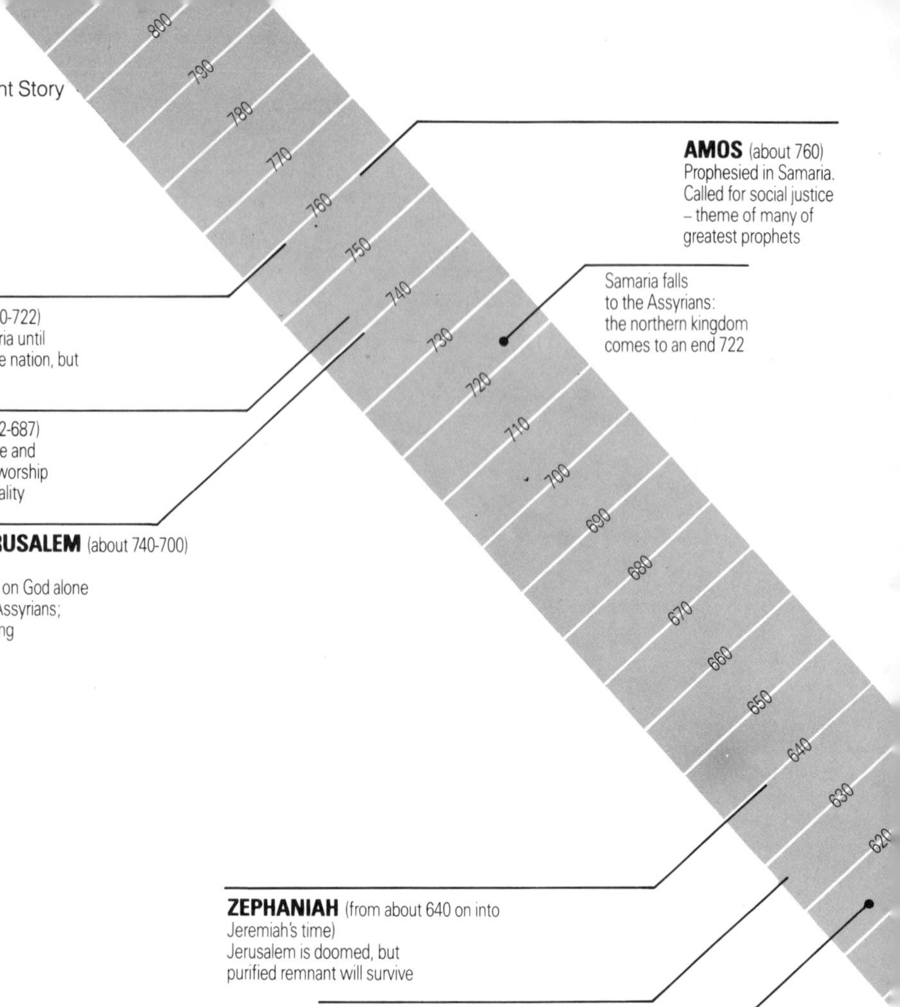

AMOS (about 760)
Prophesied in Samaria.
Called for social justice
– theme of many of
greatest prophets

Samaria falls
to the Assyrians:
the northern kingdom
comes to an end 722

HOSEA (about 760-722)
Prophesied in Samaria until
its fall. God will judge nation, but
also loves it deeply

MICAH (about 742-687)
Concerned for justice and
true religion; hated worship
separated from morality

ISAIAH OF JERUSALEM (about 740-700)
Great vision of God;
nation must depend on God alone
for protection from Assyrians;
predicts a coming king

ZEPHANIAH (from about 640 on into
Jeremiah's time)
Jerusalem is doomed, but
purified remnant will survive

JEREMIAH (about 627-587)
Jerusalem will fall; deep
concern for faith and repentance;
prophet's inward grief;
promise of new covenant

Nineveh,
Assyria's capital,
falls 612

EZEKIEL (about 593-570)
Prophesied in Babylon;
Jerusalem will finally fall;
promise of future return and revival

DANIEL
Story of Jew in exile who
refused to compromise faith;
visions of the future

ISAIAH OF BABYLON
(probably during the exile and after)
God will save, restore
and revive his people;
poems of suffering servant

OBADIAH (after 586)
Against Edomites for adding to
Jerusalem's misfortunes

LAMENTATIONS (after 586)
Five poems lamenting the
destruction of Jerusalem

JOEL? (time of writing unknown)
Plague of locusts used as
basis for call to repentance

JONAH? (time of writing unknown)
Story of prophet sent
to call Nineveh to repent

800
790
780
770
760
750
740
730
720
710
700
690
680
670
660
650
640
630
620

The Prophets:
their time and their message

There were prophets in Israel from early days,
including Moses as well as Elijah and Elisha. From
the eighth century BC to the fifth, the prophecies of
the foremost prophets were collected into books
which have survived.

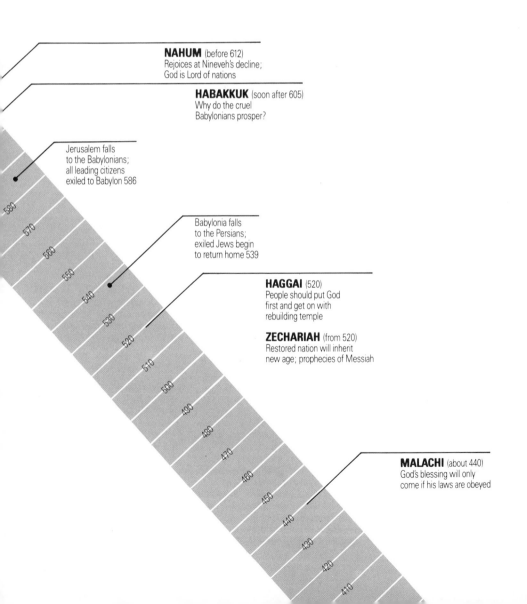

NAHUM (before 612)
Rejoices at Nineveh's decline;
God is Lord of nations

HABAKKUK (soon after 605)
Why do the cruel
Babylonians prosper?

Jerusalem falls
to the Babylonians;
all leading citizens
exiled to Babylon 586

Babylonia falls
to the Persians;
exiled Jews begin
to return home 539

HAGGAI (520)
People should put God
first and get on with
rebuilding temple

ZECHARIAH (from 520)
Restored nation will inherit
new age; prophecies of Messiah

MALACHI (about 440)
God's blessing will only
come if his laws are obeyed

580
570
560
550
540
530
520
510
500
490
480
470
460
450
440
430
420
410

kingship in a more spontaneous kind of prophetic utterance (1 Samuel 10:1–8). Yet others, like Amos, claim not to have been real 'professional' prophets at all! (Amos 7:12–15)

A number of models have been used by scholars to try to explain the form and function of Old Testament prophecy. Here we shall notice just four of the more significant approaches:

A history of religions approach

In view of our ever-increasing knowledge of social and religious situations throughout the ancient world, it is natural to compare Old Testament prophets with similar characters elsewhere. One of the earliest exponents of this view was the Scandinavian scholar Alfred Haldar. According to him, prophecy was a phenomenon found in the context of organized religion (the cult). A close analysis of texts from Babylon (Old Babylon, 1894–1595 BC) discerned two elements in it:

Mahhu priests/prophets, who specialized in wild, ecstatic trance-induced behaviour.

Baru priests/prophets, who specialized in divination. That is, they would be asked a specific question, the answer to which they would discover by throwing dice, or by astrological speculations, or by offering sacrifices and examining the entrails of the dead animals in order to discover the will of the gods.

Haldar claimed to find Old Testament evidence for this pattern, mainly in the dual functions of Samuel. He believed other isolated passages provide evidence for the work of 'divination corporations' (Isaiah 21:6–10) or sacrificial inspection (Psalm 5:3). But this view of the nature of prophecy is difficult to substantiate from the Old Testament:

● Although the Old Testament does have evidence for wild behaviour on occasion (1 Samuel 10:9–13), and of prophets giving specific answers to questions (1 Samuel 9:3–20), it is not the most obvious form of Old Testament prophecy. There is a good deal more evidence for a more 'rational' kind of prophecy. Indeed, when Jeremiah finds a message in a potter's workshop (Jeremiah 18), or in a basket of figs (Jeremiah 24), it is at least arguable that his message is essentially the result of rational deliberation on the everyday happenings of life, and has nothing at all to do with special emotional or religious experiences.

● Even when prophets do answer specific questions ('divination'), the Old Testament provides no evidence that they manipulated special objects such as dice or sacrifices in order to arrive at an answer (1 Samuel 9:17ff; 1 Kings 22).

● To use such technical means of divination required special training and a lot of practice. Again, there is no Old Testament evidence of the prophets being trained at all, and a fair amount to the contrary (for example, Amos 7:12–15).

Others have looked to Egypt and Syria as sources of possible models for Old Testament prophecy. Mari is another society in which there was evidently a kind of 'prophecy'. Texts from there speak of 'prophets' who were religious functionaries, of trance prophets, and of yet others who brought messages to the attention of the king (bureaucrats of a sort). At one time or another, all this material has been regarded as a possible 'source' of Old Testament prophecy, and there is no doubt that much of it can help us to a better understanding of the Old Testament. But there is unlikely to be any direct line of connection between them:

● Recent study has shown that the social functions performed by diviners, ecstatics, and so on can arise in any society, ancient or modern, quite independently of external direct contact.

● There is in the Old Testament a much wider diversity than in any of the comparative materials so far examined. There is far less emphasis on divination here than elsewhere – indeed, Samuel is the odd man out as far as the Old Testament is concerned.

● In general, the concerns of Old Testament prophecy are the great sweep of history and the meaning of human life on a broad scale, not the trivialities of everyday life.

A psychological approach

Julius Wellhausen (1844–1918) argued that the prophets were essentially inspired individuals, who changed the form of Israelite religious belief. The presence of apparently irrational prophetic behaviour in certain Old Testament stories seemed to suggest that a useful perspective on the prophets would be gained by asking what it was that made them such exceptional people. This line of enquiry was especially associated with the work of Hermann Gunkel (1862–1932), who concluded that the key to understanding the prophets was 'ecstasy'. By this he meant the kind of irrational, over-emotional behaviour that is familiar from many contexts the world over. Modern examples could be found in extreme forms of Pentecostalism, such as snake handlers or Holy Rollers, though this sort of wild behaviour is by no means peculiar to the Judeo-Christian religious tradition.

Gunkel described the prophetic experience in the following way: 'When such an ecstasy seizes him, the prophet ... loses command of his limbs; he staggers and stutters like a drunken man; his ordinary sense of what is decent deserts him; he feels an impulse to do all kinds of strange actions ... strange ideas and emotions come over him ... he is seized by that sensation of hovering which we know from our own dreams...'

We all know of such cases of abnormal behaviour today; and we must recognize that such mass hypnotism is

Some of the Old Testament prophets used powerful symbols to convey God's word, as when Jeremiah watched a potter making a new pot from the spoiled remains of clay that had not formed as he intended.

not difficult to produce, given the right people and the right circumstances. But is this what Old Testament prophecy is all about? To answer that question, scholars such as Gunkel looked to Canaanite prophecy (of which they knew next to nothing apart from 1 Kings 18!). Such evidence as they had for this certainly showed the prophets of Baal producing ecstatic hysteria by a series of self-inflicted moves – music, shouting, dancing, drink, drugs, and so on. And when we look at the Old Testament it is certainly possible to find such things in Israel. The best example would be the prophets whom Saul met (1 Samuel 10), though there are others (2 Kings 2; 1 Kings 22).

The real problem with this approach is that it explains only a small fragment of the total Old Testament evidence. Even Gunkel himself had to admit that, if the earliest prophets just raved in ecstasy as an end in itself, that certainly was not what the great prophets did. He reached the conclusion that prophecy must have developed from ecstatic mass hysteria into a more rational phenomenon. But others have assessed the evidence differently:

● Some identify the ecstatics with 'false prophets', by contrast to the 'real' prophets who were rational speakers. But there are many indications that the great prophets could also have unusual emotional experiences (Jeremiah 4:19; 23:9; Ezekiel 1:1–3:15).

● Recognizing this, it is possible to try to distinguish the experiences of the great prophets from the content of their messages. Perhaps the messages were delivered in a rational way after the experiences, but with no particular reference to what had gone before.

The fact is, however, that none of these explanations is wholly satisfying. The Old Testament itself makes none of these distinctions, and all the prophets mentioned there have unusual experiences of one sort or another. The way in which the experiences are related to life situations seems to depend on the circumstances of the moment. Although analysis of ecstasy and other related emotional states can shed some light on prophetic experience, it is clear that a full understanding of the prophets is not to be found there.

A literary approach

It was the search for a meaningful life situation that led Claus Westermann to begin to analyze the literary form of the prophetic messages in the Old Testament. In the ancient world, the way a person spoke was determined by their context to a much greater extent than it is today. By analyzing the forms of prophetic speech we can therefore set it in various contexts, such as the law court (Amos 7:16–17; Micah 2:1–4), the wisdom school (Jeremiah 17:5–8), the worship context (Habakkuk; Isaiah 40–55), or the royal court ('Thus says ...', a royal messenger speech-form). That being the case, it can be argued that the prophets must have been essentially ordinary people, whose background lay in the official functions of these different life situations. It has even been suggested that the descriptions of 'visions' and other 'ecstatic' experiences could perhaps be stylistic devices,

One great act of God was in bringing the Jews back to Jerusalem from exile in Babylon. The return was announced by the prophets Isaiah and Ezekiel. It heralded a fresh start for their national faith.

introduce morality into what had hitherto been a barren and empty form of ritualism. Today, many scholars would argue the exact opposite, suggesting that the religious life of Israel had started with a covenant based on a distinctly moral view of God, and that the prophets were closely associated with this covenant ideal and with its celebration in the context of worship.

There can be no doubt that the idea of a 'covenant' is at the heart of the Old Testament faith. The whole collection of Old Testament books centres on the unmistakable conviction that God had burst into the lives of his people because of his own unmerited love ('grace'), and that as a result of this his people were called upon to respond by a loving obedience in return. When we talk of 'the covenant', this is all that we mean: the responsive obedience of the people, consequent upon their experience of God's grace. In historical terms, that experience had been demonstrated most dramatically in the events of the exodus and what followed, and this is a major theme in the messages of many of the greatest prophets. It was also celebrated regularly in the great worship festivals that marked the progress of Israel's religious life.

Scholars such as Sigmund Mowinckel have no doubt exaggerated the role of the prophets in this religious worship. But it certainly makes sense to see them as guardians of the covenant faith. It explains why they spoke in full expectation that people would listen. For they were calling them back to their spiritual roots.

No one of these models by itself can fully explain Old Testament prophecy. The whole phenomenon is so diverse that perhaps we need to speak individually of particular prophets rather than trying to speak of them all in one breath. But they were all conscious of speaking in the name of God and applying the standards of the covenant faith to the events of their own day and to the lives of their contemporaries.

rather than literal descriptions of things that happened.

This way of looking at the prophets and their messages has added enormously to our understanding of them. But by itself, it can lead to a one-sided view of their functions:

● It is to some extent a reaction against the extreme 'ecstatic' view: instead of the prophet being seen as an innovator, he is here viewed as a conventional person operating within the normal structures of society. But the fact is that the element of 'ecstasy' is still there in the Old Testament, and cannot be disposed of quite so simply.

● Then there is the question of a jump from literary form to life situation. A person who uses a legal form is not necessarily a lawyer but may be just a good communicator, using language that will be especially evocative and challenging to those who hear.

A theological/cultic approach

A century ago, Julius Wellhausen was arguing that the prophets had broken completely with cultic worship in ancient Israel, and were attempting to

7 Dashed hopes and new horizons

2 Kings 25:22–30	**Isaiah 40—66**	**Joel**	**Ruth**
Jeremiah 39:11—52:34	**Haggai**	**Malachi**	**Jonah**
Lamentations	**Zechariah**	**Nehemiah**	**1 and 2 Chronicles**
Ezekiel	**Obadiah**	**Ezra**	

Exile in Babylon   Return to Judah

JUDAH

Zerubbabel and Joshua • Jerusalem temple rebuilt 520-515
Haggai   Malachi   • Nehemiah appointed Governor
Jehoiachin 597   Zechariah   Nehemiah   of Judah 445
Zedekiah 597-586   Obadiah
Jeremiah   Sheshbazzar   Joel   Ezra

BABYLON

Ezekiel
Isaiah of Babylon
Nebuchadnezzar II 605-562
Amel-Marduk 562-560   • Fall of
Nabonidus 556-539   Babylon 539

PERSIA

Cyrus 539-530
Cambyses 530-522
Darius I 522-486
Artaxerxes I 464-423

650   600   550   500   450   400

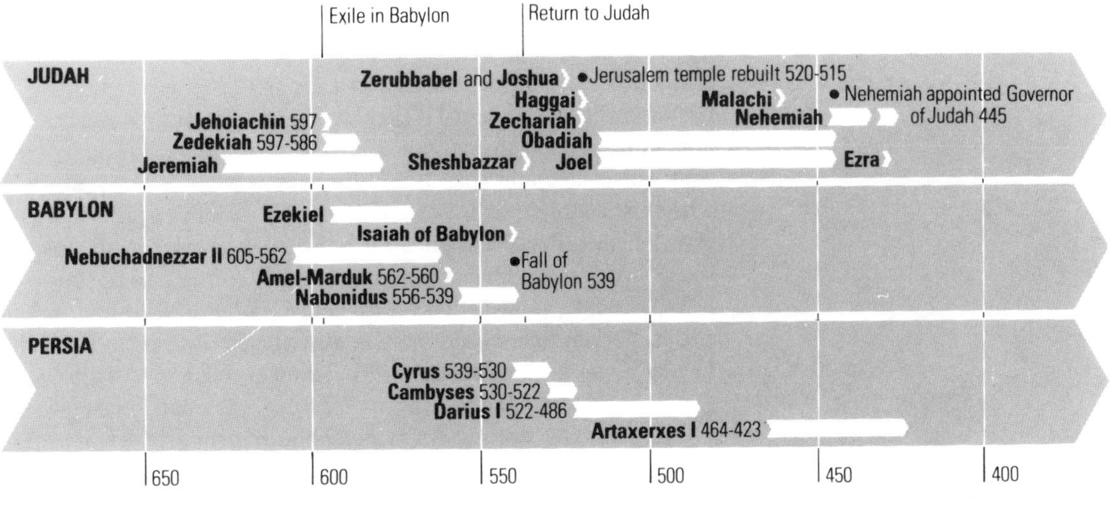

THE PERIOD following the Babylonian invasion of Judah was one of the most important in the entire history of the Jewish people and their religion. The previous millennium had seen many striking changes, as Israel first emerged as a nation, soon to become a world power, and then to sink into political and spiritual decay, so that in the years immediately prior to the fall of Jerusalem, the state of Judah had become a relatively unimportant middle-eastern kingdom. Politically, the nation was finished. Yet by the Christian era the religious beliefs based on the life of this ancient people had achieved a world-wide influence, and large groups of their descendants were making a significant contribution to the life and culture of major cities throughout the known world.

This amazing transformation, in which Judaism arose phoenix-like out of the ashes of the old kingdom of Judah, can only be explained after a careful analysis of the new currents of thought that swept through the Old Testament faith in the centuries immediately following the Babylonian exile. These centuries were an intensely creative time, as the lessons of the past were assessed and their spiritual power was harnessed to a new cause. But unfortunately for us, we know comparatively little about this period in Israel's history. We certainly know a good deal less than we do of the earlier years of the Old Testament story. There are many decades in the exilic age about which we simply know nothing at all – and even those scraps of information which we do get from the Old Testament and elsewhere are often confused and incomplete. Interpreting them is sometimes a matter of pure guesswork, and it is always a process of painstaking deductions from partial and incomplete evidence.

Facing up to disaster

We can see the nature of the problem right away, when we ask what life in Judah itself was like immediately after Nebuchadnezzar's invasion. The general outline of events is reasonably clear: the royal family was deported to Babylon, along with most of the leading citizens, after which a palace official called Gedaliah was made governor of Judah, with his capital at Mizpah. This fact suggests that neither the destruction nor the deportation was as extensive as has often been imagined. There would have been little purpose in appointing Gedaliah if there were no territory and no population over which he could rule. But at the same time, it is not at all clear what his status actually was. Was he, for example, regarded as a Babylonian official, and Judah a Babylonian province? Or was the social structure much less rigid than that? We simply do not know.

2 Kings 25:18–24; Jeremiah 40:7–12

What we do know is that his existence soon provoked opposition, and it was not long before he was assassinated by a member of the former royal family, a man called Ishmael. He was certainly one member of the Jerusalem aristocracy who had escaped the Babylonians, by fleeing to the neighbouring state of Ammon. He was not the only one to have escaped Nebuchadnezzar's invasion

2 Kings 25:25–26; Jeremiah 40:13—41:3

like this, and once the Babylonians had gone, such people came out of hiding and allied themselves with Gedaliah. The lifestyle that they anticipated for themselves was hardly at subsistence level. But it was never realized. For though Ishmael himself was put to flight after his murder of Gedaliah, those who were left at his headquarters now feared a Babylonian reprisal, and so they decided to go and live in Egypt, where they would be able to obtain employment as mercenary soldiers. Jeremiah did not want to go with them. When he had been offered a choice earlier, he had decided to stay in Judah rather than go to Babylon – and this is what he wanted to

2 Kings 25:22–24;
Jeremiah 40:7–12
Jeremiah 40:10

Jeremiah 41:11–15

2 Kings 25:26; Jeremiah 41:16–18
Jeremiah 42—43

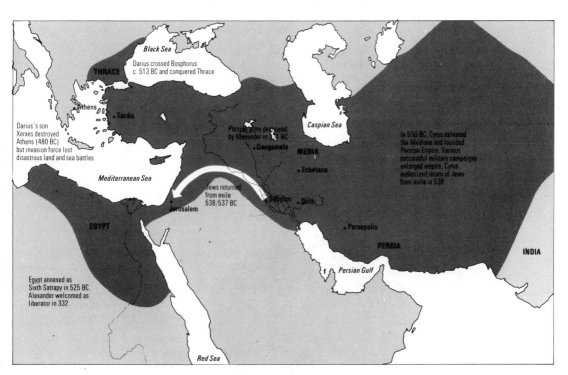

The Persian Empire

do now. He felt that his people had suffered enough, and God would soon restore their fortunes. But to be sure of that they must stay in their own land. By going abroad they would forget the God of their ancestors. Jerusalem was the place where they had lost their true faith, and it was where they must try to regain it.

Nevertheless, Jeremiah was forced against his will to join the exiles in Egypt, and he spent the rest of his life there. No doubt those who took him to Egypt felt they had done the right thing, for it seems that the Babylonians did indeed return to Judah, and a further deportation in 582 BC may well have been a reprisal for the chaos that followed the murder of Gedaliah.

Jeremiah 52:30

We know virtually nothing of life in Judah for at least the next forty years. What little we do know suggests that its people were disillusioned by what had taken place. This is hardly surprising when we recall the high expectations they had held. They never believed that Jerusalem could fall to an alien army at all: it was

God's city, and he had given it his own seal of approval through the covenant with David's family. As they faced up to the realities of their predicament, it must have seemed to these people as if very little was left of Judah's great national heritage.

The book of Lamentations

In the book of Lamentations, the full weight of Judah's grief can be felt as they experience the destruction of Jerusalem. What makes it so much more acute is that the Lord himself has turned against them in judgment.

The depth of feeling about this national tragedy is reflected with great pathos in the Old Testament book of Lamentations. The book consists of five poems, the first four of which are arranged in an acrostic pattern based on the letters of the Hebrew alphabet. This is an unusual literary device in the Old Testament, and though it may have been used here simply as an aid to the memory, it is more likely to be connected to the deeply felt message of these poems. They are essentially an adaptation of the mourning songs that were sung at every funeral, and their literary form may well be intended to reflect the all-embracing character of the tragedy which left the people emotionally and morally distraught.

The people were forced to accept the truth of what prophets like Jeremiah had been saying all along: the havoc wrought upon Jerusalem was the work of God, and it had been brought about by the disobedience and unfaithfulness of his people. Though 'No one has ever had pain like mine, pain that the Lord brought on me in the time of his anger' (1:12), nevertheless 'the Lord is just, for I have disobeyed him' (1:18). This first poem could well refer to the situation in Jerusalem after 597 BC, but before its final destruction. But the whole book gives us a striking insight into the despair of those whose arrogance and vanity are depicted so clearly in the book of Jeremiah. His message of doom had been opposed by false prophets, but their teaching now lay exposed for what it really was: 'Your prophets had nothing to tell you but lies; Their preaching deceived you by never exposing your sin. They made you think you did not need to repent' (2:14).

The pitiful trust of the people in the sanctity of their capital city and its institutions is clearly reflected here too: 'No one anywhere, not even rulers of foreign nations, believed that any invader could enter Jerusalem's gates. But it happened because her prophets sinned and her priests were guilty of causing the death of innocent people. Her leaders wandered through the streets like blind men, so stained with blood that no one would touch them.' (4:12–14). Jeremiah had seen all this coming long before the final tragedy; now those who opposed him had been forced to agree. And their unbridled despair and grief knew no boundaries.

Yet even in the midst of such shattered dreams, the tattered remnants of a once proud nation could still see cause for hope: 'The thought of my pain, my homelessness, is bitter poison; I think of it constantly and my spirit is depressed. Yet hope returns when I remember this one thing: The Lord's unfailing love and mercy still continue, fresh as the morning, as sure as the sunrise. The Lord is all I have, and so I put my hope in him. The Lord is good to everyone who trusts in him, so it is best for us to wait in patience – to wait for him to save us . . . ' (3:19–26). That in itself could never relieve the anguish

that these people felt. But it did give them the confidence to pray for restoration – and that prayer is the theme of the fifth and final poem in the book: 'Bring us back to you, Lord! Bring us back! Restore our ancient glory' (5:21).

Author and date

The Old Testament itself presents this book as an anonymous work. But other traditions, mostly within Christian circles, have attributed it to Jeremiah himself. The reason for this is to be found in 2 Chronicles 35:25, where it is stated that 'Jeremiah composed a lament for king Josiah . . . The song is found in the collection of laments.' But Lamentations has no connection at all with this early period of Jeremiah's life, and it in fact makes much better sense when viewed as a product of those elements of Jerusalem society that had been originally opposed to all that Jeremiah stood for. Various aspects of the political outlook reflected in Lamentations seem to suit Jeremiah's opponents rather than the prophet himself. It is anti-Babylonian (1:21–22; 3:59–66), and suggests dependence on Egypt (4:17), something that Jeremiah consistently opposed (Jeremiah 37:5–10). It is also difficult to imagine Jeremiah referring to Zedekiah as 'the source of our life, the king the Lord had chosen, the one we had trusted to protect us from every invader' (4:20). To the prophet, he had been one of the 'bad figs' (Jeremiah 24:8–10).

Nevertheless, the book certainly stands as a vindication of Jeremiah's message, as we see how even those who had been implacably opposed to him were forced to admit their guilt in the face of God's judgment. These five poems probably reflect the ways they did this in Judah itself, in the period immediately following 586 BC, and before the collapse of the Babylonian Empire in 539 BC.

Not everyone, however, accepted that Israel's national faith could explain the tragedy. Some people lost their faith altogether. They came to think of these sad events as a battle between Israel's God and the Babylonian gods, and they were forced to admit that the gods of Babylon had apparently won. Others felt they had been misled all along by the very prophets who claimed to speak in the name of their own God. Those who took Jeremiah to Egypt believed that the Babylonian invasion had been the fault of prophets like him. They had encouraged them to abandon the worship of the gods and goddesses to whom the land of Palestine had belonged for centuries – so why should they be surprised that the land had met with such disaster? They were convinced that the way to renewed prosperity must therefore be found in an enthusiastic return to the old ways of the Baal religion: 'We will offer sacrifices to our goddess, the Queen of Heaven, and we will pour out wine-offerings to her, just as we and our ancestors, our king and our leaders, used to do in the towns of Judah and in the streets of Jerusalem. Then we had plenty of food, we were prosperous, and had no troubles. But ever since we stopped sacrificing to the Queen of Heaven . . . we have had nothing, and our people have died in war and of starvation.'

Jeremiah 44:17–18

Jeremiah 44:23

Jeremiah would have none of this. He argued again that it was precisely this kind of worship that had led to the disaster. But who could they believe? This was a crucial question for the restructuring of Jewish society. Eventually, it was Jeremiah's argument that won the day, for his interpretation of Israel's history was embodied in the stories of the Old Testament itself. The idea that obedience and loyalty to Israel's own God led to success and prosperity is the organizing principle of the books of Joshua, Judges, Samuel and

Kings, and many scholars believe that these books were issued in a new edition in Judah itself in the years immediately following the Babylonian invasion. In previous times of national crisis, the people had often looked to their past to re-define the nature of their society, and so now they began to rebuild their shattered lives by trying to see where they had gone wrong.

The Deuteronomistic History

It was the German scholar, Martin Noth, in a book originally published in 1943, who first suggested that the books of Joshua, Judges, 1—2 Samuel and 1—2 Kings were gathered together to form an epic history of Israel at this time. He also suggested that the book of Deuteronomy, which immediately precedes these historical books in the Old Testament, was a part of them, acting as an introductory section to explain the theological basis on which Israel's history was to be understood. This is why he called these history books as a whole 'the Deuteronomistic History'. He believed that this great reassessment of Israel's history took place sometime after 561 BC (the year when Jehoiachin was released from prison, 2 Kings 25:27–30), but before the Persians came to power in 539 BC, and the subsequent rebuilding of the temple in Jerusalem in about 520 BC.

This is a bold hypothesis to explain the origin of these Old Testament books. But it is also an attractive one, and a number of facts seem to speak in its favour:

● It is not at all unlikely that those who survived the destruction of Jerusalem would begin to look at their past history as a way of making sense of their present predicament. We can see the same tendency among the exiles in Egypt, mentioned in the book of Jeremiah, and we have no reason to suppose that the same thing did not happen in Judah itself. Not only that, but in the immediate aftermath of the fall of Jerusalem there must have been an added incentive to gather together the traditions of the nation for their own sake, simply as a means of preserving the ancient records for posterity. All these books refer to other ancient sources of information from which their own stories have been extrapolated or summarized, and all of these other records have subsequently disappeared with the passage of time.

● At the same time, these Old Testament history books are more than just an anthology of extracts from older historical materials. For they also present a clear and coherent view of the meaning of the events that are recorded.

We have already mentioned the prominence of such an interpretation in the book of Judges. But it is present in many other passages too. It has not been superimposed on every detail of the narratives, but at strategic points the lessons of history are made plain: Israel was committed in a covenant relationship to God, and this placed upon her certain responsibilities. Accordingly, if she was willing to accept these responsibilities and obey the law of the covenant, she could expect the blessing that God had promised. On the other hand, deliberate disobedience would lead to failure and destruction. This message is often conveyed in the form of speeches at strategic points in the story (Joshua 23; 1 Samuel 12; 2 Samuel 7; 1 Kings 8:22–53), a device that is found in much ancient history writing.

● The fact that the covenant forms the basic framework within which Israel's history is understood in these books also gives a certain plausibility to Noth's claim that Deuteronomy was a preface for the whole work. For the literary structure of Deuteronomy is closely linked to the covenant pattern which has been traced in Hittite and Assyrian sources. In addition, the speech with which the book opens (Deuteronomy 1–4) is almost a classic exposition of the theological perspective of the so-called Deuteronomists. What is more, it seems to contain an explicit appeal and reassurance to the people for whom the exile was such a great crisis: 'The Lord will scatter you among other nations, where only a few of you will survive . . . There you will look for the Lord your God, and if you search for him with all your heart, you will find him. When you are in trouble and all those things happen to you, then you will finally turn to the Lord and obey him. He is a merciful God, he will not abandon you or destroy you, and he will not forget the covenant that he himself made with your ancestors' (Deuteronomy 4:27–31).

Noth's theory has not been universally accepted by scholars, but it has won a large measure of support. Four major issues have arisen in recent discussion of it:

● Noth regarded the Deuteronomistic History as simply an explanation of the tragedy that had befallen the people of Israel, and he therefore understood it as an essentially pessimistic work. But this is not the whole story. The main emphasis is certainly on Israel's past, but this is not simply an antiquarian interest. Indeed, there never was such a thing in ancient Israel, for the past was always seen as the theatre of God's activity, and therefore it inevitably became a mirror of the future, and a challenge to the people to face up to that future. The prophets had seen the failures of the past as an invitation to renewed obedience, and the history writers had the same perspective. Perhaps that is why they ended with the story of Jehoiachin's release, for that in itself must have generated renewed hope in the hearts of the people.

● Some have questioned whether there is such a thoroughgoing, unified presentation of the meaning of Israel's history in all these books. They point out, for example, that some passages of Samuel and Kings (like the Succession Narrative, 2 Samuel 9—20; 1 Kings 1—2) seem to have very little trace of the Deuteronomic point of view. They also ask whether the simple viewpoint of Deuteronomy itself, related to the earliest stages of Israel's history, is truly compatible with the complex position of the king and the Jerusalem temple in the later books. But these observations have more bearing on the complex way in which the various stories were gathered together. It is quite likely that the long job of writing a continuous history of Israel had already been started long before the dark days of the exile. Many scholars think that even before the time of Josiah, the outline for such a history was already in existence, and even in the earliest parts of the history, it is universally agreed that some of the stories were first written down more or less as they happened. For the later editors were not concerned to rewrite the stories (still less to invent them, as has very occasionally been suggested): they simply wanted to present them in a way that would be most meaningful to the people of their own day.

● Scholars have often asked just who these so-called Deuteronomists actually were. They have been identified in turn with groups of priests, prophets, and wise men. But they seem to have most in common with the great

A great theme of the book of Deuteronomy is that the land will be blessed if the people obey God's Law, but cursed if they disobey. This theme re-appears frequently in the history books that follow the same tradition.

prophets. Though Isaiah is the only one who is actually mentioned by name in the Old Testament histories (2 Kings 19—20), the message of these books is the same as theirs: the facts of Israel's history were taken as proof that the prophets were right. There are also a number of passages in the books of the prophets which are quite similar to parts of the Deuteronomistic History. Indeed, it is quite possible that these prophetic books were first gathered together by the same people who issued this great historical work. It is perhaps more than accidental that the Jews themselves came to regard the books of Joshua—Kings as 'the former prophets'.

● If Noth's theory is correct, then of course Deuteronomy must be detached from the Old Testament Law, or Torah, and linked instead to this Deuteronomistic History. On this, see further the special note on the Pentateuch.

By the rivers of Babylon

We know far more about the life of the exiles who were taken off to Babylon than we do about those who were left behind in Judah. They seem to have settled in a kind of Jewish ghetto in Babylon, and they evidently enjoyed considerable freedom to organize their own affairs, both socially and religiously. The fact that Jehoiachin was there no doubt helped to generate this community spirit. He was one of those taken from Jerusalem in the first deportation of 597 BC, but since he was the last true member of the royal family of David, it was to be expected that the exiles would focus their national allegiance on him. His exact position is not absolutely clear. The Old Testament states that Nebuchadnezzar's successor, Amel-Marduk, released Jehoiachin from prison and gave him a

2 Kings 25:27–30

distinctive position at the Babylonian court. That was in 561 BC, but even before that the Babylonian annals describe Jehoiachin as 'king of Judah'. Perhaps therefore his imprisonment was little more than a nominal house arrest. His presence in Babylon was certainly important for the exiles. They counted the years of their exile in

Ezekiel 1:2; 33:21; 40:1

relation to him, and his sons and grandsons continued to play an important part in Jewish affairs for a considerable time. But he seems to have been a figurehead rather than a ruler in any sense,

Ezekiel 14:1–11; 20:1

and the Jewish community itself was organized by groups of elders.

On the whole, life in Babylon was probably quite comfortable – even prosperous – for the exiles from Judah. From a slightly later period than this, we have detailed business records relating to the activities of a Jewish firm run by the Murashu family in Nippur, and the Old Testament itself suggests that about 100 years

'By the rivers of Babylon...' The exiles from Judea found the city of Babylon and the banks of the Euphrates alien territory, where they could not bring themselves to 'sing a song to the Lord'. Through the years of exile they were to discover that it is possible to worship the Lord even away from the temple and David's city.

Ezra 1:6; 2:68–69   later many of the exiles were quite rich. But they were not always happy. No matter how comfortable life in Babylon might be, it was not the same as the homeland they had left behind. The despair and dereliction felt by these people made such an impression on them that, like the story of their slavery in Egypt centuries before, it achieved a permanent place in their national consciousness:

> 'By the rivers of Babylon we sat down;
> there we wept when we remembered Zion.
> On the willows nearby we hung up our harps.
> Those who captured us told us to sing;
> they told us to entertain them:
> "Sing us a song about Zion".
> How can we sing a song to the Lord in a foreign land?
> May I never be able to play the harp again
> if I forget you, Jerusalem!
> May I never be able to sing again if I do not remember you,

Psalm 137:1–6   if I do not think of you as my greatest joy!'

By the standards of international justice, the Babylonians had been relatively benevolent. Their predecessors, the Assyrians, would never have allowed deported peoples to live in their own communities like this. But the exiles still hated them, and the same poem which contains such a moving expression of Jewish anguish ends on a note of hatred that is unparalleled anywhere else in the Bible: 'Babylon, you will be destroyed. Happy is the man who pays you back for what you have done to us – who takes your babies and

Psalm 137:8–9   smashes them against a rock.'

We get the same bleak picture in the messages of the prophet Ezekiel. He himself was one of the exiles, and he knew that this dreadful experience had knocked all spiritual vitality out of his people. They were, he said, like a valley full of dead bones, with no

Ezekiel 37   life in them at all. They were quite powerless to do anything to help themselves: their only hope for new life now lay with God himself.

Ezekiel

Ezekiel's career was roughly contemporary with that of Jeremiah. Both of them came from priestly families, but Ezekiel was far more conscious of his background, and he had much greater interest in the Jerusalem temple than Jeremiah ever had. Ezekiel was one of those who were taken to Babylon in the first deportation of 597 BC, and his carefully dated messages were given between 593 and 571 BC.

The Old Testament book of Ezekiel falls neatly into four sections:

● Messages concerning the people of Jerusalem before the city was destroyed in 586 BC (1:1—24:27)
● Oracles against foreign nations (25:1—32:32)
● Messages given in Babylon, mostly relating to the return of the exiles to Judah (33:1—39:29)
● A priestly blueprint for a future Jewish state (40:1—48:35)

This neat literary structure belies the complexity of the book and its message. Its contents are so diverse that it is not difficult to imagine many different people involved in its composition. At one time the prophet is a person who has strange visions of winged animals and of wheels with eyes (Ezekiel 1:4–28). At another he seems much more like Jeremiah, pronouncing doom on a wicked Jerusalem and laying a new emphasis on a personal relationship between God and his people (15:1–8; 20:1–49). Then there is a prophet whose messages to other nations reflect an extensive grasp of the intricacies of international politics (25:1—32:32). And there is a priest, who plans with great detail for the operation of a new temple with even stricter ritual than it had before (40:1—48:35). Because of this, some scholars have regarded the book as a compilation of the work of different people. As long ago as the first century AD, the Jewish historian Josephus mentioned 'two books' of Ezekiel (*Antiquities of the Jews X.v.1*). But it is more likely that all these messages originated with just one person.

Ezekiel was called to be a prophet in Babylon in 593 BC. He had a vision of a fiery cloud from the north containing a chariot drawn by four winged creatures of a kind familiar from many Babylonian sculptures and inscriptions (1:4—28). There was a throne on this chariot, and on the throne was the God of Israel, Yahweh himself. In the vision, Ezekiel was given a scroll to eat, which contained his message: 'cries of grief . . . and wails and groans' (2:10).

These messages are contained in the first section of the book. They were addressed to the people of Jerusalem in the dark days of the reign of Zedekiah. Ezekiel depicts the moral and spiritual decline of Jerusalem society with such realism that it is hard to believe he was not there, but in Babylon. Indeed, some scholars think Ezekiel must have paid visits to Judah at this time. But it is more likely that he had some kind of clairvoyant second sight. Ezekiel's experiences as a prophet are much closer than those of the other great prophets to the behaviour of those bands of ecstatics who are mentioned in the early period of Israel's history. He obviously had a psychic personality, for after receiving his initial vision, he lay in a trance for a full week (3:15). In view of all this, his extraordinary accuracy in portraying life in Judah could well have been due to visionary experiences rather than to actual observations made on the spot.

But Ezekiel was not an irrational prophet, and his essential message was not all that different from Jeremiah's: Jerusalem would be destroyed shortly, and its people taken off into exile. He saw no immediate hope of a return, though there are hints that the exile might be limited to about forty years (4:6).

In spite of his declaration of doom and destruction, Ezekiel's message to the exiles in Babylon after the events of 586 BC was a positive one. He had no doubt that the nation had brought ruin on itself, but he was equally convinced that the nation's fate was not in their own hands. It was God's loving actions that had made them a nation in the first place, and it was his power that would restore them, even giving them the ability to repent and start afresh: 'I will give you a new heart and a new mind. I will take away your stubborn heart of stone and give you an obedient heart. I will put my spirit in you and I will see to it that you follow my laws and keep all the commands I have given you. Then you will live in the land I gave your ancestors. You will be my people, and I will be your God.' (36:26—28). God was personally concerned for his people, just like a good shepherd caring for his sheep. They might be scattered, but he would retrieve them and lead them to a new life: 'I will take them out of foreign countries, gather them together, and bring them back to their own land . . . I myself will be the shepherd of my sheep, and I will find them a place to rest' (34:11—15).

Two distinctive features of Ezekiel's messages are worth special notice:

● When he looks forward to the restoration of a kingdom of Israel under a prince of the royal family of David, he often describes it in terms that clearly go beyond a literal nationalism. The earlier prophets had often hoped for better things to come, but they generally believed that it was at least theoretically possible that the new and better age would come through a new king in Jerusalem, who would actually obey God's will, unlike his predecessors. Ezekiel, however, implies that the inauguration of a golden age, when God and his people would live in complete harmony, could not be achieved by any ordinary king. It would have to be the direct work of God himself. Thinking of this kind led eventually to the development of a new type of Jewish religious literature: the so-called apocalyptic books, and we can see traces of its beginning in passages like Ezekiel 38—39. Here the prophet describes how the enemies of Judah under a mysterious leader called Gog would attack Palestine, only to be annihilated with torrents of fire and brimstone raining down from the sky. After that the exiled Jews would be restored to their own land, and the spirit of God would be poured out on them. The same kind of extravagant language is used when Ezekiel describes a wonderful life-giving stream flowing from the restored temple in Jerusalem out to the Dead Sea, and changing the

Judean desert into a land of great fertility (47:1–12).

● Ezekiel's messages also contain a detailed plan for a renewed temple in Jerusalem (40:1—48:35). Not only does he describe the building itself, but he also lays down the rules that should regulate its worship. Some scholars have seen this as the symptom of an arid legalism which they believe to have been rampant in the exilic age. The same influences are said to be found in other prophets of the period, and this interest in religious ritual is often contrasted with the convictions of the truly 'great' prophets like Amos and Hosea, who declared that God's will was not fulfilled through religious mumbo-jumbo, but through ordinary everyday behaviour. But this kind of view misrepresents Ezekiel's message. It owes more to modern Protestantism than it does to the Old Testament, and as a result the significant features of Israel's cultic worship are often misunderstood. Ezekiel was not emphasizing the performance of religious ritual for its own sake. But he knew that the exiles could never renew their own spiritual life. Even in the halcyon days immediately following the exodus from Egypt, obedience to God's covenant law had not been easy. Sin and disobedience were an inescapable reality. It was not the goodness of the tribes that had made them a great nation, but the unchanging presence of God. And right from the start, that presence had been represented by the formal institutions of worship – from the simple tent of worship in the desert to the elaborate temple in Jerusalem. Far from being an aberration, these things were a permanent symbol of the centralities of Israel's faith, representing not only God's own faithfulness and power, but also the way to forgiveness for his wayward people. It was for this reason that the same symbols must be an essential part of the restored community.

Ezekiel was not the only one who saw the situation in these terms. For it is widely believed that during the exile in Babylon, the Jewish leaders began to re-assess the state of their people by looking back into their past. We have already seen how the Deuteronomistic History may have been written down in Judah itself at this time, for precisely the same reasons. But the emphasis of that History on a close connection between the people's obedience and the blessing of God could easily lead to the false conclusion that the exiles themselves were responsible for their own destiny. The message of prophets like Amos and Hosea, and even Jeremiah, could easily be misunderstood to suggest that good behaviour was a way of blackmailing God into giving Israel his blessing. But when we look back to the very earliest period of Israel's history, we can see that this was only one side of the story. The prophets' demand for obedience to God's law had itself been based on the unsought goodness of God's love in events like the calling of Abraham and the exodus from Egypt. The prophets had rightly declared that the nation's religious problems had started once they settled in the land of Canaan. But the time before that had hardly been perfect. Perhaps, then, there was a lesson here for the exiles as they struggled to come to terms with their national disaster.

With thoughts like these before them, religious leaders in Babylon probably set out to write a history of the earliest experiences of their nation, starting from creation itself. They did not compile their story from nothing, any more than the Deuteronomic historians did. They had at their disposal the full riches of their nation's heritage, going back over many centuries. But as they re-told these familiar stories, they could see that the problem of human disobedience was an old one. It was part and parcel of life

Facing page: 'The Law' (*Torah*) is very holy to the Jew. He is educated in it from childhood, and it is his rule of conduct. Sometimes 'the Law' refers to the whole Old Testament, but more commonly it is applied to the first five books, the 'books of Moses', the Pentateuch.

itself. Yet in spite of that, God's living presence had been with their people. Right from the very earliest days in the desert, God had been there, even at times of disobedience. The thing that had brought the tribes from Egypt to their own land was not their own goodness, but the love of God. So a new hope and concern began to emerge from the lessons of history. As they looked at their own resources, they could see no hope. Instead, they must trust God, for his power was still supreme and all-powerful.

The Pentateuch

It is widely believed that the historical re-assessment that took place among the exiles in Babylon had strong connections with the writings of the first five books of the Old Testament, the Pentateuch. If we accept the idea that Deuteronomy was a preface to the Deuteronomistic History, then we should more accurately speak of a 'Tetrateuch', consisting of Genesis, Exodus, Leviticus, and Numbers.

In Jewish thinking, the Pentateuch was always traditionally regarded as the work of Moses. But most scholars today consider this to be impossible. At least five reasons can be given:

● **Anachronisms** Deuteronomy 34 tells the story of Moses' death, which at least makes it unlikely that he wrote this section – though both Philo (*On the Life of Moses* II.291) and Josephus (*Antiquities of the Jews* IV viii.48) claimed that he did! More significantly, however, a number of other incidental features of some of the stories in these books reflect the perspective of a later age. For instance, Genesis 36:31–39 lists the kings of Edom who ruled 'before there were any kings in Israel'. Or again, a couple of incidents in Abraham's life took place when 'the Canaanites were still living in the land' (Genesis 12:6; 13:7). And part of the land of Canaan itself is given the name 'Philistia', though it did not have that name until after the arrival of the Philistines (Genesis 21:34; Exodus 13:17).

● **Duplicate stories** The same story sometimes seems to have been recorded in two different versions. For example, Beersheba is given its name twice (Genesis 21:31; 26:33), as is Bethel – once when Jacob was running away to Haran (Genesis 28:19), and again when he was coming back (Genesis 35:15). Similarly, in the story of the covenant-making at Mt Sinai, Moses is said to have gone up the mountain three times, though there is no mention of him ever coming down (Exodus 24:9–18).

● **Inconsistencies** can be traced in certain stories. For example, in the story of creation, Genesis 1:26–31 suggests that people were created after all the animals, whereas in Genesis 2:7–20 a man is created first, and animals are later created to be his companions. Or in the story of the great flood, the number of animals to be saved in the Ark is either one pair of each species (Genesis 6:19–20), or seven pairs (Genesis 7:2). Joseph appears to have been taken off to Egypt by both Ishmaelites (Genesis 37:25) and Midianites (Genesis 37:28) – and was it Reuben (Genesis 37:22) or Judah (Genesis 37:26) who was the good brother who tried to rescue him?

● **Legal differences** Scholars have also pointed out that the laws set out in Deuteronomy are sometimes different from the laws in other books of the Pentateuch. For example, in Exodus 20:24 sacrifices can be offered to God 'in every place that I set aside for you to worship me'; but in Deuteronomy 12:14, 'you must offer them only in the one place that the Lord will choose in the territory of one of your tribes'. Exodus 28:1 suggests that only Aaron's family had the priestly qualifications to offer sacrifices, while Deuteronomy 18:6–7 allows any Levite to do so. The actual methods to be adopted also vary: in Exodus 12:8–9 the Passover lamb must be roasted, while in Deuteronomy 16:7 it is to be boiled.

● **God's name** According to Exodus 6:2–3, Moses was the first person to know God's personal name, 'Yahweh'. But Genesis 4:26 states that from the very earliest times people had used this name in their worship. Alongside this, there are many other passages which call God by the name 'Elohim'. And it has also been argued that the different names indicate different ideas about God's character: in the stories that call him Yahweh, he can be thought of as a kind of superman, speaking and meeting with people in person; while in those that call him Elohim he appears more remotely through dreams and messengers.

These five features are not all that important if we take them separately. But taken together, they have been regarded by scholars as a conclusive demonstration that the Pentateuch was not the product of just one author, either Moses or anyone else. According to the most widely accepted view, the Pentateuch as we know it today was compiled from four separate documentary sources: J (the source using the name Yahweh); E (the source using the name Elohim); D (Deuteronomy); and P (a priestly source, dealing mainly with sacrifice, etc.). This theory was most fully explained by the nineteenth-century German scholars, K.H. Graf and J. Wellhausen, and is often simply called the Graf-Wellhausen theory. Wellhausen also believed that these source documents reflect the whole course of Israel's national history, beginning with J (950–850 BC), followed by E (850–750 BC), D (621 BC), and P (about 450 BC).

In the early decades of the twentieth century, scholars set out with great enthusiasm to 'recover' and 'reconstruct' these four apparently lost documents. They concluded that J had originated among the southern tribes in the time of Solomon, and E among the northern tribes in the time of Elijah, and the two had been joined together some time after the fall of Samaria in 721 BC. D was generally identified with the law book discovered in the time of Josiah, though possibly of a northern origin. It was certainly quite a different kind of 'source' from the others, for whereas J and E could be traced more or less extensively throughout the Pentateuch, D appeared to be restricted to just the book of Deuteronomy. And P was regarded as an exclusively priestly collection, containing mainly the details of organized cultic religion, and anything connected with it – though also including certain other materials of a narrative type.

All this has been accepted in one form or another by most Old Testament scholars for the last 100 years. During that time, there have been those who pointed out the limitations of this or that detail in Wellhausen's analysis. But those who rejected it entirely were isolated individuals, usually regarded as eccentrics. The situation today, however, is quite different. The whole edifice of Wellhausen's theory is coming under increasingly heavy fire from all directions, and it is probably only a matter of time before the whole scholarly approach to these books will have to undergo a thorough reappraisal. There are a number of reasons for this radical about-turn:

● Wellhausen's view was firmly based on a particular philosophical understanding of history and its development. Along with other thinkers of his day, he believed that human society had gradually evolved from primitive beginnings to the sophisticated thinking of his own day. Wellhausen therefore took it for granted that Israel's religious experience must have started off as a simple nature worship, which later evolved into the high moral standards of the Old Testament prophets. This evolutionary theory has since been totally discredited, and it is arguable that the literary analysis which Wellhausen built upon it has therefore been left with no rational foundation.

● Since Wellhausen's day our knowledge of the ancient world in general, and of Israel in particular, has changed almost beyond recognition. Wellhausen and his contemporaries were writing before the development of modern scientific archaeology. It was easy for them to look at the Old Testament as a kind of theological source book, rather than as a body of literature to be understood in its own true-life situation. Viewed in this way, it seemed plausible to think that Israel's religion could have evolved from a primitive animism to an elevated monotheism in the course of just a few hundred years. But the more we know about the Old Testament world, the less likely it has become that Israel's faith should be thought of in these terms. According to Wellhausen's theory, for example, almost all the details of Israel's ritual worship were the invention of the P writer, late in the Babylonian exile. But the discoveries at the site of ancient Ugarit have shown that even quite technical terms used in the Old Testament were in common use in Canaan long before the Israelite conquest, let alone the exile. Far from reflecting later stages in the development of religious thought, much of the Pentateuchal material reflects precisely the circumstances of the period of which it purports to tell. Of course, this does not prove that it was all written down at an earlier period – still less does it comment directly on its historical value – but it certainly demonstrates that the assumptions on which Wellhausen argued were simply mistaken.

● Criticisms of this sort have not prevented Old Testament scholars from continuing to refine and articulate more fully the theory that Wellhausen put forward. Even today some are still arguing about the dates of the various so-called source documents. But their conclusions vary widely, with even the J source being variously dated in periods as far apart as the ninth century and the post-exilic age! Others have suggested there was no such thing as an E source, while yet others argue that the four-source theory is inadequate, and the Pentateuch in fact contains many more sources than that. Some have further claimed to be able to trace J, E and P not only in the Pentateuch, but also in Joshua, Judges, Samuel, and even Kings. Much of this debate has been engendered by the surprising fact that the so-called sources are not actually consistent in their use of the different names for God, even though this was supposed to be their characteristic feature! Considering that scholars have been trying to define the nature and contents of these source documents for a century now, it is not unreasonable to expect them to have come to some sort of conclusion on the matter. The fact that they have so strikingly failed to do so raises serious questions about their very existence.

A number of scholars have noted the strength of this particular criticism, and have accordingly directed their energies elsewhere. Gerhard von Rad, for instance, argued that this section of the Old Testament (which for him extended into Joshua/Judges, the 'Hexateuch') was centred around two major themes. One was the exodus/entry into the land; the other was the covenant ceremony at Mt Sinai. Both of these were originally related to religious celebrations in the life of early Israel, and he suggested that the continuous narrative we now have grew out of the confessions and creeds that were so often repeated in worship. This process took place, he believes, in the time of Solomon. Martin Noth also proposed his own rather different thematic origin for the same materials. But all such attempts have still been firmly based on a Wellhausen-type source analysis, and they have not successfully avoided the general criticisms noted above.

● Recent discussion of this issue has emphasized the importance of treating the Pentateuch as real literature. Wellhausen and his followers worked with a very restricted view of how ancient literature was actually written. Their understanding has often been colourfully described as a 'scissors and paste' approach, which tended to assume that the final editor of the books sat down with four documents in front of him, and chopped bits and pieces from here and there, which he then glued together (rather badly) to make a 'new' book. An idea like that can seem to make sense to a modern scholar sitting in his study. He could, after all, write a book that way himself. But this is not how a national archive like the Old Testament comes into existence. Traditional ways of handing on ancient stories – sometimes by word of mouth – are not as methodical and clear-cut as this. What is more, the whole approach to literature espoused by Wellhausen is now widely questioned.

It has always been fashionable among Biblical scholars to suppose that the only way to understand a document is to explain where it came from. We can see this clearly enough in any of the multifarious introductions to both Old and New Testaments, which tend to be preoccupied with questions of origin, date and authorship, often to the exclusion of anything else. But the meaning of a book must surely begin with the text as it stands. No matter how much a work of literature may have been edited or rewritten, its ultimate meaning is to be found in the form it now has.

In the study of English literature, it is taken for granted that William Shakespeare often took the plots for his plays from other sources. But no one would dream of looking for the genius of their meaning in the sources, rather than in the mind of Shakespeare himself. And the Pentateuch is just the same. From a purely literary point of view, it is a connected story with its own message.

Indeed some scholars have argued on this basis that some of the features that led Wellhausen to his source theory could just as easily have been stylistic and literary devices. Take, for instance, the use of different names for God: is it wholly inconceivable that the term Yahweh might have been used when the writer was talking of Israel's own national God, while the term Elohim was reserved for contexts in which a more abstract, cosmic picture of God was in view? And even the existence of duplicate stories is not a necessary indication of badly assimilated source materials. For we find a very similar phenomenon in the texts from Ugarit, where frequent repetitions of the same passages have been indispensable to scholars in helping to restore gaps in broken texts.

During the exile, the Babylonian Empire went through a period of decline. Emperor Nabonidus, seen in this relief worshipping the sun-god, rejected the national religion and spent much of his time in retreat in the desert.

The upshot of all this is that there is today a re-examination of almost all the basic issues in Pentateuchal scholarship. This is motivated partly by dissatisfaction with the Graf-Wellhausen theory, but more especially by the realization that in the literary world at large there are other, more promising methods of analysis than source criticism.

What, then, may we conclude from all this? There are those who would like to think that the imminent collapse of the scholarly orthodoxy justifies a return to belief in a Mosaic authorship for the Pentateuch. But that does not necessarily follow at all. For one thing, the Bible itself gives us no reason to link his name with all these books. Only a few scattered references in the books themselves connect Moses with their writing, and they all relate to specific parts of the narrative, rather than to the Pentateuch as a whole (Exodus 24:4–8; Numbers 33:2; Deuteronomy 31:19–29). Writing was widely used in the earliest period of Israel's history, and many scholars today would confidently link Moses with significant features of the Pentateuch, such as the Ten Commandments. So there is no good reason why this leader of the ancient tribes should not have had some connection with the traditional stories and customs of his people. But later, even those things connected with Moses himself needed to be reinterpreted and applied to new situations. As new elements joined the population of Israel, their own stories handed on over many centuries would also be incorporated into Israel's national heritage. And the inauguration of the monarchy must have necessitated a considerable reinterpretation of Israel's traditional values and ideals, in order to suit the new circumstances.

But it now seems quite likely that, instead of passing through several written stages, all this took place in a more or less haphazard fashion until the Pentateuch itself was written in its present form. It certainly makes good sense to think that this epic story of Israel's earliest days was issued during the period of the early exile, as a means of explaining the failures of the past and of charting the course for the future. But the stories and laws were not newly created at that time. The new element was the perspective that the experience of the exile had given. With that hindsight the story of God and his people could become a source of renewal for Israel's national life, and the old stories could come alive in a new way.

A new beginning

The stories of Israel's past reminded the exiles of what God had done for their nation. Even at times of great despair, God's love had never failed them, and he would not abandon them now. It was not long before things began to stir in Babylonian politics that were regarded as the actions of God himself.

When Nebuchadnezzar died in 562 BC he was succeeded by a number of very weak and inept rulers. Only Nabonidus had a reign of any length (556-539 BC). But he was very unpopular: he was opposed to the national religion of Babylon – the worship of Marduk – and he took little interest in affairs in the capital, preferring instead to live at Teima in the Arabian desert. This was a very unsettled period in Babylonian history, and life for the exiles may well have become more difficult. There is a strong tradition in Jewish literature of how the exiles were subjected to harsh treatment, almost amounting to official persecution. In the Old Testament, the stories of the first section of the book of Daniel tell how Daniel and his friends were subjected to the most harrowing treatment by the Babylonian king Belshazzar (Nabonidus's son, and his official representative in Babylon). The same kind of picture is also painted in various additions to the books of Esther and Daniel which were contained in the Greek Old Testament, as well as in books like Judith and Tobit.

Daniel 1—6

If this was a time of discomfort for the Jews in Babylon, it was short-lived. For by now, the power of the Babylonian Empire was spent, and when a little-known king from southern Persia emerged as a new leader, it was only a matter of time before he was able to take over the whole of the country. His name was Cyrus, and in 539 BC the people of Babylon actually welcomed him as their king, and he took control of the city without the use of force.

Cyrus set about the restoration of Babylonian society. The temples which Nabonidus had neglected were restored to their former glory, and Cyrus himself shared publicly in the worship of the god Marduk. But he did not become involved in sectarian arguments. Indeed, of all the ancient rulers with whom the Jews had to deal, Cyrus was the most liberal and humane. He did not see politics in terms of armed conflict between various national religions. Instead, he recognized the right of all nations to worship whatever gods they wished. Not only that, but he recognized that people should have the right to live wherever they chose. This was a massive reversal of the policies that had dominated Mesopotamian society for many centuries, but he was determined to make it work. He inherited a population with many people who had been uprooted from their own lands and settled in Babylon against their will. He decided to encourage these displaced people to go back home, and declared that he would give them financial aid to do so. The Cyrus Cylinder, now in the British Museum, contains details of all this. And the Jews were naturally included. The Old Testament book of Ezra preserves the text of an official document issued by Cyrus, dealing specifically with the plight of the Jewish exiles.

Ezra 6:3–5

The Cyrus Cylinder gives details of the reforms this Persian ruler undertook in Babylon after he had overthrown the Babylonians in a bloodless take-over. In Isaiah's prophecy, Cyrus is seen as the unwitting agent of the Lord in establishing the conditions for the exiles' return to Jerusalem.

Isaiah of Babylon

It is widely believed by modern scholars that the advance of Cyrus was seen by a Jewish prophet in Babylon, whose remarkable messages are to be found in Isaiah 40—55. As they stand, of course, these messages are a part of the book which reports the life and teaching of the prophet Isaiah, who lived in Jerusalem some 150 years earlier during the days of Ahaz and Hezekiah. A number of reasons are given for regarding these later sections of the book as originally separate:

● Isaiah 40—55 contains no mention at all of the prophet Isaiah. This is in strong contrast to Isaiah 1—39 which relate a number of stories about the prophet himself, especially his dealings with king and people in Jerusalem.

● The style and language of Isaiah 40—55 is also quite distinctive. These chapters use what is possibly the most sophisticated Hebrew in the entire Old

Testament. In addition, these messages do not have the form of the short, pointed sayings that were typical of most of the Old Testament prophets. They consist instead of sustained lyrical passages, celebrating God's sovereignty in creation and history. Because of their distinctive poetic structure, it has been thought that these messages may have originated in the context of worship. Perhaps they reflect the way that God's kingship was celebrated in the temple at Jerusalem during the heyday of the kingdom of Judah. But they are not just hymns, for they also contain many specific historical references, directly related to the message of the prophet himself.

● The fact that these specific references are based on the experiences of the Babylonian exile is one of the strongest reasons for assuming that they are the work of a prophet who lived at this time. The fall of Jerusalem is clearly stated to be a past event (51:17–23), and the fall of Babylon is imminent (43:14–15; 47:1–15). The people are encouraged to think they will soon be set free (48:20), and Cyrus himself is mentioned by name as the person who would bring this about (44:28—45:4). Other passages clearly envisage Cyrus's triumph, without actually naming him (41:2–4; 48:12–16). It is occasionally suggested that Isaiah of Jerusalem could have given such messages, and some believe he may have written them down during the reign of Hezekiah or Manasseh. But it is very difficult to see why he would have wished to do so. The Old Testament prophets were not star-gazers concerned with predicting a long-distant future, but political and social commentators wrestling with the spiritual significance of the affairs of their own day. In addition, we must face the fact that if Isaiah of Jerusalem was responsible for these messages about Cyrus, they must have been totally meaningless to the people of his own time, and also for several generations thereafter – and would anyone therefore have been likely to preserve them, especially through the turmoil of Judah's last days?

It makes much better sense to accept that the messages of Isaiah 40–55 were given to the exiles in Babylon at the time to which they relate, i.e. just before 539 BC. The prophet who delivered them had the same kind of outlook as his illustrious predecessor. Isaiah himself had gathered a group of disciples around him, so that the messages he gave could be safeguarded for later generations (Isaiah 8:16) – and these later messages may well have come from the same circle of disciples. What they were saying was a fresh application of old truths to new circumstances, and so they had no hesitation in including them all in the same book.

For convenience, we often call the prophet who delivered these later messages Isaiah of Babylon, or Deutero-Isaiah. But of course that would not be his real name. The fact that we do not apparently know his real name is the only compelling argument against his likely existence. If he was indeed one of the great prophetic figures of the Old Testament story, how is it that we have no explicit information about him? That question needs to be set against the fact that we actually know next to nothing about most of the other great prophets, apart from the messages that are recorded in their books. But the relative anonymity of this prophet in Babylon is consistent with his whole outlook. For he was concerned first and foremost with the might and power of God, rather than with himself. The change that he believed was about to take place would not be initiated by the exiles: it was to be the work of God himself, a 'new exodus' comparable with that under Moses, in which the escaping slaves (like the exiles) had been powerless, but were miraculously delivered by their all-powerful God (Isaiah 43:14–21).

A powerful God

Cyrus is seen as the instrument of this deliverance that was to come, but the people's trust should not be in Cyrus. The real power that would restore the Jewish people came from God himself. The glorious return to their homeland would be a world-wide movement, including those who had fled to Egypt (49:12). God's power would not be restricted by geography or national boundaries, as had sometimes been thought by Israel in the past. This prophet was convinced that his God was not one among many, but the only true God: 'The Lord is the everlasting God; he created all the world. He never grows tired or weary' (40:28). It was important for him to emphasize this, for some of the exiles had come to regard their plight as a direct result of the weakness of Israel's God when faced with the apparent 'power' of the gods of Babylon. Those who clung to the old covenant faith may even have been in the minority (Ezekiel 20:32; Daniel 1—6). But Isaiah of Babylon knew they were right.

Isaiah predicted that the Jews would return to their homeland with great joy. Both the journey itself and their new life in Jerusalem would see a restoration of their life as a community of God's people.

His contempt for the gods of Babylon was unbounded. In satirical vein, he points out how their own worshippers actually made them from the very same wood as they used to burn on the fire. To him, such an attitude was just blind ignorance: 'Such people are too stupid to know what they are doing. They close their eyes and their minds to the truth. The maker of idols hasn't the wit or the sense to say, "Some of the wood I burnt up. I baked some bread on the embers and I roasted meat and ate it. And the rest of the wood I made into an idol. Here I am bowing down to a block of wood!"' (44:18–19). That is not the kind of God who had revealed himself in Israel's history. He had been, and still was, a God of real power, the God of all creation: 'I am the Lord, the Creator of all things. I alone stretched out the heavens; when I made the earth, no one helped me' (44:24).

God's people and their land

With this emphasis on God's universal sovereignty, we might have expected his special relationship with Israel to have been forgotten, or at least pushed into the background. But it was not. The fact that God's power extended over the whole world meant that the exiles could go back to their homeland without worrying whether God would have the power to take care of them. Many of them probably needed this kind of encouragement. For even after Cyrus gave them permission to return, many preferred the safety and security of the life they knew to the hazards and unknown perils of a long journey and a strange land. But to those who would trust God, it was all a great spiritual adventure: 'From the distant east and the farthest west, I will bring your people home. I will tell the north to let them go and the south not to hold them back. Let my people return from distant lands, from every part of the world' (43:5–7). God had done it long centuries before in the exodus from Egypt, and he would do it again because of his great love for his people: 'Watch for the new thing I am going to do. It is happening already – you can see it now! I will make a road through the wilderness and give you streams of water there . . . (43:19). Jerusalem may be a ruined wasteland, but it would soon be restored to its former glory: 'I will show compassion to Jerusalem, to all who live in her ruins. Though her land is a desert, I will make it a garden, like the garden planted in Eden. Joy and gladness will be there, and songs of praise and thanks to me' (51:3).

God's servant and God's world

Despite this renewed emphasis on God's concern for his own people, this Babylonian prophet was convinced that God's love was not just for Israel alone.

Just as the whole world was the arena of God's activity, so all the people of the world would be the object of his love. This is the message of one of those passages that have been called 'the servant songs': 'The Lord said to me, "I have a greater task for you, my servant. Not only will you restore to greatness the people of Israel who have survived, but I will also make you a light to the nations – so that all the world may be saved"' (49:6).

There are four of these servant songs, and they seem to be separate and self-contained poems, though no doubt still the work of the prophet himself, and certainly an integral part of his message (42:1–4; 49:1–6; 50:4–9; 52:13—53:12). In these songs, the prophet talks of a specific individual, 'the servant', through whom God's plans for a great and glorious future age will come to fruition. But who was this servant? Elsewhere the prophet talks of the nation of Israel as the servant of God, and the person mentioned in the servant songs is often described in the same language as is used of Israel. Israel is 'my servant . . . the people that I have

The exile from Judah

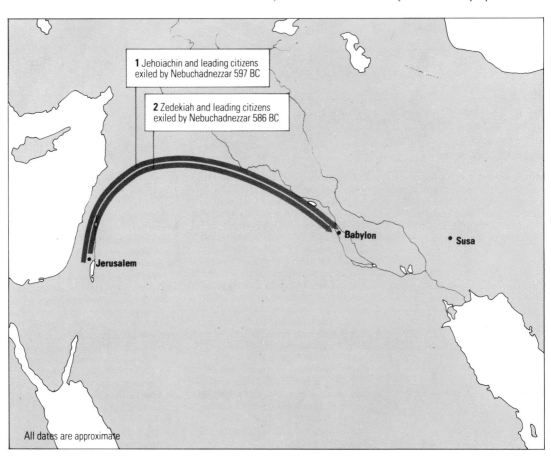

1 Jehoiachin and leading citizens exiled by Nebuchadnezzar 597 BC

2 Zedekiah and leading citizens exiled by Nebuchadnezzar 586 BC

Babylon

Susa

Jerusalem

All dates are approximate

chosen' (41:8), and so is the servant of the songs (42:1). Both of them were created by God himself (Israel, 43:1,7,15,21; 44:2,21,24; the servant, 49:5), and were endowed with God's own Spirit (Israel, 44:3; the servant, 42:1). This has led many scholars to conclude that when Isaiah talks of the suffering servant he is simply talking of God's people Israel in another way. But at the same time, things are said about the servant which are explicitly denied about Israel. The servant 'will not lose hope or courage' (42:4), nor has he 'rebelled or turned away' from God (50:5), as the nation so often did. In addition, he suffers patiently – not for his own wrongdoings like the nation, but for the wrongs of others (53:3–5). Most significant of all is the fact that while the nation needed restoration, the servant is sent to restore and renew Israel (49:5–6; 53:4–6). It is therefore difficult to see how the prophet could have identified this servant of God with the nation itself.

But who was he? Some people think the prophet had a particular living individual in mind, possibly Jehoiachin, or someone like Jeremiah, or conceivably even himself. But it is more likely that he was thinking of some future person in whose life the ideals of Israel's ancient faith would become a reality, and through whom God's intentions for his people and the world could be brought to pass. He is never actually called the Messiah in the Old Testament, nor did the Jewish people ever think to equate the two. But these passages exerted a powerful influence on the Christian understanding of Jesus as the Messiah of the Old Testament expectation. In particular, the account of the servant's suffering in the last song (52:13—53:12) has some amazing correspondences with the death of Jesus himself. This is undoubtedly the greatest insight that we have from this prophet in Babylon: that the way to the world's salvation would be the way of suffering and service.

The return of the exiles

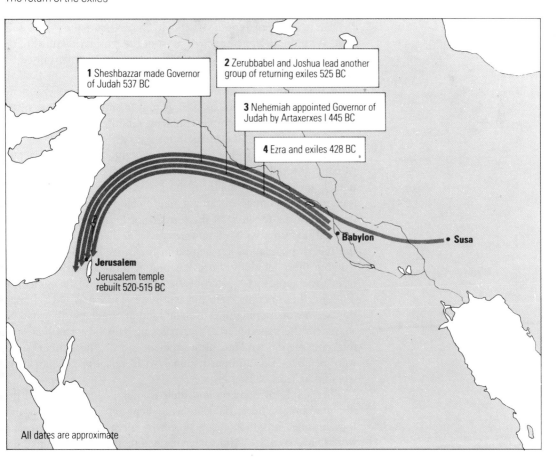

1 Sheshbazzar made Governor of Judah 537 BC

2 Zerubbabel and Joshua lead another group of returning exiles 525 BC

3 Nehemiah appointed Governor of Judah by Artaxerxes I 445 BC

4 Ezra and exiles 428 BC

Babylon • Susa

Jerusalem
Jerusalem temple rebuilt 520-515 BC

All dates are approximate

Back to Jerusalem

Antiquities of the Jews XI.i.3

Ezra 5:16

Jeremiah 41:4–5

Cyrus had issued an edict allowing the temple in Jerusalem to be rebuilt at the beginning of his reign. But there was no great rush by the exiles in Babylon to return to Judah. Josephus reports that when they were given the chance to go back home, they did not want to leave the comfortable life they had established in exile. But it was important to the Persians that their repatriation policy should be set in motion. Though they undoubtedly had humanitarian reasons for introducing it, the benefits of having loyal and grateful subjects in strategic parts of their empire can hardly have escaped their notice. Since Palestine was near to the border with Egypt, it was important for them to re-establish a friendly state there.

So they appointed a man called Sheshbazzar as governor of Judah. His name was thoroughly Babylonian, though that does not mean he was not a Jew. We know very little about him, except that he made a start on rebuilding the foundations of the temple. We are better informed about a further group of exiles who returned a little later under the leadership of Zerubbabel and Joshua. Joshua was a priest, but Zerubbabel was the grandson of Jehoiachin, the last truly legitimate king of the royal family of David. He also held an official Persian appointment, and he could have been Sheshbazzar's successor as governor. The appointment of a member of the Jewish royal family may have been a conscious effort by the Persians to persuade more Jews to return. Zerubbabel certainly saw that, with Persian help, a new Jewish state could emerge from the ashes of the past. With the disappearance of most of the familiar features of the earlier kingdom, however, there was just one thing that united the new settlers with their ancestors. That was their faith in God. In exile, that faith had been centred on customs like circumcision and keeping the sabbath day, as well as prayer and the reading of the Torah. But now the temple could be rebuilt, and its repair and renovation was to be Zerubbabel's main task.

The temple ruins had probably continued to be a place of worship throughout the period since Nebuchadnezzar's destruction. Even in the aftermath of the invasion, the book of Jeremiah mentions worshippers making a pilgrimage to the site. They had come from the territory of the former northern kingdom of Israel, centred on Samaria. No doubt people from that quarter, as well as the Jewish population left behind in Judah itself had continued to worship there all along. So it was only natural for these people to offer their assistance to Zerubbabel. But he would have none of it. To him, these people were not real Jews. They may have thought they were worshipping the covenant God of Israel, but they had not shared in the experience of the exiles in Babylon – and they were the only true descendants of the ancient tribes. These other people were of uncertain (and partly non-Jewish) racial origins, and their worship of Yahweh was suspect.

The people of Samaria and their friends in Judah realized that the newcomers from Babylon were bent on forming their own Jewish state, in which the people who already lived in the land would have no place. And so, having had their offer of co-operation turned down, these people had no option but to oppose the plans of the returned exiles. They succeeded in delaying work on the temple for something like ten years or more, by persuading the Persian officials responsible for the western empire that something illegal was afoot. By this time, Darius I was the emperor, but Cyrus's original permission still stood, and the work was allowed to proceed. The new temple was much poorer than Solomon's had been. But its completion was a milestone in the life of this beleaguered community.

Ezra 5

Ezra 3:12

Haggai and Zechariah

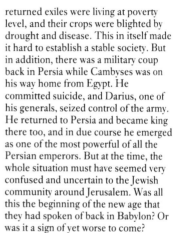

Emperor Darius I, from Media, continued Cyrus's policy of supporting the exiles' return. In his time the temple was rebuilt at Jerusalem.

Zerubbabel and Joshua were encouraged in their work by the prophets Haggai and Zechariah. Their messages give us a vivid insight into the despair and apathy of the people at this time. The wave of euphoria that accompanied Cyrus's rise to power subsided soon after his death, for his son Cambyses (530–522 BC) did not share his father's ideals. He was more interested in military conquest, and during his campaign against Egypt in 525 BC it is likely that he plundered Judah for food supplies. This would have been bad enough in good times, but Haggai's messages show that conditions were far from that. The returned exiles were living at poverty level, and their crops were blighted by drought and disease. This in itself made it hard to establish a stable society. But in addition, there was a military coup back in Persia while Cambyses was on his way home from Egypt. He committed suicide, and Darius, one of his generals, seized control of the army. He returned to Persia and became king there too, and in due course he emerged as one of the most powerful of all the Persian emperors. But at the time, the whole situation must have seemed very confused and uncertain to the Jewish community around Jerusalem. Was all this the beginning of the new age that they had spoken of back in Babylon? Or was it a sign of yet worse to come?

Haggai began speaking to the people in 520 BC, early in the reign of Darius. He urged them to make the rebuilding of the temple a real priority. They had built houses for themselves, so why should they neglect God? If he was not worshipped, they could hardly expect prosperity. But if they were prepared to put him first, then anything could happen. Zerubbabel was there as God's chosen spokesman, and the symbol of God's own presence – the temple – should also be reinstated as the centre of national life. When that happened, the scene would be set for the new age that the exiles had hoped for: 'On that day I will take you, Zerubbabel my servant, and I will appoint you to rule in my name. You are the one I have chosen' (Haggai 2:23).

Zechariah was a contemporary of Haggai, and his messages are essentially similar. He encouraged the completion of the rebuilt temple, and in a series of visions he depicted the new age that God would soon bring about. He too saw a special place for Zerubbabel in all this (4:6–10; 6:9–15), but he also emphasized that Zerubbabel's success depended not so much on the fact that he was descended from King David, but on the fact that God was with him in a special way: 'You will succeed, not by military might or by your own strength, but by my spirit. Obstacles as great as mountains will disappear before you. You will rebuild the Temple, and as you put the last stone in place, the people will shout, "Beautiful, Beautiful!"' (4:6–7).

The precise meaning of the statements made about Zerubbabel is unclear. The language used is undoubtedly what we could call 'messianic'. But at the same time, it can hardly have had a political implication, for Zerubbabel seems to have retained the confidence of the Persians. There are also hints that the high priest Joshua came to occupy an even more important place in the new community. In the days of the earlier kingdom of Judah, the temple had been under the personal

direction of the king. But with the disappearance of the kingly office, some of his functions were now carried out by the priests. In preparation for his new responsibilities, Joshua was actually crowned in a kind of coronation ceremony (Zechariah 6:9–15). This was probably a significant development in Jewish thinking. Some 400 years later the Dead Sea Scrolls seem to expect the coming of a priest who would be the Messiah, and who was at least as important as the 'secular' Messiah who would be descended from David. The same idea is also found in the letter to the Hebrews in the New Testament. Unfortunately, we have so little definite knowledge of the time of Haggai and Zechariah that we cannot trace the possible connections of this idea in any greater detail.

Confusion and despair

The new temple was completed in about 515 BC. Now at last the people had a new hope. No doubt they went about their worship with joy and expectation, believing that the new age which they had been promised must surely be at hand. But the reality was to be quite different. We have no absolutely certain knowledge of life in Judah from 515 BC until 444 BC. But we have no reason to suppose that conditions improved, either religiously or economically. A number of prophetic messages seem to reflect life at this time. The book of Obadiah is a short poem deploring the advantage that the Edomites had gained out of Judah's national disaster – and also assuring the Jewish people that better times were on the way. The book of Joel also probably relates to this period. Its immediate occasion is a plague of locusts, which led to a great famine. But Joel assured his hearers that this was just a temporary setback, and would be the prelude to the new age that God would inaugurate. The same picture of despondency is found, according to some scholars, in the final section of the book of Isaiah. Some see this as the work of yet another prophet (Third or Trito-Isaiah). But it is more likely that these messages were the work of followers of Isaiah of Babylon. Their general outlook is similar to his idealism, yet they seem to reflect the despair of this later age.

Isaiah 56—66

The only certain source of information from this period is the book of Malachi. This shows that, though the temple was indeed standing again, the spiritual realities that it should symbolize were still not being taken seriously. The priests themselves were neglecting their proper duties, and the true covenant religion of Yahweh had become mixed up with magical practices. Popular religion was just a form of practical atheism: '"You have said terrible things about me", says the Lord . . . "You have said, 'It's useless to serve God. What's the use of doing what he says or of trying to show the Lord Almighty that we are sorry for what we have done?'"' As in the past, this neglect of Israel's covenant faith was

Malachi 3:5

Malachi 3:13–14

leading to great social evils, and Malachi declared that God would step in to judge this rotten community: 'those who give false testimony, those who cheat employees out of their wages, and those

Malachi 3:5

who take advantage of widows, orphans and foreigners'. On top of that, the community of returned exiles was losing its true identity. The men were leaving their Jewish wives for more attractive younger women who belonged to the racially mixed population that had tried to stop the rebuilding of the temple. This was a serious matter, for it threatened the very existence of the fragile Jewish settlement. It would only be a matter of time before God would

Malachi 4

have to deal with these evils.

Renewing the covenant

It was not too long before moves were afoot to reform and re-establish the life of the Jewish community in Jerusalem. It began with the arrival of a man called Nehemiah. He was himself a Jew, and had risen to a position of some eminence in the Persian royal court. When he heard of the deprivation of his people in Judah and Jerusalem, he asked the Persian king, by now Artaxerxes I, to let him go there and help to rebuild the community. So he was

Nehemiah 1—2

appointed governor of Judah in 445 BC. There had probably been a succession of such governors ever since the days of Sheshbazzar about 100 years before. We know nothing of them or their work, but the brief report of their activities given in the book of Nehemiah suggests they had been more concerned with their own comfort

Nehemiah 5:15

than with the well-being of their people. The reaction of both upper-class Jews and the people of Samaria to Nehemiah's appointment certainly suggests that his predecessors did not share the commitment and religious idealism that were to be a hallmark of Nehemiah's work.

Building the walls

Nehemiah had a specific commission from the Persian emperor to rebuild the city of Jerusalem itself. But when he got there, he found that most of the Jews were satisfied with things as they were. From a social perspective, they had turned out to be model immigrants, for they had integrated almost entirely with the rest of Palestinian society. Their businessmen had established trading relations with the people of Samaria, to the mutual benefit of both groups, and this had led to co-operation over a wide range of other issues.

Of course, the people of Samaria were not total foreigners. For they too could trace their ancestry back to the original Israelite tribes. The only difference was that whereas the Jews from Babylon were of pure Israelite stock, these other people had married people of other races. Even so, they still worshipped the same God as the exiles from Babylon, and the two men from Samaria who turned out to be Nehemiah's most vociferous opponents – Sanballat and Tobiah – both felt that they had the same religious faith as their Jewish neighbours.

But Nehemiah could not accept all this. To him, integration between Jews and other people could only mean one thing: the loss

of their distinctive Jewish identity. He believed that these peopl
had abandoned the idealism that originally motivated their retur
from Babylon. The fact that he also saw the rich sections of th
community exploiting the poor only made him the more determine
to change things.

Nehemiah 5   He challenged the moral standards of the Jewish businessmen
But he could see that as long as there was easy access from Samari
to Jerusalem, the problems would persist. If there was ever to be
pure Jewish community then it would need to have its own politica
identity centred in the city of Jerusalem itself. Jerusalem must b
properly fortified, with its own city walls. That would remin
people like Sanballat and Tobiah that it did not belong to them, an
it would also give the Jews a city to be proud of. Sanballat an
Tobiah were deeply opposed to all this. Quite possibly the
themselves had exercised some sort of jurisdiction over Jerusalen
before Nehemiah came. They obviously had friendly relations witl
the Jewish leaders, and felt it was quite unjust for them to be cut of
like this by an outsider. But Nehemiah managed to gather togethe
a group of workmen from the area surrounding the city, and the
set to work – half of them building, the other half guarding th
unfinished wall. In the amazingly short time of fifty-two days, th

Nehemiah 6   wall was built. It was not as extensive as the wall that ha
surrounded the city before 586 BC, but its completion gave a grea
boost to the morale of its inhabitants. For the first time sinc
Nebuchadnezzar had destroyed their city, Jerusalem and its peopl
had their own self-contained society, and a new opportunity tc
establish their distinctive national and religious identity.

   Some twelve years after his arrival, Nehemiah returned to th

Nehemiah 13:6   Persian capital Susa to report back to Artaxerxes. He must have fel
that he had made some progress. But when he came back, h
discovered that things had not really changed. In his absence
things had returned to what they were before. Foreigners had com
to live in Jerusalem, and the people were not observing the sabbath
day. On top of that, the worship at the temple was not as strict as
Nehemiah would have liked it to be. Some of the priests had beer
forced to leave their posts to go to work on the farms, just to make
a living. At the same time, Eliashib the high priest had given a suite
of rooms in the temple to Nehemiah's enemy Tobiah! But that wa
not the worst thing. For many Jewish people were again marrying
foreigners – and even the high priest's own grandson had marriec

Nehemiah 13:4–31   the daughter of Sanballat!

Handing on the Law

Nehemiah was determined to change all this. But it was a Jewish
priest by the name of Ezra who issued the most far-reaching
challenge to the people of Jerusalem. He too was a Persian state
official, who came to Jerusalem with royal authority to reorganize
religious affairs. He was accompanied by a further group o
returning exiles from Babylon, who brought with them a consi-

Ezra 7:1–26   derable financial endowment for the temple in Jerusalem. But they
brought more than that, for Ezra was a 'scholar in the Law of th

Ezra 7:12   God of Heaven.' It was this Law that he set before the people, and

Part of the wall of Old Jerusalem is known as Nehemiah's wall. Nehemiah led the returned Jews in rebuilding the city walls, against fierce opposition from the tribes who had occupied the surrounding territory. His leadership helped to restore a sense of national religious identity to a people in danger of being demoralized by the difficult task of getting re-established in a long-neglected land.

that was to have a profound and lasting influence on their whole way of life.

It is not absolutely clear from the Old Testament just what this Law was. But it is reasonable to suppose that it would be substantially identical with the Torah as we know it today. Among the exiles in Babylon, this had become of supreme importance. Away from Judah, and unable to continue the traditional worship in the temple, the exiles had laid great emphasis on those things that could still distinguish them from other nations – things like keeping the sabbath day, observing their own special food regulations, and circumcision. And all of this was found in their Law. The exiles clearly knew a good deal more about this than the people in Judah, for their reaction to it suggests that they were not at all familiar with its requirements. They were certainly unable to read it for themselves. Ezra read it aloud to them, but a group of priests (Levites) then 'gave an oral translation of God's Law and explained **Nehemiah 8:8** it so that the people could understand it.' This was necessary because the Law itself was written in Hebrew, whereas the people now spoke Aramaic, which was the official language of the Persian Empire. The rough translation made by the Levites was the forerunner of many such translations, know as Targums. At first, a Targum was only an oral translation, but as time went on its wording became more fixed, and the term Targum came to mean just the Aramaic version of the Old Testament.

When they heard the Law that Ezra read, the people were deeply moved, and decided they must celebrate the religious festivals

Nehemiah 8:9–18

which it mentioned. But Ezra was determined to tackle the other problems too, especially the question of Jews who were married to foreigners. He was more diplomatic than Nehemiah, but also more ruthless, and he forced the Jews to agree to divorce all such partners. From a modern perspective, Ezra can easily seem intolerant and bigoted. But his view was not unreasonable for his own day. In many of the marriage laws of ancient Greece and Rome, a man was not even allowed to marry a person outside his own class, let alone from a different race.

Whatever we may think of Ezra's attitudes, it is probably true that the community in Judah may not have survived as a distinctive entity without his efforts. But the people paid a high price for their survival. For this new emphasis on racial purity and a detailed observance of rules and regulations as the heart of the Jewish religion could so easily be misinterpreted to become that self-

Matthew 23:1–36

righteous legalism and hypocrisy that was roundly condemned by Jesus and which the Christian apostle Paul later felt to be so contrary to the original intention of the covenant relationship

Galatians

between God and his ancient people. Not all Jews were narrow-minded legalists, of course. But it was almost inevitable that many of them would be tempted to lay more emphasis on the mechanical performance of religious rules than on the dynamic relationship between God and his people that had up to this point formed the heart of the Old Testament story.

Two dissidents

Not everyone accepted this new emphasis on racial purity, the Law, and the temple. When Stephen, one of the leaders of the earliest Christian church, argued that the building of the temple was a mistake because 'The Most High God does not live in houses built by men' (Acts 7:48, quoting Isaiah 66:1–2), he had a long line of Jewish protest behind him. But at this earlier period, more criticism was focussed on the policy of rigid separation from other races.

Many scholars believe that the Old Testament book of Ruth may have been published at this time, as a protest against Ezra's actions. The fact that the Jews placed it in the third section of the Old Testament – the Writings – certainly suggests that it may have been among the later Old Testament books. But in our English Bibles it is placed after Judges, because its story is set in that age. It tells how Elimelech, a native of Bethlehem, emigrated to Moab at a time of famine. He was accompanied by his wife, Naomi, and his two sons, both of whom married Moabite women. The father and the two sons all died in

Moab, and Naomi returned to Bethlehem along with her daughter-in-law Ruth. There, Ruth met Boaz, who was a relative of her husband's family, and they got married. As a result, Ruth, a Moabite woman, became the great-grandmother of King David.

Like other parts of the Old Testament, this story may have originated in earlier times. But the opening phrase of the book, 'Long ago, in the days before Israel had a king . . .', shows that it was written down much later. And though there is no positive evidence to prove it, it is plausible to think that it could have been written as a protest against the legislation of Ezra and Nehemiah: if a Moabite woman married to an Israelite could have been the ancestor of King David himself, then surely there was nothing wrong with mixed marriages!

The book of Jonah may also have originated in the same context. A prophet called Jonah is mentioned briefly in the time of Amos (2 Kings 14:25), but the book contains none of his messages. It tells the story of how

Jonah was sent by God to go to Nineveh, the capital city of the Assyrian Empire. Jonah, however, did not want to go, and boarded a ship going in the opposite direction. A great storm blew up, and the crew decided he must be the cause of it. At his own suggestion they threw him overboard, but he was swallowed by a fish which later deposited him on dry land. Again Jonah was sent to Nineveh, to announce the destruction of the city. But his preaching resulted in such a dramatic and thoroughgoing repentance that God withdrew the threat of destruction.

Jonah was dispirited at this, and went to sit alone outside the city. A plant grew up to give him much-needed shade from the sun, only to disappear as quickly – much to Jonah's annoyance. But his frustration then becomes the occasion for the book's message to be hammered home: 'The Lord said to him, "This plant grew up in one night and disappeared the next; you didn't do anything for it and you didn't make it grow – yet you feel sorry for it! How much more, then, should I have pity on Nineveh, that great city. After all, it has more than 120,000 innocent children in it, as well as many animals!"' (Jonah 4:10–11)

There are some indications that this book was written after the city of Nineveh had fallen (in 612 BC), and a few Aramaic expressions seem to date it in the Persian period. Its message would certainly be a corrective to the narrow exclusiveness of many Jews at that time. Like Jonah, they were often prepared to go to any lengths to avoid sharing their faith with others, preferring that non-Jews should be destroyed rather than repent.

The Chronicler and his history

The Old Testament books 1 and 2 Chronicles were written during this post-exilic period. In them, we have yet another view of the Old Testament story, a story which this time begins with Adam, the first man (1 Chronicles 1:1) and ends with Cyrus the Persian (2 Chronicles 36:22–23). The first nine chapters of 1 Chronicles consist entirely of various family and tribal lists and genealogies, and the story proper begins with the death of Saul, the first king of Israel (1 Chronicles 10). But he is mentioned only as a prelude to the story of David, and the main interest of the author of these books ('the Chronicler') centres on the history of Judah from the time of David onwards.

Inevitably, therefore, the stories of the books of Chronicles parallel those of the Deuteronomistic history books. Indeed, at many points the Chronicler shows that he has actually used the books of Samuel and Kings in the writing of his own story. This fact should make it easy for us to discover his own special reasons for telling the story yet again, simply by comparing his accounts of the same events described in the earlier books. Unfortunately, it seems likely that he was using a slightly different version of Samuel and Kings from the one that is now part of our Old Testament. We know of the existence of such a version from the Dead Sea Scrolls, a collection of scriptural and other writings preserved by a Jewish sect in the century immediately preceding the Christian era. But because of the doubt concerning the edition of Samuel and Kings used by the Chronicler, reconstructing his own historical method is not a straightforward business. Chronicles also contains other historical information not found in Samuel and Kings, much of which is of independent value in helping us to understand the events of Israel's earlier history.

On the whole, however, the Chronicler sets out not so much to record the facts about the past, as to comment on their meaning and significance. And though there may be doubt about some of the details, his main concerns are not difficult to discern. He looks back to the reigns of David and Solomon as a golden age in Judah's history. The kings who followed them were all disobedient to God's Law, and the northern kingdom of Israel is scarcely mentioned at all, for it was believed to be so corrupt right from its inception. The Deuteronomic picture of Solomon and David gives us a more realistic, balanced account of their reigns than we have in Chronicles. Not that the Chronicler necessarily invented his facts: he simply omitted significant elements from the story, and emphasized other aspects that to him were more important. So, for instance, there is no mention here of David's struggle for the kingdom against Ishbaal, Saul's son. Nor is there any mention of David's adultery with Bathsheba – or anything else that might cast David in a bad light. The same is true of the presentation of Solomon. The court intrigues that brought him to power are not mentioned, nor is his worship of false gods, or his involvement with foreign wives. Instead, both David and Solomon are praised because they built the temple. David's preparations for doing so, and Solomon's execution of his father's plans are described in far greater detail than in the earlier history books. Then, against this background, the later kings of Judah are all depicted as men who led their country to ruin because they neglected this all-important feature of Judah's national life.

The fact that Cyrus's edict is mentioned in the last paragraph of 2 Chronicles has led some to suggest that the two books may have been written to provide support for the work of Zerubbabel in rebuilding the temple after the exile. The fact that the issue of racial purity – so important later – does not feature in Chronicles may also support such a date. On the other hand, this may be too early, for the list of Jehoiachin's descendants in 1 Chronicles 3:17-24 goes well beyond the time of Zerubbabel, and possibly takes us to about 400 BC. In that case, the two books could have been written in support of Ezra's reforms. They certainly stress some of the same things – and in that context, the ignoring of the life of the northern kingdom of Israel could be seen as an encouragement to the people of Jerusalem to have nothing to do with their descendants who now lived in Samaria. On the other hand, some scholars have argued that we should not try to link Chronicles up to specific events and situations in this way, but simply see it as the product of a number of different political and theological currents in the post-exilic Jewish community.

Ezra and Nehemiah

The date of 1 and 2 Chronicles is closely bound up with their relationship to the books of Ezra and Nehemiah. Many scholars believe that all four of them together were originally written as a history of the Jews from creation itself up to the Chronicler's own day. If that is the case, then we would need to think of all four books as written about 400 BC, or possibly even later. The only substantial reason for seeing a connection between 1-2 Chronicles and Ezra/Nehemiah is the fact that the closing words of 2 Chronicles are identical with the opening paragraph of Ezra. But in other ways, their concerns are rather different. In particular, the deep interest of 1-2 Chronicles in David's family is not reflected in Ezra

and Nehemiah.

The style and general organization of material is also strikingly different. Whereas 1-2 Chronicles contain a coherent, well-organized account, Ezra and Nehemiah contain a very disjointed collection of stories and other materials. Temple records are quoted (Nehemiah 7:5; 12:23), as is the decree of Cyrus – in Hebrew (Ezra 1:1-4) and Aramaic (Ezra 6:3-5). Various other Aramaic letters are also included in Ezra (4:7-22; 5:6-17; 6:2-12; 7:12-26), while the actual story of Ezra's exploits is partly contained in the book of Ezra (7—10) and partly in Nehemiah (7:73-10:39) – and some of it has the appearance of being extracts from Ezra's own diary (Ezra 7:27—8:34; 9:1-15). Likewise, much of Nehemiah's story appears in the form of extracts from his own personal diary (Nehemiah 1:1—7:73, and sections of 11—13).

Then as the stories stand, there are complex issues involved in understanding the relationship between these two men. According to Ezra 7:7, Ezra went to Jerusalem in the seventh year of Artaxerxes' reign, and Nehemiah in his twentieth year (Nehemiah 1:1). That would place Ezra's arrival in 458 BC, and Nehemiah's in 444 BC. But this seems to imply that Ezra's reforms were a miserable failure, for when Nehemiah arrived he certainly found all the same abuses as Ezra fought so strenuously to overcome. There are other facts which further complicate matters. For instance, when Nehemiah arrived he set to work building a wall round Jerusalem, though Ezra 9:9 implies that there was already a wall there when Ezra arrived. There is also the fact that in Nehemiah's time, the high priest was Eliashib (Nehemiah 3:1), whereas in Ezra's time it appears to have been his grandson, Johanan (Ezra 10:6; Nehemiah 12:11,22).

Various attempts have been made to overcome this problem. Some suggest that Ezra perhaps came in the reign of Artaxerxes II, which would place his arrival in 398 BC – long after the time of Nehemiah. Others emphasize the fact that their careers do seem to have overlapped at some points (Nehemiah 8:9; 12:26,36). They have therefore suggested that the correct date for Ezra was the *twenty*-seventh year of Artaxerxes I, i.e. 428 BC. All three dates for Ezra – 458, 428, and 398 BC – have supporters today, and it is difficult to decide which is likely to be correct. In our account of the work of these two men, we have assumed that Nehemiah did precede Ezra, but probably not by a long period of time.

Perhaps the reason for this confusion can be found in the disjointed nature of the narratives of these two books. For as we read them carefully, they seem to be not so much a continuous story of Ezra and Nehemiah, as a kind of preliminary collection of information such as a historian might make before writing his polished account. The first six chapters of Ezra are more or less continuous, but between them and chapter seven there is a time gap of at least sixty years, and possibly more. The further fact that some parts of Ezra are written in Aramaic, while other parts are in Hebrew, also reinforces this impression of a collection of notes rather than a finished story.

If this is a correct understanding of the nature of Ezra and Nehemiah, it would then be possible that 1 and 2 Chronicles were written early during the period of the exile, and that these other materials were gathered together by some later author – perhaps a follower of the original Chronicler – as a means of bringing the story up to his own day. We have so little knowledge of this period that it is difficult to be certain. But this does not detract from the usefulness of these books, for all scholars are convinced that Nehemiah and Ezra contain important and valuable historical materials from the period which they describe.

This papyrus letter was written by Jews who were living in Elephantine, in southern Egypt near Aswan. It mentions Sanballat, governor of Samaria in the time of Nehemiah. Documents found at Elephantine show that Jews who lived there at that time continued to worship the Lord.

Jews in Egypt

The Jewish community in Jerusalem was not the only context in which the God of Israel was being worshipped at this time. We have already noticed that the inhabitants of Samaria felt themselves to be a part of the ancient covenant faith – and in a series of Aramaic documents discovered at the island of Elephantine, near Aswan on the River Nile, we are given a fascinating glimpse of life in another Jewish community at roughly the time of Nehemiah and Ezra.

The Jews who lived here were a military settlement. At the time of these documents, Egypt was a part of the Persian Empire, and they had perhaps been sent to guard the southern frontier of Egypt and the trading post of Syene, where traders from further south met the ships of Egyptian traders on the Nile. These Jews may well have been in this area long before Cambyses the Persian conquered Egypt in 525 BC, but they certainly had a military function rather than being (as some have supposed) the descendants either of a group of religious dissidents who left Jerusalem in protest at Josiah's reforms (621 BC), or of those Jews who took Jeremiah to Egypt after the fall of Jerusalem in 586 BC.

There are many different kinds of documents in this collection, including deeds for property, marriage contracts, and other legal transactions. But the most interesting ones to us are those that describe the religious practices of this group. For it soon emerges from them that the Judaism of this Egyptian garrison was very different indeed from the Judaism that was being taught at the same time in Jerusalem by Nehemiah and Ezra.

● In spite of the Deuteronomic law that sacrifices were to be offered only in Jerusalem, there was a Jewish temple in Elephantine at which sacrifices were offered. The priests who officiated here are not said to have belonged to the tribe of Levi, nor is there any evidence that they knew the Torah. After their temple had been destroyed in 410 BC, the governors of Judah and Samaria advised them to limit their sacrifices to meal offerings and incense. This could have been a gesture intended to show that the Elephantine temple was inferior in status to that in Jerusalem – but it could also have been because animal sacrifices were particularly offensive to the Egyptians.

Various explanations have been offered to account for the existence of this temple. Perhaps the Deuteronomic law of a single sanctuary applied only in Palestine. Or possibly the Jews of Elephantine had left Palestine already before the reforms of Hezekiah and Josiah had really taken a grip. We simply do not know, though some scholars have suggested that there may be a veiled reference to this Egyptian temple in Isaiah 19:19, which reads 'When that day comes, there will be an altar to the Lord in the land of Egypt and a stone pillar dedicated to him at the Egyptian border'. We know very little about this temple, except that it had pillars of stone, five gateways made of carved stone, and a roof of cedar wood. But there is not the slightest suggestion that the Jews of Elephantine thought there was anything wrong in having such a temple outside Jerusalem. Indeed, when it was destroyed they appealed for help in its rebuilding both to the Jewish leaders in Jerusalem, and to the people in Samaria who were so hostile to Nehemiah!

● Though this temple was definitely dedicated to Yahweh (or Yaho as he is called here), other gods and goddesses had some part in it. Some believe there were five deities worshipped here, represented by the five gates of the temple. Others believe there were only two or three, of whom Yaho was certainly one. Most of the other gods and goddesses mentioned in the texts are Canaanite. When we recall the habits of the people in Israel itself, we need not be surprised by this. The prophets were constantly complaining because the worship of Yahweh was mixed up with the worship of other gods and goddesses. And when Jeremiah met up with such people after his flight to Egypt, they justified their worship of 'the Queen of Heaven' by reminding him that this was 'just as we and our ancestors, our king and our leaders, used to do in the towns of Judah and in the streets of Jerusalem' (Jeremiah 44:17).

● One of the most interesting texts is the so-called 'Passover Papyrus'. This dates from 419 BC, and contains a decree said to have been issued by Darius, laying down regulations for the celebration of the festival of Passover. This suggests that the annual observance of Passover was not so regular in early times as it came to be in later Judaism. But the very existence of this text is itself unusual, though it is of the same type as other edicts contained in the books of Ezra and Nehemiah, which also give directions for the establishment of Jewish religious practices.

It is naturally tempting to try to find clear links between these documents and the Old Testament story. There is for example mention of people by the name of Hanani, as well as Johanan and Sanballat – all of whom figure in the stories of Nehemiah and Ezra. But there is no way of being certain that they indicate the same people. One of the things that is quite clear from these texts is that there were some people who believed it was possible to be a good Jew without necessarily following the rigid lines that had been drawn in Jerusalem. And in the next few centuries, this strand of Judaism was to be increasingly important in many parts of the Mediterranean world, not least in Egypt itself.

8 The challenge of a new age

Daniel

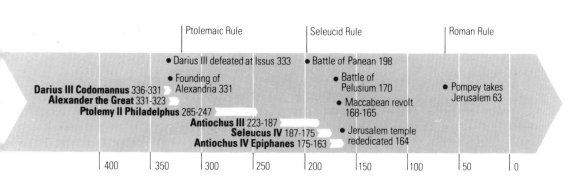

Ptolemaic Rule   Seleucid Rule   Roman Rule

● Darius III defeated at Issus 333   ● Battle of Panean 198

● Founding of   ● Battle of
Alexandria 331   Pelusium 170

Darius III Codomannus 336-331

Alexander the Great 331-323   ● Maccabean revolt
168-165   ● Pompey takes
Jerusalem 63

Ptolemy II Philadelphus 285-247

Antiochus III 223-187

Seleucus IV 187-175   ● Jerusalem temple
rededicated 164

Antiochus IV Epiphanes 175-163

| 400 | 350 | 300 | 250 | 200 | 150 | 100 | 50 | 0 |

THE HISTORY books of the Old Testament tell us nothing about events after the times of Nehemiah and Ezra. But the Old Testament story does not end there. Life in Judah continued, and changing attitudes and experiences may well be reflected in some of the Old Testament books. We have very little specific knowledge of what life was really like in Judah in the seventy or eighty years following the work of Ezra. But the community which he founded on the twin principles of religious and racial exclusivism probably continued along the same lines. Judah was still a Persian province, but it was allowed to mint its own coins, and enjoyed other privileges that the community based on Samaria never had. During this period the differences between Jerusalem and Samaria eventually forced the two populations of Palestine to go their own separate ways.

A high priest, from the small community of Samaritans still living in Israel today. Their origins reach back at least to Sanballat and Tobiah in Nehemiah's time and possibly even to the racially mixed community who survived the fall of Samaria and the northern kingdom to the Assyrians. Though kept at a distance by mainline Judaism, the Samaritans have always looked on themselves as heirs to the Old Testament traditions.

Jews and Samaritans

The people of Samaria realized they would never again be allowed to worship God in Jerusalem. Yet they still felt themselves to be a legitimate part of the great national and spiritual movement that could be traced back to the Israelite tribes of the earliest days. As they read the ancient stories of Abraham, Isaac, Jacob, and Moses, they recognized them as their own story – and the God of whom they spoke was worshipped with as much fervour in Samaria as he was by the settlers in Jerusalem.

As they reassessed their own national life in the wake of Ezra's reforms, the people of Samaria gradually developed their own distinctive beliefs and culture. The New Testament mentions people called 'Samaritans', and they may well have been the descendants of the people led by Tobiah and Sanballat, who were so fiercely opposed by Ezra and Nehemiah. On the other hand, it is perhaps more likely that the Samaritans of New Testament times were a completely new sect that emerged in the days just before the beginning of the Christian era.

The Samaritans got their chance to establish their own national identity in 333 BC. This was the year when the Persian king Darius III Codomannus was defeated in battle at Issus in north-west Syria. The victor was a young, enthusiastic warrior from Macedonia (the northern part of modern Greece) – Alexander the Great. Having overcome the main Persian army, he moved south towards Egypt. The Samaritans seized this opportunity, and got permission to build a temple of their own on Mt Gerizim. At first they were more eager to co-operate with the Greeks than were the high priest and the ruling classes in Jerusalem. But for some unknown reason they soon revolted, and their city was made into a Greek military colony.

A new empire

The empire created by Alexander the Great's fourth-century conquests took in Judea. For the next centuries the dominant influence in the whole Eastern Mediterranean was 'Hellenism' - a culture based on Greek language and thinking.

Alexander's progress was spectacular. Egypt put up no resistance to him, and in 331 BC he was able to found a new city on the Nile delta. This was the city of Alexandria, and it was to have a considerable influence not only on Egypt, but on the Jewish people living in various parts of the Mediterranean world. It later became an important centre of early Christianity.

The establishment of new cities played an important part in Alexander's strategy. For he was not just out for political power: he also had an almost fanatical fervour about spreading Greek culture and the Greek language. He was remarkably successful in doing so, and although his empire did not last long as a united political entity, the cultural world that he created, based on all things Greek – 'Hellenism' – lasted for nearly 1,000 years.

Alexander himself died of a fever in 323 BC. By then his empire stretched from Greece in the west to Pakistan in the east. But it did not survive intact. After much feuding among Alexander's generals, Judah – or Judea as it was now to be called – came under the control of Ptolemy, who established himself and his successors as a new ruling dynasty in Egypt. From about 320 BC until 198 BC, the Jews came under the jurisdiction of these Greek rulers of Egypt. On the whole, they were tolerant of the religious scruples of the Jewish people. They forced many Jews to emigrate to the city of Alexandria, which was at the time under-populated. Many others also went voluntarily, and there was soon a thriving Jewish community in this new Egyptian city. The language of the city was Greek, of course, and it was there that the Old Testament was translated from its original language into Greek.

According to one ancient legend, the Jews of Egypt managed to persuade the Egyptian king, Ptolemy II Philadelphus to sponsor the project. He sent to Jerusalem for seventy men who knew both Hebrew and Greek, and locked them up in seventy cells while each one produced his translation. When the work was finished, to everyone's amazement the seventy men not only expressed the same ideas, but also used the very same Greek words to do so – whereupon Ptolemy was so impressed that he was immediately convinced of the divine origins of their work! In reality, the work of translating the Old Testament into Greek was more humdrum than that. The Greek Septuagint version (the LXX) probably just evolved over many generations. But it certainly seems to have had some connection with Alexandria, and it became increasingly important not only for the spread of Judaism in the Mediterranean world, but also for the earliest Christian believers, who adopted it as their own Bible.

The Septuagint and the Deutero-Canonical books

It is customary today to speak of 'the Septuagint' as if it were simply a Greek Old Testament. But the facts are not so simple. A modern translator begins with a complete Bible in Hebrew and Greek, and produces its equivalent in his own language. But what we now call the Septuagint was never a complete Bible until the early centuries of the Christian era. Before that, no one knew the techniques necessary to bind such a large volume of literature into one single volume. Writing materials were painstakingly made by hand, and individual sheets would then be glued or stitched together to make a strip long enough to contain a single book. This would then be rolled up for storage, and to possess a complete Old Testament required a large number of different rolls. In addition to this, different people were busy making their own translations of the Old Testament books into Greek – and when the Christians eventually produced a single-volume Greek Old Testament, they simply made a selection from the translations that were available to them. Even today, we have a great number of ancient translations of Hebrew Old Testament books into Greek, not to mention several revisions and new editions of the Septuagint itself, all of them made by early Christian authors.

This complex state of affairs has also led to considerable debate about the actual contents of the Old Testament. How many books should it contain? At first, this may seem an odd question to ask. But we only need to compare a selection of modern versions of the Old Testament to see that though they all contain the thirty-nine books of the Hebrew Bible, some also contain other books, called either 'The Apocrypha' or 'The Deutero-Canonical books'.

These writings are: 1—2 Esdras (also called 3—4 Ezra), Tobit, Judith, additions to Esther, Wisdom of Solomon, Ecclesiasticus, the Letter of Jeremiah, Baruch, Song of the Three Young Men, Susannah, Bel and the Dragon, Prayer of Manasseh, and 1—2 Maccabees. Like the thirty-nine Old Testament books, they represent many types of literature. Some are clearly history books (1—2 Maccabees), others are books of philosophy and religious poetry (Wisdom of Solomon, Ecclesiasticus), while others are moralistic novels (Tobit, Judith, Susannah, Bel and the Dragon), and yet others provide additional material for books in the main body of the Old Testament, or purport to give a clairvoyant view of the future (2 Esdras).

Almost all these books are known to us primarily from early Christian copies of the Greek Septuagint version of the Old Testament. But we know that not all of them came from the same sources. Fragments of some of them have been discovered written in Hebrew. Others were originally composed in Greek, while yet others were probably first written in Hebrew, but have only survived in their Greek versions.

If we knew more about the origins of the Septuagint itself, we might be able to say with certainty how the Egyptian Jews thought of these books. But there is no evidence at present that suggests they regarded them as a part of the Old Testament itself. That argument only became important when Christians had collected together the various Greek translations of Old Testament books into one volume. Once the Septuagint had become the Bible of the Christian church, a long debate began about the value of these 'extra books'. Roman Catholic Christians accept them as a true part of the Old Testament, though most others do not. Some, like the Episcopal churches, use them selectively, accepting the guidelines laid down in the *Articles of Religion* of the Church of England, that 'the Church doth read (them) for example of life and instruction of manners; but yet doth it not apply them to establish any doctrine.'

So are these books a part of the Bible or not? No doubt the final answer to that question will have to be a theological one. But as a historical question, their existence can be explained quite easily. For in the days before the Old Testament was literally one book, the various rolls in which its writings were contained needed to be stored safely, and were often kept in small boxes. These boxes were used as a classification system, and if there was room the owner would store similar kinds of writings in the same boxes. This was probably how the books we now call the Apocrypha came to be associated with the other Old Testament books. In content and style, they were not all that different from the books of the Hebrew Bible, and it was natural to keep them all together. In time, they came to be accepted as part and parcel of the books that collectively made up the Greek version of the Old Testament. So when the early Christians came to bind all these books into one volume, it was natural to include them – even though they had probably never been included in the Hebrew Old Testament used by most Jewish people.

Jews and Greeks

Ptolemy had not been the only one of Alexander's generals with designs on Judea. Seleucus, who ruled from Antioch in north Syria, was not too happy that Judea and Lebanon should belong to Egypt. Throughout the third century their respective successors were engaged in a kind of cold war, and actually became involved in a number of military encounters over this issue. The matter was

The Greek Empire

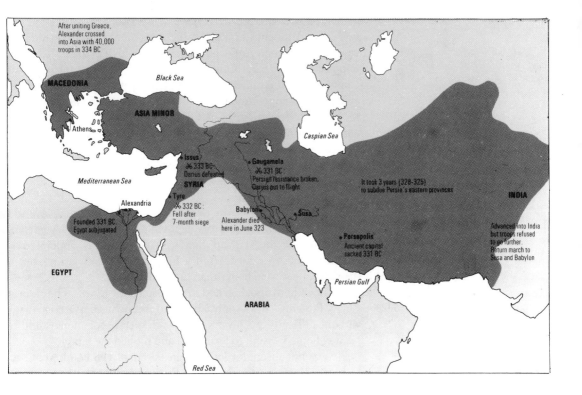

After uniting Greece, Alexander crossed into Asia with 40,000 troops in 334 BC

MACEDONIA

Black Sea

ASIA MINOR

Athens

Caspian Sea

Issus
333 BC
Darius defeated

Gaugamela
331 BC
Persian resistance broken.
Darius put to flight

It took 3 years (328-325)
to subdue Persia's eastern provinces

INDIA

Mediterranean Sea

SYRIA

Tyre
332 BC
Fell after
7-month siege

Babylon
Alexander died
here in June 323

Susa

Alexandria

Founded 331 BC.
Egypt subjugated

Advanced into India
but troops refused
to go further.
Return march to
Susa and Babylon

Persepolis
Ancient capital
sacked 331 BC

EGYPT

Persian Gulf

ARABIA

Red Sea

finally decided in 198 BC, when the Seleucid Antiochus III defeated Scopus, the general of Ptolemy V, at the battle of Paneon.

At first Antiochus adopted a tolerant policy towards the Jews. He reduced their taxes and made a generous grant towards their temple in Jerusalem. Unfortunately, he was soon forced to change his attitude. Having extended his power to the south, he tried to expand his empire in the west. But he had reckoned without the growing power of Rome, and in 190 BC he was defeated in a land and sea battle at Magnesia, near Ephesus. The peace treaty that he subsequently signed was a great humiliation, for he was forced to abandon his territory in Asia Minor. The loss of face was bad enough. But this territory had always been the wealthiest part of the Seleucid Empire, and the loss of its revenue led him to the brink of bankruptcy. He was soon desperate for money and just a year after signing the treaty with the Romans, Antiochus himself was killed in Elam while in the act of robbing a temple. He was succeeded by his son, Seleucus IV – who promptly despatched his chancellor, Heliodorus, to plunder the temple in Jerusalem.

2 Maccabees 3

Religion and politics

In the meantime, new tensions had emerged in Jewish society. Even before the Seleucids gained control of Judea, two of the leading families of Jerusalem – the Tobiads and the Oniads – had emerged as rivals, the one representing a rigid Jewish orthodoxy, and the other being more in sympathy with the new Hellenistic culture.

The climax of this power struggle within the Jewish hierarchy coincided with the murder of Seleucus IV and the accession of a new king, Antiochus IV Epiphanes. A member of the Oniad family called Jason bribed Antiochus to make him high priest in Jerusalem in place of his brother Onias. This suited Antiochus, for Jason was committed to the same policies of Hellenization as he was himself. With Jason's appointment, a thoroughgoing plan was set in motion to establish Jerusalem as a Greek city. Even the priests in the temple were soon hurrying through their work to have time to go off to the wrestling arena. The Greeks wore no clothes on such occasions, and to avoid possible embarrassment when they took part, the Jewish men even went so far as to try to disguise the fact that they had been circumcised. All this was too much for those who wanted to remain true to the traditions of their people, and it was not long before Jason was deposed and replaced by Menelaus, a member of the Tobiad family. Menelaus was appointed by Antiochus because he offered a higher bribe than Jason – but to the pious, he was no better than his predecessor.

Meanwhile, Antiochus had set his sights on Egypt. The ruler of Egypt, Ptolemy VI, was only a boy, and Antiochus defeated his army without difficulty. As always, he was desperate for money, and on his way home he went to Jerusalem and robbed the temple.

He was not absent for long. In the spring of 168 BC he went back to Egypt. But this time, he found the Romans there, and they soon

2 Maccabees 4:13–15

1 Maccabees 1:10–15;
2 Maccabees 4:7–17

2 Maccabees 4:23–50

1 Maccabees 1:16–28

In the days of Antiochus IV Epiphanes, there was a great struggle between the Jews and their Seleucid rulers over whether Jewish life and religion should continue its distinctive existence. The Seleucids wanted to make Jerusalem a purely Greek city, but the Jews fought strongly to retain the right to keep their Law.

2 Maccabees 5:1–20

2 Maccabees 5:11–14

1 Maccabees 1:41–50;
2 Maccabees 6:1–6

sent him packing. In the meantime, a rumour had spread in Jerusalem that Antiochus was dead. Jason seized the opportunity to try to get rid of Menelaus. But Antiochus was in no mood for compromise. He had already been humiliated by the Romans, and he was determined to keep his grip on Judea. So he moved to Jerusalem again, and took what treasure was left in the temple, assisted this time by Menelaus himself.

Antiochus was determined to show who was in charge. His visit to Jerusalem was accompanied by great slaughter and destruction, and some of the people were taken off as slaves. But Antiochus knew that this was not just a political struggle: it was also a dispute among the Jews themselves about their own religion. This was something he neither understood nor cared for. But since it was causing trouble, he was determined that its power would have to be diminished. Circumcision, sabbath keeping, and reading the Law were all banned, and it was only a matter of time before Antiochus had arranged for the temple in Jerusalem to be given over to the worship of the Greek god Zeus. To add insult to injury, he opened the temple to the whole population of the land, including those who were not Jews. With this, Antiochus embarked on a comprehensive policy of enforced Hellenization. This had always been culturally desirable to the Seleucids, but now it was politically essential. Whether they liked it or not, the Jews would have to accept on equal terms the other racial groups with whom they lived – and the only practical way to achieve such integration was by everyone being united under the Greek religion and Greek way of life.

National pride and religious zeal

Antiochus had underestimated the strength of the Jewish resistance to all this. It was one thing to set up altars to the Greek gods – but it was to be another thing altogether to persuade the Jews to worship at them. Their resistance was fanatical, and was only strengthened by the fact that pigs (unclean animals to the Jews) were offered on

2 Maccabees 6:7–31

2 Maccabees 7

1 Maccabees 2:1–26

1 Maccabees 2:29–38

1 Maccabees 2:39–41

2 Maccabees 11:27–33

1 Maccabees 4:36–59;
2 Maccabees 10:5–8

these altars. Many pious individuals were prepared to die rather than take part in such ceremonies. Their resolution was matched only by the cruelty of Antiochus's soldiers, who on one occasion skinned and fried alive an entire family who refused to submit to this compulsory Hellenization.

Such passive resistance may have been morally praise-worthy – but it was hardly effective, and an armed resistance movement soon sprang to life. It began at the village of Modein near Lydda. A priest by the name of Mattathias was ordered to offer a sacrifice at a pagan altar. When he refused, another Jew stepped forward in his place – whereupon Mattathias killed both him and the Seleucid officer who had given the order. That was the sign for one of the most remarkable resistance movements in Jewish history.

Mattathias and his five sons fled to the hills and began a guerilla war under the leadership of Judas. He was nicknamed 'The Hammer' *(Maccabi)* , and from that the whole movement came to be called 'the Maccabean revolt'. A particularly despicable act by the Seleucid soldiers soon brought support from other sources. Many Jews had no wish to become involved in an armed struggle, and among them was a large ultra-religious group (the Hasideans) who had tried to withdraw from the conflict by going into the Judean desert. The Seleucid army went after them, and challenged them to battle on the sabbath day. Naturally, they refused, for they would not work on the sabbath. But they were mercilessly butchered. It was obvious then that passive resistance was going to be useless – and equally obvious that if all Jews continued to uphold the Law like that, there would soon be none of them left! So the Maccabees decided that they would sometimes need to be prepared to break the Law, and fight even on the sabbath.

This realistic policy attracted new supporters, including the Hasideans themselves. Under the daring leadership of Judas, the rebels had an amazing success, and it was not long before the weary Antiochus was forced to reverse his policies. The Jewish Law could be reinstated as the foundation of Jewish society, and the temple itself was restored to its rightful purpose and rededicated on 1 December 164 BC – an occasion that is still celebrated by pious Jews today, in the annual feast of Hanukkah.

The Hasideans were happy. They had won the freedom to practise their own religion and keep their own laws. But Judas's family (the Hasmoneans) wanted more than that. This limited victory had given them the taste for power, and it was not long before they had more or less thrown off Seleucid rule and established themselves as a ruling dynasty in Judea. Under their leadership, Judea enjoyed a period of relative political independence until the Roman general Pompey took the city of Jerusalem in 63 BC. But the Hasmoneans did not always remember the religious struggle that had originally brought them to power, and as a result they soon lost the support of the Hasideans.

The Hasideans disappeared altogether as a united religious

group. Some of them found the corruption and Hellenism of the Hasmonean kings intolerable, and withdrew into the Judean desert, just as they had done in the days of Antiochus. It was probably a movement of this kind that led to the foundation of the Essene community at Qumran by the shores of the Dead Sea. Other Hasideans did not go that far, but regrouped as a protest movement within mainstream Jewish society. Many scholars believe that they were connected with the rise of the Pharisees in the centuries before the birth of Jesus. The Hasmoneans, for their part, often seem to have favoured the Sadducees – another religious grouping of the time of Jesus – though they themselves were perhaps the precursors of the intensely anti-Roman zealot movement that emerged in Palestine during the first century AD.

The ruins of Qumran, a Jewish monastic community on the shores of the Dead Sea. This Essene community formed a distinct tradition within Judaism, based on the idea of withdrawing into the desert to preserve a religiously pure way of life.

The book of Daniel and the Maccabean crisis

The story of these stirring and difficult times for the Jewish people is not contained in any of the history books of the Old Testament. But the book of Daniel seems to reflect and comment on them. It is an obscure and complex book. Indeed, it is more like two books. For the first section contains a number of stories about a young Jew named Daniel who, along with his friends, faced opposition to their religion and way of life during the exile in Babylon (Daniel 1—6). But then the character of the book suddenly changes, and instead of real people in plausible real-life situations, we read about a series of grotesque visions. They relate the exploits of various mythological animals, and contain complicated speculations about the chronology of other Old Testament passages as they relate to the reigns of various unspecified kings (Daniel 7—12). In addition to this division in the book's contents, Daniel also has a linguistic division. It is written

in two languages, neither of which corresponds exactly to the two major sections of the book's message. Hebrew is used in 1:1—2:4 and 8:1—12:13, with Aramaic in 2:4—7:28. In addition to this, the vocabulary of Daniel is sprinkled with Persian, and even Greek loan-words.

What, then, does the book mean, and why was it written? The answers to these two questions are very closely connected, for our understanding of the book's message will determine when we think it was written. We must therefore examine the two aspects of this book in some detail.

Stories about Daniel and his friends

Many people will be familiar with this section of the book of Daniel. It tells of the adventures of a young Jew called Daniel. According to the story, he was taken off to exile in Babylon by

Facing page: The story in the first part of the book of Daniel concerns young Jews among the exiles in Babylon. They were given privileges within the Babylonian Court, but refused the temptation to compromise their Jewish religion and laws.

Nebuchadnezzar in the course of an otherwise unknown attack on Jerusalem in 605 BC (1:1), and he stayed there until at least after the triumph of Cyrus in 539 BC (6:28). Daniel and his friends were given the unexpected privilege of being educated in the king's own court. But this presented them with problems right from the start. For one thing, they were expected to eat food that pious Jews would never have eaten (1:3–17). They were also required to worship a great statue that Nebuchadnezzar set up. But they could not do that and still remain faithful to their own religion. As a punishment, Daniel's three friends – Shadrach, Meshach and Abednego – were thrown into a furnace to be roasted alive. But they were miraculously saved from destruction, and eventually even Nebuchadnezzar himself had to admit the great power of their God (3:1–30). Daniel found himself in a similar situation during the reign of King Darius. He was thrown into a den of lions because he insisted on worshipping his own God. But again, he was unexpectedly delivered and Darius was forced to accept the supremacy of the God of Israel (6:1–28).

Many other stories about Daniel are found in other Jewish literature. But we know nothing else about him. Some have suggested he may have been an ancient legendary figure, perhaps to be identified with the Danel mentioned in Ezekiel 14:14, whose exploits are also recorded in the texts from Ugarit. But whoever he was, his experiences were probably typical of some Jews during the

Babylonian exile. For many of the exiles, this was a time of great prosperity and new opportunities. But we have already seen that traces of a less comfortable existence can also be found in other parts of the Old Testament.

Visions of the future

The significance of these stories about Daniel and his friends begins to come out in the second part of the book. For the two sections are linked together by visions of four great empires. There is a story of how Nebuchadnezzar had a dream that he could not understand and, in the way of ancient oriental rulers, he sent for his advisers to explain it to him (2:1–13). When they failed, Daniel succeeded – and told Nebuchadnezzar that the dream was about four great empires, represented by a statue made of four different metals – gold, silver, bronze, and iron. Nebuchadnezzar's own empire was the first of them – the golden one – and the others were to be empires that would follow on in turn (2:24–45). The fourth one would be the most terrifying of all, for 'it will shatter and crush all the earlier empires'. But it will also have a weakness, for 'it will be a divided empire . . . part of the empire will be strong and part of it weak' (2:41–42).

The first of the visions in the second half of the book is very similar to that. This time, the four empires are pictured as four animals: a lion, a bear, a leopard, and a fourth animal modelled on a goat. Again the fourth one is to be even more terrifying than the others: not only did it have teeth of iron with which to crush its victims, it also had a number of horns, capable of much terror. Indeed, the horns contended among themselves, until finally ' a little horn' with 'human eyes and a mouth that was boasting proudly' sprang up and 'tore out three of the horns that were already there' (7:1–8).

The precise identity of these kingdoms has been one of the most hotly disputed issues in the whole of the Old Testament. But the book itself tells us clearly that the first empire was Nebuchadnezzar's (2:37–38), and if we start there the identity of the others becomes plain. The story of Belshazzar is probably meant to be a part of the first empire, for he is described as Nebuchadnezzar's son (5:2). But then comes a ruler of a different race, 'Darius the Mede' (5:31), and it therefore seems reasonable to suppose he was the representative of the second empire. We certainly know that the

A Persian and a Median nobleman depicted on a frieze among the ruins of Persepolis. The second and third of the four empires in the apocalyptic vision in Daniel 7 have been identified with the Medes and the Persians.

A wall painting found in the ruins of Pompeii shows Alexander the Great in battle with Darius at Issa. The fourth of Daniel's visionary empires is probably Alexander's.

power of the Medes was increasing in the years after Nebuchadnezzar's death, and they eventually joined with Cyrus the Persian in 550 BC, and thereafter were able to take over the Babylonian Empire. Cyrus's Persian Empire is the next one to feature in Daniel (6:28), and can therefore reasonably be identified with the third empire of the visions. The fourth one would then be the empire of the Greeks, set up by Alexander and later divided among his successors.

The symbolic language used of the fourth beast seems to allude clearly to the events following Alexander's death. One vision tells how ' . . . at the height of his power his horn was broken. In its place four prominent horns came up, each pointing in a different direction. Out of one of these four horns grew a little horn, whose power extended towards the south and the east and towards the Promised Land . . . It even defied the Prince of the heavenly army, stopped the daily sacrifices offered to him, and desecrated the Temple. People sinned there instead of offering the proper daily sacrifices, and true religion was thrown to the ground' (8:8–12). This is obviously a detailed description of how, at the zenith of Alexander's power, his empire was divided among four of his generals, and of how out of one of those kingdoms (the Seleucid) great persecution came upon the Jewish people, culminating in the defiling of the temple under Antiochus IV Epiphanes.

Later visions describe the precise events which led up to Antiochus's arrival in Jerusalem, including the story of his visits to Egypt, his humiliation at the hands of the Romans, and his erection of 'the Awful Horror' in the temple itself (11:21–31) – presumably the statue he set up there. The Maccabean revolt which followed is also implied here: ' . . . those who follow God will fight back . . . God's people will receive a little help, even though many who join them will do so for selfish reasons. Some of those wise leaders will be killed, but as a result of this the people will be purified' (11:32–35). The fact that the hope of purification is in the future may well indicate that the book itself was written while the war was still in progress. It is perhaps a little odd to find the brave efforts of Judas and his band of guerillas described as only 'a little help', but some have concluded from this that the book of Daniel may have been the work of a Hasidean, who was still slightly uneasy with the Maccabean approach.

As we shall see, this identification of the kingdoms of the book of Daniel makes the best sense out of other aspects of its message. But some have argued otherwise. They point out that there never was a separate Median and Persian empire – and therefore the fourth empire would not be Alexander's Greek empire, but Rome. Others have wished to identify Alexander with the fourth empire, but used the same argument to suggest that Daniel's historical sense is inadequate, and that he simply got it wrong when he seemed to infer that the Medes and the Persians were two separate kingdoms. But neither of these inferences is necessary:

● The Medes did develop their power even before the end of the Babylonian Empire. Indeed, their position began to strengthen just after the death of Nebuchadnezzar in 562 BC. They subsequently united with the Persians under Cyrus in 550 BC – after which the two combined were able to achieve their imperial ambitions. They would probably not have been able to succeed separately – and in some places Daniel seems to reflect this quite clearly (5:28; 6:8; 8:20).

● We must also recognize that Daniel was using here a traditional literary scheme to describe these four kingdoms. It was quite common at the time to depict the activity of great nations by using the symbolism of the four metals gold, silver, bronze, and iron. This literary device in effect required Daniel to have four kingdoms rather than three – whatever the facts might actually be. So he accommodated them by giving the Medes a semi-autonomous position which, had he been writing in a more straightforward style, he would probably not have done.

The book and its message

Modern interpreters of the book of Daniel are virtually unanimous in regarding it as a message of encouragement to those people who were suffering for their faith under the oppression of Antiochus IV Epiphanes. The visions of the second part of the book assure their readers that, though things might seem to be out of control, their future – indeed, the whole of history – is in the control of a loving and all-powerful God. For the final terrifying beast is not overcome by their own efforts, but by the direct activity of God himself (8:25; 12:1–13), just as the great statue mentioned earlier in the book was destroyed by a stone without any human intervention (2:31–35). That stone did not disappear, but 'grew to be a mountain that covered the whole earth' (2:35). And, after these great empires had done their worst, God himself 'will establish a kingdom that will never end. It will never be conquered, but will completely destroy all those empires, and then last for ever' (2:44).

This assurance that the world was not out of control must have meant a great

deal to the beleagured Jews in the early second century BC. But the book contains even more specific encouragement than that. For the earlier stories about Daniel himself have also obviously been selected with an eye to the circumstances that faithful Jews now had to contend with. Indeed, the prominence of Nebuchadnezzar in these stories may be intended as a conscious reference to Antiochus himself:

● The form of Nebuchadnezzar's name here is not the same as that found elsewhere in the Old Testament. But the word used in Daniel may have been intended to symbolize Antiochus. In Hebrew, as in many other ancient languages, names and words often had a numerical value, for each letter of the alphabet was also a number. And it is unlikely to be a coincidence that when the numbers represented by 'Nebuchadnezzar' are added up they come to exactly the same figure (423) as the numbers of the name 'Antiochus Epiphanes'.

● The issue of food which features so largely in the opening story of Daniel (1:3–17) was one of the crucial points at issue in the whole argument about Hellenism. Much of the opposition that sparked off the Maccabean revolt was concerned with the unwillingness of pious Jews to eat pork and other unclean foods.

● The worship of the great statue set up by Nebuchadnezzar (3:1–18) also involved the same principles as Antiochus's action in setting up an image of Zeus in the temple at Jerusalem. Indeed, in both cases it may be implied that the images were actually statues of the kings themselves. Even the story of Nebuchadnezzar's subsequent madness (4:19–33) may have been intended to be reminiscent of the commonly held belief that Antiochus himself was mad, because he thought of himself as an incarnation ('Epiphanes') of Zeus.

● Other details of the stories in the early chapters of Daniel are also similar to the conditions prevailing in the early Hellenistic age. Belshazzar, for example, falls from power because he defiled the sacred objects taken from the temple in Jerusalem (5:1–4) – just as Antiochus repeatedly robbed the temple. The people of a later age would also recognize the Jews who collaborated with the pagan Seleucids in the duplicitous figures of the spies and informers who plotted against Daniel and ensured that he was shut up in the den of lions (6:1–14).

The book in its context

The book of Daniel is unique in the Old Testament. Its detailed descriptions of visionary experiences are found nowhere else in such a concentration. But books like this were to become increasingly popular in the two centuries before the birth of Jesus, and in the New Testament the book of Revelation is of a similar type. These books have come to be known collectively as 'apocalypses', from a Greek word which means 'a revealing of secret things'. A number of special features make them readily recognizable:

● They are essentially literary works. In this respect they are quite different from the work of the earlier Old Testament prophets, who always used plain language that could be readily understood by anyone. The prophets also frequently used pithy poetic sayings that people could remember. But the apocalyptic books are complex prose compositions. They have long connected discourses, with many quotations and obscure allusions. Everyday events are usually described in a symbolic way, often with many references to real or imaginary animals and monsters.

● They also often portray God as a transcendent, remote figure. Indeed their whole emphasis is on the life of heaven rather than the everyday world of human experience. Events in this world are mentioned, but usually they are important only insofar as they are thought to reveal something about events taking place in another, spiritual world. Because of this, the apocalyptic writings often emphasize dreams, visions and communications given to people by angels. God's plan for the nations is fixed and unchanging. The Old Testament prophets often give the impression that the future course of history in some way depends on how people respond to the prophet's message. But for the apocalyptic writers nothing can ever change the predetermined course of history as it moves to a final climax.

● This final climax is also to be revealed in a distinctive way. The new age is never thought of as part of the ongoing life of this world. Instead, it is either something that exists only in a different, heavenly world – or . something that breaks into this world from outside by the direct intervention of God himself. This too is significantly different from the future hopes of most of the Old Testament prophets. For they generally expected a new age to dawn as a result of God's actions in the course of ordinary history – and it would be inaugurated by a human prince of the royal family of David, rather than by the kind of supernatural figures who appear in some apocalyptic books.

The apparent differences between apocalyptic and what seems to be the mainstream of Old Testament thinking have led many people today to think of all this as a rather eccentric and unprofitable sideline of Jewish religious thought. It has often been dismissed as the result of foreign (and therefore pagan) influences being incorporated into the Jewish faith as a result of the exile. But there is more to it than that:

● For a start, we need to remember that some of the most distinctive Christian beliefs seem to have originated among people who thought like this. It is unlikely that Jesus himself had too much sympathy for the apocalyptists of his day, but there can be no denying that the Christian understanding of life as a struggle against evil forces, together with the hope of future resurrection – not to mention the belief that history is moving towards a definite and meaningful goal – are clear developments of ideas that we first find in the writings of Jewish apocalyptists.

● We must also set the growth of apocalyptic in its own historical context. It is easy for us to criticize it from the relative comfort of our own perspective. But the hard realities for the people of Palestine at this time were quite different. The Old Testament prophets had suggested clearly enough that obedience to God would lead to prosperity, and disobedience would lead to hard times. The course of Israel's history up to the time of the Babylonian exile seemed to confirm that. But in the days following the collapse of the Persian Empire, things were quite different. With the arrival of a rampant Hellenism, new questions began to present themselves. As time went on, the way to prosperity seemed to lie more in collaboration with people like Antiochus than in continued faithfulness to the old values of the Jewish religion. Those who tried to keep the Old Testament faith alive found themselves more and more in a minority, and those who prospered often did so by neglecting their fathers' faith, or even abandoning it altogether. There were urgent questions to be answered: why did faithfulness not lead to prosperity? Why were the righteous suffering? Why did God not put an end to the power of evil forces? And to add more point to such questions, there seemed little sign of God's activity on the political and military front. He may well have raised up Cyrus in a previous generation, but in the period between Alexander the Great and Antiochus IV Epiphanes, Jerusalem had been captured at least ten times, while scores of major battles had been fought all over the country – and God seemed to be absent from the scene. In facing up to facts like these, the apocalyptists asserted that all the present difficulties were only relative. They needed to be set in the broader context of God's overall control of the world and its destiny – and in that time scale, the righteous would eventually triumph and the oppressive domination of evil would soon be relaxed.

● There is an increasing body of opinion today that would regard apocalyptic not as an alien intrusion into the religion of the Old Testament, but as a legitimate – indeed, inevitable – development of the work of the great prophets themselves. Even in the earliest of the prophets – Amos – we find the expectation of a great day of crisis, 'the Day of the Lord', when God would step into history and inaugurate a new age of justice for his people (Amos 5:18–20). The same idea was developed by others, and passages in both Isaiah (e.g. 2:1–4; 9:1–7; 11:1–9) and Micah (e.g. 4:1–5) are couched in such idealistic terms that they almost demand the apocalyptic perspective to give them some meaning. With the passage of time, these themes took on a greater importance, and when viewed from the perspective of Jewish experience during the exile and after, it is not difficult to see how these earlier expectations were transformed into an altogether grander vision. Some scholars have tried to link apocalyptic with the wisdom books of the Old Testament, through their common use of encyclopedic lists, and interest in astronomy and chronology. If this could be sustained, it would again anchor it firmly in the centre of Old Testament thinking. But it is unlikely that its roots lie there. It is more significant that the messages of Daniel are presented as in some sense a reinterpretation and new application of the messages of the earlier prophets (Daniel 9:1–2).

The end of the story

From the time of the Maccabees through to the New Testament period, Jewish history was dominated by the issues that emerged in the course of the early struggles with Hellenism. The twin issues of politics and religion were to become inextricably interwoven. The Jewish people tried to reconcile their aspirations for a society in which God would be all-important with the plain fact that their world was dominated by unbelieving pagan rulers. Within Jewish society itself, one political intrigue followed hard on the heels of another, until eventually the Romans stepped in and destroyed the temple at Jerusalem in AD 70, and by the early part of the second century AD, Jerusalem itself had become a pagan city.

In the midst of this constant turmoil many ordinary people no doubt wondered what had happened to the ideals of the Old Testament story. At the beginning of that story stood their ancestor Abraham, a man in whose life God was a living reality – a person who could be known as a friend to be loved, as well as a God to be worshipped. The same themes of God's love and his people's response had been contained in the work of the great prophets. But now, by common consent, the time of direct communication between God and his people seemed to have ended. In the closing decades of the first century BC, many groups in Jewish society were desperately searching for the word from God that would speak to them in their own situation. Some sought for meaning in the solitary silence of the desert. Others looked in vain to the lurid speculations of the apocalyptists. And yet others concluded that

At one level the Old Testament closes with the Jewish world in ruins. But it was not a world without hope. God's promises to Israel still held and many still believed them. They were a gateway to a better future.

their ancestral faith had lost its relevance, and looked for fulfilment in political opportunism.

At the end of the Old Testament story we have an unforgettable picture of God's people in turmoil. But we also have an unfading reminder of God's continuing love even for people like this. Out of their failure of nerve the author of the book of Daniel fashioned a picture of a kingdom in which God alone would be the supreme sovereign.

For Christian readers of the Old Testament, the whole of the Old Testament story needs to be seen in the light of Jesus Christ. The earliest Christians certainly viewed his life, death and resurrection as the climax without which the Old Testament story would be incomplete. They saw him as the one person in whose life God was truly king – the ideal son of David, the Messiah, of whom the prophets had dimly spoken. They identified him with 'the Son of man' to whom the authority of God's kingdom had been given in the visions of Daniel. They saw him also as the true descendant of Abraham himself. The Old Testament story began with God's promise to Abraham, that 'through you I will bless all the nations' – and for Christians, in Jesus' life, death and resurrection God did precisely that. But we have already jumped ahead – and before we can usefully assess the authority of the Old Testament for the Christian, we must pay more detailed attention to the main features of the Old Testament faith itself, in its own original context.

Section Two
The Old Testament Faith

9 The living God

Who is God?

THE QUESTION 'Who is God?' is as old as the human race itself. Philosophers and theologians, as well as countless multitudes of ordinary people down through the ages, have tried to find an answer to it. To some, God is a kind of invisible 'force' who keeps things ticking over smoothly. They may even think of him in the same terms as 'the laws of nature'. To others, God is associated with the various features of the natural world, such as the sun or moon, trees or rocks. Yet others suggest that since the most significant aspect of existence is the human personality itself, then God must be found in the depths of human experience. There are also many others who claim that to talk of God at all is quite irrelevant. Human life, the atheist believes, is complete in itself. It may not always make sense, but there is nothing more to existence than what we can feel and see and handle.

The Old Testament deals with the question in a completely different way. Its answer is clear and straightforward. Far from arguing about God's existence, it simply takes him for granted. We will look in vain to find in the Old Testament any real discussion of the case put forward by the atheist. To be sure, the Old Testament expresses many searching questions about God's reality and his activity. It contains at least one book which never mentions his name (Esther), and another which puts a serious question mark against his concern for the world and its inhabitants (Ecclesiastes). But even these books assume that God is there, and their questionings and probings are carried out in the context of a community which was well aware of the reality of the God whom it worshipped.

The actual statements made about God vary from one Old Testament book to another. New opportunities and fresh experiences of life pose new questions about many aspects of God's being and activity. In the 'Song of Moses', an ancient poem celebrating God's greatness and goodness to his people Israel, we find this rhetorical question: 'Lord, who among the gods is like you? Who is like you, wonderful in holiness? Who can work miracles and mighty acts like yours?' The implied answer, of course, is 'No one', and the poem ends with a commitment that 'You, Lord, will be king for ever and ever'. Even at this early period in Israel's experience, they were certain that their God was more powerful than any other, and so they must give him their undivided allegiance. They did not stop to ask whether other so-called 'gods' really existed. That was hardly necessary, for they knew in their own lives the reality and power of their own God.

The changing fortunes of their nation over the next 700 years, however, brought that question into clearer focus. In the face of great national disaster, some wanted to suggest that Israel's exclusive worship of just one God had contributed to their decline. But, taking their inspiration from the great prophets who had preceded them, the Old Testament history writers were convinced that this was quite wrong. Far from allowing the events of Israel's history to turn them away from the exclusive worship of their own God, they categorically denied that any other gods really could exist. The God of Israel was

Exodus 15:11

Exodus 15:18

Opposite
The Old Testament people had no doubt God existed. But they had the same questions as people everywhere and always: What is God like? How does he affect our lives?

not one God among others – not even the most powerful. He was, in the words of a later Old Testament prophet, 'the first, the last, the only God; there is no other god but me'.

Isaiah 44:6

Although the details of Old Testament beliefs about God were redrawn from time to time, the whole picture is consistent and quite clear in its main outlines. The God of whom it speaks is an all-powerful God, whose concern extends not only to the world of creation, but also to the events of history and to the lives of individual people.

Three things in particular distinguish Old Testament beliefs about God from other ideas current in the world of ancient Israel.

God is invisible

Every nation with which Israel came into contact depicted its gods and goddesses in the shape of idols. They frequently portrayed them as animals. The native religion of the land of Canaan, which was often so attractive to Israel, generally portrayed its god Baal in the form of a young bull, the symbol of life and sexual virility. The Egyptians also used this, and other symbols, to represent their gods. Right from the start, Israel was under constant pressure to do the same.

Exodus 32:1–35; Deuteronomy
9:7–21

While Moses was on Mt Sinai receiving the Law, his people were down below melting their gold jewellery to make a calf which they could worship! Idol-worship became an especially pressing problem after the once-proud empire of David and Solomon had disintegrated to become the two states of Israel and Judah. At that time, the creation of two national shrines became a political as well as a religious necessity. King Jeroboam of Israel gave religious backing to his political stance by erecting golden bulls at the northern sanctuaries of Bethel and Dan. He could see good reasons for doing this. Some of his subjects were not Israelites at all, but Canaanites, and what better way of gaining their support than by erecting religious images to represent their favourite god, Baal? And since the Israelites had long been familiar with the ark of the covenant – a portable 'holy box' giving visible form to the invisible presence of God – why could they not think of the bulls in the same way? But however sophisticated Jeroboam's reasoning, he received the unbridled condemnation of the Old Testament history writers for his actions. Whether he had intended it or not, his people worshipped these bulls as idols, and Jeroboam went down in history as the king who had 'led the people of Israel into sin'.

1 Kings 12:28–33

1 Kings 14:1–16

It was a serious mistake to create any kind of statue that could be worshipped as a god. The belief that God is invisible is firmly embedded in every strand of the Old Testament. Idols are prohibited in the second of the Ten Commandments, and the book of Isaiah contains one of the most sophisticated condemnations of idolatry to be found in any literature anywhere.

Exodus 20:4–5; Deuteronomy 5:8–9

Isaiah 44:9–20

God is not a natural force

Most of the religions of the ancient Near East were means of explaining and controlling the world of nature as it affected the lives of men and women. In Egypt, the annual flooding of the Nile was essential to the well-being of its people. Much Egyptian religion was therefore concerned to ensure that this would continue. Elsewhere in the Fertile Crescent, the fertility of fields and flocks was bound up with the appearance of the rains at the right time of year. This was the case in Canaan, the land in which the people of Israel settled after their dramatic escape from slavery in Egypt. We have already looked in some detail at the stories of the Canaanite gods and goddesses – El, Anat, Baal and others – contained in the Ras Shamra texts, found at the site of the ancient city of Ugarit (see chapter 3 above). Many features of the story are unclear, but it is obvious that the activities of the gods personify the cycle of the seasons. For instance, the story of how Baal dies, and is returned to life by the sexual attentions of his lover Anat, has close connections with the apparent death and rebirth of the life of nature that took place year by year as one season succeeded another.

The people of Israel were often tempted to worship Baal instead of their own God. For this the Old Testament condemns them roundly. By so doing they misunderstood the character of God in a fundamental way. He is above nature, not a part of nature. And though he can on occasion be described in imagery derived from natural phenomena such as light or fire, he can never be identified with the forces of the natural world.

Psalm 104:2; Ezekiel 1:27–28
Exodus 19:18; Deuteronomy 4:32, 36

God is not an abstraction

Canaanite religion centred on worship of Baal, god of fertility, sometimes portrayed as a young bull. Resheph, seen in the statue below, was a god of plague and disasters.

The Old Testament never tries to define God. In one sense this is hardly surprising, for if God is greater than the sum of human intelligence then he must be beyond description. But that has not generally prevented people from making the effort. In the early Christian centuries readers of the Bible spent much time and energy trying to decide how to describe God. Modern books of systematic theology often begin in the same way, by trying to define God's being

Greek philosophers, such as Plato, speculated about God's being. The Hebrews were interested in how to relate to God.

in abstract terms – almost as if there is some chemical or mathematical formula that, if only we can find it, will give us access to the innermost depths of his existence.

This approach has a long and venerable history going back at least to the work of the great Greek philosophers. They tried to explain God in an abstract, or metaphysical, way. To answer the question 'Who is God?' it was therefore necessary to ask a further question, 'What is God made of?' This is not the way the Old Testament thinks about God. Its writers do not try to analyze God as if he was a specimen under a microscope. The world of abstract thought is quite foreign to their concept of God. Instead of defining God metaphysically, by asking what he is made of, they defined him functionally, by exploring his relevance to human life and experience. They were asking the same questions as the modern theologian or philosopher, but they took a very different route to get to the answer.

A simple example will explain the difference. If someone asks me to describe my lover I can give two rather different answers. I can describe her appearance – height, weight, colour of hair, colour of eyes, and so on. This would certainly answer the question, and it would allow the questioner to form a mental picture of her appearance. But it would also leave many things unanswered, and if the questioner really wanted to get to know and understand my partner, it would be an altogether unsatisfactory sort of answer. A more useful answer would include some description of the kind of person that she is, illustrated with personal anecdotes to show how she has reacted to life in particular circumstances. To give that sort of answer I need never mention things like the colour of her hair and I might well refer to undefinable notions such as 'love' as the key to her personality. The philosopher would find great difficulty with all that, but most people would accept this rather emotive description of my partner as a good deal more helpful than a series of abstract observations about her external appearance.

This is how the Old Testament speaks about God. It answers the question 'Who is God?' by laying all the emphasis on the way he relates to the world and its people. It never analyzes him in an abstract, factual kind of way.

What is God like?

In one sense, the entire Old Testament is the answer to this question. As we read its books we can see how they are all concerned to describe the different ways in which God has revealed himself to his people. At the very beginning of Genesis we have a series of ancient stories that tell how God relates to the world of creation. These are followed by the long and complex accounts of his dealings with the nation of Israel from the time of Abraham in the Middle Bronze Age (2000-1500 BC) right through to the time of the Persian Empire and beyond, just a century or two before Christ. Then in addition to God's revelation through nature and history, the Old Testament contains many books showing how God relates to the

One way God has shown himself to humanity is in the world he created. The beginning of Genesis says repeatedly of the creation that 'it was good'.

more mundane circumstances of everyday life – either the corporate life of society or the personal spiritual experience of individuals. With such variety in its literature the Old Testament contains many different perspectives on the involvement of God with his people. But some themes are so common that they are obviously fundamental to the total Old Testament picture of God.

An active God   The Old Testament is distinguished from most other religious books by its great emphasis on the facts of history. The messages of the prophets, as well as the history books, declare that God is to be encountered in the varied events of Israel's national life. Other nations in the world of ancient Israel sometimes thought of their gods as being involved in political life. But what distinguishes the Old Testament is that God's activity is seen not in isolated incidents, but throughout the whole story. Indeed, it is only because God is at work there that the history has a coherent meaning at all.

Scholars of a previous generation often saw this as the main key to understanding the Old Testament. They laid all the emphasis on the notion of a 'God who acts'. This is perhaps too simplistic a way of describing the Old Testament faith, for some of its books scarcely mention God's actions in Israel's history. But there can be no doubt that this is one of its more distinctive features. Life is not just a meaningless cycle of empty existence. It has a beginning and an end, and events happen not in a haphazard sequence but as part of a great design that in turn is based on the character of God himself. And this God is encountered by his people in the ordinary events of everyday life, and not through tortuous intellectual debate.

This confident assertion dominates the Old Testament story. From the early accounts of the call of Abraham, right through to the apocalyptic visions of the book of Daniel, it is God who is in control of history. In bad times as well as good, all that happens is part of God's plan for his people. Because of this overriding conviction, the way the Old Testament writers tell the story of their people is quite different from the approach of the modern historian. A modern reader may look for historical explanations of a particular event, assuming that if history makes sense at all it is a sense that comes from within itself rather than depending on the external influence of God.

It is, of course, possible to read the Old Testament in this way, and to some extent this is what we have been doing in the first section of this book. But if we restrict our thinking to historical cause and effect we will miss an important dimension of what the Old Testament writers were saying.

● **God chooses his people** Their story begins with Abraham, a pagan merchant who leaves his homeland in Mesopotamia and heads west and south to make a new life for himself. Abraham's journey was, in fact, typical of many such journeys that were being made in the Middle Bronze Age (2000-1500 BC). People were

This standard was found in the city of Ur, on the River Euphrates, from which Abram set out in faith.

moving in all directions through the Fertile Crescent, and Abraham was certainly not alone in making the journey from east to west in search of a new way of life. But this is not important to the Old Testament. Abraham's migration was not just a symptom of demographic changes: it was an integral part of God's plan for his life. Not only was he to have a new lifestyle: he was also to become the ancestor of a great nation. Through him God would 'bless all the nations'. The driving force in Abraham's life – as in that of his successors – was the intention of a loving and all-powerful God to share his love with the whole world and its people.

Genesis 12:3

This belief found its classical expression in the story of how a group of Abraham's descendants were released from slavery in Egypt (the exodus). This is the heart of the Old Testament faith. For centuries afterwards the people of Israel looked back to this event to remind them of God's goodness and their responsibilities. Here again, it may well be that various details of the exodus story can be explained by reference to features of the geography or natural history of the area. But this is not the way the Old Testament describes it. For Israel, it was more than just a story. The dramatic escape from slavery and their settlement in the land of Canaan was due not to social or geographical factors. It was the action of God himself. Without his intervention it could never have taken place.

When later generations wanted to remind themselves of the character of their God, they turned to the exodus story. This event

The Assyrian army, seen here using a siege-engine and battering-ram to attack a city, was a formidable force. Yet the prophet Isaiah could assure the people of Jerusalem that God would protect them from Assyrian invasion.

Archaeologists believe they may have found remains of the wall Nehemiah persuaded the exiles to rebuild when they returned to Jerusalem. This leader took all his decisions in the context of prayer to God who was personally concerned for his people.

was celebrated in poetry and in song, and reported in family groups at every opportunity. It became the central focus of their faith. Not only did it remind them that God was active in history: it also gave a unique insight into the nature of that activity – and therefore into the character of God himself.

● **God's love** is a major theme that runs through the whole story. The slaves were powerless and weak. Even their leaders were uncertain of the future, and had the nation depended for its survival on human ingenuity and courage, then it would have failed. When later generations celebrated this great event, God's generous actions towards his people (his 'grace') were always in the centre of their thoughts. An ancient creed, recited as the first-fruits of later harvests were offered, puts it like this: 'We cried out for help to the Lord, the God of our ancestors. He heard us and saw our suffering, hardship and misery. By his great power and strength he rescued us from Egypt ...' This theme was given a powerful social dimension by the prophets to remind the people that God has a particular care for those who are the victims of unjust oppression. The exodus was not just a demonstration of God's powerful actions in history: it was also an experience of his love, which found its truest fulfilment when it centred on those who were past helping themselves.

Deuteronomy 26:7–8

● **God's power** over the whole of life is another dominant theme in the exodus story. God acts not only in the lives of his people to bring about their salvation: he also controls the powers of nature itself. He meets Moses in the burning bush; he sends the plagues on the Egyptians; he parts the Sea of Reeds – and later the River Jordan – to allow the escaping slaves to cross on dry land. He provides food and water in the course of the long desert journey – even flocks of birds can be sent at his command to feed those who are hungry. Nations are also in his control. Both Egyptians and Canaanites are used by God to accomplish his purposes. Sometimes they become instruments of judgment, at others of blessing – but always as part of God's loving purpose for his people.

Exodus 3:1–10

Exodus 7:14 — 11:9

Exodus 14:1–31; Joshua 3:1–17

Exodus 15:22 — 17:7

● **God's justice** is a prominent element in the story of the exodus. At the heart of the story we find the Old Testament Law, the *Torah*. It is significant that this is an integral part of the story of God's actions on behalf of his people. At the heart of the Old Testament faith is the belief that God acts in accordance with his own clearly defined standards of justice – never in an arbitrary or unpredictable fashion. The core of God's relationship with his people is morality and when a person encounters God it is always in the context of moral challenge. When Isaiah had a vision of God in the temple, it was not the other-worldly, supernatural aspects of the experience that impressed him: his first response was to confess his own

Isaiah 6:1–5 inadequacy in the face of the great moral purity of God. When God reveals himself, whether in temple or in exodus, his people must face up to the demands of his justice.

● **Finding God in later history** These three features of God's activity dominate the rest of the Old Testament story. It was in the process of trying to relate God's love, power and justice that the prophets hammered out some of the most distinctive elements of the Old Testament faith. As time went on, it became increasingly clear that Israel's fortunes were closely connected to the international power politics of the day. Israel and Judah were just pawns in the strategic manoeuvres of the two superpowers based in Egypt and Mesopotamia who vied with each other for domination of the Fertile Crescent. It often seemed as if these powers were in control of things, not God. What then was the value of God's promises – not only his promise to Abraham and his mighty acts in the exodus, but his bold assurance to David that 'I will make you as famous as the greatest leaders in the world ... You will always have descendants and

2 Samuel 7: 8–16 I will make your kingdom last for ever. Your dynasty will never end'?

Viewed in this light, the facts of history raised many awkward questions. If Israel had been chosen by God, should they not be triumphant in all their battles? And if God was in control of things, why should other nations be able to get the upper hand? The prophets had a clear answer to these questions. The fact that God had revealed himself to Israel, showing his love in so many ways, imposed great responsibilities. As Israel were faithful to their calling, so they would prosper. But when they were unfaithful, then they needed to return and ask God's forgiveness. The misfortunes they suffered were a reminder of that. This is how the author of the book of Judges assessed Israel's early history. It was a lesson that the prophets hammered home in many a crisis of the nation's later life.

The people often misunderstood the nature of God's involvement in their history. They imagined that his dealings with them were a sign that they were God's favourites. But the prophets knew that God's purposes were never so restricted. His intention was firm and

Following pages
Much like nomadic peoples today, the Israelites retained a sense of being together before God – the group or the nation mattered every bit as much as each individual person.

clear: the salvation of all peoples, as he promised to Abraham. And though Israel had been the special recipient of God's love, and had witnessed his great acts of power, both love and power could only operate within the framework of God's justice.

This conviction often brought the prophets into direct conflict

with the politicians of their day. And they did not always take the same side. Isaiah, for example, could advise the king in Jerusalem that God would protect his city and all would be well in the face of an Assyrian invasion. But a few generations later, Jeremiah said exactly the opposite. What united them was the knowledge that history was in God's control, and he was ordering things in accordance with his own absolute standards. Those who arrogantly set themselves up against him – whether Assyria or Judah herself – would be judged. And when the Babylonians took the king of Judah off into exile and later destroyed the city of Jerusalem, that was as much the work of God as the exodus itself had been.

Many people found that hard to understand. After all, their entire history seemed to suggest that God was on their side. And if he was, how could he allow a catastrophe such as the exile to befall them? It was at this time that Israel's historians compiled the story of their nation as we now have it in the Old Testament. The Deuteronomistic History, stretching from Deuteronomy to 2 Kings, retold the familiar stories in an effort to explain why God had apparently deserted his people. Following the prophets, it declares that Israel had been disobedient. They had failed in their God-given responsibilities, and had suffered the inevitable consequences. Others compiled the story of Israel's earlier experiences, from creation to the exodus. And they too had a message for their people: disobedience had been a part of human life from the very beginning. But it was always balanced by God's grace and forgiveness. God's justice and God's love could not be separated. And whereas the Deuteronomistic History had a sad and depressing tale to tell, the message from Genesis to Numbers was more encouraging, assuring those in exile that God's love would ultimately triumph.

But what about God's power? Had not the final days of Judah been in effect a battle not between two armies but between two gods – and had not the gods of Babylon won? Where did the God of Israel stand in relation to the apparent power of other gods? This question had been faced in a practical way right from the earliest days, when the tribes had decided to worship only one God. But they had not denied that other gods might exist. Indeed, the eagerness with which they often worshipped Baal suggests that some of them were not at all convinced that their own God was all-powerful.

Some of the earlier psalms, as well as prophetic messages from the time of Amos, had hinted that God was in control of the lives of people everywhere, and not of only Israel's destiny. But with the exile the question had become ever more urgent. And it was given a very clear answer in some of the most remarkable passages anywhere in the Old Testament. In a series of prophetic messages, the God of Israel is declared to be the God of the whole world. He is all-powerful, and those who worship other gods are not only misguided but stupid. Far from being a sign of God's defeat, the exile had itself been God's punishment for his people. He had used the Babylonians to do his will, but they too had been punished for their excessive violence. God's power was in no way diminished, and

Isaiah 31:4–5
Jeremiah 7:1–15

Jeremiah 24

Joshua 24:1–28

Psalm 47
Amos 1:3 — 2:5

Isaiah 44:1–20

Isaiah 47:1–15

Isaiah 45:1–4

he would raise up a new deliverer for his people – this time, not a Moses from among them, but Cyrus, the emperor of Persia. The future would be even greater than the past had been, as God would move in a new way to fulfil the original intention of his promise to Abraham. God's servant, through whom this would be accomplished, would bring blessing to Israel, but he would also be 'a light

Isaiah 49:6

to the nations – so that all the world may be saved'.

A personal God

The fact that God reveals his character in the great sweep of history may lead us to wonder if he was not just a personification of 'fate', or even of 'history' itself. Many gods and goddesses of the ancient world were personifications of various aspects of the world of nature. Could it not be that the God of the Old Testament was just a personification of Israel's history?

Things are not quite as simple as that. To the Canaanites, for instance, the world of nature seemed to go its own way regardless of human interest, and there was very little anyone could do to change things. The best one could hope for was to escape the most vindictive aspects of nature by avoiding too much personal involvement with the gods who control it. The Old Testament accepts that God is to be given the honour that is due to him, and recognizes that his ways are often beyond human understanding. But it also emphasizes that he does not relate to people in a purely mechanical way. Quite the opposite. He is intimately interested in both the world and its inhabitants, not remote from people and their needs. All the great events of the Old Testament stress that God does not act in a capricious, unpredictable way. He is not concerned to manipulate events for his own advantage. He is concerned for people and their good. Even more striking is the way he expresses his love. For it is not the patronizing care of a moralist who knows what is best, and is prepared to ride roughshod over human need in order to achieve his ends. Some of the most striking, and unexpected, stories in the Old Testament depict God entering into discussion with his people, and

Genesis 18:16–33; Amos 7:1–6

even changing his mind as a result. We may find all this a little difficult to understand. But it explains why morality and justice are so fundamental to the Old Testament view of God. For it is in the context of personal relationships that such qualities are most important.

● **The individual and society** How then does God relate to his people? There is no doubt that the Old Testament lays much emphasis on the fact that he relates to Israel as a nation. When the tribes escaping from Egypt arrived at Mt Sinai, it was only Moses who went up the mountain to receive God's laws. In that sense, it was only one person who had a direct encounter with God himself. Yet what happened there was not something private and personal: it was a representative experience in which all the people were included. The idea that one person could represent a whole nation in this way was widely held in the ancient world, where kings could be the very embodiment of their nation. The term 'corporate personality' is sometimes used to describe this sense of national solidarity, though it is not a term used by the Old Testament itself and its importance has often been exaggerated.

But it does draw attention to an aspect of Old Testament thinking that is sometimes difficult for modern Western people to grasp. Most of us are accustomed to thinking in terms of the work of an individual – and when we talk of 'society', we mean just the sum total of individuals living in a particular time and place. The Old Testament knows nothing of this kind of narrow individualism. The family, the village, the tribe and the nation were all of crucial importance. A person found fulfilment in life as he or she was in the proper relationship with others. Both happiness and misery were shared with other people, and a sense of social solidarity runs deep in the Old Testament, just as it does in many Asian cultures today. We find this most strikingly in the story of Achan, whose entire tribe was implicated in the sin of just one man. There were clearly risks involved in being closely identified with others! But compared to the fear of being alone, such risks were very small. To have no friends, and to be an outcast, was the final indignity that an Israelite could suffer, for life only found its fullest meaning when a person was a part of society.

Joshua 7:1–26

Jeremiah 15:17; Psalm 102:6–7

It was once fashionable to suppose that people of Old Testament times could see no meaning or purpose in life except as part of a large social unit. But this is to press the idea of corporate personality to a logical conclusion that is never drawn in the Old Testament itself. We would be quite mistaken to imagine that God only deals with people in large numbers. The book of Psalms is an anthology of materials used in the worship of God over generations, and it contains many examples of prayers and hymns which show just how much worshippers in ancient Israel felt that God was personally interested in the details of their own everyday life. The prophets also stressed the importance of individual commitment to the God who revealed himself through the events of their national heritage.

The same theme is prominent in many of the Old Testament's best-known stories. God is personally concerned for the welfare of Abraham and his wife when they find themselves in a hostile land. Later, he takes care of Joseph, saving him first from the jealousy of his brothers and then from the plots of the Egyptians. Nor is his personal interest restricted only to members of the nation of Israel. It extends to the boy Ishmael who, with his mother Hagar, is expelled from Abraham's family circle. Much later in the Old Testament, God's pity covers not only the innocent children of the great city of Nineveh but even the suffering animals in it.

Genesis 12:10–20

Genesis 37:39–41

Genesis 21:9–21

Jonah 4:11

● **Describing God** The importance of recognizing God as a person comes out clearly in much of the imagery that the Old Testament uses to describe him. The messages of the prophet Hosea apply the terminology of personal relationships to God and his people in a particularly sensitive way. God is a loving father to his people, who protected them and directed their footsteps from the very beginning of their national history. He not only guided them, he also cared for them: 'I drew them to me with affection and love. I

Opposite
The love of God for Israel is sometimes likened to a parent's love for a child.

Hosea 11:4

picked them up and held them to my cheek; I bent down to them and fed them.' According to the book of Exodus, this was the message that Moses had given to the pharaoh of Egypt when he reminded him that Israel was God's 'first-born son. I told you to let my son go, so

Exodus 4:22

that he might worship me ...' And centuries later, Isaiah depicts God as a broken-hearted father whose children have rejected his

Isaiah 1:2

guidance.

Hosea 2:14–23; Jeremiah 31:32

At other times God can be depicted as the husband of his people. After the fall of Jerusalem Ezekiel portrays him as a generous stepfather who had rescued the city and its people from certain

Ezekiel 16:3–8

death. Other prophets of the same generation boldly applied the

Isaiah 49:15; 66:13

imagery of motherhood to God's love for his people.

In spite of statements such as these, many people feel that the Old Testament picture of God is unsatisfactory and primitive, and especially that it is radically different from the Christian New Testament. This is a misconception of the teaching of both parts of the Christian Bible. God's love for his people and his concern for them in the dangers and difficulties of life was as fundamental to the Old Testament faith as it is to the life and teaching of Jesus.

At the same time, we must not hide the distinctive elements of the Old Testament picture of God. For although it occasionally describes God in terms of close personal and family relationships, it more often portrays him as the ruler, master and lord of his people. He is their sovereign, often in a very literal way. In some early narratives, God leads his people into battle as their army commander ('the Lord of hosts'), his invisible presence symbolized by the ark of

1 Samuel 4:1–4; Psalm 24

the covenant. And though from the time of Saul onwards a human king plays a leading role in the affairs of the people, there is still a considerable emphasis on the fact that God himself is Israel's only true king. Indeed, the Old Testament historians pass their verdict on the various kings of Israel and Judah mainly in relation to whether they have been prepared to recognize the greater kingship of God himself.

Even when the idea of kingship is not explicitly mentioned, much of the imagery used in speaking of God comes from such a background. The well-known Psalm 23 refers to God as the 'shepherd' of his people. To us this suggests a different background of thought. But in the ancient world the king was often referred to as the 'shepherd', and this is almost certainly what the psalmist had in mind.

● **The king and his people** It was perfectly natural for the Old Testament writers to think of God as their king. In rescuing the slaves from Egypt, God had done for them what any good king would do for his people. We have already noted in chapter 2 some striking similarities between the covenant formulations of the Old Testament and the way in which a subject nation would define its relationship to a greater power that had delivered it from an enemy. Israel's allegiance to God as king was the grateful obedience of those who have been set free, not the fear of those who have been defeated.

If God is the king, then human relationships with him must

Right from the time when he rescued Israel from Egypt, God acted towards his people as a good king to his subjects.

Psalm 113:1; 123:2

Psalm 19:9

naturally be described in terms of obedience and service. God's people are his 'servants', and their attitude towards him is often described as 'fear'. Sometimes the 'fear of the Lord' is just a name for religious worship. But more often it indicates an attitude of mind which recognizes the difference between God and people. We might talk of 'reverence' or 'honour' rather than 'fear', and this is how many modern versions of the Old Testament translate the word. To fear God in this sense has little connection with popular pictures of an angry God before whom men and women can only cower in insignificance. It is rather a matter of giving God his appropriate place. The importance of recognizing that God is so much greater than men and women is a common Old Testament theme. Even the prophets, who claim to have access to God's innermost secrets and to be on close personal terms with God, nevertheless display a strong sense of awe and reverence as they stand in his presence and hear his word.

No doubt there are many reasons why the Old Testament most often describes God in terms of the king/subject or master/slave imagery. But there was one particularly strong reason for avoiding the language of the family. For much of the Old Testament story Israel was resisting the inroads of Canaanite religion, which laid great stress on the physical relationships of its deities. Gods and goddesses could be portrayed as fathers, sons, mothers, and lovers. They were all related in some way or another, and physical characteristics were an important part of such relationships. The key to unlock life's mysteries could be found in the sexual relationships of gods and goddesses. There was always a strong temptation for

Hosea 2:16

Israel to think of their own God like this. But to talk exclusively of God as 'father' or 'husband' in that context could have suggested little more than a merely physical relationship. It is not surprising therefore that, with one or two striking exceptions, most of the references to God as 'father' are found in the later Old Testament books, coming from an age when the battles with Canaanite religion had receded into the past.

We must remember that all these images are attempts to describe a person who is essentially indescribable. They help to portray some of his characteristics but must all be understood by reference to their broader context. Emphasizing some aspects of the picture at the expense of others leads to distortions. By concentrating on the descriptions of God as a father or husband and his people as children or wife it is easy to miss the sense of reverence and wonder that pervades the Old Testament. But to dwell exclusively on the picture of God as a master and his people as servants is just as misleading if it suggests that he is a harsh, cruel and unpredictable tyrant. The Old Testament recognizes that God is different from men and women. But it declares that the gap between God's perfect being and the imperfect world of humanity is bridged by God's loving actions in saving and blessing. And these actions find their ultimate meaning in the fact that God is not just a force or an abstract will, but a person – with all that that involves.

God's name

The fact that God is a person comes out in the way the Old Testament emphasizes his name. Only people have names, and in the ancient world a person's name was more than just a label.

● A person's name established a person's identity, and revealed their character. So, for example, in the early stories of the book of Genesis, Eve (3:20), Cain (4:1), and Noah (5:29) are all given names that indicate something about their personalities. Later, all twelve ancestors of the Israelite tribes have names that reflect either the nature of the recipients or the experiences of their parents (Genesis 29:31–30:24).

● Knowing a person's name, or giving a name to someone, is often a way of gaining authority over that person. God himself gives the stars their names because he is their Creator (Psalm 147:4). He gives Israel their name, and in doing so asserts his authority over them (Isaiah 43:1). Similarly, when Jacob wrestles with an unknown deity, he wants to know his name so that he may establish a proper relationship with him (Genesis 32:29–30). To know the name of a god could therefore be very important, for a god's name gave the worshipper access to his power. By calling a god's name, his presence could be assured.

The Old Testament attitude to God's name is distinctive. Using God's name in this semi-magical way is expressly forbidden in the Ten Commandments (Exodus 20:7). God's

name is not something to be discovered and manipulated by men and women: it is something that God himself reveals in his love to his own people.

What is God's name?

Because of this, there is an extraordinary reverence for God's name throughout the Old Testament. The reticence to mention the name of God is so widespread that we do not even know for certain how his personal name was pronounced. Hebrew has no vowels, and this name was written down as YHWH. Vowel sounds are needed to pronounce it, of course, but we do not know precisely which sounds were used. When the Old Testament was written down in its present form, Jewish religious teachers regarded the personal name of God as too sacred to say. Whenever they found it they would substitute the Hebrew word *Adonai*, which means 'my lord'. In this way, the vowels of *Adonai* came to be pronounced with the consonants of God's name YHWH, to produce something like the English term 'Jehovah'. Nowadays it is customary to write this name as 'Yahweh', and this is the form we have used here.

It is often supposed that this avoidance of God's personal name was a relatively late development in Judaism. But we can find traces of it throughout the Old Testament. For example, in the stories of Joseph, God's name Yahweh is never found on the lips of non-Israelites (Genesis 37–50), and there is a whole section of the book of Psalms which avoids it (Psalms 42–83). Other parts of the Old Testament use the expression 'the Name', instead of speaking directly of God himself (for example Psalm 5:11; 7:17; 9:2, 10; 18:49) This usage is taken up in a particularly constructive way in Deuteronomy, where it is God's 'Name' that is bestowed on the temple in Jerusalem to signify God's presence and blessing there (Deuteronomy 12:11; 14:23, and so on). By having 'the Name', and not Yahweh himself, dwell in the temple, the Old Testament avoids the idea that God was restricted to just one locality, and yet still assures the people that he could be found in the context of worship at Jerusalem.

What does Yahweh mean?

From a purely linguistic point of view, a number of suggestions can be made. The word Yahweh could, for example, be related to an Arabic word meaning 'blow'. Some scholars have argued from this that Yahweh was therefore originally the name of a storm god. Others have suggested that the clue to its meaning is to be found in a shortened form of the name, Ya'u, which is known in Babylon and other parts of the ancient world. Or perhaps it was originally just a shout of excitement used in the context of religious worship, which was subsequently taken as a proper name.

Suggestions such as these are of little use for our purposes here. Explaining where a name comes from is not the same as explaining what it means. And the Old Testament gives a quite distinctive meaning to it. When Moses asks on whose authority he is to go and demand the release of the slaves from Egypt, he is told: 'I am who I am. This is what you must say to them: "The one who is called I AM has sent me to you"' (Exodus 3:14). Even this is not absolutely clear. Several centuries later, when the Old Testament was translated into Greek (the *Septuagint*), this phrase was taken as an indication of God's eternal existence, along the lines of Greek philosophical speculation about God. But it is obvious in the context that, although the name Yahweh is related to the Hebrew verb 'to be', all the emphasis is on God's activity rather than on his existence as such. It is, like the rest of the Old Testament story, a declaration that God is characterized by his actions. His name indicated his nature, and with it came the assurance to the slaves in Egypt that God was active on their behalf. He was the Lord of time itself, and what he had done in the past, he was doing in the present – and would continue to do in the future.

Descriptions of God

As well as the many words, names and titles used for God in the Old Testament, the writers employ numerous evocative images to describe him. These are sometimes missed in the newer translations. Some of the best known are:

Revised Standard Version	Key Reference	Good News Bible
Rock	Deuteronomy 32:4	Mighty defender
Shepherd	Psalm 23:1	Shepherd
Shield	Psalm 18:2	Shield, or sometimes protector
Light	Psalm 27:1	Light
Strength	Psalm 28:7	...protects me
Refuge	Psalm 46:1	Shelter
Sun	Psalm 84:11	Glorious king
Father	Psalm 89:26	Father
Help	Psalm 115:9	Help
Shade	Psalm 121:5	...protects
Song	Isaiah 12:2	(doesn't translate)
Redeemer	Isaiah 41:14	The one who saves you
Husband	Isaiah 54:5	Husband
Fountain	Jeremiah 2:13	Spring
Dew	Hosea 14:5	Rain

This detail from an ancient scroll of Isaiah shows important alterations, from 'adonai' to 'Yahweh' in one case and from 'Yahweh' to 'adonai' in the other. Hebrews often used the title 'adonai', 'my lord', in place of the holy name of God.

Other names for God

According to Exodus 6:3, Abraham and the other patriarchs did not know God by his personal name Yahweh. Instead, they worshipped a God called El Shaddai (Genesis 17:1). But scholars have noted that in the Old Testament the name Yahweh not only appears right from the beginning of the story, but is expressly given to Abraham as the name of the God who led him out of Mesopotamia (Genesis 15:7). In addition, the patriarchs are often said to have worshipped a deity who is called 'the God of the ancestors'.

These differences can be explained by reference to the theory that the first five books of the Old Testament consist of a number of different sources, one of them using the name Yahweh from the very beginning, and another not introducing it until the time of Moses. On this, see the discussion in chapter 7 above

But others have suggested that the matter is not quite as straightforward. They draw attention to four features in particular:

● The research of Albrecht Alt has shown that the worship of gods identified as 'the god of my father' (that is 'the god of the ancestors') was widespread among many tribes in the ancient world.

● We also know that the name 'El' was widely used as a name for local gods. In Canaan itself, the Ras Shamra texts depict El as the father of the gods and head of the pantheon at Ugarit.

● Moses apparently knew nothing of the worship of Yahweh until his meeting with Jethro in the desert of Midian. It was certainly in that area that Moses had his experience at the burning bush (Exodus 3:1–6). It is notable that after the exodus from

Egypt Jethro reappears in the story and offers a sacrifice to Yahweh (Exodus 18:10–12).

● When Joshua and his people enter into a solemn agreement to worship only Yahweh, he suggests that both in Mesopotamia and in Egypt their ancestors had worshipped other (pagan) gods (Joshua 24:14–15).

There are two main ways of explaining these apparently diverse facts:

● Some (notably O. Eissfeldt and R. de Vaux) argue that worship of El and worship of Yahweh were originally quite distinct and separate. El was identified by the patriarchs with the high god of Canaan, of whom we know from other sources, and Yahweh was originally the mountain god of the Kenites, whose worship was taken over and reformed by Moses on the basis of the exodus events. Then eventually, either in the days of the judges or in the later monarchy, the worship of Yahweh became dominant and took over its more primitive predecessor.

● Professor F. M. Cross takes a completely different line, arguing that all these names (and others) used for God by the patriarchs referred to the one deity later called Yahweh. To speak of 'the god of the ancestors' was, in his view, just another way of referring to 'El', and 'Yahweh' was the way to address this one God in the context of worship.

Cross's position is certainly closer to the theological stance of the Old Testament itself. As we shall see in a later chapter, the Old Testament was never averse to taking over imagery and ideas from other religious contexts if it could be useful in describing Yahweh and his activities. The patriarchs may well have used traditional ideas from their cultural environment when thinking and speaking about their own experiences of God. But that did not diminish Yahweh's power. It even enhanced it, for it showed that Yahweh was able to do all that the Canaanite El was supposed to do, and much more besides. Whether they knew it or not, it was none other than the God of the exodus – Yahweh himself – who had been the guiding force in their lives from the very beginning.

A hidden God

The Old Testament is dominated by the conviction that God's character is revealed most fully in his dealings with his people, both in history and in personal experience. It is in the common round of everyday life that people meet God. The fact that God is related to the world in which we all live, rather than being relegated to some esoteric, 'heavenly' world, is one of the great strengths of the Old Testament faith. But to many modern people it also seems to be one of its greatest weaknesses. For the plain fact is that we do not normally see events such as the exodus taking place all around us. Nor do many of us have experiences similar to that of Isaiah when he stood in awe before God's glory in the temple. So how realistic and relevant is the Old Testament's picture of God?

Isaiah 6:1–7

It is important for us to observe here that the triumphalist view of God's activity in history and personal experience is by no means the only element in the Old Testament picture of God. To many people in the Old Testament world, God often seemed to be hidden. At the very time when they needed his assistance to make sense of life they found it most difficult to find traces of his activity. The facts of history did not always portray the inevitable progress of an all-powerful God. Nor did the facts of everyday life always give Israel the assurance that a living and personal God stood alongside them. There were times when life seemed to be quite the opposite, with evil and suffering as the dominating influences of human existence. How then did God relate to this darker side of life? Was he a God for bad days as well as for good?

The Old Testament writers held a realistic view of life, with all its suffering and darkness as well as light. God carried his people through some bleak years.

The writer of the Book of Job contrasted hope in the natural world – that new growth might come from the stump of a tree – to despair in his personal world. God seemed to have gone for ever.

Psalm 23:4

Psalm 44

The Old Testament takes full account of the fact that there are times when it seems that God, far from being powerful and active, is lost in the depths of human pessimism and despair. This honest recognition of God's apparent absence from the scene is most striking in the book of Psalms. Here we have a series of fascinating glimpses into the life of a nation at prayer. Many psalms are great celebrations of joy and optimism, telling the people of God's mighty works and great love for them. These psalms were no doubt used at the great religious festivals, as Israel looked back on the great events of her history and traced God's goodness in them. But for every jubilant psalm there are two or three others in which the worshippers express not joy but sorrow and dismay. Even those with a quiet confidence in God often recognize that he has to be sought in times of 'deepest darkness'. Others complain that life's realities seem inconsistent with the reports of God's mighty deeds in the past.

We have already looked at Hermann Gunkel's classification of the psalms into five main types (see chapter 4 above). It is significant that only two of these five categories celebrate the triumphs of God in an unreserved way. The other three are all concerned to varying degrees with the fact that God's activity and presence were not always obvious. And when we look closely at the psalms, there are far more of the individual songs of lament than of any other type. Other poems included in this collection express the feelings of the whole nation, as it tried to come to terms with the difference between the great promises that God had made and the less thrilling realities of ordinary life. There is a strong thread of moral and religious realism running through the whole fabric of the Old Testament. God's apparent absence from the world and from human experience is one of its major themes.

● **Personal alienation** This is prominent even in the most striking Old Testament stories. Though Abraham is indeed depicted as a man of great faith who 'put his trust in the Lord', he also finds God's intentions so puzzling and so difficult to reconcile with what he believes about God's character that he is even found arguing with God himself. Moses' experience is quite similar. He had a closer and more direct experience of God than any other Old Testament character, for 'the Lord would speak with Moses face to face, just as a man speaks with a friend'. But at the same time, Moses' life was full of questions and complaints, as he tried to reconcile God's promises with what he saw going on around him.

Nor are the prophets exempt from feelings of doubt and uncertainty about God's intentions. Take Elijah, for example. He won a great and famous victory in the name of God, as the prophets of Baal were put to flight and their specious beliefs were repudiated. But almost immediately after that, it seemed as if God had deserted him, and Elijah suffered an extraordinary attack of uncertainty and doubt about the reality of God's power. And for Jeremiah, doubt and uncertainty were a major influence in his life. On the one hand, God had explicitly told him, 'I chose you before I gave you life, and before you were born I selected you to be a prophet to the nations'. In addition, God had assured him of his continuing love and protection. And yet on the other hand, God seemed singularly reluctant to back him up. A quarter of a century after Jeremiah had first announced the doom of Jerusalem, nothing had happened except that a new mood of national optimism and self-confidence had swept over the city. Jeremiah had to question God's ways: 'Why are wicked men so prosperous? Why do dishonest men succeed?' At another time he even wondered why God allowed him to be born at all: 'Was it only to have trouble and sorrow, to end my life in disgrace?' Of course, the prophet knew that God had indeed spoken to him, but that did not make it any easier to come to terms with God's apparent remoteness. The passages in which Jeremiah addresses his complaints to God (the 'Confessions') are remarkable for their frankness, and show the depths of despair and questioning to which even those with a personal knowledge of God in their lives can be driven.

Margin references:
Genesis 15:6
Genesis 18:16–33
Exodus 33:11
Exodus 5:22–23
1 Kings 18:1–40
1 Kings 19:1–18
Jeremiah 1:4
Jeremiah 12:1
Jeremiah 20:18
Jeremiah 11:18–23; 12:1–6; 15:10–21; 17:14–18; 18:18–23; 20:7–18

Wrestling with a hidden God

The apparent hiddenness of God is a major theme of one of the great masterpieces of the Old Testament: the book of Job. The book itself begins with an idyllic description of the life of its hero. He was a successful man in every respect, surrounded not only by the material trappings of prosperity but also by an affectionate family group. He was also exceedingly upright and religious.

His lifestyle and disposition both show him as a paradigm of virtue. But then things change. God, depicted here as the president of a heavenly court, receives a formal request from the prosecutor (Satan) who suggests that Job is righteous only because he finds that it pays handsome dividends. And so the prosecutor is given permission to put him to the test to ascertain the value of his faith. One calamity after another comes upon Job and his family, until he is reduced to misery and poverty – the exact opposite of what he was at the beginning (Job 1:1–2:10).

At this point, the ancient story is left behind. The author of Job was not just a storyteller. We saw in an earlier chapter that his book belongs to the 'wisdom' literature of the Old Testament, and its main concern was to answer the questions that were raised by the story. It was a simple and well-known problem: If God rules the world, why do good people suffer so much? Wisdom teachers from Babylon to Egypt and beyond had wrestled with

this problem long before the author of Job. But two things gave it special urgency in Israel: Israel believed that God was active in controlling the life of this world; and Israel also believed that God acted in accordance with strict concepts of morality.

The standard answer to the problem was easy, and is in fact represented in some other wisdom books, notably Proverbs: those who were prosperous must be good, and those who suffered must be evil. But it is often difficult to reconcile that with the facts, especially in the case of a person like Job. Of course, his friends could not see that. For although they sympathized with Job

The Jews exiled in Babylon longed to return home. But during this time of heartache they learned new truths about God's relationship with them wherever they were.

in his suffering they were quite sure that, whatever he thought, he must have sinned against God and brought his suffering on himself. Job knew he had not done so, and he was convinced that the easy theology of his friends was quite misguided. Not that this made it any easier for him to see God at work in his own life: 'I have searched in the east, but God is not there; I have not found him when I searched in the west.' But he never abandoned his certainty that, though God may be hidden for a time, he is still there: 'God has been at work in the north and the south', and it is just that 'I have not seen him' (23:8–9). Indeed, it was worse than just

being blind to God's purpose, for it was God's very hiddenness that concerned Job most of all: 'It is God, not the dark, that makes me afraid ...'(23:17).

The meaningless circle of Job's existence is eventually broken when, after more conventional wisdom from his friends, God himself confronts the sufferer in a great storm (38:1–41:34). God reminds Job of his own greatness and might by drawing his attention to the complexity of the world and its workings. In the face of this, Job can place his own questions in their proper perspective: 'I know, Lord, that you are all-powerful; that you can do everything you want' (42:1).

But what is the answer to the main question? Certainly there is no intellectual discussion here of the presence and power of evil in the world. But it is typical of the Old Testament that even a topic such as this should not be dealt with in an abstract, philosophical way. God is known to men and women not in flights of fancy but in the reality of divine encounter. Job had appealed to God to answer him – and he did. Not in a way that he might have expected, but in a way that ultimately reminded him that, however difficult it might be to understand life's bitterest experiences, and however hard it might be to perceive God at work, nevertheless he was there. And to those who were prepared to seek him out – unlike the friends who looked for easy answers – God would ultimately reveal himself.

Another Old Testament book which tackles similar questions is Ecclesiastes. But its answer is very different. Indeed, it lays so much emphasis on God's apparent absence from the world that the Jewish rabbis were reluctant to accept it as a part of scripture. Like Job, this book has no mention of the great events of Israel's history in which God's hand had so clearly been seen. But unlike Job, it has no clear conviction that God's workings can be seen anywhere in the world at all. Job never actually loses sight of God, even if only in the negative sense that he blames God for his misfortune. But for Ecclesiastes, life is essentially meaningless in itself. That is not to say that life need be miserable and uninteresting. Ecclesiastes does not actually deny that God exists, for all life's goods come from him (2:24–26; 3:13; 8:15). But the whole book is shot through with a kind of practical atheism. Whether or not God exists is really irrelevant, for the author does not see much evidence of his involvement in the practical issues of everyday living. The most anyone can do is to try to enjoy what they have while they are here to enjoy it.

This might seem a very negative attitude to take towards God. But it is more faithful to human experience than the fanciful and unsatisfying theology of Job's friends. The fact is that human life cannot be reduced to simple formulas. Nor can faith in God. Not only Ecclesiastes but the whole of the Old Testament bears witness to the fact that a faith which comes too easily has a certain lack of reality. The experience of honest and searching doubt is often the prelude to a deeper and more satisfying understanding of God and his ways and not to a loss of faith.

● **National despair** It was not only individuals who often had to look hard to find God at work in their lives. The whole Jewish nation found itself in a similar crisis after the fall of Jerusalem to the Babylonian king Nebuchadnezzar in 586 BC. A once-proud nation had been brought to its knees by events that shattered all their expectations of God. Looking to the past, they could recall God's gracious actions through the great heroes of their nation. They could remind themselves of God's unfailing promises to previous generations. But what value could be placed on such a glorious past in the light of the harsh realities of exile in a strange land? The promises had apparently failed, and evidence of God's involvement with his people was hard to find.

Much of the Old Testament story was hammered into shape on the anvil of this experience. Its pages often reflect the deeply felt anguish of those who survived this great tragedy, as they asked the inevitable question: Why should this have happened in a world controlled by God? In response to that the Deuteronomistic History asserted quite plainly that national disgrace was the outcome of national sin. But in looking to the past it did not give a simplistic explanation of the present. For although it emphasized God's great goodness to his people in events such as the exodus, or the establishment of David's throne in Jerusalem, it also reminded them that there had been many a crisis in the past too. The exodus itself had been God's answer to a grave crisis faced by the enslaved tribes in Egypt. God can hardly have seemed very real to them in Egypt – but one of the lessons of history was that God's mighty power had often burst in to change the lives of those who were least expecting it.

There could be no doubt that the exiles were suffering as a result of their nation's disobedience. A God whose character was defined in terms of justice and moral standards could not easily turn a blind eye to the rotten state of Jewish society. But though it might seem as if the stringency of God's justice was greater than the power of his love, nevertheless he would still be faithful to his promises and in the end would bring blessing to his people.

This was the view that finally triumphed and transformed the dead husks of exile into the seed corn of new life. Just as in the experience of the prophets and of people such as Job, so here there is no real effort to explain why God seemed to be hidden from his people. But there is a clear practical message for those who found it difficult to see God at work in their lives. As men and women contemplated the suffering and injustice of their present existence, they were forced to confess that God really is inscrutable in his ways. Yet alongside this they could place the evidence of his mighty acts in history and in personal experience, both of which gave the assurance that though God may be hidden by the gloom of present experience, he was still active in his world. To those who trusted him the future would present something even more glorious than what had been lost.

At Mount Sinai, in the wilderness between Egypt and Canaan, God made himself known to his people as the giver of the law. It was an encounter that permanently changed their understanding of themselves and of God.

How is God known?

Finally, we must turn briefly to consider some of the assumptions behind the Old Testament's view of God and his relationship to his people. Two themes are especially important here.

God's grace

It was not unusual in the ancient world for the gods to be portrayed almost as if they were a race of superhumans. In one way it is almost inevitable that when people talk about God they should use human analogies to do so. The Old Testament is no exception. It describes God in very bold figures of speech, asserting that he has hands and eyes, and that he cries or laughs, and has emotions comparable to human feelings. But for all that, there is a clear consciousness that in his essential being God is quite different from people. His actions are not therefore rationalizations of the way men and women behave. Nor is he to be bullied and cajoled by magic, as if he could easily be blackmailed. If God makes himself known in the lives of men and women, it is because he has taken the initiative.

This affirmation is central to the Old Testament faith: all relationships with God are based on God's own actions in grace and love. God wishes to commit himself to the whole human race and as a means to that end he calls Abraham. In doing so, he acts freely, and his only motive is to share his love with the people who live in his world. At every significant point of the story thereafter, the Old Testament emphasizes that God's own gracious actions are the starting-point for a meaningful relationship with him. The exodus itself happens because God sees their plight and takes pity on them, not because the enslaved tribes ask for it. And individual men and women can enjoy fellowship with him simply because of God's love for them and not because of any inherent claim they might have on God. No one can work up a sense of God's presence for themselves. He is not found by personal introspection: God bursts into a person's life from outside. He is, to use theological jargon, transcendent. The Old Testament uses more picturesque language to describe the same thing: 'The Lord is great and is to be highly praised; his greatness is beyond understanding.'

Genesis 12:1–3

Psalm 145:3

God's word How then does God communicate? A simple answer would be: through his mighty acts. There is much truth in this, and the Old Testament often claims that God has revealed himself to his people through his great actions in history and personal experience. Indeed, much of the Old Testament's moral law is based on the assumption that the way God acts displays the kind of God he is. But a moment's thought will show that this answer is not entirely satisfactory.

Take the exodus, which for Israel was the greatest revelation of God's character and will. For the escaping slaves, and later generations who shared their perspective, this was the crucial event in which God was made known. But what did it mean to the Egyptians? We do not know, of course, for Egyptian annals nowhere mention such an event. But it is quite certain that the exodus was not for them a means of divine encounter in which the God Yahweh met them and changed their national history. Something else was needed to transform the bare happenings of history into a message from God.

This is always the way, of course. The 'bare facts' of history only gain significance when they are placed in an appropriate context. A modern historian does not simply record isolated incidents from the past, but tries to explain them in relation to other incidents, in order to make sense out of what has taken place. The Old Testament does the same, and what makes its story so distinctive is the interpretation that is given to the events which it describes. As historians and prophets looked back to the nation's past they did not view it as just a historical chain of cause and effect. They saw God himself at work.

If that was the end of the story, we might conclude that the Old Testament faith was little more than a historian's theory – a neat way of giving coherence and meaning to a rather amorphous collection of events that had happened at different times and places over many generations. But there is more to it than that. For the prophets did not interpret the history of their people in retrospect. They claimed to announce it before it took place. When Amos issued his scathing denunciations of Samarian society, and declared that it would soon come to an end, there was no sign of such an end. Indeed, the nation was enjoying a period of prosperity unparalleled at any other time in its history. When Jeremiah announced the doom of Jerusalem, the mood of self-satisfaction that was sweeping the city led people to regard him as a madman. But they – and the other prophets – persisted with their message because they were convinced that what they were saying was the word of God to their people. The earlier story of the exodus was no different. For Moses himself is portrayed as a prophet – indeed, the greatest of all prophets – announcing the exodus while the people were yet in slavery!

Deuteronomy 34:10–12

It is difficult for us today to grasp this, and still more difficult to understand it. But it is an essential part of the Old Testament's picture of God. The Old Testament never claims to be able to fathom all the depths of God's personality, and there are many aspects of his work that can never be fully understood. But this one conviction runs throughout all its writings: the living God is not a static being, remote and irrelevant to the lives of ordinary people. He is a God who acts, and a God who speaks in order that men and women might have a full and meaningful relationship with him and with one another.

10 God and the world

Discovering God in nature and history

IN THE last chapter, we saw that God's most characteristic method of communication in the Old Testament was through the events of history: the exodus from Egypt; the establishment of David's royal city in Jerusalem; even the exile. When correctly understood and explained, all these things told the people of Old Testament times what God was really like.

We would be quite wrong though to think that the Old Testament faith is concerned exclusively with the events of Israel's history. The heart of the Old Testament is certainly to be found in the stories that begin with Israel's ancestor Abraham and end with Judah's exile in Babylon. But there is a lot more than this in its pages. The early

Genesis 1 — 11

stories of the book of Genesis, most of the psalms, and all the 'wisdom' books (Proverbs, Ecclesiastes, Job, Song of Solomon) are only loosely related to the great themes of Israel's salvation history. In their own way, they all deal with the universal experience of men and women everywhere as they try to come to grips with the world in which they live. Moreover, these particular parts of the Old Testament have many close connections with the religious literature of other nations of the time. Their central concern is not with the unique and unrepeatable experience of Israel. Instead, they place God's activities in an international perspective, and suggest that his claims over people's lives are universal because his handiwork is evident in the very stuff of which the world is made.

Some scholars have suggested that the Old Testament faith developed an interest in God's relationship to the world at quite a late date. It is certainly true that during the years of the Babylonian exile (which began in 597 BC), many aspects of the Old Testament faith were worked out in their final detail. The majestic poetry of the

Isaiah 40 — 55

second part of the book of Isaiah certainly reflects that period. One of its most striking features is the imagery in which it celebrates God's power over the world of nature. Some of this language, and

Genesis 1:1 — 2:4

that found in the creation story of the book of Genesis, seems to have connexions with Mesopotamian stories of how the world was made. On that basis, it is suggested that the Old Testament faith was expanded at this period, moving the emphasis away from God's acts in history at a time when he seemed to be doing very little for his people.

This is a widely-held view, repeated by many Old Testament scholars. But it is far too simplistic. Some of the Old Testament's most sophisticated thinking about God and creation may well have been articulated during the exile. But a number of factors suggest that God's relationship to the natural world must have been an important part of Israel's life long before that:

● Most of the psalms reflect the worship and liturgy of pre-exilic Israel. They show quite clearly that Yahweh was worshipped as the Creator of the world long before Israel had any firsthand dealings with Babylon. There is no creation story as such in the psalms, but creation imagery (often drawn from the religious traditions of other nations) is used so often that belief in God as Creator was obviously a fundamental theme of worship in the temple at Jerusalem.

● We also know that the gods' role in relation to the natural world was fundamental to most other religions of the time. The texts from Ugarit have not so far disclosed a fully developed Canaanite creation story comparable with those found in ancient Babylon, but all the activities of the Canaanite gods and goddesses were related to the workings of the natural world. One of the first questions the invading tribes had to answer was whether Baal or Yahweh was in control of their world. It is inconceivable that they should have waited for half a millenium before giving an answer. As the Old Testament story unfolds, one of its major concerns is how Yahweh, the God of the exodus, related to the demands of settled agricultural life. The prevailing popular view was that the world of nature and the world of the gods were one and the same. So the actions of gods such as the Canaanite Baal would explain the mysterious workings of the world of nature in which Palestinian farmers had to eke out a precarious living. Was Yahweh only a God of history – and did that mean the natural world was controlled by worship of deities such as Baal and Anat? The story of Elijah shows that this was a pressing issue as early as the ninth century BC. A hundred years later the prophet Amos denounced the behaviour of non-Israelite people in a way that would

1 Kings 17:1 — 19:18

The Israelites began to discover the character of God in their time as nomads in the wilderness. But the discovery continued as they settled in the fertile land of Canaan and began to live an agricultural life.

Amos 1:3 — 2:3

only have made sense on the basis of a coherent set of beliefs about God and the world which he had made.

● Similar questions must also have presented themselves on a personal level. After all, only one relatively small group of people had witnessed the amazing events of the exodus and the conquest of the land. Not many had any direct contact with the great promises made to David. And, mercifully, few had been left in Jerusalem to witness its final humiliation at the hands of Nebuchadnezzar. If these were the key events in which God revealed himself to his people, then how could the rest of them hear his voice? Though the great events of the past could be celebrated in regular religious festivals, the fact was that the everyday experience of ordinary people was more closely tied to the world of nature than to the world of great and unrepeatable historical events. And that in itself must have required the development of some coherent belief about Israel's God and his relationship to the natural world.

Genesis 12:1–3

● From as far back as the call of Abraham, the Old Testament suggests that God's intervention in Israel's history was to be a means to the salvation of all nations. This insight was clearly central to the Old Testament faith, and is underlined by all the great prophets. It was often misunderstood, of course. The easy-going national optimism that often dominated popular thinking in both Israel and Judah could easily lead people to conclude that other nations were of no concern to God. But to overcome such misunderstanding, it must have been necessary to know precisely how Israel was related to other nations. The stories of creation are the only parts of the Old Testament which answer that question.

Genesis 2:4–25

● At least significant parts of the Genesis stories were certainly composed long before the exile in Babylon, for their imagery, and the assumptions made about the countryside and the moods of the weather, clearly point to a Palestinian background.

In the light of all these considerations, we must conclude that belief in God as the Creator was a significant and integral part of the Old Testament faith from relatively early times. Like other aspects of that faith, it developed and matured as time passed. But one of its basic convictions was that 'The world and all that is in it belong to the Lord ...' Its importance is stressed by the fact that we meet this subject on the opening page of Genesis. For here, and in what follows, Israel's ancient thinkers have preserved for us some of the most fundamental aspects of their faith.

Psalm 24:1

Thinking about the world

Genesis 1 — 11

The first section of the book of Genesis is one of the most important parts of the whole Old Testament. In the stories of creation, the fall, Cain and Abel, the flood and the tower of Babel, we have a concise summary of the whole of the Old Testament faith. Such basic themes as the character of God, the nature of the world, and the meaning of human existence are presented here with an imaginative subtlety that has given these chapters a place among the great classics of world literature. Yet we need be neither theologians nor literary critics to grasp their message. Like the parables of Jesus, these stories have a universal appeal to people in all times and places, for they speak to the deepest needs of men and women, and give an honest answer to questions that have perplexed the world's greatest thinkers.

Understanding the Genesis stories

This makes it all the more surprising that the early chapters of Genesis should ever have become a subject of controversy. Yet it can hardly be denied that in the last 200 years they have been the subject of so many complex debates that ordinary Bible readers are often at a loss to know what to do with them. Huge volumes have been written in answer to this question, and anything we can say here must inevitably be brief and incomplete. But two things may be taken as basic for a satisfactory understanding:

● Ever since Charles Darwin published his *Origin of Species* in 1859, the Genesis creation story has been used by the protagonists in many debates about science and religion. Scientists imbued with a materialistic world-view have sometimes claimed that these chapters demonstrate the naivety of religious belief – and fervent believers have just as often replied that the creation stories prove the inadequacy of modern scientific endeavour. In some Christian

Many ancient peoples have their myths, as is shown in these mysterious carvings on Easter Island. But how well does the category of 'myth' fit the stories at the beginning of Genesis?

circles, it is taken for granted that Christian doctrine requires these chapters to be taken as a scientific account of the origins of the universe. This position inevitably sets the Old Testament at variance with the findings of science, and identifies a biblical faith with what most people would regard as an outmoded view of how the world works.

We need to remember that all this is a fairly recent development. Earlier generations of Bible scholars were much less inclined to try to force the book of Genesis into the strait-jacket of a scientific textbook. The great sixteenth-century scholar, John Calvin, was asked by the literalists of his day how he could make sense of the statement that the dome of the sky ('firmament') was separating 'the water under it from the water above it'. Even to scientists at that time, it seemed unlikely that there could be waters above the sky. In his *Commentary on Genesis*, Calvin agreed with them, describing such a notion as 'opposed to common sense, and quite incredible'. He found those who regarded Genesis as a book of science equally incredible, and went on to assert that 'to my mind, this is a certain principle, that nothing is here treated of but the visible form of the world. He who would learn astronomy, and other recondite arts, let him go elsewhere ...' Calvin was quite clear that the Old Testament was never intended to be a book of science, and that reading it as if it was would only confuse and distort its essential message. The Old Testament writers, he argued, simply took for granted the sort of world-view that was widely held in their day. This assumed that the world was like a flat disc, set upon pillars below, and with the sky arching over it like a dome. The Old Testament writers never discuss whether this was scientifically correct or not: it was unnecessary for them to do so, for this was not why they were writing. Calvin describes details such as this as only props on the main stage – background detail to reinforce the fact that the Old Testament's message was relevant to the world in which ordinary people lived.

Genesis 1:6–7

● The message, here as elsewhere in the Old Testament, is about God. We have already seen this when we considered the meaning of the great events of Israel's history. The story of the exodus, for instance, was recorded not just because it happened, but because it demonstrated God's active and loving concern for his people. A casual reader can see that even in the Old Testament's history

The great ziggurat at Ur on the Euphrates was built in about 2100 BC. It has recently been partially reconstructed. Such a structure may lie behind the story of the tower of Babel.

books, the main emphasis is on theological explanation, not on historical analysis. The great Deuteronomistic History which forms the core of the Old Testament story certainly explains and applies the lessons that are to be drawn from what it records. So do the books of the Chronicler. And Genesis itself was no doubt compiled and issued in its present form as a tangible answer to the problem faced by a generation far removed from the events which it describes.

Deuteronomy — 2 Kings

Nor does the Old Testament always use historical events to convey its essential message. The hymns and prayers of the psalms, the sermons of the prophets and the writings of Israel's wise men, all explain important aspects of God's dealings with his people. As the prophets loved to point out, the message ('the word of the Lord') was the really important thing, not the medium through which it was communicated. Of course, those who do not share the prophets' faith could read the Old Testament histories and see nothing more than a diffuse account of a small and second-rate Middle Eastern power. We can do the same with the creation stories, and see nothing but an apparently factual account of the doings of two people in a garden full of plants and animals. At a more sophisticated level, we can join those modern scholars who think of these stories as a collection of folk tales designed to answer such everyday questions as why snakes have no legs, why weeds grow in fields, or why in ancient Israel it was better to be a shepherd than a farmer. But if these are the only things we see as we read the book of Genesis, then we have missed the most crucial points that its author was intending to make. For he was not concerned with the needs of ancient farmers, nor even with some kind of primitive sociology, but with God himself. Just as Jesus often explained important aspects of his message by using the familiar experiences of everyday life, so the editor of Genesis starts from the common experiences of human life, and goes on to show how God can relate to both the joys and the miseries of the world and its people.

The stories as literature

The Old Testament is a library of many different kinds of literature. In its pages we find not only history, but law, drama, poetry, sermons, political tracts, and much more. They are all held together by their common conviction that God is at the centre of all human life and activity. But before we can fully understand the significance of any particular passage, we must obviously decide what sort of literature we are dealing with. We would not read a political tract in the same way as we might read legal documents. The kind of analytical judgment required to understand history would be quite out of place in the more aesthetic world of poetry and drama. So how can we classify these early stories in Genesis?

● **Myth?** Many books on the Old Testament refer to them as 'myths'. But this is not a particularly helpful term to use. Most people think of a myth as something that is untrue. Scholars do not normally use it in this sense, but even they have no agreed definition of it. It is commonly used to mean at least three different things:

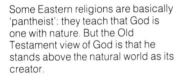

Some Eastern religions are basically 'pantheist': they teach that God is one with nature. But the Old Testament view of God is that he stands above the natural world as its creator.

1. A myth can be simply a story about gods and goddesses and their doings, described as if they were human beings. There are many examples of this in Greek and Hindu mythology.

2. Myth can also be a technical term for what takes place during a religious rite. In ancient Babylon, for instance, the annual New Year Festival was the most important religious event of the year. Here, the Babylonian story of creation would be recited, while the king acted out the story as it was told. The recitation was a 'myth', to accompany the 'ritual' carried out by the king.

3. Yet others use the term 'myth' to describe a story which expresses a truth about human life that cannot adequately be described in terms of science or history. In this sense, myth is as valid and respectable a way of thinking about life's deepest meaning as science, art, or philosophy. This is the type of 'myth' scholars have in mind when they use this term of the Genesis stories.

The trouble is that with so many possible meanings, 'myth' has become a very slippery term, and for that reason alone is unlikely to be of much help to us here. In addition, not all the stories in the early chapters of Genesis can easily be accommodated even within the three definitions of 'myth' listed above. For although many people would be happy to think of the stories of creation and the fall as a kind of 'theology in pictures', the stories of the flood and the tower of

Babel seem to have some connection with historical events. Archaeologists have found mud deposits from a number of great floods which swept over the ancient world from 4000 BC onwards, and the description of the tower of Babel recalls towers (ziggurats) that have been unearthed in the same areas of Mesopotamia.

● **How many stories?** The conventional way of explaining these stories has been to suggest that Genesis is actually a composite document, and what we now have has been put together out of a number of sources. Old Testament scholars have often claimed to be able to distinguish not one, but two (or even more) accounts of creation and the flood. The reasons for this have been fully explored in chapter 7 above. But even supposing that this analysis is correct, it is difficult to see how it can help us to understand what Genesis is trying to say. To explain where an author got his materials is not the same as explaining what he wanted to say. Unless we read these stories as they are, we are unlikely to make much headway in discovering their message.

● **What kind of stories?** If we take the stories of creation and the fall, it is easy to see that the beginning of the story is quite different in character from its sequel. This is not because they are variant accounts of the same thing (as some think), but because they are different literary forms. The first section has many close similarities to the poetic style that we find in the psalms, and especially in certain passages in the book of Isaiah. It is written in poetic style, with a repetitive refrain. From a literary standpoint it is a hymn in praise of creation, celebrating God's greatness and his concern for every living thing. It takes the observable features of the world, and asserts that God is in control of them all. It is the sort of confession of faith that may well have been formulated and used in the context of worship in ancient Israel. When we come to consider its message these are the terms in which we need to try to understand it.

What follows is quite different. The dramatic action takes place in a different setting altogether. No longer is it reported in the measured language of lofty poetry, but with the directness of an expert story-teller. In a straightforward account, we read of how the man and woman who enjoyed a perfect relationship with God rejected that relationship, and chose instead to be the controllers of their own destiny.

Their choice was simple, but its consequences incalculable. As the story unfolds, we are soon made aware that this is no ordinary story. The garden, the trees, and the creatures are all described in superlatives, as befits the momentous implications that stem from the action. For the effects of the human action described here were not restricted to the earliest age of human existence, but were to have repercussions for men and women at all times and places. It is no coincidence that the author names the central actors Adam (meaning 'mankind') and Eve (meaning something like 'humanity'). For the experience of all subsequent generations was enshrined in their act of disobedience. Their story is theological writing at its best and most imaginative, simple yet profound. No reader with even a

Genesis 1:1 — 2:4

Genesis 2:4 — 3:24

Genesis 1:1 — 2:4

Genesis 2:4 — 3:24

glimmer of aesthetic appreciation can fail to grasp what the author is saying.

The message of the stories

What then is the message of these chapters? We shall look at some specific aspects later. But the overall theme is well summed up in the refrain repeated throughout the creation hymn: 'God was pleased with what he saw.' It is not surprising that the composer of the hymn should have repeated this statement so many times. In his own day, it was distinctive enough, and it makes an emphasis that even today is often avoided by religious people. It is a basic assumption of many oriental religions that the world as we know it – indeed, our whole bodily existence – is quite incompatible with spiritual enlightenment. Down through the centuries, this has been a dominant theme in much Christian thinking too, and has led many people to opt out of the world in the hope that by so doing they would somehow get closer to God.

Attitudes such as this within Christianity owe more to the influence of Greek philosophy than to the Bible. The Old Testament stands fundamentally opposed to this idea. Unlike the Greeks, the Israelites did not see this world as a 'prison' from which they needed to escape in order to find God. It was, rather, their home, and God was to be found not beyond the created world, but in it. One of the basic affirmations of the Old Testament faith is that 'the world and all that is in it belong to the Lord; the earth and all who live on it are his'. Moreover, the creation stories emphasize that God is directly involved with the life of this world. He is, of course, all-powerful, and his word alone is sufficient to bring his will to fruition. But in describing the place of men and women in creation, God's own personal involvement is always emphasized. He is like a potter, who takes soil from the ground and with his own hands forms a human being out of it. Unlike many of the traditional gods of the Middle East, Yahweh can never be identified with nature: he is beyond it and above it. But at the same time, he is directly involved in the work of creation, thus demonstrating his close concern not only for Israel, but for people and animals in general, and even for the very stuff out of which the universe is made.

Psalm 24:1

Genesis 1:3, 6, 9, 11, 14, 20, 24

Genesis 2:7

Genesis in its context

Just over 100 years ago, archaeologists uncovered the library of the seventh-century BC Assyrian emperor Ashurbanipal. Politically, he was a failure, but his library survived and is one of our major sources of knowledge of the Old Testament world. It was written on cuneiform tablets, which are virtually indestructible: flat bricks of river mud written on with a wedge-shaped stick while still soft, and then baked hard in the heat of the sun. The contents of these stories were ancient even in Ashurbanipal's day, and go back almost to the dawn of civilization.

It soon became apparent from these documents that stories of creation and a great flood had circulated in ancient Babylon long before the Old Testament was written. In a wave of enthusiasm for new discoveries, the scholars who first deciphered these texts concluded that the Old Testament stories were taken from them, and were therefore of relatively little value. Things have changed a lot since then, and modern experts are now far less confident that we can trace a direct line of descent from the Babylonian documents to the stories in Genesis. One of the main reasons for this has been the more recent discovery of other religious texts from the Canaanite stronghold of Ugarit. These texts tell the stories of

Baal and other Canaanite gods and goddesses, and have shown that in many crucial respects Canaanite religion was rather different from its Babylonian counterpart. Though Ugarit's heyday had passed long before there was a nation called Israel, it is still likely that the religious context in which the Old Testament developed must have had more in common with such Canaanite beliefs than with the developed religious traditions of ancient Babylon. As a result, scholars now find it far more productive to compare the Old Testament with what we know of the religion of Ugarit.

Imagery from other religions

Many ordinary readers of the Bible may feel uneasy with the idea that it contains materials connected with the documents of other religions. But in fact this kind of religious borrowing is found not only in the stories of creation and the flood, but in many other parts of the Old Testament. The wisdom books are often very similar to wisdom books found in Egypt and elsewhere, and much of Israel's case law resembles the precepts of other nations. Parallels are perhaps to be expected, for they concern matters of morality and social organization that are common to people all over the world. It is more surprising to discover that the Old Testament's religious imagery is also quite similar to the language used of other gods. As we shall see in a later chapter, the Old Testament's language of sacrifice was essentially the same as that used in Ugarit. And the psalms in particular use many concepts that were not exclusive to Israel:

● For instance, the statement that the temple hill in Jerusalem is 'in the far north' (Psalm 48:2) has puzzled many people, for Jerusalem was not in the north, but right in the middle of the country!

But the Hebrew word for 'north' is virtually identical with the Ugaritic word 'Zaphon'. In the stories of Baal Mt Zaphon is frequently mentioned as the traditional home of the gods. So when the psalmist penned these words, it is almost certain that he was not making a (false) geographical statement about the location of the temple, but was claiming that whatever was supposed to happen at Mt Zaphon was actually taking place on Mt Zion. There are other references to this home of the gods in Isaiah 14:13, and perhaps also in Psalm 89:12.

● Psalm 46:4 speaks of 'a river that brings joy to the city of God'. There is

no literal river in Jerusalem, but this statement makes perfectly good sense when we learn that the same imagery was used throughout the Middle East to illustrate the life-giving powers of divine beings. In a scene from the palace at Mari, for example, the king is shown being invested by a god. In one corner stand two figures holding a vase with the tree of life, from which comes a stream, dividing into smaller streams, and so dispensing the blessing of the gods among the people. The same theme is taken up and developed further in Ezekiel 47:1–12, where the stream that flows from the temple in Jerusalem transforms the life of everything that comes in contact with it.

● In many passages celebrating God's triumphant power, he is depicted as winning battles over the sea and monsters which lived in it. Some of these passages depict unruly waters which are threatening to bring chaos into the world which he has made (Psalms 18:15; 29:3–4,10–11; 77:16–18; 93:3–4; Habakkuk 3:8). Others speak of monsters emerging from the unruly depths to challenge God's power (Job 7:12; Psalm 74:12–14; 89:10; Isaiah 27:1). These are obviously allusions to incidents that must have been well known to the people of ancient Israel. Yet the Old Testament nowhere contains a simple descriptive account of them. For that we need to look elsewhere. These references to a battle between God and the powers of the sea are drawn from the general religious ideas of the time, rather than belonging uniquely to the Old Testament faith.

Some of the closest parallels with the Old Testament statements can be found in the texts from Ugarit. When Isaiah speaks of Yahweh using 'his powerful and deadly sword to punish Leviathan, that wriggling, twisting dragon, and to kill the monster that lives in the sea' (27:1), he uses words virtually identical with a text which speaks of Baal: 'You have killed Lotan the primeval dragon, you have seen off that twisting snake, the powerful one with the seven heads.' Other Old Testament passages attest the belief that such monsters had multiple heads (Psalm 74:13–14), and that they can be called Rahab as well as Leviathan (Psalm 89:10; Isaiah 51:9).

So what are we to make of all this? After the outspoken prophetic condemnation of Canaanite religion, why does the Old Testament use this language? Was the Old Testament faith perhaps not as distinctive as we would like to think? Some have certainly

This Babylonian account of creation tells of a time when nothing existed except the gods and the great Deep. Then a movement took place in the waters and the god Marduk formed first the earth and then the living world.

suggested that, regarding this imagery as the remnants of what was once a highly developed nature mythology in which Yahweh played much the same role as the Canaanite Baal. But there is no real evidence, either historical or religious, to support such a contention.

The way these materials have been adapted for Israelite use is far more subtle than that. In Middle Eastern thinking, the waters of chaos were essentially personifications of the natural forces that seemed to bring productive life to a standstill at the end of each season. But in the Old Testament, this imagery is either set very clearly in the context of God's firm control over the powers of nature (Psalm 74:12–17; 95:5; 135:5–7; Isaiah 51:15–16), or else is given a completely different reference altogether by being applied to the great events of Israel's history. In particular, the waters of chaos are often transformed into the waters of the Reed Sea, controlled by Yahweh to allow his people to escape from Egypt (Psalm 77:16–18; Isaiah 51:9–11). And the monsters become symbols of the more tangible enemies with whom Israel had to deal throughout her troubled existence (as in Isaiah 27:1). In other words, the imagery has been separated altogether from its original context, and in its new setting is given a new emphasis to celebrate some of the most distinctive aspects of the Old Testament faith.

A 'Babylonian Genesis'?

The same thing has happened in the early chapters of Genesis, with the stories of creation and the flood. It is natural that here the Old Testament should have many elements in common with other texts of its day. For although the events of history were the unique possession of just one nation, the facts of creation were part of the common heritage of humanity. When the Old Testament describes the world, it does so in conventional terms. But in the process, it reinterprets these traditional ideas in such a way that they become a means of explaining its own distinctive beliefs about God.

● **The creation story** (Genesis 1:1–2:4) has often been compared with an old Akkadian tale called *Enuma Elish*. This was recited in the temple at Babylon at the annual New Year Festival, and was a hymn in praise of the god Marduk. It tells how at the beginning nothing existed except the dark waters of primeval chaos, personified as Apsu and Tiamat. In their turn they reproduce a series of other gods representing the various elements of the universe. Later, a revolt against these forces of chaos led by the younger and more active gods brought into existence the ordered world. Apsu was killed by magic, and Tiamat was cut in two. With one half of her body Marduk made the solid sky (firmament), and with the other the flat earth. The gods were then divided between heaven and earth, and people were made to perform menial tasks for the gods on earth.

It is unlikely that there was any direct connection between this and the Old Testament account, though there are some superficial similarities. In both, light emerges from a watery chaos, followed by the sky, dry land, sun, moon and stars, and finally people. After this the creator or creators rested. There are, of course, many differences. But even at the points of closest resemblance, the Genesis account deliberately undermines the assumptions of the Babylonian story.

Scholars of an earlier generation often linked the 'raging ocean' of Genesis 1:2 (Hebrew *tehom*) with the Babylonian goddess Tiamat. This is linguistically unlikely. But in addition, the Old Testament idea of 'the raging sea' is quite different, with not the least suggestion of a conflict between God and the watery chaos. Instead, 'the power of God' was 'moving over the water' from the very beginning, and the 'great sea monsters' are explicitly said to have been only a part of what God created. The Hebrew word used to describe their creation is carefully chosen, to indicate that God's control over these creatures was quite effortless and in no way the outcome of some cosmic battle.

Nor is there any idea that this 'raging ocean' would somehow again get the upper hand and plunge things back into chaos. This was basic to the whole idea of the Babylonian stories. Genesis makes it clear that creation is not something needing to be repeated in the ritual of an annual New Year Festival. It happened once and for all. Once the days of creation were passed they could not be repeated.

Many ancient people thought the sun, moon and stars had powers over people. Many modern readers of horoscopes think the same thing, but such beliefs are quite specifically undermined here by describing the heavenly bodies as nothing more than 'lights' (Genesis 1:14–19). They were

The Babylonian myths had a story of a Great Flood, parallel in some ways to the story of Noah. It forms part of the Epic of Gilgamesh, and tells of a man whom the gods instructed to make a boat and survive a flood.

eternal life. He seeks out his own ancestor Ut-napishtim, who had himself gained immortality, and asks him about it. He is told that first he must get a plant from the bottom of the ocean which will renew his youth. But at this point in the story, Ut-napishtim goes on to tell Gilgamesh how he himself had escaped from a great flood.

He had been warned by Ea, the god of magic wisdom, that the other gods, especially Enlil, had decided to send the flood. Ut-napishtim was advised to build a boat, which he did. The 'boat' was in fact a large cube, and in important respects was therefore rather different from Noah's 'ark'. After coating this cube inside and out with bitumen, he stocked it with food and brought all his family and belongings into it, together with animals and skilled craftworkers. The storm raged for seven days, at the end of which nothing but water could be seen. Twelve days later, Ut-napishtim's 'boat' ran aground on a mountain. He sent out a dove and a swallow in turn, both of which came back. Then he sent out a raven, which did not return as the waters had subsided. When he left the 'boat', he made a sacrifice to the gods, who crowded round like flies to smell it. They promised that never again would they send a flood, and gave immortality to Ut-napishtim and his wife.

certainly not gods themselves.

The picture of people is also quite different. In many ancient stories, they were created as an afterthought to serve the gods, so they would not have to gather their own food. But in the Old Testament men and women are not only central to the whole of God's purposes: they are the pinnacle of his creation. Far from being made for God's selfish benefit, he provides other things for theirs – and so the plants and grains are available for food (Genesis 1:29). As in the rest of the Old Testament, the destiny of people is in the hands of a loving and powerful personal God, and not in the control of either nature or superstition.

● **The Flood Story** (Genesis 6:9–9:17) displays essentially the same characteristics. Neither Egyptian nor Ugaritic literature contains an account of a great flood, but again several such stories have been found in Babylon.

The most complete of these is in a poem known as *The Epic of Gilgamesh*. This tells how Gilgamesh, king of Uruk (Erech in Genesis 10:10), shattered by the death of his friend Enkidu, realizes that he himself must soon die and decides to try to find the secret of

Here again, there is no compelling evidence to suggest that the Genesis story is in any way based on the Babylonian account. But there are sufficient resemblances to make it likely that both depend on the same general stock of ideas. Where they differ, they do so because the Old Testament story is based on a different understanding of the nature of God himself. In the Gilgamesh story, no explanation is given for the flood, though in another Akkadian source (the *Atrahasis Epic*), the gods decide to destroy men and women because they are making too much noise! In Genesis, however, God sends the flood as a judgment on human disobedience. Throughout the story the recurring theme is that there is only one God. Unlike the Babylonian gods he is not afraid of the flood: he is in complete control of it. Nor does he deal with men and women in an arbitrary way. The saving of Noah is as much the outcome of his own just nature as is the destruction of everyone else. The Genesis God is essentially a moral God, and his dealings with men and women depend solely on his own standards of justice and love, not on capricious self interest.

Men, women and God

Psalm 8:4

Psalm 144:4

Psalm 103:15–16

Psalm 8:5

Psalm 103:17

Genesis 1:27

'What is man, that you think of him; mere man, that you care for him?' As people compare their own meagre existence with the greatness of the world around them, this question often sums up the basic problem of human existence. Why are we here? Some parts of the Old Testament emphasize the apparent insignificance of men and women, referring to life as 'a puff of wind ... a passing shadow', or 'like grass. We grow and flourish like a wild flower; then the wind blows on it, and it is gone ...' Others reflect a more positive mood, declaring that people are only a little lower than God himself, 'crowned with glory and honour'. Yet all would agree that the life of men and women finds its true fulfilment when they are living in personal fellowship with God. This is why we were made, and no matter how insignificant or powerless a person may feel, we can be sure that God is still interested in their life and experience: 'for those who honour the Lord, his love lasts for ever, and his goodness endures for all generations.' Men and women are the pinnacle and crowning glory of the world and all its affairs. In the Babylonian creation stories people were made last of all, almost as an afterthought, and always for menial duties. But the Old Testament will have none of this.

The heart of the Genesis creation stories is to be found in the simple statement that 'God created human beings, making them to be like himself' – or, as other translations put it, 'God created mankind in his own image'. When we recall that the Old Testament expressly forbids making images of God, this may come as a rather unexpected sentiment. But in the previous chapter we saw that the imagery of the Old Testament is always specific and positive, never abstract and philosophical. God is described in relation to what he does, not by reference to what he is made of. This is precisely the emphasis that is intended here. When God makes men and women 'to be like himself', he does not mean them to look like him, or to be made of the same stuff. Rather he intends them to be a kind of extension of his own personality, and a fundamental part of his own activity in the world. They are his representatives. In this claim at least three important ideas are put forward about the relationship between people, the world, and God himself:

In relation to the earth

Genesis 1:28

Men and women are given God's blessing and told: 'Have many children, so that your descendants will live all over the earth and bring it under their control. I am putting you in charge of the fish, the birds, and all the wild animals.'

This statement has often been misunderstood, especially by modern Christians who have taken it as a licence to exploit the natural world in any way that is to their benefit. Older Bible translations may have encouraged this, by articulating God's instructions in terms of 'subduing' the earth, and 'having dominion' over its creatures. But the Genesis story implies nothing of this kind, indeed, quite the opposite. The whole point of the story is that God has made a world of order and balance out of a state of chaos. Men and women are here called upon to maintain and preserve the world

Opposite
The Genesis creation story shows humanity as both part of the created order, in harmony with nature as a whole, and also the summit of creation, responsible for the proper care of all life.

Amos 4:13; 5:8; Isaiah 45:12

Isaiah 40:26; 48:13

Psalm 104:10

Psalm 104:14–15,28–30

as God intends it to be. God has not wound the world up like a mechanical toy. He continues to be actively involved in its workings, changing night to day. He controls the sun, moon and stars, the rivers, and gives life to crops and animals. Any human activity which disrupts the life of nature is contrary to the will of God, for God intended there to be a mutual respect and service between people and the world in which they live.

Genesis 2:7

This is strikingly emphasized when Genesis depicts God as a divine potter forming a person out of the ground. There is a subtle play on words here, for the Hebrew word for man (*adam*) is very similar to that for 'ground' (*adamah*). This similarity is used here to emphasize that people are a fundamental part of the world system in which they live. Men and women are not above nature: they are a part of it, and are responsible to God for the way they care for their world and the other creatures with whom they share it. Denis Baly lucidly captures the spirit of this word-play in English: 'Man was never intended to be the proud ruler of conquered and enslaved territory ... he is human, taken from the humus, and therefore he must act with humility.'

In relation to God

Men and women are distinctive because God can and does speak to them. Though they are part and parcel of the world in which they live, that is not the only dimension in which life finds meaning. Indeed, a materialist view which tries to make sense of human existence by only analyzing the world of our senses and reason is, in biblical terms, meaningless. Being made 'in God's image' means that people are incomplete without God. They are intended for

An important part of the meaning of our creation 'in the image of God' is that people have a capacity for intimate relationships – with each other and with God.

fellowship with him, and it is this which gives meaning and direction to life. Communication with God is of vital importance to human satisfaction.

It is important to notice that by fellowship the Old Testament does not mean a kind of conventional religiosity. One of the most striking features of these early stories in Genesis is the way God comes and talks with people. He arrives in the evening to discuss with Adam and Eve the affairs of the day. This statement is not to be regarded with embarrassment as either hyperbole or exaggerated anthropomorphism. It is a moving affirmation of the fact that communication between God and people was intended to be delightful and personal, not formal and rigid. In ancient Israel, God's word came to his people through many different channels. The priest would interpret the Law (*Torah*); the wise man would give advice on everyday affairs; and the prophets most characteristically brought a direct word from God to particular situations in his people's life. But underlying all these modes of communication was the conviction that God and his people related to each other on a personal level. Like the characters in the Garden of Eden, each individual was made for direct encounter with God himself.

Genesis 3:8

In relation to each other

There are important lessons here about human relationships to the world and to God. But some of the most striking points of these stories concern relationships between human beings themselves at different levels.

● **In social relationships**, the fact that all human beings are made 'in God's image' implies that all are of equal value and importance. The Bible solves the problems of race by declaring that we all belong to the same race! Israel often found it difficult to grasp that. But the prophets were adamant that no one race was better than another, and no one group in society was of more importance than another. So far as God is concerned, all men and women are equal. Though Israel was specially privileged to receive God's Law (*Torah*), this did not mean that others had no access to God's will. However imperfectly they might have perceived it, every person knew the difference between basic issues of right and wrong just because they were made 'in God's image'.

● **In sexual relationships**, the Old Testament takes a realistic view. There is here no hint of the narrow asceticism that has often marked Christian views on sex. The idea that sexual knowledge only emerged in the context of broken relationships after the fall is clearly contradicted in Genesis. Human sexuality is an essential part of God's design for his people. And it is worth noting that procreation is not the only reason given for this. Though it is true that men and women are told to 'Have many children ...', great emphasis is laid on the fact that a sexual partner is to be 'a suitable companion'. Nor is there any suggestion here that in such a relationship one partner is intrinsically more important than the other. A man is incomplete without a woman, and it is only the two of them together who can work out the full potential of human existence. Sex is a part of God's

Genesis 1:28
Genesis 2:18

gift to men and women. But it is also something to be enjoyed and developed for its own sake – a point that is made most forcibly by the inclusion in the Old Testament of a book of erotic love poems, the Song of Solomon.

●**In family relationships**, there is again an emphasis on the mutual sharing of one person with another. In the Old Testament world, the patriarchal family was the norm. Men as well as women were often seen as chattels to be disposed of to suit the head of the family. The Old Testament itself gives many examples of family heads doing just that. But here in this basic exposition of God's plan we find a rather different emphasis. There is nothing here that would give grounds for the exploitation of one sex by the other. Instead, there is a very strong emphasis on the mutual commitment of men and women to each other in the context of a sexual relationship. Moreover, this relationship takes precedence over all other traditional family commitments. The book of Genesis issues a very strong challenge to the ancient supremacy of the family patriarch when it states that 'a man leaves his father and mother and is united to his wife, and they become one ...'

Genesis 2:24

Broken relationships and new beginnings

The book of Genesis paints an idyllic picture of life in this world, with nature, people and God all working together in perfect harmony and mutual understanding and support. But, of course, life is not like that. Though most people have on occasion glimpsed the idealistic possibilities that are presented here, human experience is more often marred by exploitation, disharmony, and suspicion. The real world is a world of broken relationships.

The root of the problem

Genesis 3:1–24
Genesis 11:1–9

Genesis 11:4
Genesis 3:4

Genesis 2:17; 3:4–5

Deuteronomy 1:39; Isaiah 7:14–15

So what has gone wrong? Two stories here answer that question: the story of the fall, and the story of the Tower of Babel. Both of them declare that the reason for human misery is that the delicate balance between people, nature and God has been disturbed. Instead of being content to accept God's will, men and women have tried to set themselves up as controllers of their own destiny. They are not content to accept even the benign guidance of a power greater than themselves. Instead, their chief concern has been to 'make a name for ourselves' or, as the story of the fall puts it, to 'be like God'.

One story expresses this as seeking after the fruit of 'the tree that gives knowledge of what is good and what is bad'. The fact that God bans the human pair from eating this fruit has suggested to some that there was a built-in unfairness in God's original design. After all, why should God want people to be kept in ignorance like this? But a comment like that misses the point. For elsewhere in the Old Testament, the same term is used with a distinctive connotation. To be ignorant of the difference between right and wrong indicates that a person is yet a child, depending for guidance and direction on his or her parents. In the case of a child, of course, it is important that they grow up and eventually gain independence from their parents. But in a person's relationship with God this can never happen. To have a meaningful relationship with God, men and women must be prepared to recognize his greatness and love, and relate to him as a child to a generous parent.

People who do not have a childlike trust in God are in revolt against their Creator. God has given limits within which life can prosper. When human selfishness tries to overstep these limits, disaster will soon follow. One of the most moving aspects of these stories is the contrast between the world as God intended it to be and the world of broken relationships so familiar to us all. The Bible's understanding of the nature of sin at this point is, of course, quite different from the view taken by many people today. It is often assumed that the history of the human race is one long story of continuous improvement, as people moved from primitive and savage beginnings to the so-called sophistication of our own day. Christians adopt various positions on the question of biological evolution. But there can be no argument about the possibility of moral evolution. The facts of history prove conclusively that people are getting worse, not better. Genesis explains it by saying that human life has moved from a position of fellowship with God to a position of rebellion. And it traces it all back to the disobedience of the man and woman in Eden who knew God so well.

The results of their disobedience and selfishness are simple:

● **Disharmony in nature** Mutual service and interdependence between people and the natural world is replaced by hostility and mutual distrust.

Genesis 3:14–21

● **Alienation from God** Instead of meeting God in a close personal relationship, the man and woman avoid him, and are ultimately sent out of the garden.

Genesis 3:8–10
Genesis 3:22–24

The charter for family life laid down in the creation story is of a marriage of equals, bringing different attributes into a partnership. Within this setting children find their secure place.

● **Broken society** With broken relationships between people, the world and God, even brothers can become enemies – and so Cain goes out and kills his brother Abel.

Genesis 4:1–16

Searching for the answer

The people of Israel knew well enough what all this meant in the ordinary details of everyday life. By the time these stories were finally written down, they could look back on a long history which amply illustrated the tragedy of human disobedience. But they had also learned that even when his judgment was well deserved, God could never leave people to languish in the results of their own sin. These early stories contain a vivid portrayal of broken relationships. But

A spoiled creation

People's good relations with each other
in marriage and the family, in social harmony and co-operation . . .

. . . are broken by human sinfulness,
so that marriages break up, social and racial divisions arise, and wars kill millions

People's good relations with the land,
so that by caring for the created world and sharing its resources we can all have enough . . .

. . . are broken by human greed,
resulting in plenty for some, deprivation for others, and a polluted world

People's good relations with God,
in direct awareness of him, and in worshipping him as he really is . . .

. . . are broken by human pride,
so that we have a distorted understanding of God, and worship the creation rather than the Creator

they also have an underlying emphasis on the ever-present possibility of a new beginning. Sin and disobedience are a tragedy. Judgment is inevitable – and well deserved. But God's love and forgiveness for the world and its people will never be defeated.

Even in the earliest stories there are hints that God cannot just abandon people. When Adam and Eve feel the need for clothing, **Genesis 3:21** God provides it for them. When Cain kills his brother Abel, God condemns him – but then forgives him and takes steps to keep him **Genesis 4:15** safe from the vengeance of others. This theme comes to full expression in the story of the great flood. At a time when men and women were so determined to go their own way and disturb the delicate balance of relationships between God and his world, **Genesis 6:5–8** judgment was the only possible answer. Yet even here, God's purpose is not ultimately destructive, and Noah is saved. He is spared because of God's love, grace, and forgiveness – all of which is encapsulated in the promise freely given by God to all humanity. The rainbow, given at that time, is a sign of his continuing love even **Genesis 9:8–17** through the worst excesses of human disobedience.

It is little wonder then that these stories came to form the opening pages of the Old Testament. In them we have a profound and picturesque summary of all the essential features of the Old Testament faith. Here we meet a God who is both totally different from men and women, and yet deeply involved with them. We are given a glimpse of a world in which people and nature can relate meaningfully to each other, because both of them relate to God. And we see the tragic results when that relationship breaks down.

The tragedy is familiar enough to us all. But the Old Testament has its own diagnosis of the problem. The world is out of joint because men and women are in revolt against their Creator. Human sin affects both human life and the life of nature. Disobedience is a tragedy, and wilful neglect of God's will leads to judgment. The

The story of humanity's fall into sin speaks of a breakdown in relationships at every level. There is evidence of this breakdown throughout history, particularly in the cruelty and waste of wars.

The task God gave humanity, of working for the good of the whole living world, can only be achieved through co-operation. Sinfulness shatters that co-operation and brings bitter hostility.

course of human history has demonstrated all this often enough. But the Old Testament does not leave it there. For God wishes to bring order out of this chaos. He intends to replace alienation with healing. And his forgiveness and love are always available to those who in childlike simplicity acknowledge their dependence on the Creator.

Looking to the future

The Old Testament clearly asserts that human existence finds its true fulfilment only in a close personal relationship with God. But where are the boundaries of that relationship to be drawn? Does it end with death – or does it extend further, into an after-life?

To modern people this is a natural question to ask. For one thing, we tend to think of people as individuals rather than as a part of some much larger group, and the fate of each person is therefore of considerable importance to us. In addition, we have been nurtured in an environment where popular ideas about death often incorporate the ancient Greek view that a person is composed of two parts: a body, which is mortal and comes to an end, and a soul (or spirit) which is immortal and can last for ever quite independently of the body.

Neither of these assumptions would have meant very much in the Old Testament context. Although we should not over-emphasize the corporate aspect of Old Testament thought it is certainly true that ancient Israel thought far less in terms of the individual than we do. And at the same time, the Old Testament contains not a trace of the bipartite view of human nature that leads to the conclusion that people are souls imprisoned in bodies. For the Old Testament writers, all aspects of human existence were just different facets of the same reality. Though it was possible to speak of a person's 'heart', or even 'spirit', terms of this sort did not refer to independent entities, but were only a graphic way of describing a person's emotions and general motivation. A person's bodily existence could in no way be distinguished from other aspects of the human experience.

With such an outlook, death is simply taken for granted as part of the whole business of human existence. It may be regrettable, but is a perfectly natural thing (2 Samuel 14:14), and there is nothing anyone can do about it (Job 7:9; Psalm 89:48). Two of the great heroes of the Old Testament story – Joshua and David – express the general view in their final speeches: 'I am about to go the way of all the earth' (Joshua 23:14;

The Israelites set great store by the continuance of the family name in future generations.

Old Testament people accepted death as a natural part of life. But are there some hints of belief in life hereafter?

1 Kings 2:2). The author of Psalm 90 defines the human life span as 'seventy years ... eighty years, if we are strong' (Psalm 90:10). With characteristic coolness the author of Ecclesiastes states that 'For everything there is a season, and a time for every matter under heaven: a time to be born, and a time to die ...' (3:1–2). And when the time comes, 'No one can keep himself from dying or put off the day of his death. That is a battle we cannot escape ...' (8:8). Even if we try to understand it, 'no one can tell us what will happen after we die' (Ecclesiastes 10:14; 3:22). Of course, Ecclesiastes has its own cynical viewpoint, and we need to make allowances for that in reading these passages. But when we look to the rest of the Old Testament, comments of this sort are not altogether inappropriate. For although many Old Testament passages seem to allude to the continued survival of dead people, there is no consistent picture. We can trace a number of different emphases in the Old Testament:

● At a popular level, it seems likely that many ordinary people shared much of the superstition of the ancient Middle East. Egyptians and Babylonians, as well as the people of Ugarit in Canaan, all believed that there was another life after death. The Egyptians made the most elaborate preparations for the comfort of the deceased in this new environment, and it was widely believed that the dead should be given sufficient provisions to ensure a comfortable life. Tombs discovered at Ugarit were equipped with channels through which living worshippers could pour food and drink

to their dead ancestors. Such offerings were often motivated by the view that the dead could influence the lives of the living, and if they were kept well fed then their influence would be good rather than evil. The Old Testament provides evidence for similar attitudes in Israel. The most striking instance of this is Saul's belief that the dead Samuel could somehow affect the course of his own life (1 Samuel 28:3–19). Saul was roundly condemned for this – and other Old Testament passages condemn similar reverence for the dead as alien to the true Old Testament faith (Deuteronomy 26:14; Ezekiel 43:7–9; Isaiah 8:19–20; 65:1–5).

● A more orthodox view suggested that a person could in some way survive through the continuation of their family line. This assumption seems to lie behind the book of Ruth, and is hinted at in many passages which suggest that a person who dies without children to preserve the family is at a particular disadvantage.

● The most common description of the dead is that they live a shadowy, indeterminate existence in a place called Sheol. Sheol is not to be confused with later Christian ideas of heaven and hell. It is a morally neutral term, and what actually goes on in Sheol is never really made clear. Sometimes, existence there is spoken of as an imprisonment, with those who are there isolated from God and completely unaware of anything (Psalm 30:9; 88:10–12; 115:17; Job 14:20–22; Ecclesiastes 9:5–6). At other times, God's power is said to extend even to Sheol (Amos 9:2; Psalm 139:8), but these sentiments are essentially poetic and rhetorical. They are meant to encourage the living rather than to make definitive statements about the state of the dead.

● Yet other Old Testament passages have been taken to refer to the idea of resurrection from the dead. There is only one absolutely clear statement of belief in a resurrection, and that is Daniel 12:2. Because of this it is often supposed that the idea of resurrection was a relative latecomer in the Old Testament faith, articulated at a time when the deaths of good people were especially hard to accept – as they were at the time Daniel was written. But this is difficult to sustain, and it is more likely that the idea of resurrection emerged naturally from a much earlier period. Some of the oldest poetry in the Old Testament seems to imply resurrection (Deuteronomy 32:39;

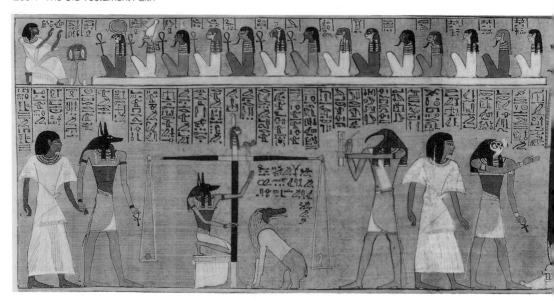

The Egyptians certainly believed in life after death. In this papyrus a man's heart is being weighed against a feather, as he prepares for his final journey.

1 Samuel 2:6), and there are three stories of resurrections from the dead told in the Deuteronomistic History (1 Kings 17:8–24; 2 Kings 4:8–37; 13:20–21). Though these stories raise other questions, the way they are told suggests that their readers would be familiar with the possibility of resurrection from the dead. The same can also be said about other passages, for instance, Hosea 6:1–3, Ezekiel 37:1–14, Isaiah 53:8–12, and Job 19:25–27. Some scholars have also argued that the references to Sheol could at least imply resurrection. Existence there is characterized as a sleep in silence and darkness – and in Daniel, resurrection is referred to as an awakening from the sleep of death.

It certainly seems likely that this later articulation of a resurrection belief emerged from the earlier faith of Israel, rather than coming in from some other source, as was once believed. We know that it was the subject of continual argument for a very long time. Even in the time of the New Testament, the Sadducees still could not bring themselves to accept that resurrection of the dead was an authentic part of the Old Testament faith. The Pharisees, and probably most ordinary Jewish people, took a different view. But we should notice that, where the Old Testament does mention resurrection is essentially the reversal of physical death, and the restoration of the life in this world that was there before. The idea that resurrection life could have a distinctive and different quality is not found in the Old Testament. Nor is the belief that resurrection signified the defeat of death. Both those developments were to come later, and grew out of the Christian belief in the resurrection of Jesus.

11 God and his people

THE OLD Testament faith emerged from the corporate history of Israel's people. This meant it could be tested in the affairs of everyday life. It was not a series of abstract speculations about God. Though Israel's theologians were constantly questioning and refining their understanding of God and his ways, their faith was never merely an intellectual process. At the centre of the Old Testament faith is a relationship between God and his people. Israel's faith and Israel's style of life could not be separated. How then, in practical terms, did God and his people relate to one another?

Belief and behaviour

It seems to be almost endemic within human nature that people express their deepest convictions in those special forms of behaviour that we would normally call 'organized religion'. Israel was no exception. Worship at the local and national sanctuaries took place in strictly defined circumstances, and included a wide variety of activities. Prayer, praise, sacrifice – all these things were just as typical of the Old Testament faith as they are of many other religions. When Israelite people met for organized worship, they were expressing their appreciation for all that God had done for them.

We shall leave this aspect of the Old Testament faith until later. For in the Old Testament, a person's response to God was always intended to be much broader than that. Many writers emphasized

The life of the market-place was never intended to be distinct from the life of worship. Repeatedly the prophets condemned a religiosity which made no difference to everyday behaviour.

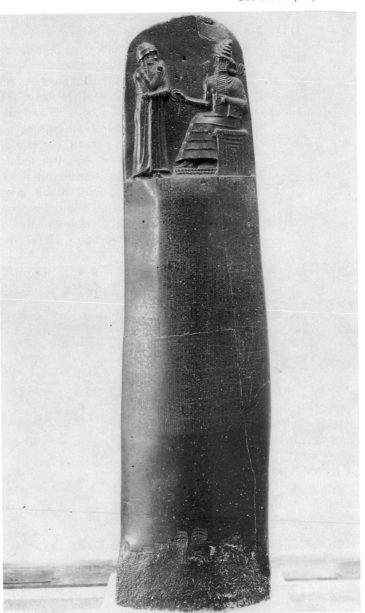

The law-code of King Hammurabi of Babylon is inscribed on this column (or *stele*). This ancient code bears a considerable likeness to some Old Testament laws.

that what went on in the shrine must never be separated from the way people lived day by day in the market-place, on the farm or at home. The prophet Micah was outspoken in condemning the empty performance of religious rituals, and emphasized that true worship of God was quite different and far more demanding: 'the Lord has told us what is good. What he requires of us is this: to do what is just, to show constant love, and to live in humble fellowship with our God.' Most of the prophets made similar statements. So too did the history writers, as well as the poets and the wisdom teachers.

Micah 6:8
1 Samuel 15:22
Psalm 51:16–17
Proverbs 21:3

God had shown by his actions in history and nature that his love and concern extend to every area of human life. So too, every aspect of Israel's experience was to be affected by their commitment to him. The relationship between God and his people was to have a moral, as well as a cultic basis. The nation's response to God must be shown in the way they behaved, not just in what they believed.

This conviction runs deeply throughout the Old Testament. Even those books which relate to the formalities of organized worship are founded on moral and spiritual values. At the heart of the book of Deuteronomy is the instruction to 'Love the Lord your God with all your heart, with all your soul, and with all your strength'. Love for neighbours is also advocated in another section of Old Testament Law – and it is notable that the Ten Commandments sum up Israel's duty to God predominantly in terms of social and personal morality.

Deuteronomy 6:5

Leviticus 19:18
Exodus 20:1–17; Deuteronomy 5:6–22

At one time, scholars imagined that this emphasis on behaviour was a late development within the Old Testament faith. Many nineteenth-century thinkers believed that the sort of biological

These pillars of salt in the Dead Sea are close to a possible site for Sodom and Gomorrah. This early story shows a deep concern that religion and morality should go together.

evolution popularized by Charles Darwin had been paralleled by a moral and spiritual evolution, as human attitudes had developed and matured. Theories such as this encouraged people to take it for granted that Israel's religious experience must have begun as a simple nature worship, which only evolved into high moral standards under the influence of great thinkers such as the Old Testament prophets, who tried to persuade their people to move from superstition to a more sophisticated understanding of God and his ways.

This sort of view of the Old Testament faith has had many supporters. But it is simplistic and superficial:

● The whole concept of evolutionary philosophy has now been discredited. The idea that people began in primitive savagery and are getting better all the time simply does not square with the facts. The violence and brutality of our own generation makes it perfectly obvious that people are not improving. The madness of the nuclear arms race suggests they might even be getting worse.

● In the last seventy-five years, our knowledge of the ancient world in general, and of Israel's neighbours in particular, has changed considerably. Earlier scholars did not have the benefit of these insights, and it was correspondingly difficult for them to understand the Old Testament in its own true life setting. We now know that some aspects of Old Testament morality were familiar to people throughout the ancient Middle East. Much of Israel's civil law in particular bears a close resemblance to concepts of justice going back at least as far as the law code of King Hammurabi of Babylon (about 1700 BC).

● Literary analysis of the Old Testament stories has shown that a concern for good behaviour is central to many of the oldest traditions. The story of the destruction of Sodom and Gomorrah is

The Old Testament books of Wisdom instruct the rich to have a care for the poor.

The Book of Proverbs is full of concern for children to be wisely brought up in a secure family environment.

Genesis 18:16–33

Exodus 2:11–13

certainly much older than the time of the prophets – and yet it condemns immorality in no uncertain terms. The stories about Moses also go back to ancient sources, and show his anger at moral injustices as they affected both himself and his people.

● The Old Testament law codes themselves contain instructions about the conduct of religious services alongside clear instructions about maintaining a just society. Such references were once dismissed as later additions to bring the laws into line with the message of the prophets. But further study has shown that even the very earliest strands of the Old Testament's legal material emphasize the importance of everyday behaviour as a way of serving God.

Exodus 23:1–9; Deuteronomy 16:18–20; Leviticus 19:15–18

Everyday behaviour was always a crucial factor in the Old Testament faith. But even today, religious people the world over know how easy it is to depend on the performance of familiar rituals as a means of trying to please God. Israel was no different. When the great prophets reminded them that faith in God should affect the whole of life, this was no new revelation: it was the recalling of the people back to the ideals of their ancient covenant faith.

Discovering God's will through wisdom

What exactly were these ideals – and how were they expressed in terms of everyday life? There are two main sections of the Old Testament where we can find the answer to these questions: the wisdom books; and the books of Law (Genesis to Deuteronomy), supplemented by the messages of the prophets. We have already dealt with the literary and historical contexts of these various writings. Here we are concerned with their message as it related to the discovery of God's will, and the doing of it.

Against Apion I.8

The Jewish historian Josephus (first century AD) described the wisdom books as 'precepts for the conduct of human life'. Josephus was probably thinking especially of the book of Proverbs, which contains many memorable observations on how people should behave in order to enjoy a satisfying life. Here we find advice of the sort that parents throughout the world might give to their children. Many of the instructions of the book of Proverbs would not have been out of place in quite different cultural contexts. Indeed, one whole section of Proverbs is at many points identical with an Egyptian document of about the twelfth century BC, the *Teaching of Amenemope*.

Proverbs 22:17 — 23:11

Understanding 'wisdom'

In the ancient world, the pursuit of 'wisdom' seems to have involved many different skills. Sometimes a 'wise' person was a good diplomat; at other times, a person with specialist knowledge about the world and its workings – perhaps a botanist or zoologist. When Solomon prayed for 'wisdom', he asked to be given the ability 'to rule ... with justice and to know the difference between good and evil'. But he could also be called a 'wise man' because of his literary and artistic interests.

1 Kings 4:33

1 Kings 3:9

1 Kings 4:32

'Wisdom' was obviously a very wide-ranging series of skills. Perhaps it was a term used simply to denote the possession of whatever abilities were necessary for a particular individual to be successful in their own sphere of life. For some, that meant technical training in the art of international relations. Israel no doubt had schools attached to the royal courts where this kind of formal education would be given. For others, it meant the study of science and philosophy – a sort of ancient university education. But for most, it meant the cultivation of those personal qualities that would result in happy and meaningful relationships in the everyday life of home and work-place.

There were 'wisdom' traditions in some of Israel's neighbouring cultures. The *Teaching of Amenemope*, an Egyptian document, is quoted almost verbatim in a section of Proverbs.

Deuteronomy 6:6–7

Nowadays, most people learn these social skills in school. There is some evidence that the Canaanite city-states had a formal education system. But in Israel, the family was the main influence in the life of a growing child. Young people would learn most of what they needed to know from their parents, grandparents, and the village elders. The practice recommended in the book of Deuteronomy almost certainly continued through most of the Old Testament period: 'Never forget these commands that I am giving you today. Teach them to your children. Repeat them when you are at home and when you are away, when you are resting and when you are working ...'

Wisdom in practice

The Old Testament wisdom books contain examples of all these different kinds of 'wisdom'. Job and Ecclesiastes are the product of a well-developed intellectual approach to the great imponderables of human existence: the problem of evil, and the apparent meaninglessness of so much of life. As such, they do not tell us much in a direct way about everyday behaviour in ancient Israel – though they do, of course, take certain moral standards for granted. In the book of Proverbs we find a much greater emphasis on 'practical wisdom'. Yet even here, there seems to be a good deal of interest in scientific study, for moral lessons are often reinforced and illustrated by reference to the life of the animals and events in the natural world.

The book of Proverbs is itself an anthology of materials emanating from various wisdom teachers. But its contents are remarkably consistent, and deal with personal relationships in a number of different contexts.

● **The family** It is not surprising that this should be a basic concern in Proverbs, since many of its precepts almost certainly originated in the context of advice handed on from one generation to another.

As elsewhere in the Old Testament, a stable sexual relationship between husband and wife is seen as the key to family stability. Adultery is singled out as a particularly destructive evil whose repercussions affect more than the two individuals involved: 'A man can hire a prostitute for the price of a loaf of bread, but adultery will cost him all he has.' As we might expect in view of what we have already seen in the Old Testament creation stories, wisdom teachers in Israel spoke frankly and freely about both the attractions and perils of sexual unfaithfulness: 'The lips of another man's wife may be as sweet as honey, and her kisses as smooth as olive-oil, but when it is all over, she leaves you nothing but bitterness and pain.' But the advice is never narrow-minded or prudish. The love poems in the Song of Solomon have a number of connections with the wisdom books, and the way they depict a developing sexual relationship has often alarmed modern Christian readers by its frankness. But the same open and joyful acknowledgment of human sexuality as part of God's creation is found also in the everyday advice of the book of Proverbs. For at the same time as its readers are warned against the dangers of adultery, they are also encouraged to develop and renew relationships within the marriage context: '... be happy with your wife and find your joy with the girl you married ... Let her charms keep you happy; let her surround you with her love ...'

Out of a happy marriage will come happy children – and the responsibility for bringing them up is to be shared between husband and wife. Indeed, the guidance of growing children is one of the major themes of Proverbs. Such guidance should be positive, by both example and precept, aiming to 'Teach a child how he should live, and he will remember it all his life'. Even when parents need to correct their child, that should always be done from a concern to promote moral maturity in the family: 'If you don't punish your son, you don't love him. If you do love him, you will correct him.' If the right course is followed in all these matters, then the whole family will be able to share in the mutual joy of a developing relationship in which 'Old men are proud of their grandchildren, just as boys are proud of their fathers'.

● **Friends** Next to a good family, a person needs good friends and neighbours. In practice, a friend can often be more valuable than members of the family: 'Do not forget your friends or your father's friends. If you are in trouble, don't ask your brother for help; a neighbour near by can help you more than a brother who is far away.' Of course, in order to acquire friends we need to show ourselves to be friendly: 'Never tell your neighbour to wait until tomorrow if you

Margin references:

Proverbs 6:26

Proverbs 5:3–4

Proverbs 5:18–19

Proverbs 1:8–9; 6:20–23

Proverbs 22:6

Proverbs 13:24

Proverbs 17:6

Proverbs 27:10

Proverbs 3:28
Proverbs 25:17

Proverbs 26:18–19, 24
Proverbs 18:8; 26:22

Proverbs 6:16–19

Proverbs 26:5

Old Testament laws are strongly concerned for the disadvantaged, especially widows and orphans, whose care should be taken over by the whole community.

can help him now.' We also need tact: 'Don't visit your neighbour too often; he may get tired of you and come to hate you.' Above all, a relationship between friends needs to be based on honesty: 'A hypocrite hides his hatred behind flattering words ... A man who misleads someone and then claims that he was only joking is like a madman playing with a deadly weapon.' Gossip, then as now, was one of the commonest threats to wholesome friendship. Indeed, the way people speak to each other is one of the major themes of the wisdom literature. A slogan in one of the early chapters of Proverbs sums up 'seven things that the Lord hates'– and most of them are related to the way people speak: 'A proud look, a lying tongue, hands that kill innocent people, a mind that thinks up wicked plans, feet that hurry off to do evil, a witness who tells one lie after another, and a man who stirs up trouble among friends.'

Those who behave like this are the opposite of 'wise': they are fools. And there is only one way to deal with them: 'Give a silly answer to a silly question and the one who asked it will realize that he's not as clever as he thinks.' The wise person, on the other hand, is characterized by prudent thought and speech: 'Be careful how you think; your life is shaped by your thoughts. Never say anything that isn't true ...'

● **Society** Wisdom teachers were not only concerned with the

behaviour of people in small groups: they also gave much teaching on how society as a whole should operate. At the very beginning of the book of Proverbs, we learn that its advice 'can teach you how to live

Proverbs 1:3

intelligently and how to be honest, just, and fair'. Honesty, justice and fairness in society were among the key themes in the preaching of the prophets – and they are just as important here. We may find this somewhat surprising, for most scholars are agreed that the wisdom books must have originated in fairly well-to-do circles. The fact that the wisdom teachers of Israel had international connections supports that assumption, for wealth is required to make and sustain worldwide contacts of this kind. We certainly know that later Jewish wisdom teachers must have been quite rich. Writing about 180 BC,

Ecclesiasticus 34:9–12
Ecclesiasticus 31:12 — 32:13
Ecclesiasticus 33:24–31
Ecclesiasticus 51:23–28

the wise man Ben Sirach tells of his wide travels, and gives advice on such things as behaviour at banquets and how to treat servants. He also mentions the large fees that he charged for tuition at his school! In the Old Testament itself, the description of Job certainly suggests

Job 1:1–3

that the authors of that book moved in high-class circles. Even in Proverbs, some pieces of advice suggest a context of relative

Proverbs 21:14

affluence.

It is therefore all the more surprising to find here a morality which recognizes the limitations of wealth. 'Wisdom' itself is more

Proverbs 3:13–15
Proverbs 17:1
Proverbs 22:1

important than riches. So is 'peace of mind' and 'a good reputation' – all of which suggests that it is 'Better to be poor and fear the Lord than to be rich and in trouble. Better to eat vegetables with people

Proverbs 15:16–17

you love than to eat the finest meat where there is hate.' The other Old Testament wisdom books make exactly the same points. Even the pessimistic author of Ecclesiastes declares that amassing money

Ecclesiastes 2:11

is pointless: 'It was like chasing the wind – of no use at all.' And the book of Job asserts quite bluntly that trust in money is incompatible with a living relationship to God himself: 'I have never trusted in riches or taken pride in my wealth ... Such a sin would be punished

Job 31:24–28

by death; it denies Almighty God.'

The imagery of the wisdom books may be less picturesque and dramatic than the words of the prophets, but their social perspective is remarkably similar. Many of the abuses condemned by the wisdom teachers were the same as those that caused so much concern to the

Proverbs 11:1
Proverbs 15:27
Proverbs 28:8

prophets: unjust business practices, bribery, and taking advantage of people by charging interest on loans – all of it summed up in the slogan that it is 'Better to be poor and honest than rich and

Proverbs 28:6

dishonest.' On a positive note, the wisdom literature is full of instructions to those who are rich to share what they have with the

Proverbs 13:23
Job 31:19–20
Proverbs 14:21, 31

poor – whether it be sharing access to their land and crops, or giving them clothes, or just general exhortations to be generous to others. As elsewhere in the Old Testament, this generosity is to apply especially to those with no other visible means of support – which in

Proverbs 23:10–11; Job 31:16–18
Proverbs 14:4

ancient Israel meant especially widows and orphans. And even animals were to be treated with due concern for their welfare.

Besides charity, the wisdom books also advocate justice. It is one thing to give freely to those who are poor. But social justice is a more basic human need. The wisdom books are conscious that it is people

Proverbs 30:13–14

Proverbs 31:8–9

(usually rich people) who actually create divisions within society. So they advocate a positive effort to correct social injustices: 'Speak up for people who cannot speak for themselves. Protect the rights of all who are helpless. Speak for them and be a righteous judge. Protect the rights of the poor and needy.'

Here, in the wisdom books, we have much clear guidance on how God's people should behave. Morality, like charity, was to begin at home. But its effects went wider than the individual person: they were as broad as society itself.

Wisdom and faith

The law-keeping aspect of Old Testament faith has survived into modern Judaism. This boy wears the phylactery, a box fixed to his forehead in which are copies of a part of the law.

People have often thought that the wisdom books present a different message from the prophets or the Old Testament laws. The main strands of the Old Testament faith emphasize God's actions in the life of his people, whereas the wisdom books are said to be more 'secular', based not on God's revelation of himself but on human reason. In addition, it is often asserted that whereas the prophets and lawgivers of ancient Israel were concerned with the shape of society, the wisdom books are concerned more with personal morality. We can certainly agree that some features of these books seem to justify such observations:

● They are part of an international way of thinking, and as such have a number of similarities with literature from both Babylon and Egypt. They are not, therefore, unique to Israel, and in that sense cannot be said to be exclusively based on the unique aspects of the Old Testament faith.

● They rarely, if ever, refer directly to the great events of the Old Testament story. Instead, their teaching tends to be based on commonsense and on observation of the world of nature.

Some scholars have thought of the wisdom books and their moral teaching as a secular, humanistic intrusion into the Old Testament faith. They regard them as the religious side of those social and political changes that accompanied the institutionalization of the monarchy in ancient Israel, and the adoption of a lifestyle suited to the world of international politics.

But this is too simple an analysis.

Is wisdom secular?

To say that the wisdom books are 'secular' is imposing modern ways of thinking on the ancient world. Certainly, the wisdom writers take their starting-point from human experience of life. But in the ancient world in general, this was never 'humanistic' in the sense of being purely secular and non-religious. Throughout the ancient world, 'wisdom' was always based on an understanding of how the world works – but it was everywhere taken for granted that the world only worked at all because of the intentions of the gods or, in the case of the Old Testament, of one all-powerful God. To refuse to take account of this was something that only a 'fool' would do. A really wise person would never forget that even the ordinary world of everyday experience was sustained by God himself. Even a pessimist like the author of Ecclesiastes, who frankly confesses that he sometimes finds it hard to discover God at work in the world, nevertheless takes his existence for granted as a fundamental part of his view of life. Other writers were more positive: 'To be wise you must first obey the Lord... If you know the Holy One, you have understanding' (Proverbs 9:10).

Wisdom and natural law

In view of the importance the Old Testament attaches to the relationship of God and his world, it is not surprising that contemplation of the way the world is should lead to personal encounter with God himself. If, as the writer of the first few chapters of Genesis suggests, God can be found in the realities of the natural world, then it is hardly surprising that the discerning moralist can discover there God's demands of his people. This kind of 'natural law' is a widespread phenomenon. Even today, questions relating to human rights are often decided on the basis of some notion of 'natural justice' rather than by appeals to standards handed down from God or anyone else. The Old Testament wisdom books often appeal to precisely this sort of argument. Job, for example, asks for justice for himself because he has been just to his servants – and 'The same God who created me created my servants also' (Job 31:15).

Scholars have sometimes supposed that this sort of appeal to 'natural justice' is unique to the wisdom books. But in fact it is found throughout the Old Testament. When the prophet Amos denounces the war crimes of the nations of his day, he does so on the basis of natural justice (Amos 1:1–2:3). When the writer of Genesis condemns murder, he does it because people were made 'in God's image' (Genesis 9:6). And when Isaiah complains about the disobedience of his people, he concludes that their behaviour is unnatural and irrational because it is so different from the way that things work in the world of nature (Isaiah 1:2–3).

Apart from specific examples such as these, much of the imagery of the messages of the Old Testament prophets is also drawn from the world of nature – just as is the imagery in books such as Proverbs. At one time it was fashionable to think that the prophets had 'borrowed' ideas from the wisdom teachers. But it is much more likely that both of them were independently basing their teaching on the clear 'creation theology' of the Old Testament faith.

Wisdom and social ethics

It has also been claimed that a 'wisdom' morality is inconsistent with an emphasis on social justice. It is certainly true that teaching on the shape of society is presented more forcibly by the prophets and lawgivers in relation to the great themes of Israel's salvation history. But we do an injustice to wisdom teachers in ancient Israel to suppose that they were interested only in themselves. Indeed, in the wider wisdom literature of the ancient world, social justice was a major concern. Protecting the poor and disadvantaged members of society was a major theme in Babylonian and Egyptian literature, as well as in the texts from Ugarit which tell of Canaanite kings showing the same sort of consideration. At the very beginning of the Old Testament book of Proverbs, its aims are summed up as teaching people 'how to live intelligently and how to be honest, just, and fair' (1:3). And the hero of the book of Job is a perfect example of a person who always did the right thing by those less fortunate than himself (Job 31:13–23). Questions about social justice are certainly a major concern of both prophets and history writers in the Old Testament. They emphasized that the shape of society should reflect God's dealings with his people. The wisdom books give different reasons for promoting equality and justice – but their ethical stance is none the less 'religious' for that.

Wisdom and the covenant

In point of fact, the actual ethical advice of the wisdom writers is often identical to the lessons of Israel's history. Caring for the poor, consideration for animals, justice in society, concern for orphans, as well as prohibition of false witness, adultery, bribery and vengeance – all of these things are as common in the wisdom literature as they are in the Old Testament laws. Indeed, the wisdom writers often express these ideas more concretely by showing how they relate to specific situations in the life of the family or the community. Time and time again, the wisdom writers apply the same lessons as the prophets and others who stood in the 'covenant' tradition. For they were all consciously serving the same God – a God whose will could be made known to his people in both the created world and the great unrepeatable events of history.

Discovering God's will in the Law

The wisdom books reflect the standards of decent behaviour that ordinary people might take for granted. But in any organized society, this kind of moral consensus needs to be clearly defined, and this is what we find in the Old Testament law books.

The first five books of the Old Testament, from Genesis to Deuteronomy, were often referred to simply as 'the Law'. Much of the material in these books is not at all like the kind of law most people would be familiar with today. Genesis in particular is a collection of stories, which at first sight we might expect to be regarded as some sort of history. But the Old Testament notion of 'law' was much more comprehensive and wide-ranging than ours. When we talk of 'the law' we generally have in mind sets of rules that can be interpreted by lawyers with special professional training, and applied in a court of justice by a judge. It would certainly be unusual for a modern person to agree with one of the Old Testament poets who wrote, 'I take pleasure in your law'.

Psalm 119:77

But the Hebrew word for law *(Torah)* meant far more than just rules and regulations. It really included everything that God had revealed to his people – but especially the 'guidance' or 'instruction' that he would give to their lives. In the Old Testament, the Law is the place to discover what people can believe about God, and what he requires of them in return. This is why the *Torah* is so closely bound up with the stories of Israel's early history. Knowing and obeying God is not just a matter of blind obedience to religious and moral rules: it is a question of experiencing God's concern and love in a personal and social context. God's undeserved love to his people – shown in events such as the exodus – is basic to the Old Testament laws. Israel did not keep the Law in order to become God's people, but because they were already living in a close relationship to him.

The German scholar Albrecht Alt believed that some of the Old Testament's most distinctive laws emerged in this way out of Israel's experience of God. Many Old Testament laws are similar to laws in other ancient societies, for they concern the everyday happenings of rural life. Alt called these 'casuistic' or case laws – laws in which very specific situations were envisaged, and guidance given as to how disputes may be resolved. A typical law of this kind might deal with violent assault, or with the processes of responsible farming.

Exodus 21:20
Exodus 22:6

But the Old Testament also contains other, more absolute regulations, such as the Ten Commandments, where worship of other gods, murder, adultery, theft, lying and adultery are all prohibited without any further qualification or explanation. Moreover, such prohibitions seem to be based on a simple statement about God's nature as Israel had experienced him in the course of their history. In a previous chapter we have reviewed the evidence suggesting that in giving the commandments this precise form, the Old Testament writers may have had in mind the kind of covenant treaties that small struggling nations often made with more powerful states, in exchange for protection and security. Such covenant agreements would be reaffirmed at regular intervals. Alt believed that 'apodictic' laws of this kind formed the centre of Israel's renewal

Exodus 20:1–17; Deuteronomy 5:6–22

of their faith in God every seven years at the Festival of Shelters, or Tabernacles. It was this form of absolute law that was most characteristic of the Old Testament, for it was nothing less than an explanation of the everyday ramifications of Israel's covenant faith.

But there are difficulties with this view:

● Casuistic law is a distinctive literary form. But this so-called 'apodictic' law is not strictly a literary form at all. These absolute laws are expressed in a variety of literary formulations.

● Alt believed that these absolute rules were unique to Israel. But we now know that similar terminology could also be used in legal contexts elsewhere, especially among the Hittites, but also in Egypt and Babylon. It was not always the same actions that were prohibited there, of course, but the form itself was certainly found outside the Old Testament faith.

● There is no real evidence that these 'apodictic' laws either originated in or were regularly repeated at the great religious festivals in Israel.

● These statements are not really 'law' in the technical sense at all. They are more a general listing of accepted standards of behaviour, and in this respect the 'apodictic' law is not all that different from the teaching of the wisdom books. It is at least arguable that they could be based on Israel's understanding of the 'natural law' revealed in the work of creation, and not on the covenant at Mt Sinai.

The books of *Torah* in the Old Testament, like all modern collections of law (and many other parts of the Old Testament), are an anthology of laws relating to different situations and different periods during the whole span of the Old Testament story. They are not meant to be read from start to finish as a consistent account of Israel's legal system. All scholars would agree that within the books of the Law there are at least four quite different collections of material. The precise way in which we relate these separate law codes to one another will be determined by our view of how the first five books of the Old Testament came to be written, and our discussion here takes account of what has already been said on that subject in chapter 7.

The Ten Commandments

Most people who know anything at all about the Bible will recognize this collection of moral rules as a basic part of the Old Testament's view of human behaviour. Its principles have been enshrined in many national law codes since Old Testament days, and in many respects form a charter of fundamental human rights. It was obviously intended to be learned by heart, and often repeated. The fact that there are ten commandments is certainly not accidental, but is a learning device so that they could be counted off on the fingers of both hands as they were repeated. This was a popular way of remembering things.

There are other groups of laws which may originally have been organized in the same way, though they are mostly concerned with the conduct of organized worship. The book of Psalms contains at least one such list of ten things that summarize good behaviour. This is the main subject of the Ten Commandments themselves. They are not technically law, for they contain no mention of penalties for those who break them. Rather, they are a kind of policy statement – a bill of rights – showing how relationships between God and his people were to be viewed within the Old Testament faith community. It is widely agreed by scholars that this list must have originated at a very early period in the Old Testament story, quite possibly with Moses himself.

Exodus 34:12–26; Leviticus 20:2–16; 18:6–18

Psalm 15:2–5

The book of the covenant

Exodus 20:22 — 23:33

Many parts of the book of the covenant are similar to other ancient law codes, especially the codes of Ur-Nammu of Ur (2050 BC) and of Hammurabi, king of Babylon (1700 BC). Though there are many differences of detail between the Book of the Covenant and these other laws, their general outlook is the same and simply reflects widespread customs in the ancient Middle East. So this is much more like a code of law in our modern sense. It is widely believed to be very ancient, going back to the time of Israel's earliest leaders, Moses and Joshua. The essential concern of these laws is with the life of the community. They are mostly a 'casuistic' type of legislation, though there are also some rules relating to the conduct of organized worship.

Crimes of violence are punished in nearly all societies.

Deuteronomy

The word 'Deuteronomy' means 'a second law'. Here we find an amplification and application of earlier law codes, showing how they could apply to the changing circumstances of Israel's national life. As such, it is obviously based on ancient materials. Some scholars believe that it found its present form as a liturgy for a covenant renewal festival at which the worshippers in ancient Israel would regularly 'relive' the events of their national past, and commit themselves afresh to their God Yahweh. Much of the book certainly reads like sermons, preached as a prelude to the presentation of the actual Law itself, and followed by the people's commitment to it. The book of Deuteronomy was a major influence in the reform of temple worship carried out by King Josiah of Judah, though its actual origins were certainly earlier than his day.

Deuteronomy 5 — 11
Deuteronomy 12 — 26
Deuteronomy 27 — 28

2 Kings 22:3–20

Priestly laws

These are found in Exodus, Leviticus and Numbers. They include all the rest of the Old Testament laws, among which are large sections dealing with the tent of worship and its contents, and various regulations for the priests there. There are also detailed regulations for the conduct of worship, together with rules governing the preparation and eating of food as well as matters of domestic and personal hygiene. It was once believed that these rules concerning worship were relatively late developments in the Old Testament story, partly because the message of the sixth-century prophet Ezekiel contains some similar notions. But closer investigation has shown that many of the practices referred to here are very similar to practices known elsewhere in the ancient world at a much earlier date.

Exodus 25 — 30
Exodus 35 — 40
Leviticus 1 — 10

Leviticus 11 — 16

Ezekiel 40 — 48

Leviticus 17 — 26

One section of the book of Leviticus is often thought to be another separate law code — the 'Holiness Code'. There are several reasons for this:

● These chapters begin with rules about organized worship, but then make no reference at all to the very full legislation on the matter found in the preceding chapters.

● The statement that 'All these are the laws and commands that the Lord gave to Moses on Mt Sinai for the people of Israel' seems to be a formal ending, which does not relate to what follows in the next chapter.

Leviticus 26:46

● The theme of 'holiness' runs everywhere through these chapters but is not a prominent theme at all in the rest of Leviticus.

From theory to practice

Life in the ancient world was totally different from life today, and most modern readers find the laws of the Old Testament dull and tedious. But they can still give us a number of insights into important aspects of the Old Testament faith. There seem to be so many collections of laws that it comes as a surprise to discover they are far from comprehensive. Many situations are not mentioned at all. Other ancient law codes were the same, perhaps because the laws that were written down were only intended as samples of how justice should be administered. Or it could be that the written laws were to give guidance in cases of particular difficulty, and alongside them other more straightforward procedures were simply taken for granted.

There are many ways of classifying laws. For our purpose here it will be helpful to consider how they related in general terms to the life of Israelite society. One area of life controlled by the Law was what we would call religion. Many Old Testament laws are cultic (or religious) laws, describing how worship is to be conducted. This is considered more fully in the next chapter – though we must never forget that religion and everyday behaviour can not easily be separated in the Old Testament. But in addition to that, we can trace four other types of law in the Old Testament codes.

Criminal law

Covenant treaties, like this one found in Alalah in modern Syria, were common in Old Testament times, and the 'covenant' is a basic Old Testament theme. Some believe the Ten Commandments take their form from the typical covenant treaty.

Every society has certain actions that are so thoroughly and universally disapproved of that the community itself feels it necessary to punish those who do them. Civil law deals with arguments between individuals, about which there can be room for different judgments. But criminal law concerns principles of right and wrong that are taken as self-evident. This does not mean that the criminal law of one nation will always be the same as the criminal law of another. Indeed, there are often striking differences. Even today, activities that are branded as criminal in one state may well be regarded as fundamental human rights in another. So by examining those actions which a particular state regards as criminal, we can soon understand the basic attitudes and fundamental values of its people.

As far as we can see, the only penalty actually exacted by the state in ancient Israel was the death penalty. Fines were unknown, and though a person could be put under arrest while his case was decided, imprisonment as such was not introduced until after the exile in Babylon. Monetary sanctions could be imposed, but they were regarded as restitution by the wrongdoer to the victim – and therefore came within the jurisdiction of the civil law. Even crimes such as personal assault or theft were dealt with in this way.

It is probably significant that every crime punishable by death was related in some way or another to the Ten Commandments. This is why Dr Anthony Phillips describes these Commandments as 'Ancient Israel's Criminal Law'. We have noticed that the Ten Commandments are not strictly 'law' at all in the technical sense. But this description is still a useful one, for all those actions punishable by the community as a whole were closely related to Israel's understanding of her position as the people of God. To commit a crime was, quite simply, to deny the reality of the covenant faith. Such crimes included:

● **Offences against God** Examples of these offences are

Exodus 22:20; Leviticus 20:1–5;
Deuteronomy 13:1–18
Leviticus 24:10–16
Exodus 22:18; Leviticus 20:27
Leviticus 21:9
Exodus 31:14–15

idolatry, blasphemy and magic – all of which in one way or another deny the very basis of the relationship between God and his people. Other offences, such as the prostitution of a priest's daughter or not keeping the sabbath day might seem less serious to us. But the Old Testament Law views them in the same light because both priesthood and sabbath are 'a sign of the covenant'.

Exodus 31:16

● **Offences against human life** Intentional murder was a particularly serious crime, though accidental killing was subject to other arrangements. No less serious was the case of a person who kidnaps another, intending to make him a slave. Human liberty as well as human life is of great value. Many scholars believe that the eighth commandment refers not to stealing in general but to kidnapping. The theme of personal freedom is certainly important in other sections of Old Testament Law.

Exodus 21:12; Leviticus 24:17; Numbers 35:16–21
Numbers 35:22–29
Exodus 21:16; Deuteronomy 24:7

Exodus 20:15; Deuteronomy 5:19

● **Offences against the family** If unnatural termination of life is a criminal offence, so is interference with the natural context in which life is created: the sexual relationship between husband and wife. Other kinds of sexual relationship, whether incest, homosexuality, buggery, or even adultery are all regarded as serious criminal offences, along with disdain for parents.

Leviticus 20:10–16
Exodus 21:15, 17; Leviticus 20:9;
Deuteronomy 21:18–21

Civil law

Old Testament civil law has many similarities to other laws of the ancient world. It deals with everyday affairs such as the treatment of employees, violence of various sorts, and the duties of owners to protect third parties from injury caused by either animals or property. The Book of the Covenant consists entirely of this sort of law. It is instructive that in this law code God is usually referred to as 'Elohim', meaning 'God' in general, rather than by his personal

Boundary stones marked the limits of a person's land; this one comes from Babylon in the time of Nebuchadnezzar I. Some Old Testament laws were aimed at preventing the absorption of smallholdings into great estates.

name 'Yahweh'. This may well suggest that Israel simply took over this legal form from the general stock of commonly accepted norms without making too many detailed changes to it.

Punishment is generally understood as compensation for the wrong done, and many penalties are similar to those in other codes such as the laws of Hammurabi. But there are some differences. Bodily mutilation, for example, was quite a common punishment in the ancient world, but there is only one specific example of it in the *Deuteronomy 25:11–12* Old Testament. The Old Testament certainly states that punish- ments should be exacted 'life for life, eye for eye, tooth for tooth, *Exodus 21:23–24; Leviticus* hand for hand, foot for foot, burn for burn, wound for wound, bruise *24:19–20; Deuteronomy 19:21* for bruise'. But this seems to be almost a symbolic statement, emphasizing that the punishment should always be in proportion to the wrong that has been suffered. In the ancient world, even this apparently ruthless retribution could be a means of limiting what would otherwise be excessive vengeance. In the light of Lamech's *Genesis 4:23* boast that 'I have killed a young man because he struck me', even a basic law of equal retribution would be an improvement! In the event, though the principle is stated in the Book of the Covenant, it is both preceded and followed there by laws which show that in general other forms than physical punishment could and should be preferred – generally financial compensation. The payment of compensation to the victim in place of physical punishment was probably quite a widespread practice.

Family law

The whole of Israelite society was family and clan based, and the importance of the family unit is reflected in many Old Testament laws. Relationships between family members had a far-reaching effect on the overall shape of Israelite society.

A stable relationship between husband and wife was basic to the Old Testament view of family life. Marriage itself was generally of one man to one woman (monogamy), though kings and other leading figures often seem to have had more than one wife (polygamy) – and this practice is never actually banned anywhere in the Old Testament. Marriages were generally arranged by parents, though *1 Samuel 18:20* love marriages are not altogether unknown. But alongside his legal wife, a man could also have any number of 'concubines'. These were slave wives, and had a correspondingly lower status than the main wife. Divorce was taken for granted, though in practice it could often leave a woman destitute and was probably not very frequent for that reason.

But all these matters were entirely a family affair. The Law was not involved at all, except that the civil law contains a number of guidelines relating to circumstances that might arise with a breakdown of normal relationships, and the criminal law of course *Exodus 21:7–11; Deuteronomy* forbids adultery. Detailed regulations are given for the proper *21:10–14* treatment of concubines. Guidance is also given on what should *Deuteronomy 24:1–4* happen after a divorce.

Wilful disregard for parents was in certain circumstances dealt with by the criminal law, but usually the authority of the father or patriarch of the family was absolute. In the earliest period, a father could even condemn members of his family to death. Later legislation provided for such cases to be referred to the village elders, and some passages suggest there was an ultimate right of appeal to the king.

Genesis 38:24
Deuteronomy 21:18–21

2 Samuel 14:4–11

On the positive side, members of a family also had obligations to each other. If one member was forced to sell himself into slavery to pay off a debt, then it was the duty of one of his close relatives to buy him back – circumstances which are well illustrated in the story of Ruth. Family life in Old Testament times could have definite advantages; but it also carried with it awesome responsibilities.

Leviticus 25:47–49

Social law

The Canaanite city-states which preceded the emergence of Israel as a nation were essentially feudal societies, with a powerful and wealthy ruling class. This was in strong contrast to the tribal structure we find in the Old Testament, which ensured that Israelite society was not dominated by a powerful hierarchy. Instead, it was a self-consciously egalitarian society in which all citizens enjoyed the same fundamental rights and privileges.

The conflict between these two models of society runs deep in the Old Testament. In the earliest Israelite settlements, local elders were the leaders of their own communities. As things developed authority became more centralized until the need for a king was obvious. The Old Testament story documents the way the kingship was strenuously resisted. Even then, the power of the king was stringently regulated by the Law. When the great kingdom split in two after Solomon's death, it was largely the result of tensions between the Canaanite, bureaucratic ideal and the Israelite ideal in which every individual was equal – his freedom restricted only by the mutual obligations imposed by the family group.

1 Samuel 8
Deuteronomy 17:14–20

In practical terms, the central issue was the possession of land. In the Canaanite city-states all land was ultimately owned by the king. But in Israel, all land ultimately belonged to God himself. It was given in trust to the family group as something that could be neither bought nor sold, but must be handed on from one generation to the next. In this way Israel hoped to avoid the emergence of a land-owning class, and to preserve the relative equality of people. Those who tried to amass land for themselves were tirelessly condemned by the prophets. Even the king himself was not exempt. This is why apparently tedious lists of people and land play an important part in the Old Testament.

1 Samuel 8:11–17

Leviticus 25:23

Isaiah 5:8
Micah 2:1–2
1 Kings 21

Numbers 26; 34; Joshua 13 — 19

Many laws set out to preserve the freedom of the individual to live unmolested on the land which God had given to the family. The Law banned actions such as moving boundary stones, and many other prohibitions relating to loans and debts also find their real significance in this context. Charging interest on loans was forbidden. But what often happened was that a person would give either clothes or property as security for a loan. Then, if the loan could not be repaid, the borrower soon became virtually a slave of the lender – and though technically living on his family land, he was reduced to a

Deuteronomy 19:14

Exodus 22:25; Leviticus 25:35–38;
Deuteronomy 23:19–20

state of destitution. This is why the Law tried to regulate what could be used as securities for loans. It also provided for debts to be written off every seven years (the sabbatical year), or every fifty years (the Jubilee).

Exodus 22:26–27; Deuteronomy 24:6
Deuteronomy 15:1–11
Leviticus 25:8–17

The Old Testament social ethic shows great concern for many disadvantaged groups – foreigners, the poor, the oppressed, widows, orphans, and even personal enemies. This emphasis has led some recent scholars to think of early Israel as a proletarian protest movement against the elitist structures of Canaanite power. There is a good deal to be said in favour of this view of Israel's social perception. But we must not exaggerate its uniqueness. Concern for despised people was not an exclusively Old Testament interest. In the laws of Ur-Nammu we read the following list of the king's achievements:

Exodus 22:21–27; 23:1–9

> The orphan was not delivered up to the rich man, the widow was not delivered up to the mighty man, the man of one shekel was not delivered up to the man of one mina.

The Old Testament is most distinctive in its treatment of slaves, who were clearly regarded as persons in their own right. Not only could they expect to be set free, but they also had rights even if they ran away from their master. The master must give his slaves a regular day off, and he must recognize the limits to his power over a slave's life. The master who injures his slave can be forced to compensate him by giving the slave his freedom.

Exodus 21:1–6
Deuteronomy 23:15–16
Exodus 23:12; Deuteronomy 5:12–15

Exodus 21:26–27

If a master kills his own slave, that is a particularly serious offence, and is to be avenged by the community acting on behalf of the slave, presumably because he has no family of his own to defend him. Some scholars believe that the death penalty was prescribed for this. If so, such concern for the welfare of slaves would be absolutely without parallel in the ancient world. It would also suggest that the killing of a slave represented a spiritual as well as a social challenge to the community. The religious background to the slavery laws is certainly made clear in at least one law code, where special treatment of slaves is justified by the statement that 'you were slaves in Egypt and the Lord your God set you free; that is why I am now giving you this command'. The distinctive nature of Israelite society emerged not out of purely humanitarian motives: it was part and parcel of Israel's experience of their God in the formative events of the nation's history.

Exodus 21:20

Deuteronomy 15:15

Explaining God's will

The impact of Israel's history can be seen most clearly in the sort of society envisaged by the Old Testament. In one way or another, all the most distinctive features of Old Testament morality have been determined by Israel's encounter with God on the stage of human history. The great events which helped formulate Israel's understanding of God's character also gave a special insight into what God required of his people. Events such as the escape from Egypt and the entry into the promised land had their effect on God's people and

These slaves in Assyria at the time of Sennacherib were far worse off than slaves in Israel, where the laws protected them at many points.

their behaviour. In the Old Testament, correct behaviour, like so many other things, was based on history.

But how can the facts of history tell you how to behave? As we read the messages of the great prophets and explore the teaching of the books of Law, the answer to the question soon emerges. For the Old Testament ethic is not only historical: it also has other characteristics that can be identified by an appreciation of God's involvement in the lives of his people.

The Old Testament ethic is theological

It is 'theological' in the strict meaning of that word, for the Old Testament code of behaviour always refers us back to God himself. Correct human behaviour is closely related to the kind of God who had revealed himself in the events of Israel's history. It is, of course, always true that the kind of god people believe in affects the way they behave. Many people today look on religion as a kind of insurance policy for the future. They think of God as more concerned with the next world than with this, and as a result their lifestyle now is often motivated by pure self-interest. But others who understand God as a person to be known and loved here and now will have quite a different attitude to contemporary social realities, and their lifestyle will reflect their concern. The Old Testament stresses that God is a personal and active being who can be known both by individuals and societies in the context of their everyday experience of life. It takes these characteristics of God and applies them directly to the life of his people. In the Old Testament human goodness finds its authority, example and inspiration in the person of God himself. Nowhere is this summed up more eloquently than in the book of Leviticus: 'Be holy, because I, the Lord your God, am holy.' God's

Leviticus 19:2

people are to behave like God behaves. The German scholar Emil Brunner summed it up concisely when he described Old Testament morality as 'the science of human conduct as it is determined by divine conduct'.

The Old Testament ethic is dynamic

How does God express his own personality? We have already seen that the Old Testament never tries to analyze or define God in an abstract way. He is never described 'metaphysically', by asking what he is made of. He is always described 'functionally', by reference to what he does. Obviously, the two are closely related, because the way people are will be reflected in the way they work. But the Old Testament God is not just a 'God who is' – he is a 'God who acts'. He is a dynamic God rather than a static one.

So what can we learn about human behaviour by looking at the characteristic actions of God himself? Three terms are often used in the Old Testament to describe God's moral disposition:

● **Justice** This might seem a very abstract idea to us. 'Justice' is the kind of thing that lawyers and judges argue about in law courts. In the Old Testament, 'justice' includes this concern for fair play. But more characteristically justice is not something to talk about – it is something to be done. The leaders of early Israel were not 'judges' in the modern legal sense: they were leaders of their people who saw something wrong, and did something to put it right. Indeed, the Hebrew word that is normally translated 'justice' in our English Old Testament really has a much wider meaning. It refers to everything that a ruler might do to ensure that his people would enjoy a stable

One of the great formative experiences of Israel's history was their entry into the promised land, seen here from across the north end of the Dead Sea. The people were called to remember that their land was held in trust from God.

and satisfying way of life. God, therefore, is like a 'just' ruler: he

Deuteronomy 32:4; Isaiah 5:16; 61:8 — improves the quality of life for his people.

● **Mercy** When this word is used to describe God, it is emphasizing that he deals with people in a loving and personal way. God's justice is not determined by the stringent requirements of some legal system: it always operates in a context of personal love and trust. The entire Old Testament story shows how, against all expectations, God has initiated a relationship with people who by nature are weak and often morally and spiritually powerless. God never abandons them. Instead, he stands alongside them to help in their weakness, and will never reject them despite all their inadequacy and imperfection. 'How can I give you up, Israel? How can I abandon you? ... My heart will not let me do it! My love for you is too strong ... For I am God and not man. I, the Holy One, am with

Hosea 11:8–9 — you. I will not come to you in anger.'

● **Truth** This is also something that we tend to think of in abstract terms. But in the Old Testament, 'truth' is more often a characteristic of people. When the disguised Joseph put his brothers

Genesis 42:16 — in prison, he did so to find out 'whether there is truth in you' – in other words, whether they could be trusted or not. In the world of the Old Testament the gods were notoriously unreliable. They did whatever they wished, and all too often their human worshippers had to pay the price. But the God of the Old Testament is quite different. He is wholly trustworthy, and it is upon God's faithfulness that his people can stake their own destiny: 'I have complete confidence, O God! ... Your constant love reaches above the heavens; your

Psalm 108:1–4 — faithfulness touches the skies.'

In these three respects, God's people are called upon to imitate him. Following his example is not just a matter of believing certain things about God: it is supremely a matter of behaving as he behaves.

The Old Testament ethic is social

In what context is God's will most truly done? Is God concerned with the moral goodness of individuals – or with the shape of society? Inevitably, these two concerns are not mutually exclusive. Individual people are called upon to respond for themselves to the will of God. When Isaiah was confronted with the moral grandeur of God in the temple, he confessed to his own shortcomings and became intensely aware of his own personal inadequacy to do the work to which God

Isaiah 6:5 — was calling him. The story of Abraham pleading for the deliverance of two evil cities makes a similar point: that God cares about the

Genesis 18:16–33 — behaviour of individuals. Yet throughout the Old Testament, there is also a major emphasis on the whole of God's people. God's will is to be shown not just in pious individuals, but in the structures of national life.

We have already seen this strong emphasis on social justice in both wisdom books and law codes, and it was born out of the formative events of Israel's history. On a social level, the exodus had demonstrated God's concern for those who were unjustly oppressed by the forces of imperialism. The God of the Bible was not like the paternalistic God of the cotton growers of the American south, who

The Israelites were instructed to teach each generation the laws God had given.

in the nineteenth century used to encourage their black slaves by telling them that life would be better in heaven. Yahweh saw that things were bad in Egypt – and stepped in to change the situation. This is why the ideal Old Testament society always had a special place for the dispossessed, the oppressed and the disadvantaged. Moreover, the very fabric of society should reflect this concern. The prophets loved to remind their people that in Israel all men and women must be equal. They had all started out as equals – they were all slaves – and therefore economic and social exploitation of one class by another was not only deplorable: it was a fundamental denial of the very heart of the Old Testament faith.

The Old Testament ethic is personal This brings us to the crux of the whole matter. Behaviour in the Old Testament is always seen in the context of the covenant that Israel had entered into with God. God was deeply involved in every aspect of the life of this world. He was not aloof from the human predicament. And his involvement was expressed in the notion of the covenant. For as Israel looked back to the foundation events of their national life, they saw the events of the exodus and what followed as the culmination of God's purpose for his people. In the memory of that momentous event, Israel found the meaning of their national life. As the freed slaves had stood before Mt Sinai they had been reminded of God's great and loving actions on their behalf. In return they were called upon to fulfil his commands and to be loyal to him. Israelite society was based on this mutual relationship of love and responsibility. As Israel met for worship in the annual cycle of the great religious festivals, each generation was able to commit itself afresh to this personal relationship between God and his people. This was where life found its deepest meaning. God had called his people in love when they were neither expecting nor deserving it – and succeeding generations would respond to that love by following the example of God himself.

When the Old Testament demands justice, mercy and truth in human relationships, it does not appeal to some abstract notion of morality. Instead, it goes back to the roots of the covenant faith, in the justice, mercy and truth of God himself. When the prophets call for righteousness in society, they look back to the actions of God himself in caring for outcasts and strangers. And it is no surprise that one of the most eloquent statements of God's will – the Ten Commandments – begins not with a command, but with a statement: 'I am the Lord your God who brought you out of Egypt, where you were slaves.' Right behaviour should stem naturally from the response of a grateful people to what God has done for them. Morality and theology are inextricably interwoven with each other – for it is within the context of a personal relationship between God and his people that the ethical principles of the Old Testament can most fully be understood.

Exodus 20:2

The administration of justice

We have examined the content of the Old Testament law codes in some detail. But how were these laws put into practice? What sort of legal structures existed in ancient Israel?

The answer to that question is quite complex, for Israelite society underwent a number of profound changes in the course of the events documented in the Old Testament. The life of the tribes in the days of the judges was socially and politically quite different from life in the kingdom of David and Solomon. Things changed again after their kingdom divided, and then following the demise of the northern kingdom of Israel. Changing circumstances inevitably led to changes in national institutions, and the administration of law varied from one century to another in the course of the Old Testament story.

But a number of individuals are mentioned in relation to the administration of justice, and consideration of their functions will give us an insight into some aspects of this complex subject.

The elders

Israelite society was always regarded as an extended family group. The head of each family had jurisdiction over his own relatives and household. The town or village elders were just the leading members of the various families. The Deuteronomic code mentions them quite specifically as acting as a regular court where disputes about the Law could be settled (Deuteronomy 19:12; 21:1–9,19–21; 22:13–21; 25:5–10). All the evidence suggests that this was the main law court throughout the entire history of Israel. The elders would meet at the gates of the town, which was a regular meeting place for serious discussion of the affairs of the community (Genesis 23:10–18; Job 29:7–10).

There was no official prosecutor, and the complainant would present the case against the accused in person. Some Old Testament passages suggest there would be an official 'defender' of the accused person (Psalm 109:31). Both prosecution and defence would call witnesses and produce material evidence (Exodus 22:13; Deuteronomy 22:13–17). Accusations and evidence would normally be presented verbally, though written statements could also be accepted (Job 31:35–36). The elders

Opposite
The law was held in great honour by the people of Israel, as it has been by orthodox Jews through the generations since.

would be seated during the trial, rising to pronounce their verdict. If a penalty was involved, then the elders would impose it and would usually carry it out on the spot (Deuteronomy 22:13–21).

The whole of this procedure reflects the view that most cases were essentially civil disputes between citizens. The job of the town elders was to adjudicate between them, and thereby see that justice was done. The story of the book of Ruth is a good illustration of how it worked in practice (Ruth 4:1–12).

The corruption of such local courts is a major theme in the prophets (Amos 5:10–15). It was all too easy for local elders to be swayed by their own prejudices, or even to accede to the wishes of a king who wanted to act unconstitutionally. The story of Naboth's trial and subsequent execution is a striking illustration of how the whole system could be abused by the powerful for their own advantage (1 Kings 21:1–16). Though false witnesses could be liable to severe penalties (Deuteronomy 19:15–20), this does not seem to have deterred perjury, and there is plenty of evidence to show that justice at the city gate was sometimes rough and ready.

The judges

As well as the courts of elders, the Old Testament also mentions professional judges (Deuteronomy 16:18–20; 19:16–18). The laws of Deuteronomy seem to envisage a system of local judges, with a final court of appeal in Jerusalem itself (Deuteronomy 17:8–13).

Albrecht Alt believed that the professional judge was important even in the earliest days of Israelite society. He equated them with the 'minor judges' (Judges 10:1–5; 12:8–15), and suggested that the law they administered was the casuistic law contained in the Book of the Covenant. Martin Noth incorporated this insight into his theory that early Israel was organized into a tribal amphictyony, and these 'minor judges' thereby became the guardians of the covenant theology which held the various tribes together. This view has been considered in detail in an earlier chapter. But the main difficulty is that neither Alt nor Noth was ever able to produce any really compelling evidence to support it.

Others have argued that professional judges were a later development, perhaps originating in the southern Kingdom of Judah with the political and religious reforms of Jehoshaphat (875–851 BC) (2 Chronicles 19:4–11). They believe that the king always had

an important part to play in both establishing and maintaining the Law, and that when Jehoshaphat set up a legal system of professional judges he was merely formalizing a state of affairs that had existed for a long time.

The king

The king certainly had a role in the legal affairs of his people. All the ancient Middle Eastern law codes known to us are associated with kings, though quite often their function was limited to classifying customary procedures rather than actually originating the Law. Since the laws of a state are a vital part of its self-understanding, it was vital for the king to be involved in this way if his own position was to be maintained. But the Old Testament gives no real indication that the kings of either Israel or Judah operated in this way. Josiah perhaps came closest to publishing a law (2 Kings 23:1–3). But the story makes it clear that he was acting as an intermediary in a covenant renewal ceremony between God and the people, in much the same way as Moses (Exodus 24:3–8) and Joshua (Joshua 24:1–28) had done earlier, and as Ezra was to do later (Nehemiah 8:1–12). When the Old Testament explains the function of the king, there is no mention of law-giving, and he is himself firmly stated to be subject to the law of the covenant (1 Samuel 8:10–18; Deuteronomy 17:14–20).

Some scholars suggest this reflects the ideals of Old Testament kingship, rather than what actually happened in practice. But incidents in which the king overturns the normal course of justice always seem to be the exception rather than the rule in the Old Testament story. There is no substantial evidence that the king was in control of the legal process unless we are prepared to set aside almost the whole of the Deuteronomistic History as worthless and unreliable.

This need not mean that kings never issued law codes as part of their activity. Josiah was certainly involved in re-establishing the laws of Deuteronomy. There is also good reason to think that the Book of the Covenant may have been collated and issued in the time of David and Solomon as a kind of constitution for their kingdom. But this did not make it 'state law', because it ultimately rested on a religious understanding of the life of the nation. It could just as easily be argued that when kings became involved in promoting the Law they were acting in a religious capacity rather than as purely political leaders.

There is also evidence that kings had a judicial function. The kingship itself apparently originated within the general framework of family and tribal life (1 Samuel 8:4–5). In that context the king would automatically be one of the 'elders' of the extended family of Israel. As such he would have a part to play in the administration of the law, probably acting as a final court of appeal (2 Samuel 12:1–6; 14:1–11; 1 Kings 3:16–28; 7:7).

The priests

Deuteronomy makes a close connection between judges and priests, when it provides for a court of appeal in Jerusalem staffed by both priests and judges apparently operating on a rota basis (Deuteronomy 17:8–12). Priests and judges are found together elsewhere in the Old Testament (Deuteronomy 19:17; 2 Chronicles 19:8–11). In other ancient Middle Eastern states priests often had judicial functions. In Israel, the close connection between Law and the covenant religion

The laws of Israel covered every aspect of daily life. But how were they to be applied and enforced in practice?

made it inevitable that priests should be involved in interpreting and applying the Law.

No doubt this priestly function went back to a very early period of Old Testament history. Whatever may be the truth about the 'minor judges', there can be little doubt that like the 'major' judges they had a religious as well as a political and social function. Samuel, who appears as their successor, was essentially a priest operating from the shrines of Bethel, Gilgal and Mizpah. But his typical activities at these centres of worship were what we could call judicial (1 Samuel 7:16).

The precise judicial function of the priest is unclear from the Old Testament. Priests would certainly pronounce on religious affairs (Leviticus 10:10; 13:1–14:57). There are also hints that they could operate in a wider legal context (Leviticus 10:10–11; Deuteronomy 21:5; Ezekiel 44:24), though apart from the stories of Samuel there is no evidence of them ever doing so. Their more usual function would be as guardians of the final court of appeal: God himself. The Law allowed that in cases where a normal court could reach no verdict, God should be called in as the final judge. His will was discerned either by a procedure of judicial oaths (Exodus 22:6–13) or by drawing lots – something probably associated with the manipulation of urim and thummim (sacred stones or dice) by the priests (Joshua 7:1–19; 1 Samuel 14:41–43).

Individuals and the community

The Old Testament faith lays great emphasis on groups: the family, the clan, the tribe, and ultimately the nation, are all of fundamental importance both religiously and morally. The covenant itself is a relationship between God and the whole people of Israel, and salvation and judgment are both corporate experiences.

The processes of justice also take account of this corporate solidarity. When Achan stole some goods from the Canaanite city of Jericho, his entire family and all their goods shared in his punishment (Joshua 7:1–26). Some passages seem to elevate this to a general principle, that children will always be punished for the wrongs of their parents (Exodus 20:5; Deuteronomy 5:9). As a matter of common experience, it is true that any generation inevitably shares the legacy of the past. But the Old Testament makes a very clear connection between past and present, the individual and the community. The prophets also emphasize corporate responsibility, pronouncing judgment on the whole nation because of the wrongs of some of its members (Amos 3:12–15; 5:16–24).

This emphasis was perhaps inevitable in a religion which was anchored to the events of history. If the exodus was to be relevant to later generations, then they had in some way to identify themselves with the experience of their ancestors. And when they went along to organized worship at the shrines, they often did precisely that (Deuteronomy 26:5–10). This same connection between the experience of an individual and the state of the community also comes out in some of the psalms. But the best example of it is in the passages referring to the suffering servant. For here, this one person both represents the community and fulfils its true destiny in his own spiritual experience (Isaiah 42:1–4; 49:1–6; 50:4–9; 52:13–53:12).

This way of thinking has often been described as 'corporate personality', and it has been assumed that the Old Testament has a unique way of looking at people and their relationships. On this view, the idea of personal responsibility only came into the Old Testament at a relatively late stage, when the group was in danger of disappearing altogether as an identifiable national entity. Jeremiah (31:29–30) and Ezekiel (18:4, 20) certainly emphasize that each person is responsible to God. But they do not really contradict the earlier Old Testament position. In their day, the people were blaming their problems onto past generations. In response to that Jeremiah and Ezekiel both emphasized that it was not that simple, for each individual must accept some share of responsibility for the state of society as a whole. In any case, there is plenty of evidence that individuals were believed to have moral and spiritual responsibility long before their time:

● Many individuals in the earlier parts of the Old Testament story are praised for their own personal response and commitment to God. Enoch (Genesis 5:21–24), Noah (Genesis 6:9–12) and Hannah (1 Samuel 1:9–2:11) – as well as the prophets – are all specifically described in terms of their own personal spiritual experience.

● Individuals are also condemned and judged for their own wrongdoing. When David committed adultery with Bathsheba, he himself suffered the penalty (2 Samuel 12:1–23). And when

Opposite
The memorial to the 'Unknown Soldier' in Washington, United States, is a modern counterpart to the sense of national togetherness felt by the people of Israel.

Jezebel met her death beneath the ramparts of Jezreel, that was considered a fair punishment for her malicious judicial murder of Naboth (2 Kings 9:30–37). Moreover, the law codes are full of instructions about how individuals are to be dealt with in the light of their own behaviour. The case of Achan, whose entire family was punished for his theft, is in fact exceptional. It was almost certainly considered to be a specifically religious crime – and for that reason was punishable under different rules.

● Amos seems to have condemned the whole nation without regard for personal responsibility, though he may have expected some to repent and avoid judgment (Amos 5:4–7,14–15). But other prophets clearly distinguished between the majority of the people who had broken the covenant and a small group who had not and who for that reason would escape punishment (Isaiah 10:20–22; Micah 5:7–8; Zephaniah 2:3; 3:11–13).

The idea of corporate solidarity is both less precise and less extensive than has often been thought. But it is also less distinctive than has sometimes been suggested. Many modern states have a parallel in their memorials to an 'unknown warrior'. This is a soldier who has been buried in a public place to be a lasting reminder of thousands of others like him, who died in battle and were buried in unmarked graves where they fell. When people pay their respects at such national monuments, they are not primarily honouring the soldier who happens to be interred there. Through him, they are honouring the memory of all those whom he represents. The analogy is not exact, for people in ancient Israel obviously felt this strong sense of solidarity at many other levels of everyday life. But a person's place in the nation never encompassed everything, and there was always a belief that people were morally and spiritually responsible to God as individuals.

12 Worshipping God

Worshipping a holy God

IN THE Old Testament, the need for worship is related to the fact that God is 'holy'. Today, the word 'holy' often has a rather vague meaning, sometimes indicating little more than 'religious'. But when the Old Testament describes Yahweh as 'holy' it is saying some very specific things about God and his relationships with people.

God is infinite

In the Old Testament story, God made himself known to his people in the events of their history and of their own everyday life. Because of this, we can understand a good deal about his nature and personality. But this never meant that ordinary people could know everything about God. When Job was trying to make sense out of his own frustrating life, he was forced to admit that in the last analysis there are hidden depths to God's workings that defy human

Job 30:1–31

understanding. Though God had revealed himself so clearly in events such as the exodus, there were still other aspects of his existence that were deeply mysterious. Nor was Job the only one to

Psalm 139:6
Isaiah 40:13–14

feel this way. Both poets and prophets knew that God was different from people. In chapter two we saw how God's apparent 'hidden-ness' was a major part of Israel's experience on both a personal and a national level.

This feeling of perplexity and wonder in the face of an awe-inspiring divine presence is, of course, common to religious people the world over. So is the use of the word 'holy' to describe the difference between God and people. The literal meaning of the Hebrew word translated 'holy' is not certain, though many scholars think it is related to a word that means 'to divide'. When people describe the gods they worship as 'holy', they often think of the universe being divided into two quite different modes of existence. There is the place where God is – and people, things and events connected with it can be called 'holy'. Then there is also the world where we are – and that is 'profane' or 'common'. In this context, the words 'holy' and 'profane' do not indicate moral judgments: they are simply terms used to convey the fact that God and people are not the same. The Old Testament shares this widely-held view with other

Leviticus 10:10

nations of both the ancient and the modern world.

Within this frame of reference, one aim of worship is to enable these two domains to meet and relate to each other. Even apparently 'common' things can be made 'holy' – places, times, people and objects. But once they have been consecrated to God in this way, special care must be taken by 'common' people in dealing with them. 'Holiness' is often spoken of in the Old Testament as if it were a great power or force, emanating from the very person of God himself. It is not easy for modern people in a technological society to understand this idea. But a parallel might be found in our own respect for the contents of the core of a nuclear reactor. Though most of us do not understand its workings, we all know that at the centre of the process are materials radiating out invisible rays of power that, if not properly contained and controlled by those competent to deal with them, could be disastrous for us all.

The Old Testament often uses similar sorts of imagery to describe

God's holy presence. When God revealed his will to Moses at Mt Sinai, his awesome presence was something that ordinary people must avoid. The place became so saturated with the divine power ('holiness') that only specially equipped people could cope with it. Ordinary people such as Moses could readily be set aside and themselves made holy, but if they came into contact with such holiness before that the results could be catastrophic. The Philistines learned this to their cost when they tried to meddle with the Ark of the Covenant.

Exodus 19:9–25

But even an Israelite could suffer the same fate when he as a 'common' person came into contact with the 'holiness' of the divine presence.

1 Samuel 5:1 — 6:19

2 Samuel 6:1–8

God's majesty and power must be respected, and to call God 'holy' is one way of emphasizing that. Though God can be known in a direct and personal way by his people, he is still God, to be esteemed and treated with due reverence.

Exodus 15:11; Job 11:7–12; Psalm 139:6–12

God is good

Many religious people think of their gods only in terms of awe-inspiring power. But Israel's covenant faith led to a distinctive understanding of what it means to be holy. In the world of religions, the mysterious, numinous, all-powerful kind of holiness has often been advanced as an explanation for the irrational and capricious actions of the gods. But the events of Israel's history had shown that the God of the Old Testament was faithful and trustworthy, not

Throughout the Old Testament the call to worship is sounded. People are summoned to come together and be joyful before God.

fickle and unpredictable. In the light of that, God's holiness was a way of behaving, not just a state of being. To say that God is holy means that he is good. And since people are by nature the very opposite of what God is, to describe him as 'holy' is also a confession of human failure.

Isaiah 55:8

These two aspects of God's holiness – the numinous and the ethical – are brought together most clearly in the experience of the prophet Isaiah as he went to the temple to worship. By definition, what went on in the temple was holy in the numinous sense – for the temple was a holy place, set apart for God's own use, and only those who were ritually holy themselves could cope with it. As the prophet stood there with the other worshippers, he had an awe-inspiring experience of God's greatness and power. But in response to this revelation, he at once recognized that a state of ritual cleanness was not enough by itself to equip him for God's presence. God's majestic holiness and his moral goodness could not be separated from each other, and Isaiah instantly knew that he was unfit to encounter God because of his own sinfulness.

Isaiah 6:1–7

This recognition was one of the greatest insights of the Old Testament prophets. In the various Canaanite cults it was widely assumed that God's holiness had only a cultic, numinous dimension, and that people could be made fit to deal with God by means of appropriate rituals. The people of Israel were constantly tempted to think the same way. But the prophets declared that they were wrong. God was concerned with everyday behaviour, not just with ritual at the shrine. Personal and social sin were incompatible with true worship.

Amos 5:21–24; Micah 6:6–8

It was not only the prophets who saw sin as a barrier to fellowship with God. The law codes make the same connection between morals and worship – indeed, words that worshippers used in the temple itself often reminded them of precisely the same fact: 'Who has the right to go up the Lord's hill? Who may enter his holy temple? Those who are pure in act and in thought ...'

Psalm 24:3–4

God is love

For Isaiah, the painful awareness of God's moral holiness was inextricably linked to his need for forgiveness. A way must be found by which the sinful prophet could be made fit for the presence of such a holy God. In numinous terms, a person could be made fit to deal with holiness by undergoing the required cultic procedures. But how could moral reformation be brought about? Like others both before and after him, Isaiah knew only too well that human effort could not improve things. If he was to be morally right with God, then God himself would have to do it. And so the means of Isaiah's spiritual reconciliation comes from God himself. A burning coal is brought from the altar. Through this symbolic act he is told 'your guilt is gone, and your sins are forgiven'.

Isaiah 6:5

Isaiah 6:7

The book of Isaiah frequently calls God 'the holy one' precisely because he forgives sin and brings salvation to the lives of his people. Yes, God is the Almighty, the Infinite. Yes, he is morally perfect. But he cares for sinful people. To say he is 'holy' not only defines his

Isaiah 43:14–15; 45:11–13

awesome power: it also implies his perfect love. God's holy presence condemns human sin – but it also provides the means whereby sin can be forgiven: 'I am the high and holy God, who lives for ever. I live in a high and holy place, but I also live with people who are humble and repentant, so that I can restore their confidence and hope.'

Isaiah 57:15

This is the background against which we must understand Old Testament worship. Sincere worship reflects the response of God's people to the revelation of God's nature – and the nature of God's holiness determines the character of the human response. Because God is almighty, true worship must always respect the barriers between the sacred and the secular, the holy and the profane. Because he is good, true worship must honestly face up to the reality of human sin. But because he is love, the repentant worshipper can always look for God's forgiveness and the promise of a renewed life. The precise way in which these themes are related to each other varies from one occasion of worship to another. But all worship begins from the recognition that God is holy and people are not. It is a celebration of the many ways in which they can be made fit for God's presence.

Places of worship

Modern Christian places of worship are simply buildings where large numbers of people can meet together. Their size, shape and location are often determined by social convenience rather than by any particularly religious considerations. In principle, a Christian place of worship could be built anywhere. Indeed, Christians can (and often do) meet for worship without special buildings – in schools, public halls, or even the open air.

But in ancient Israel things were quite different. A legitimate place of worship needed to be a recognizably 'holy' place – a spot at which God had revealed himself in a specific way, and which men and women could therefore assume was a place where the holiness of God's presence could safely meet the profane life of the world. When Moses encountered the burning bush in the desert, he recognized it as just such a place. That particular spot never became a regular place of worship, presumably because of its distance from the main centres of population in later Israel. But later generations had many such places where they could worship God, because he had previously met there with the leaders of their nation. Inevitably, the most popular places of worship changed with the passage of time. As we read the Old Testament story we can trace a number of significant stages.

Exodus 3:5–6

The tent of the Lord's presence

In the earliest days of Israel's history, the tribes who escaped from Egypt worshipped God in a special tent erected in the centre of their camp. The Old Testament uses a variety of terms to describe this tent. It is often referred to as the tent of the Lord's presence, or 'tabernacle'. The practice of having such a place for worship is not

Exodus 33:7 – 40:38

unusual among nomadic tribes in the Middle East even today. God's presence in this sanctuary (his 'holiness') was symbolized by the cloud which covered it. The movement of this cloud provided the signal for the tribes to move on.

The Old Testament provides detailed instructions for the erection and use of this portable sanctuary. There is considerable debate among scholars as to the precise origin of these instructions, but the general picture they give is typical of many ancient places of worship. A central enclosure marked the most holy part of the tent (the holy of holies). It was surrounded by various other enclosures until the boundary of the shrine was reached. Beyond this were the tents of the priests and those of the people. Such an arrangement was found in every place of worship throughout the whole of the Old Testament story. It was designed 'to separate what was holy from what was not', and to ensure that only those who were properly qualified would come into contact with the awesome holiness of God's presence at the very centre of the sanctuary.

Ezekiel 42:20

The sacred tents of bedouin tribes would normally have an image of their god within the most holy place. But Israel never portrayed God as an idol. Instead, the holy of holies contained the Ark of the Covenant. There is a good deal of uncertainty about the precise significance of this Ark, but it was certainly identified very closely with God's personal presence.

Numbers 10:35–36; Joshua 4:5,13

We do not know for sure what happened to either the Ark or the tent of the Lord's presence. The Ark is mentioned a number of times after the desert period. It was present at the crossing of the River Jordan. Later it was kept at Bethel, but was then captured from the sanctuary at Shiloh by the Philistines in the time of Samuel. Still later, it was taken to Jerusalem by David, where Solomon finally installed it in the temple he built. It may well have been used in religious festivals at Jerusalem, and it was probably either destroyed or taken away by the Babylonian Nebuchadnezzar when he overthrew Jerusalem in 586 BC. In any event, after the exile its place in the temple was probably occupied by a gold plate, and by New Testament times the holy of holies was completely empty (Josephus *Jewish Wars* V.v.5).

Joshua 3:1 – 5:1
Judges 20:18–28
1 Samuel 4:1 – 7:1
2 Samuel 6:1–23
1 Kings 8:1–9
Psalm 24:7–10; 48:12–14;132:1–18

The tent of the Lord's presence disappeared from sight even earlier than the Ark. There are no certain references to it after the tribes had settled in the land of Canaan. Some passages seem to imply that it was at one stage erected at Shiloh. But if that was the case it cannot have lasted long, for by the time of Samuel Shiloh had a permanent building for worship. There is also a reference to 'the tent of the Lord' at Gibeon in the time of Solomon, though the precise meaning of the phrase there is uncertain. David placed the Ark of the Covenant in a tent when he first took it to Jerusalem. But although this was undoubtedly intended to recall the tent of the Lord's presence, there is no suggestion that it was this original tent that he erected.

Joshua 18:1; 19:51; 1 Samuel 2:22

1 Samuel 1:7,9; 3:15
1 Chronicles 16:39

2 Samuel 6:17; 7:2; 1 Kings 1:39

Both Ark and tent played an important role in the development of the Old Testament faith. By their very nature they were a challenge to the widespread view that gods were restricted in power and influence to particular places and peoples. It was always a temptation for the settling tribes to imagine that God's power extended only over the desert – and as a result they found themselves worshipping the gods and goddesses of Canaan. Later on, in the time of Jeremiah, just before the final collapse of the kingdom of Judah, the people of Jerusalem were tempted to suppose that their city would never fall because God lived there – in the temple. Both attitudes were understandable. But both were false, and when a later prophet declared that Israel's God was in reality the God of the whole world, he was articulating something that had been implicit in the Old Testament faith from a very early period.

Jeremiah 7:1–15

Isaiah 44:1–8

Local sanctuaries

During the Israelites' time as desert nomads, the central place in their camp was given to the 'tent of the Lord's presence' or 'tabernacle', with the Ark of the Covenant in its holy of holies. The altar for sacrifice stood on open ground outside the tent itself.

People always like to worship where they live, and the local sanctuaries in towns and villages throughout the land had an important part to play for most of the Old Testament period. Almost every settlement must have had its own place of worship. Not all of them would be buildings. A majority may have been little more than altars in the open air at which regular sacrifices could be offered. A great many such altars have been discovered by archaeologists throughout Palestine. Sometimes they were constructed from heaps

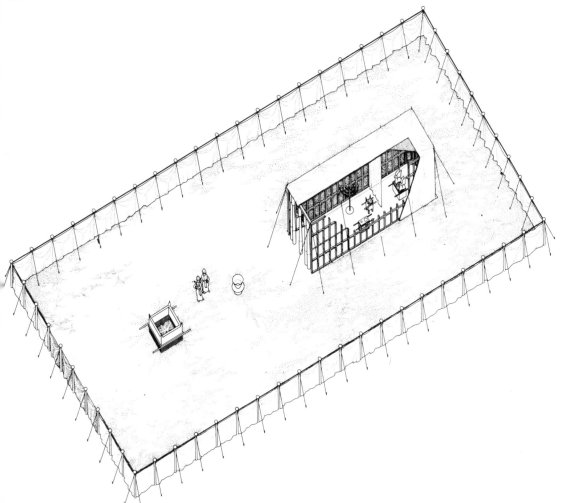

of stones. At other times a natural feature of the landscape or a particularly striking rock would be used for the purpose.

The stories of the patriarchs show the earliest ancestors of Israel worshipping at a great number of such local sanctuaries right across the country – places like Hebron, Beersheba and Mizpah. These places were most likely Canaanite places of worship long before the Hebrew patriarchs arrived in the land, though the Old Testament generally points out that it was really the covenant God Yahweh whom they worshipped there. At other times the patriarchs are depicted establishing new centres of worship. When Jacob had an unusual dream in the open air, he recognized it as a holy place because God met him there. As a result, he called it 'Bethel', meaning 'the house of God'. Later generations of Israelites regarded it as a particularly holy place. After the collapse of Solomon's united kingdom, Bethel became one of the major sanctuaries of the northern kingdom of Israel.

Local places of worship play an important part in the Old Testament story. The stories about Samuel associate him with the sanctuaries at Bethel, Gilgal, Mizpah, Ramah and Shiloh. The shrine at Shiloh seems to have been of sufficient importance to be called a temple. After its destruction by the Philistines in about 1050 BC the centre of attention moved to other places, notably Gilgal and Mizpah, both of which are connected with significant stages in Saul's career as king. Later, King Solomon was a regular visitor to a sanctuary at Gibeon. On one occasion there he had a dream in which he met God and was promised the gift of wisdom.

Gibeon is described as 'the most famous altar' of all. But that situation soon changed, when Solomon built his great temple in Jerusalem. After that, the local sanctuaries must have been put in the shade by the splendour of worship in the temple. The large staff of priests and other officials there made worship so much more impressive and exciting than what went on in smaller towns and villages – and it was not long before large crowds were making regular pilgrimages to Jerusalem. This was what Solomon had wanted – for political as well as religious reasons. But it meant that smaller shrines had to struggle to survive. Many local places of worship probably fell into disuse at this period. Many more tried to get the worshippers back by reviving Canaanite forms of worship that the Old Testament denounces as departures from the true covenant faith. Such worship was certainly widespread. Looking back at this time, Jeremiah could later comment that 'On every high hill and under every green tree you worshipped fertility gods'. This complaint had particular relevance to the sanctuaries of the northern kingdom. But even in Judah every later attempt at religious reform involved the forcible closure of these local sanctuaries which had become centres of alien worship.

The temple

The temple in Jerusalem came to occupy a special place in the devotion of the people. Its unique position was celebrated in much of

Genesis 13:18; 18:1–15
Genesis 26:23–26
Genesis 31:43–55

Genesis 28:10–22
Judges 20:18–28; 1 Samuel 7:16; 10:3
1 Kings 12:29 – 13:32; Amos 3:14; 4:4; 5:5–6; 7:10–13

1 Samuel 1:1 – 3:21; 7:16–17

1 Samuel 11:14–15; 13:8–15; 10:17–27

1 Kings 3:4–15
1 Kings 3:4

1 Kings 5:1 – 6:37

Jeremiah 2:20

2 Kings 18:1–8; 21:3; 23:1–20

ancient Israel's best-loved poetry. It symbolized all the distinctive features of the Old Testament faith, uniting the political and the religious aspirations of the people, centred on the kings who ruled from Jerusalem as the successors of David. Devotion to the temple could sometimes lead to misplaced nationalism.It did so in the days of Jeremiah when the inhabitants of Jerusalem were certain that

Jeremiah 7:1–15

nothing could happen to their city because the temple was there. The prophets had to remind them that God's holy presence in the temple could bring judgment as well as salvation. It was possible to preserve the external appearance of true worship when in reality

Ezekiel 10:1–22

God's presence was no longer there.

The Old Testament gives fairly detailed accounts of the building

1 Kings 6:1 – 7:51; 2 Chronicles 2:17 – 5:1

of the temple by Solomon. But the details of the design are obscure, and when modern scholars have tried to reconstruct models of the temple they have produced a number of different proposals. It is clear that the general layout was similar to many other temples throughout the ancient Middle East (though no precisely identical temple has been found elsewhere). This general similarity is not surprising, as Solomon needed to import workers from Phoenicia to

1 Kings 5:1–12; 7:13–14

design and build it – presumably because Israel had no previous experience of a large-scale building project.

In general terms, the layout of the temple was similar to the design of the tent of the Lord's presence, with a central holy of holies surrounded by other spaces and enclosures. Indeed, some scholars believe that the Old Testament's descriptions of the temple and the tent are quite closely related to each other. The basic structure consisted of three rooms: an entrance hall, a main room and, at a slightly higher level, the holy of holies. Whereas the entrance hall and main room were rectangular, with the doors on the shorter sides, the holy of holies was a cube. As in the tent of the Lord's presence, the holy of holies contained the Ark of the Covenant – with two large golden cherubim suspended from the ceiling over the place where the Ark was kept.

Most of the worship, however, took place not in the holy of holies but in the other parts of the temple building and courtyards. The actual contents of these areas varied from time to time, and the religious symbols and altars used there were often as much an indication of the nation's political alliances as of its spiritual commitment. When Ahaz wanted to seal his alliance with Assyria, he

2 Kings 16:10–18

adjusted the temple contents to prove his intentions. His successor Hezekiah, on the other hand, wished to reassert Judah's indepen-

2 Kings 18:1–7
2 Kings 21:1–18

dence, and set about removing such signs of external religious influence. Manasseh later brought them all back. Josiah eventually inaugurated a thoroughgoing religious reformation, and completely refurbished the temple as well as terminating local shrines

2 Kings 23:1–20

throughout the country.

There was obviously a close connection between the kings of Judah and the temple. Solomon played a major part in erecting the building and in organizing worship there. But he also had his own

2 Kings 16:18

palace next door, linked to the temple by a private passage. The temple was more than a national place of worship: it also symbolized the power of the royal family of David. David and Solomon had political reasons for wanting to build a temple in Jerusalem. In the ancient world politics and religion were often two sides of the same coin. Various buildings mentioned on the perimeter of the temple precinct may well have housed the king's personal treasury. Certainly, much of the nation's wealth must have been kept there, for invaders often went to the temple to plunder it.

As well as priests, the temple had a large staff, including administrators of various kinds and temple slaves who kept the fires burning on the various altars used in worship. Some of these workers may well have been non-Israelites, for the prophet Ezekiel later complained about the practice of allowing foreigners to be involved in the life of the temple.

Not everyone was happy with the temple. There were always radicals who felt that it was a backward step in Israel's spiritual pilgrimage, and that the covenant faith would be better served by adherence to the less settled ways of worship represented by the tent of the Lord's presence. But most people were committed to it. They knew well enough that God did not literally 'live' in the temple, but still this was the place where they felt most directly in God's presence. Their anguish was real and deeply felt when it was destroyed by the Babylonians. After the exile, a replacement was built, of which we know only very little – but it was obviously a much less impressive place.

1 Kings 14:25–28; 15:15; 2 Kings 16:7–8; 18:15–16; 24:12–13

Ezra 2:40–42
Joshua 9:27; Ezra 2:43–54; 8:20

Ezekiel 44:6–9

2 Samuel 7:5–7; Jeremiah 35:1–19; Isaiah 66:1
Psalm 11:4; 1 Kings 8:27–30
Psalm 63:1–5; 84:1–4; 122:1; 26:8

Psalm 137

Ezra 1:2–4; 3:1 – 6:18

Some details of Israelite worship echoed the cults of the surrounding peoples, though Israel's monotheism made the central thrust quite different. The pomegranate decorations (right) are Canaanite, and the cult stand (centre above) is Philistine. But the cherub and the shrine with pillars (model) are Israelite.

The synagogue The exile was in many ways a great watershed for the people of Israel, and their worship was never again to be quite the same as it had been in the days of the great kings. The temple was rebuilt in Jerusalem, and it always had a special place in the affection of the Jewish people. But the effective centre of worship shifted to the synagogue. By the New Testament era there were synagogues in all the important towns of the Mediterranean world, and Jewish people went there week by week for regular worship.

Synagogue worship was quite different from temple worship. For one thing, it was on a much smaller scale. And in addition, it never

included sacrifice. Prayer and the reading of the Old Testament Law and Prophets came to be all important. Naturally, there was no Ark of the Covenant or a holy of holies, though later synagogues had their own 'Ark of the Law' which contained the sacred scrolls of Scripture.

Almost all our evidence for life and worship in the synagogues is later than the Old Testament period – much of it a lot later. It shows the synagogues were more than places of worship: they were social and educational centres for the many Jewish communities scattered throughout the world in the early centuries of the Christian era. The synagogues emerged to fill a need which had not existed when Israel was an independent nation with their own land.

We have no real evidence to show how the synagogues originated. A number of ideas have been suggested:

● Some believe they began in Judah itself even before the exile. We know that in the course of his religious reforms, Josiah made a concerted effort to close down the local sanctuaries throughout his kingdom and to centralize all worship in Jerusalem. Of course, that could not eliminate the need for people to worship where they lived. And so, the argument goes, they went to Jerusalem only when they needed the sort of sacrificial worship that went on there. At other times they met for more informal local worship that was the forerunner of the synagogue. There is, however, no evidence to support this view. Indeed, it is doubtful whether Josiah's reformation was quite that successful, for less than twenty years later Jeremiah provides plenty of evidence of worship continuing at traditional sites throughout the country.

● It seems undeniable that the synagogue must have originated after the temple at Jerusalem was not available for worship. After the destruction of Jerusalem by Nebuchadnezzar, the remnants of the population left in Judah probably worshipped on the temple site from time to time. But those who were transported to Babylon had no further access to Jerusalem. Possibly, therefore, synagogues first began as places of prayer and contemplation for these exiles in Babylon itself. We know these people certainly had a close interest in gathering together the books of the Law and Prophets. But here again there are no real facts to go on, and a certain amount of evidence to the contrary. In Psalm 137 the exiles bemoan their fate but with no reference at all to the possibility of synagogue worship. Archaeology has uncovered comparatively few remains of synagogue buildings in Babylon, none of them relating to the Old Testament period.

● It has also been suggested that the synagogue began in Palestine after the return of some of the exiles under Nehemiah and Ezra. There is a good deal of archaeological evidence for the existence of synagogue buildings in Palestine, though none of it goes back to this period. Perhaps the most we can say is that the need for regular worship, combined with the strong emphasis of Ezra on reading and interpretation of the Law could have provided the conditions for this new form of worship to evolve.

Jeremiah 41:4–5

Nehemiah 8:1–12

Wherever the synagogues came from, the simple worship carried on there was an authentic reflection of an important strand in the Old Testament faith. For though the people rejoiced in the splendid magnificence of the temple at Jerusalem, it had always been recognized that God's presence could not be restricted to one place. The consciousness that God was with them (symbolized by the Ark of the Covenant) was more fundamental than the need for a holy place like the temple. There are many stories in the Old Testament which show that God's presence could be enjoyed anywhere. Joseph met God in a prison, Jeremiah in a well. When the Jewish people began to worship in synagogues throughout the world, not only were they coming to terms with the political realities of their national life: they were exploring new dimensions in the covenant faith itself. Perhaps that is why Jewish writers insisted that the synagogue began with Moses (Philo, *Life of Moses*, ii:39; Josephus, *Against Apion*, II:xvii). Historically, they were certainly wrong. But ideologically they were giving expression to an important aspect of the Old Testament faith.

Genesis 39:21
Jeremiah 38:1–13

The character of worship

What was worship like in Old Testament times? We have already referred in passing to prayer in the synagogue and sacrifice in the Jerusalem temple. Other passages mention the use of incense and

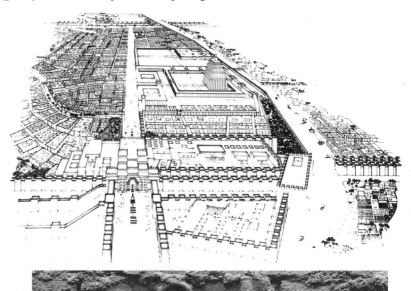

When the Jews were exiled in Babylon, they were surrounded by reminders of Babylonian mythology, like this dragon from Ishtar Gate (right). The whole city, shown in this artist's reconstruction (above right), was dominated by temples. Yet the Jews kept their own beliefs intact.

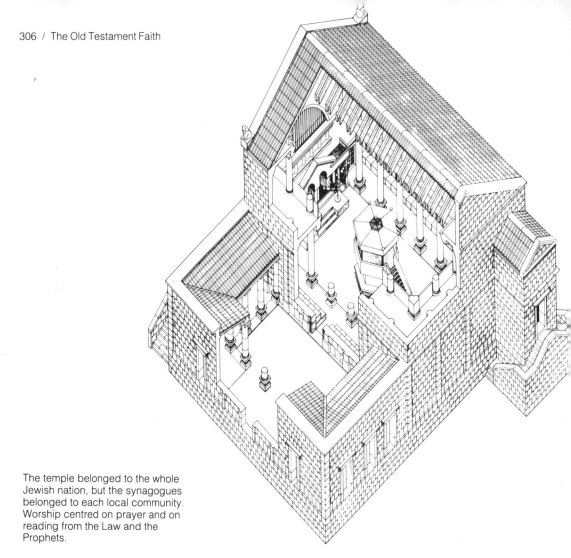

The temple belonged to the whole Jewish nation, but the synagogues belonged to each local community. Worship centred on prayer and on reading from the Law and the Prophets.

Jeremiah 6:20
Amos 4:4

Leviticus 1:1 — 7:38; Numbers 15:1–31; 28:1 — 29:40

the giving of monetary offerings. But the Old Testament never gives us a fully detailed account of a complete worship service. The most specific instructions refer to the offering of sacrifices, but worship obviously included a lot more than that. What went on in the local sanctuaries and in the temple was probably so familiar a part of life that it was unnecessary to spell it all out in detail. Of course, it was

The temple area in Jerusalem today has some remains of Herod's temple, built between 19 BC and AD 64. The original temple, known as Solomon's temple, was destroyed when the Babylonians sacked Jerusalem in 587 BC. The second temple was built after the Jews returned from exile in Babylon, and stood for almost 500 years.

These remains are of a synagogue at Capernaum. From the time when the Jews returned from Babylon, the synagogues began to play an important part in regular Jewish worship.

Old Testament worship had its services for the 'rites of passage' – birth, marriage and death. The box shown here is an ossuary, in which the deceased person's bones would have been interred. It dates from after the Old Testament period.

inevitable that the Old Testament should ignore some aspects of worship in ancient Israel. We know from the prophets that all too often the people worshipped their own God Yahweh using the rituals of the local Baal religion – and though this was popular, it was a denial of the true covenant faith.

In spite of the absence of any comprehensive set of instructions for the conduct of public worship, scholars agree that the Old Testament does contain a good deal of material that was regularly used in that context, especially in the book of Psalms. Some have called this 'the hymn book of the second temple'. It may well have been compiled at that time, for some psalms clearly refer to the exile and what followed. Not all psalms are hymns in the normal sense. Some of them are more personal and individual expressions of piety. Yet others refer to the great ceremonial events of national life. But whatever their form, the psalms give us an invaluable glimpse into the way God was worshipped in the temple at Jerusalem in the period before the exile. Sometimes we see individuals at worship. At others, we can catch sight of great national occasions involving the whole community. Some psalms centre on the king and God's promises to the royal family of David. One thing we do not find, however, is worship for the so-called 'rites of passage' – birth, marriage, and death. Most nations celebrate these events in the context of religious worship. But in ancient Israel they were all essentially family matters, and in the time before the exile they had no particular connection with formal worship.

Understanding the psalms

At one time, scholars tried to understand the psalms either as purely personal poetry, or as poems composed on particular historical occasions in the course of Israel's history. But more recent study has suggested that most of them had their roots in the worship of Solomon's temple, and quite possibly in the worship at local sanctuaries as well. There are a number of reasons for accepting this:

● At least one Old Testament passage shows psalms being used in the course of worship. When David first brought the Ark of the Covenant into Jerusalem, its arrival was accompanied by dancing and singing (2 Samuel 6:5). One account of this incident includes an example of the songs that were sung on the occasion – and this turns out to be surprisingly similar to several of the psalms (1 Chronicles 16:8–36).

● Other Old Testament passages also confirm the important part played in worship by religious songs and poetry of the type found in the book of Psalms (Amos 5:23).

● Much of the imagery used in the psalms is very similar to imagery used in specifically religious poetry and songs elsewhere in the ancient Middle Eastern cultures. There are particularly close linguistic connections between many of the psalms and the songs used to worship Baal as depicted in the texts from Ras Shamra. The theological ideas are completely different, of course, but a judicious comparison of the psalms with these other texts has led to enormous advances in our understanding of the meaning of many obscure Hebrew words used in the Old Testament.

● The Jerusalem temple and its worship provide many of the basic themes of the psalms, reflecting the centrality of the temple as a symbol of God's presence (Psalm 11:4; 46:4–6; 50:2) and the eager longing of the people to share in its worship (Psalm 26:8; 84:1–4; 122:1). Indeed, some of them even seem to refer directly to sacrificial worship (Psalm 36:8) and to the various days over which the great national festivals would be held (Psalm 118:24).

● The structure of some psalms seems to indicate that they were used as comprehensive liturgies for worship on particular occasions (Psalm 118:1–4). Some depict a number of participants in the worship, asking questions and receiving responses (Psalm 24). It is quite likely that many of the obscure references in the psalm titles are really instructions about how they were to be used in worship, and the Hebrew word *Selah* which appears in a number of psalms is almost certainly an instruction to the temple singers to increase the volume and sing louder.

Psalm 42 shows how much someone steeped in the worship at Jerusalem could miss the temple services. It is like drowning in the waterfalls of the Jordan submerged by 'waves of sorrow'.

When we analyze the psalms and other references to worship, we soon discover that it included many different activities.

Singing and music

This was a vital element in all worship, and it appears throughout the Old Testament as an appropriate way for God's people to praise him. It was, of course, an important activity in many ancient religions. When Elijah confronted the prophets of Baal on Mt Carmel, the Baal worshippers used music to stir themselves up into a frenzy. On occasion, prophets of Yahweh could use it for the same purpose. Not all religious singing was necessarily pleasing to God but without it his people could not truly praise him. His holy character found its natural response in this kind of worship, and the awareness of God's presence must inevitably lead to worshipping him in 'glad songs of praise'.

1 Kings 18:27–29
1 Samuel 10:10–13
Amos 5:23
Psalm 22:3

Psalm 63:5

1 Chronicles 15:16–24; 16:4–7; Ezra 2:40–42

Psalm 42:5,11; 43:5; 46:7,11

2 Samuel 6:5; Psalm 43:4; 68:25; 81:1–3; 98:4–6; 150:3–5; Isaiah 30:29; 1 Chronicles 25:1–5

Psalm 42:4

Singing became especially important after the exile, and the Old Testament mentions the names of several choirs in this connection. Some of the psalms have refrains, which suggests that one part of the song would be sung by the worshippers, and the rest by the choir.

Musical instruments are mentioned in connection with the praise of God: tambourines, harps, lyres, trumpets, rattles, horns, flutes, and cymbals. Worship was obviously a joyful business, and the carnival atmosphere of the temple is captured in one of the psalms which speaks of 'a happy crowd, singing and shouting praise to God'.

Prayer

This was to become one of the characteristic activities of the synagogue. By the New Testament period there were also regular daily times of prayer in the temple at Jerusalem. It is unclear whether this custom originated in Old Testament times, though prayer was certainly a vital element in worship right from the start. The belief that ordinary people could have direct access to God was a fundamental part of the Old Testament faith. Not only prophets such as Elijah, or kings such as Solomon, but ordinary people such as Hannah could bring their everyday problems to God. The Old Testament Law contains prayers to be said on special occasions, and the book of Psalms contains many examples of prayers that were no doubt used by individuals, as well as by groups of worshippers, to

1 Kings 18:36–37
1 Kings 8:22–61
1 Samuel 1:1–18
Deuteronomy 26:5–10

Music was important in the worship of Israel and her neighbours. The musicians above are from an Egyptian mural, and those in the picture centre right are Elamites (a relief from Ashurbanipal's palace in Nineveh). The cymbals are from Luristan (in modern Iran), but the photo far right shows a reconstruction of the kind of lyre King David would have played. But not all worship is music and singing; prayer is always central.

give thanks and to express their trust and confidence in God.

Sometimes the worshipper would kneel to pray, or even bow low to the ground. At other times prayers would be said in a standing position, occasionally with hands raised up above the head. But the important thing was not the posture for prayer, but 'a humble and repentant heart'.

1 Kings 8:54
Psalm 5:7
1 Samuel 1:26
1 Kings 8:22,54;
Psalm 63:4; Isaiah 1:15
Psalm 51:17

Dance and drama

Psalm 26:6
Psalm 149:3; 150:4

Given the importance attached to singing and music in Old Testament worship, we are not surprised to discover that dancing could also be used in praise of God. Some of the psalms seem to presuppose it, and others specifically encourage it. On one occasion even King David himself took part in public dancing as the Ark of

the Covenant was brought into his city of Jerusalem. Indeed, he danced so vigorously that his wife thought his behaviour was indecent, and rebuked him for making a fool of himself.

There is also evidence for the use of drama in worship. There are many indications of processions in which the worshippers would march in and out of the temple and the city of Jerusalem. Sometimes, God is depicted accompanying the worshippers as they march – perhaps in the form of the Ark of the Covenant, carried at the head of the procession. Other passages suggest that God's mighty acts in the past could be re-enacted in the course of worship, to bring home their lessons to new generations. At the great annual Passover festival, drama also played an important part. At the most solemn moment of the festival, the worshippers ate a fellowship meal dressed ready to go on a journey, just as the slaves in Egypt had done at the time of the exodus. Symbolic actions could also play an important part in more ordinary acts of worship. Drama has always been a powerful medium through which people can express their deepest convictions, and when the worshippers of ancient Israel reminded themselves of God's goodness to their nation they did so in action as well as in word.

2 Samuel 6:1–22

Psalm 26:6; 42:4; 48:12–14; 118:19,26–27

Psalm 68:24–27; 132:7–9

Psalm 46:8–10; 48:8; 66:5

Exodus 12:21–28
Psalm 26:6

Sacrifice
2 Kings 16:15

To many people, this is the most characteristic activity of Old Testament worship. Certainly, it was a daily ritual in the temple. But it was only one element among many. Modern Western people tend to give so much attention to it simply because it is generally remote from our own experience. To us, the gratuitous death of animals in the course of religious worship is something repugnant – and we are not aided here by the fact that the Old Testament never explains exactly why this form of worship was used. As with so many other things, it simply takes it for granted that everyone would know why sacrifice was an appropriate way to worship.

Sacrifice is a worldwide phenomenon, and is not restricted either to the Old Testament or the Middle East. Anthropologists have tried hard to understand the need for sacrifice in different cultural contexts around the world. To appreciate the importance of sacrifice, we need to return to the observations about 'holiness' with which we began this chapter. Wherever it is practised, sacrifice is always understood as a means of relating the visible, tangible world in which people exist to the invisible, intangible and uncontrollable world in which God or the gods exist. It is a means whereby people can encounter the powerful 'holiness' that radiates out from the presence of God, without suffering the horrific consequences that would normally follow such an encounter. This is why animals (particularly domestic animals) were appropriate as sacrifices, for they are themselves living, have a close relationship to people, and could therefore serve as a suitable symbol of the worshippers themselves.

A religion's view of God will always affect its view of sacrifice. In many primitive religions, sacrifice is thought of as a way of feeding the gods. But this is a view that the Old Testament rejects. The Old

Psalm 50:7–15

Testament's understanding of sacrifice is dominated by its perception of the meaning of holiness. This means that an important function of sacrifice was concerned with securing ritual purity. But the moral dimensions of God's holiness were never far from view. As time went on and the events of history made the need for forgiveness of sin more obvious, this came to be the predominant meaning attached to sacrifice.

This does not mean, of course, that sacrifice and sin were related only at a late date. At an earlier period, even sacrifices that were not identified as 'sin offerings' could be accompanied by great repentance. The prophets and others often reminded the people of the need for true confession and repentance to accompany sacrificial worship. As in so many other things, the actual practice of ancient Israel varied from time to time and place to place. And there was always the temptation to offer sacrifices to gods other than Yahweh, using rituals that were fundamentally alien to the Old Testament faith.

The Old Testament mentions many different types of sacrifice. In some ways, they defy comprehensive analysis. But anthropologists have identified three major types of sacrifice, and it will be helpful to use these divisions in our discussion of the Old Testament.

● **Gift sacrifices** Sacrifices would often be given to God as a way of saying thank you for some particular benefit that the worshipper had received. The very first sacrifices mentioned in the Old Testament were of this type, as also was the sacrifice of Noah after the great flood had subsided. At the other end of the Old Testament story we find the exiles who returned from Babylon offering the same sort of sacrifices. They are also mentioned in many of the psalms.

On other occasions, gift sacrifices would be offered in order to secure God's guidance for the future. But quite often a gift sacrifice would be given as a simple expression of joy on the part of the worshipper. Such offerings would usually be given in their entirety to God, by being burned on the altar of the sanctuary – hence the term sometimes used to describe them, 'whole burnt offerings'. Offerings of grain could also serve the same purpose, and the annual offerings of the first-fruits of the crops were in effect gift sacrifices given to celebrate a successful harvest.

● **Fellowship offerings** Not all sacrifices were given completely to God as whole burnt offerings. Often, only a part of the animal was burned on the altar, and the rest was eaten in a fellowship meal at the sanctuary, shared by worshippers and priests. A shared meal is a symbol of friendship throughout the world. But the worshippers of ancient Israel were doing more than simply expressing their mutual affection. For the most important event of their history, the covenant ceremony at Mt Sinai, had been accompanied by a fellowship offering like this. Whenever this event was celebrated a fellowship offering was usually at the centre of things. No doubt the same themes would be in the worshippers' minds whenever fellowship offerings were made. In these meals the people were constantly

Leviticus 11:1 — 15:33

Ezekiel 45:18–25

Judges 20:26; 21:1–4; 1 Samuel 7:2–9; Job 1:5

Micah 6:6–8; Amos 5:21–24; Psalm 51:16–19

Jeremiah 44:24–25; Amos 5:25–27

Genesis 4:3–4

Genesis 8:20

Ezra 6:16–18
Psalm 54:6–7; 56:12–13

1 Samuel 7:9

1 Samuel 6:14; 2 Samuel 6:17; Psalm 96:8

Leviticus 1:1–17

Leviticus 2:1–16

Leviticus 23:1–25

Leviticus 3:1–17

Exodus 24:1–8
Joshua 8:30–35; 2 Samuel 6:17; 1 Kings 8:63–64

reminded of the keynote of their covenant faith: that God and his people enjoyed a personal relationship whose repercussions influenced the whole of life.

● **Forgiveness of sins** The Old Testament mentions two sacrifices that were designed to remove the barrier of sin that made fellowship between people and God impossible: the sin offering and the guilt offering. The precise difference between these two classes of sacrifice is not very clear. But in view of the way that God's holiness was equated with moral perfection, it is not surprising that sacrifice and forgiveness should have been related to each other. Human sin broke the covenant relationship between God and his people. But fellowship could be restored by offering an appropriate sacrifice.

An awareness of the seriousness of sin seems to have developed most fully in the later stages of Israel's history. The earlier prophets often found it difficult to convince the people that worship and behaviour belonged together. But when the awful events of the exile had proved them right, everyone could see that disobedience to God was a real problem that needed to be dealt with. The Old Testament never specifically discusses how a sacrifice could deal with sin. But it is clear that it was taken for granted that those who sinned deserved to die, and that a sacrifice in some way substituted for the condemned sinner. Certainly, the blood of these sacrifices (representing the life of the animal) played an important part. It was only as this was daubed on the altar that the worshipper could be pronounced forgiven. Depending on the identity of the sinner, different altars would be used.

There was one occasion when the whole nation was united in seeking forgiveness: the annual Day of Atonement. On this occasion, the blood of the sacrifices would be taken into the holy of holies itself, and applied to the top of the Ark. This was why the lid of the Ark came to be known as 'the mercy seat'. After the exile it was replaced by a gold plate which served the same purpose. When the

Leviticus 4:1 — 5:13

Leviticus 5:14 — 6:7; Numbers 5:5–8

Ezekiel 18:20

Leviticus 17:11

Leviticus 16:1–34; 23:26–32; Numbers 29:7–11

main sacrifices had been offered, a second ritual took place. This involved the selection of two goats, one to be sacrificed in the temple and the other to be sent away into the desert beyond the inhabited land. The priest laid his hands on the head of the goat which was to be sent out and confessed the sins of the nation. These two procedures were quite different, but they both emphasized the same facts: that sin is a serious business as it disrupts fellowship between God and his people. They were also a dramatic declaration that sin could be forgiven, and removed from the lives of God's people as surely as the goat was driven out into the desert, never to be seen again.

Understanding sacrifice

So far, we have looked at the ways in which sacrifices were used in the worship of God in the Old Testament. But what is sacrifice all about? Just what did the worshippers think they were doing when they engaged in this sort of activity? At one time, it was thought that sacrifice was based on superstition and ignorance, and that it was only relatively late in Israel's history that it came to have any theological significance, as sacrifice became a way of making amends for sin. But modern anthropologists studying sacrifice in

Israel and her neighbours sacrificed animals as part of their worship. The sacrificial animals being carried in procession (left) are from a relief at Carchemish on the upper Euphrates; the sacrifices on the right are being made by the small group of Samaritans who remain today; and the horned altar below was probably used for Israelite burnt offerings.

many different cultures have shown that, whatever else it is, sacrificial worship certainly is not unsophisticated.

Wherever it is practised, sacrifice is a means of reaffirming the structures of civilized life: it declares that God and people are united in a relationship of mutual interdependence, and, by means of the meal which often follows a sacrifice, it affirms the importance of good social relationships as a basis for a contented life. In the context of the Old Testament faith, those affirmations are central. Peace and harmony with God is a fundamental requirement for a good life – and peace and harmony both in nature and in human society stem only from God himself. Sacrifice, therefore, needed to be offered at those points in a person's life when they were out of tune with the 'holiness' which characterized God's own being.

Sacrifice and holiness

Just as God's holiness was defined in a number of ways, so sacrifices could be offered for a number of purposes.

● In relation to the mysterious, numinous holiness that radiated out from the divine presence, sacrifice was the means by which a person who was 'unclean' could be made 'clean' and fit to encounter God's holy power. In this context, the notion of 'unclean' was not related to morality or behaviour. Things

Different kinds of sacrifice

Category of sacrifice	Example of category	How sacrifice conducted	Spiritual meaning
Gift sacrifices	Firstfruits Grain offerings Offerings in thanks for particular blessings	Burnt in entirety on the altar (whole burnt offerings)	Gratitude to God Joy in him
Fellowship offerings	Events of national significance e.g. sealing covenant, dedicating temple, covenant renewal	Part burnt, part eaten in fellowship meal with priests and worshippers	Reminder of covenant relationship with God
Sacrifices for forgiveness of sins	Sin offerings Guilt offerings Sacrifice on Day of Atonement	Blood daubed on the altar	Animal is dying in place of sinner

such as illness, touching a dead body, giving birth, menstruation, even having mildew in houses or clothing, all rendered a person 'unclean' in a ritual sense (Leviticus 11–15). To us, this seems rather an odd collection of things. But what unites them seems to be the fact that they are all things that happen occasionally, and are not a part of everyday life. In this context, those things that are 'clean' are perhaps what we might call 'normal' – and any unusual occurrence renders a person 'unclean'. The precise reasons for this are no doubt lost in the mists of antiquity. But before a person could approach the holy presence of God in the sanctuary, such uncleanness had to be dealt with by the offering of appropriate sacrifices.

● There was also a moral side to God's holiness. Wrongdoing also made people 'unclean', and therefore unfit to deal with God. An inadequate understanding of this led to many problems in the history of ancient Israel. The people were naturally inclined to think that worship was concerned only with the ritual aspects of holiness – and the prophets were continually reminding them that ritual worship and everyday behaviour could not be separated. There can be no doubt the nation as a whole took a long time to learn this lesson – and that is the reason why offerings for sin came to assume more importance as time went on. For sacrifice was also the way that sin could be forgiven, and people could be restored to fellowship with God.

Making a sacrifice

The worshipper who made a sacrifice in ancient Israel did so out of a consciousness of being alienated from God, for whatever reason. Reconciliation with God had to be achieved in order for life to proceed as God intended it to be. This sense of alienation is familiar enough to modern people. Modern Christians would tend to place all the emphasis on internal spiritual change as the means of overcoming it. But in the Old Testament, this change of internal disposition was always displayed externally. Here, sacrifice became a visible symbol of change in a person's life. We can trace a number of stages in the process whereby this change was brought about.

First of all, the sinner would approach the altar of God with the sacrifice. He then laid his hand on the animal's head, to indicate that he wished to be identified with the animal. This was most important, for it meant that from this point onwards the animal was to be a symbol of the worshipper: whatever happened physically and outwardly to the animal was to happen to the worshipper spiritually and inwardly. Four things then took place:

● The animal was killed. In this action, the worshipper was reminded of the consequence of uncleanness: death, separation from fellowship with God. The worshipper himself would perform this action, declaring that he was fit only for death himself.

● The priest then took the blood of the sacrifice (which now represented the sinner's life given up to God) to the altar. Depending on the identity of the sinner, different altars would be used. For an ordinary person, it was the altar of burnt offerings in the temple courtyard; for a priest, the altar of incense in the temple itself; and for the whole nation (on the Day of Atonement), the lid of the Ark in the holy of holies. This action constituted the moment when the worshipper's uncleanness was removed (Leviticus 17:11) – the moment of reconciliation, or 'atonement' as it is sometimes called. God and his people had been reunited in fellowship.

● After this, the animal's body was placed on the altar in the temple, as a sign that the forgiven sinner was offering his whole life to God. In the case of a gift offering, the whole sacrifice would be burned there.

● Finally, depending on the nature of the sacrifice, some of the meat still left was eaten in a meal. Not only were things right between God and the individual worshipper: true fellowship with other people had also been restored.

We can see from all this that sacrifice was a very important part of worship. It both represented basic aspects of the Old Testament faith (people made for fellowship with God and with one another), and also externalized the faith in such a way that no one would be left in any doubt about what it meant to address Yahweh as a holy God.

Times for worship

We have already seen that worship involved a whole style of life, including daily behaviour as well as what went on at the sanctuaries. It was, therefore, a continuous activity. One of the major themes of the Old Testament faith is that God is available to people at every time and in every place. Formal worship was one way of expressing this, and the sanctuaries would be open every day. But there were also special times when the great national festivals would interrupt the normal run of things and the people would join together to celebrate God's goodness to them. The significance of the different festivals changed with the passage of time, but we can trace a number of important occasions in the Old Testament.

The sabbath day

Many nations in the ancient world had a regular day of rest, and the celebration of the sabbath every seventh day was an important part of Old Testament life from a very early date. There is no single passage which describes what a sabbath should be like. But it probably began as a day of rest, so that every member of the population (including slaves and foreigners) could renew themselves for their daily work. Worship was a part of this renewal process, and no doubt it was an occasion when crowds would throng to the various sanctuaries throughout the land – though what they did there was not always pleasing to God. On the sabbath, no regular work would be undertaken, though it would not necessarily be a day of complete rest for everyone.

Exodus 23:12; 34:21

Leviticus 19:30; Numbers 28:9–10
Isaiah 1:13; 2:11
Amos 8:5; Jeremiah 17:21–22
2 Kings 11:5–8

The main emphasis was on the sabbath as a day to look back to the nation's roots, to celebrate God's goodness and greatness, and to renew a commitment to the covenant faith. This is no doubt why its observance is required in the Ten Commandments. The whole day was specially dedicated to God ('holy'), because it was a reminder of his greatness both in creation and history. It was also a reminder to them that belief in God meant concern for other people. In the period after the Babylonian exile, the sabbath became very important in the synagogues. Eventually it became a day that was rigidly controlled by many prohibitions. But in the Old Testament period it was a day for joyful celebration.

Exodus 20:8–11
Exodus 31:12–17
Exodus 20:11; Deuteronomy 5:15
Deuteronomy 5:13–14

Isaiah 58:13–14

The Passover

The greatest event of all to which the people looked back was God's deliverance of the slaves from Egypt (the exodus). This was marked in an annual festival at which an animal was sacrificed, and a meal was shared. In this respect, the Passover was just a special form of fellowship offering, celebrating the relationship inaugurated between God and people in the exodus events. These events themselves had a profound impact on the way the festival was celebrated. The people dressed up in the same way as their ancestors had done – 'with your sandals on your feet and your stick in your hand' – as if ready for a long journey.

Exodus 12:11

According to the story of the exodus, the people prepared to leave Egypt in their family groups. This is how the Passover was celebrated in the earlier part of the Old Testament period. A lamb was sacrificed in the home, with none of the splendour of worship found in the sanctuaries. The animal's blood was daubed not on an altar but on the doorposts of the house. At this time, the animal was always a lamb roasted for the fellowship meal – a custom perhaps

The great Old Testament festivals have carried over into modern Judaism. This Jewish family are celebrating Passover, recalling their ancestors' deliverance from slavery in Egypt.

going back to the origin of the festival in the days when Israel had been a nomadic sheep-rearing people. Later, it became a national occasion, centred on the temple in Jerusalem, with all the impressive pageantry associated with worship there. The ritual naturally changed to suit the different circumstances. Both sheep and cattle could be used in the celebrations, boiled rather than roasted. There was also a provision whereby anyone who missed the Passover because they were ritually unclean could celebrate it a month later than the proper date. It has been suggested that the worshippers in the temple may have recited the story of the first Passover and exodus, perhaps acting out the events and culminating with the singing of the great 'song of Moses'.

Deuteronomy 16:1–8; 2 Kings 23:21–22; 2 Chronicles 30:1–22; 35:1–19

Deuteronomy 16:2
Deuteronomy 16:7

Numbers 9:1–14; 2 Chronicles 30:23–27

Exodus 1 — 15
Exodus 15:1–18

In the New Testament period, both the family and the national elements of the occasion were united. The sacrifices were killed in the temple but the fellowship meals then eaten in a family home.

The harvest festivals

Exodus 23:14–17; 34:18–23

The Old Testament mentions three major religious festivals that relate to the agricultural year. These celebrations had probably always been a part of the national life of the inhabitants of Canaan. Similar occasions are celebrated by farmers all over the world. But the Old Testament links each of them to the great and unrepeatable events of Israel's history, not to the cycle of the seasons and the inevitable concern of farmers for the continuing fertility of their land.

Leviticus 23:9–14; Numbers 28:10–23

● **The festival of Unleavened Bread** was apparently related to the barley harvest and the offering of the first-fruits. But this was celebrated at the same time of year as Passover and that, together with the fact that unleavened bread features in the passover story, meant that the two festivals came to be closely connected, and together served to commemorate the escape from Egypt.

Numbers 28:26–31

Leviticus 23:15–21

● **The Corn Harvest** (or Feast of Weeks) celebrated the end of the wheat harvest. Special offerings would be made in the sanctuaries, though the central action was the ceremonial presentation of the first sheaf that had been cut. Following this, individual worshippers could bring offerings from their own crops. The events

Festivals of the Jewish Year

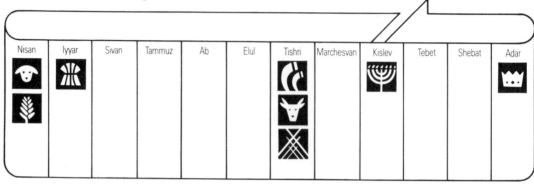

Nisan	Iyyar	Sivan	Tammuz	Ab	Elul	Tishri	Marchesvan	Kislev	Tebet	Shebat	Adar

 Passover (evening)/**Unleavened Bread** (whole week). Remembering deliverance from Egypt

 Firstfruits (last day of Unleavened Bread). First sheaf of barley harvest presented to God

 Weeks/Pentecost (fifty days after Passover). Rejoicing for corn harvest

 Trumpets/New Year (first day of seventh month). Tishri celebrated as specially solemn month

 Day of Atonement (ten days after Trumpets). Day of national repentance and fasting; in Old Testament, annual sacrifice and scapegoat

 Shelters/Tabernacles (at end of fruit harvests). Families camped out in shelters for a week

 Dedication/Lights (began after Old Testament period). Celebrated cleansing of second temple

 Purim (another festival of later origin) Recalls story of Esther

Three other celebrations were not annual:

Sabbath Seventh day of each week kept as special day of rejoicing

Sabbatical Year Every seventh year, ground intended to lie fallow

Jubilee Year Every fiftieth year, all property intended to revert to original owner or descendants

Deuteronomy 16:12

of the exodus were also in the minds of the worshippers on this occasion, though after the exile the harvest festival came to be used as a time for celebrating the giving of the Law at Mt Sinai.

Leviticus 23:33–43; Deuteronomy 16:13–17

● **The Festival of Shelters** (or Tabernacles) came at the very end of the growing season, and was a celebration of the fruit harvest from vineyards and orchards. This was a particularly joyful festival,

The Festival of Shelters is in direct continuity with the Jews of Ezra's day. As well as celebrating the fruit and vine harvest, it reminds participants of the Israelites' wilderness days and the beginning of their covenant faith.

and took its character from the practice of the farmers, who would stay out all night to guard their crops, with only flimsy huts to protect them. For the seven days of the festival, the worshippers lived in similar structures.

The main feature of this occasion was the simple expression of joy at the safe gathering of the harvest. But there also seems to be a close connection between the Festival of Shelters and the renewal of the covenant faith. The Old Testament identifies the temporary shelters with the tents in which Israel lived in the desert. Some have suggested that this association only came in later, when the shelters traditionally used at this time of year no longer had any practical relevance to the essentially non-agricultural life of the exiles. But many more are of the opinion that the covenant theme was always an important part of this festival, even from the earliest days of Israel's life in the land of Canaan. Allegiance to the covenant certainly seems to have been the bond that united the various tribes in the days of the judges. It is likely that they renewed their commitment to God and to one another in annual ceremonies which would include the reading of the covenant law. The Old Testament indicates that this covenant law could be read out as a part of the Festival of Shelters, and many scholars therefore believe that this would be followed by a solemn moment when the people committed themselves once again to the demands of God's covenant and his Law.

Leviticus 23:33–44

Exodus 24:7; Deuteronomy 27:9–10; Joshua 24:1–28

Deuteronomy 31:9–13; Nehemiah 8:13–18

Old Testament worship was a varied experience. But one thing we do not find in it is preaching. After the exile the *Torah* was regularly expounded during organized worship. But in the earlier Old Testament period, the main emphasis was always on praise and celebration. Like daily behaviour, worship was a response to God as he had made himself known in the events of Israel's history and the everyday experience of ordinary people. As the joyful worshippers went to the sanctuaries, they were reminded of God's past goodness, and given fresh inspiration for their own lives. But they were also challenged by his holiness, as they faced the central need for repentance and forgiveness – and offered sacrifices in order to secure it. As time went on, it was this repetitive nature of much Old Testament worship that led prophets and others to question its lasting effectiveness, and to see it as but one stage on the road to a closer relationship with God. Could God not forgive sin in a more comprehensive way, they asked, so that his people could really praise him as men and women 'pure in act and thought'?

Nehemiah 8:7–9

Psalm 24:4

The Old Testament never really gives an answer to that question, though some of its writers looked forward to a time when the covenant would be renewed in such a way that the past would be forgiven, and the future could hold out the hope of real victory over the power of evil. They never spelled out the meaning of that in detail. But they were sure that God could be trusted to work for the benefit of the whole world, which he had made and on which he set his love. When men and women commit themselves to God in humble trust, whether it be in great corporate acts of worship or in

Jeremiah 31:31–34

the private recesses of their own lives, they will always learn more about the true meaning of life and faith:

> Don't you know? Haven't you heard?
> The Lord is the everlasting God;
> he created all the world.
> He never grows tired or weary.
> No one understands his thoughts.
> He strengthens those who are weak and tired.
> Even those who are young grow weak;
> young men can fall exhausted.
> But those who trust in the Lord for help
> will find their strength renewed.
> They will rise on wings like eagles;
> they will run and not get weary;
> Isaiah 40:28–31   they will walk and not grow weak.

Kings, priests and prophets in worship

The existence of a regular system for public worship inevitably requires full time officials to look after the places of worship, and to supervise what goes on there. In the Old Testament a number of figures appear to be important in this connection.

The Kings

Throughout the ancient Middle East, kings had a special role in religion. Their precise function varied from place to place. In Egypt, for example, the pharaoh was often thought to be himself a divine being. In Babylon, on the other hand, he was more often regarded as a sort of messenger of the gods – an intermediary between people and gods, though not himself divine. Although some have argued otherwise, it is unlikely that the kings of either Israel or Judah were ever thought of as gods themselves. Indeed, when the Syrian Naaman assumed that one of them was a god, he was quick to disclaim it (2 Kings 5:7). The psalms contain ample evidence to show that the people prayed not to the king, but to God on his behalf (Psalm 20:1–9; 72:1–19). From the earliest days of Israel's arrival in the land of Canaan, God himself had always been regarded as the king. The tension between this belief and the political need for a military leader was recognized in the stories of Saul's appointment (1 Samuel 8:1–22; 10:17–27), and occasionally features in the message of the prophets (Hosea 8:4). But even when the idea of kingship was accepted, God himself was still regarded as the supreme sovereign of his people, and the king as his servant (Deuteronomy 17:14–20).

The special nature of the king's position was symbolized in the fact that he was anointed. This ritual signified his close relationship with God, and declared that he was, in effect, a 'holy' person. David recognized this quality even in Saul (1 Samuel 24:5–7), and when Saul was killed in the heat of battle his murderer had to be punished for killing 'the one whom the Lord had chosen to be king' (2 Samuel 1:14–16). This special relationship between God and the king was expressed in the idea of a 'covenant' existing between God, the royal family of David, and the people of Judah (2 Samuel 7:8–16), and the king could on occasion even be called God's 'son' (Psalm 2:7).

The king could also be called a priest (Psalm 110:4). Kings in general often had an important part to play in organized worship, and the Old Testament depicts the kings of Israel and Judah engaged in such activities. Throughout the whole history of both kingdoms, the kings played an important part in public worship. David established centres of worship (2 Samuel 6:17; 24:25), and Solomon, of course, built the temple itself (1 Kings 5:1–6:14). The first king of the northern kingdom of Israel also set up sanctuaries in his own land, and decreed the sort of worship that should be carried out there (1 Kings 12:26–33). As a result, these shrines were thought of as 'the king's place of worship, the national temple' (Amos 7:13). But the same was true of the temple in Jerusalem, for the kings of Judah controlled the worship there too. The priests were effectively members of the royal household, under the control of the king (2 Samuel 8:17; 20:25; 1 Kings

'Those who trust in the Lord for help will find their strength renewed. They will rise on wings like eagles' (Isaiah 40:31).

2:26–35; 4:4; 2 Kings 12:4–16).

The kings also took charge of religious policy-making. Asa (1 Kings 15:11–15), Ahaz (2 Kings 16:1–18), Joash (2 Kings 12:1–19), Hezekiah (2 Kings 18:1–7), Manasseh (2 Kings 21:1–9) and Josiah (2 Kings 22:3–23:23) are all specifically credited with having reorganized temple worship in one way or another.

As well as being responsible for the general tenor of organized worship, the kings could also on occasion conduct worship. Saul (1 Samuel 13:8–10; 14:35), David (2 Samuel 6:13; 24:25), Solomon (1 Kings 3:3–4; 8:62–63), Jeroboam 1 (1 Kings 12:32—13:1) and Ahaz (2 Kings 16:1–16) all offered sacrifices regularly. Kings could also pray on behalf of the nation, and issue blessings in God's name (1 Kings 8:14–66; 2 Kings 19:14–19). On one occasion, David offered sacrifice and gave a blessing while clothed in the apparel of a priest (2 Samuel 6:12–19).

The kings obviously had an important role in the religious life of their people. Since they were believed to be appointed by God, this is not surprising, for they had the power to encourage their people to maintain the covenant faith – and, on occasion, to corrupt it. There have been many arguments as to the precise nature of the kingship, in view of the many 'priestly' functions that kings could carry out. But a number of factors suggest that we need to be cautious in claiming that the king's main function was religious rather than political:

● Religion and politics were always closely related in the ancient world. In particular, the various superpowers of the day often imposed their own religions on their vassals, as a means of demonstrating the vassals' subservience. This fact alone explains why the kings of Judah were so often involved in changing the equipment used in the temple. Restoration of the covenant faith meant reasserting Judah's independence.

● The exclusive functions of the priests were not so well defined during the time of the monarch as they were later to become after the exile. As we shall see below, any head of the family could offer sacrifices or establish a new place of worship – and when the kings engaged in such activities they could well have been acting mainly in that capacity.

● It is perhaps significant that the only occasions when we have specific reports of kings conducting worship were particularly important times in the life of the nation. Even today, monarchs

tend to be involved in religious celebrations at important moments, although they themselves have no regular 'priestly' functions. No doubt, in general, the day to day conduct of worship in ancient Israel would be left in the hands of other religious officials, appointed by the king for the job.

Priests

We have already seen that during the period of the monarchy the priests often had a close relationship with the king himself. Some experts have suggested that the priesthood itself only emerged at this period. But its existence and functions must go back further than that.

It is certainly true that the Old Testament shows a lot of flexibility in worship at an earlier time. A number of stories show the heads of families offering sacrifices (Genesis 22:13; 31:54; 46:1; Judges 6:19–27; 13:19–23; 1 Samuel 1:3; 2:12–13; 9:12–13). But this is not of itself evidence that there were no priests, for even much later the actual act of sacrifice was always performed by the worshipper himself and not by the priest.

More surprising, perhaps, is the way that in this early period it was apparently possible for clans and other groups to appoint and dismiss their own priests at will (Judges 17:1–18:31). But incidents of this kind may well have been exceptions, for it would be odd if Israel had no organized priesthood at this time. Other nations certainly had well developed priesthoods, and the Old Testament mentions some of them: the Canaanite priest Melchizedek (Genesis 14:17–24), the Egyptian priest Potiphera (Genesis 41:45–46), the Midianite Jethro (Exodus 18:1), and the Philistine priests of Dagon (1 Samuel 5:5). In the context of the religious ideas of the time, the existence of the Ark of the Covenant and the tent of the Lord's presence almost necessitate the existence of professional priests to take care of them.

So what did priests do, and how did they operate? The answer to that question naturally changed with the years. After the exile, with the disappearance of the kings, the priests came to occupy an important political place. But in the earlier period, they must have operated in a more restricted religious capacity, at least in the great national sanctuaries that were closely controlled by the kings. Some aspects of their work are unclear, especially the relationship between priests and

Levites. But the Old Testament gives information about several of their functions.

● Priests cared for the sanctuaries throughout the land (Judges 17:1–13; 1 Samuel 1–3:21; Amos 7:10–13). They would get their living from the gifts of worshippers – and, of course, they also had their share of the meat from the sacrifices (Numbers 18:8–32; 1 Samuel 2:12–16). They could also have their own lands and property (1 Kings 2:26; Amos 7:17).

● People would also consult the priests in order to get advice for particular situations. One story tells how Saul first met Samuel while he was asking for advice about some lost donkeys (1 Samuel 9:3–16). The account does not tell us precisely how Saul expected Samuel to know where they were, but other passages seem to imply that the priest would use a set of special dice (Urim and Thummim) to give the answer to such questions (1 Samuel 14:41–42; Deuteronomy 33:8; Exodus 28:30). It is not known exactly how this procedure operated, but it seems to have died out quite early in any case. After the time of David, it is the prophets who give direct advice and instruction of this kind (1 Kings 20:13–14; 22:6; 2 Kings 3:11–19).

● More generally, the priests would give instructions (*Torah*) on questions relating to worship. They were able to pronounce on whether things, places or people were clean or unclean, holy or profane, and so give guidance to the worshippers (Leviticus 10:8–11; 13:1–8; Ezekiel 22:26; 44:23; Haggai 2:11–14). Some scholars believe that moral law such as the Ten Commandments may also have been 'preached' in this way by the priests. After the exile, the Levites had the job of teaching. But their 'Torah' was different from the earlier priestly teaching, since it now consisted of exposition of parts of the written Old Testament books (Nehemiah 8:7–9). Priests could also have certain judicial functions, as we saw in a previous chapter.

Priests were involved in the offering of sacrifices. It would be the worshipper who actually killed the animal. But the priest gave advice about the appropriate form of sacrifice to be offered on different occasions, and it was always the priest (as a specially 'holy' person) who took the blood to the altar. In this context, he was a mediator – representing God to the people, and the people to God.

● The priest could also mediate between God and people when he gave answers in God's name to the prayers of the worshippers (1 Samuel 1:17), or pronounced a blessing upon them (Numbers 6:22–26).

It was this function as mediator which was most characteristic of the priest's work. He was specially consecrated to God, and as such was able to deal with the awesome holiness of a place of worship. Through his presence, God and people could be brought together in a tangible way.

Prophets

When the people of Jerusalem were plotting to get rid of Jeremiah, they commented that even if they disposed of him, 'There will always be priests to instruct us, wise men to give us counsel, and prophets to proclaim God's message' (Jeremiah 18:18). At one time, scholars were surprised to see prophets and priests mentioned in the same breath, as if they were complementary to each other. A hundred years ago it was an 'assured result' of Old Testament study that priests and prophets were implacably opposed to each other. They represented different kinds of religion: priests being concerned with the arid and mechanical performance of pointless ritual, and prophets with the communication of a vital and life-giving message from God. It was widely supposed that the great Old Testament prophets were moral preachers, with no interest in organized religion at all – and it was only after the exile that a lesser breed of prophets emerged, who then became involved in formal worship because the fire of the original prophetic message had been all but extinguished.

It is certainly true that some of the prophets were outspoken in their criticism of empty formality (Amos 5:21–24; Hosea 6:6; Micah 6:6–8; Isaiah 1:10–17). But we can now see that it was wrong to dissociate them altogether from the cult. Closer Old Testament study has shown that the prophets as a group often were closely linked with organized worship. A number of factors have led to this conclusion:

● As we have seen throughout this book, formal worship and everyday behaviour were closely linked in the Old Testament faith. Both of them were part of the people's response to God's goodness. The prophets could not have denied outright the importance of organized worship without also denying the very foundations of the covenant faith.

● The general picture often shows

This reconstruction of a Jewish high priest's breastplate shows twelve stones with symbols for the twelve tribes of Israel.

priests and prophets working alongside each other. Samuel and Elijah are the only prophets whom we know carried out priestly functions (1 Samuel 7:9; 11:15; 1 Kings 18:36–39). But other passages connect them quite clearly (Jeremiah 5:31; 23:11; 26:7,16; 29:26; Lamentations 2:20; Zechariah 7:1–3). And we know of at least one prophet who had his own room in the temple at Jerusalem (Jeremiah 35:3–4).

● The prophets often delivered their messages in the context of organized worship, and their themes were often related to the great festivals. For example, when Amos spoke of the coming 'Day of the Lord', he was probably taking up the popular expectations in the mind of the worshippers as they approached the climax of one of the great festivals – though Amos turned their expectations upside down (Amos 5:18–24). When the priest Amaziah challenged Amos, he

suggested that he should go and proclaim his message somewhere else, because he could not expect to be employed in Bethel – thus implying that prophets would on occasion be employed there (Amos 7:10–13). Then we also need to take account of the fact that both Jeremiah (Jeremiah 1:1) and Ezekiel (Ezekiel 1:1) were themselves members of priestly families.

Observations of this kind have been taken to indicate that Jeremiah, Ezekiel and others were actually on the staff at various places of worship. But there is no real evidence to support that. The evidence only shows them in the temple to speak and to attend worship. In a later age, Jesus did both – but no one ever thought he was a priest! It was just good sense to go where the people were, and to use familiar motifs to present a message. In any case, the prophets never restricted their preaching to cultic occasions, but went

Several prophets compared themselves to watchmen in their watchtowers, set to give warning when the people left God's ways. The prophets hated empty, formalized worship with no moral content.

into the market-place, the fields, and anywhere else that people would listen.

● Certain psalms seem to imply that someone spoke in the name of God during the liturgy of worship. A number of psalms that begin as lamentation end in thanksgiving – implying that at some point during the prayer the worshipper has been reassured of God's continuing presence (Psalm 20; 22; 86). Others contain such messages of reassurance said to have come direct from God himself (Psalm 12:5; 85:9–13; 91:14–16). One psalm clearly says that such messages were delivered by 'an unknown voice' in the course of temple worship (Psalm 81:5–16). We have seen that worship often included drama, and since other parts of the Old Testament show the prophets to be speakers on God's behalf, who better than a 'cultic

prophet' of this kind to play such a part in worship?

There is some evidence for this in the work of the Chronicler, who in one passage gives the title 'Levites' to people who were designated 'prophets' in the earlier account of Kings (compare 2 Chronicles 34:30 with 2 Kings 23:2). In other passages, these same 'Levites' are expressly given prophetic functions, including the deliverance of messages on God's behalf during worship (1 Chronicles 25:1–6; 2 Chronicles 20:13–19). Scholars have naturally speculated on the exact tasks performed by such cultic prophets. Unfortunately, apart from these rather vague references in Chronicles, and the implications of certain psalms, there is no specific information to help us further.

13 The Old and the New

The problem

THE OLD Testament has always been highly important for Christians: it is quoted on nearly every page of the New. And yet it has also presented them with a problem, and even in the very earliest days of the church its meaning and relevance were subjects of heated debate and controversy. In the years immediately following the death and resurrection of Jesus, this was the one issue that caused most friction and dissension in the lives of the young churches. Jesus himself had claimed that his own life was a 'fulfilment' of the Old Testament. Yet many of his actions seemed to set aside its most distinctive teachings, especially on subjects such as sabbath-keeping and the food laws, but also some of its moral teaching. What kind of authority then should the Old Testament have in the lives of Jesus' followers?

Matthew 5:17
Mark 2:23–28
Mark 7:14–23
Matthew 5:21–48

The very first generation of Christians were also Jews, and for them there was no particular problem. For the most part they continued to observe the way of life in which they had been brought up, based on the Old Testament as it was understood in first-century Judaism. But once it became clear that the Christian message was for non-Jewish people, and that Romans and Greeks could also become followers of Jesus Christ, the question of the Old Testament's authority presented itself in an altogether more pressing form. Was it necessary for a Gentile person to become a Jew in order to be a Christian? Paul and other New Testament writers answered that question with a firm 'no'. But they still kept the Old Testament as their sacred scriptures, and often used these ancient books as a basis for their own exposition of the Christian faith.

Galatians; 1 Peter; Hebrews

And therein lies the problem. For if certain parts of the Old Testament can be set aside as no longer relevant to Christian faith and action, how can we tell which those bits are – and what should we do with the rest of it?

Searching for solutions

The question of the relationship between Old Testament and New was put in an outspoken way by a second-century Christian called Marcion. Not only did he see the ambiguities in the position evidently taken by the apostles. He also noted other problems for Christian belief in the Old Testament. Jesus had spoken of a God of love who was concerned for the well-being of all men and women. But as Marcion read the Old Testament he often saw there a rather different picture of God, in which he seemed to be associated with extreme savagery and cruelty. Far from seeking the salvation of people, he sometimes seemed to be associated with their annihilation. Of course, Marcion had the picture slightly out of focus: stern judgment was an important part of Jesus' teaching, and God's love was never absent from the Old Testament faith, as we have seen in many different ways.

Nevertheless, modern readers have often felt the same way, and some Christians today would find it difficult to reconcile some aspects of the Old Testament's view of God with what they take to be the mainstream Christian view of the New Testament. As well as the matters to which Marcion drew attention, they might also refer to the contrast between the universal message of God's love in Isaiah 40–55 and the apparently narrow-minded nationalism of a book such as Ezra. And even the most ingenious interpreter would find it exceedingly difficult to reconcile the sentiments of Psalm 137:8–9 with the statements about loving enemies in Jesus' Sermon on the Mount (Matthew 5:43–48). Then again, many people today find some aspects of Old Testament worship difficult to understand – especially sacrifice which (at least to Western people) seems primitive and cruel, if not completely incomprehensible.

Marcion's solution to all this was simple: tear up the Old Testament and throw it in the dustbin! But his view found no widespread support in the early church, not least because Marcion wanted to dispose of much of the New Testament as well, and that seemed to put a serious question mark against the reality of his Christian faith.

But the leaders of the early church could understand well enough the point that Marcion was making. There was a real question about the Old Testament. If the coming of Jesus was God's new and decisive action in the life of the world, then what relevance could the history of an ancient people have for faith in him?

The usual answer was that when the Old Testament was correctly understood it could be seen to be saying exactly the same thing as the New Testament. But in order to demonstrate this, it was necessary to interpret the Old Testament in such a way as to show that its real meaning was somehow hidden from the casual reader.

By coincidence, Jewish scholars had already faced this question in a different context. A century and more earlier, the great Jewish interpreter Philo (about 20 BC–AD 45), who lived in the Egyptian city of Alexandria, had taken up the challenge of reconciling the Old Testament with the thinking of the great Greek philosophers. There were few obvious connections between them. But by applying a mystical allegorical interpretation to the Old Testament, Philo had succeeded in demonstrating (at least to his own satisfaction) that Moses and other Old Testament writers had actually declared the truths of Greek philosophy several centuries before the Greeks thought of them!

Some of the early Christian leaders, especially those in Alexandria, adopted this approach with enthusiasm. Soon, they were using the same techniques to show that the Old Testament books also contained everything that was in the New Testament, for those with the eyes to see it.

Even apparently insignificant details in the Old Testament stories were taken up as symbols of the Christian gospel. Anything red could be understood as a reference to the death of Jesus on the cross (for example, the

How far did Jesus set aside the Old Testament's detailed teachings? His disciples were criticized for picking and eating ears of wheat on a sabbath day.

red heifer of Numbers 19, or Rahab's red cord, Joshua 2:18). References to water soon became pictures of Christian baptism. The story of the exodus, with its combination of blood (on the doorposts at Passover) and water (in crossing the Sea of Reeds), engendered many complex explanations of the relationship between the cross and Christian salvation, as well as the two Christian sacraments of baptism and the Lord's Supper!

Hilary, bishop of Poitiers in France (AD 315–68), explained this way of reading the Old Testament in the following terms:

> Every work contained in the sacred volume announces by word, explains by facts, and corroborates by examples the coming of our Lord Jesus Christ ... From the beginning of the world Christ, by authentic and absolute prefigurations in the person of the patriarchs, gives birth to the church, washes it clean, sanctifies it, chooses it, places it apart and redeems it: by the sleep of Adam, by the deluge in the days of Noah, by the blessing of Melchizedek, by Abraham's justification, by the birth of Isaac, by the captivity of Jacob ... The purpose of this work is to show that in each personage in every age, and in every act, the image of his coming, of his teaching, of his resurrection, and of our church is reflected as in a mirror.
>
> (Hilary, Introduction to *The Treatise of Mysteries*)

Not all church leaders were happy with this approach to the Old Testament, especially those connected with the other great Christian centre at Antioch in Syria. But it was generally taken for granted that the Old Testament was basically a Christian book, and in one way or another its contents were related to the fundamental beliefs of Christian theology.

During the Protestant Reformation the whole subject was once again opened for fresh examination. Martin Luther (1483–1546) and John Calvin (1509–1564) both emphasized the need to understand the Old Testament faith in its historical and social context. In that respect their approach was not dissimilar from that of many modern scholars. But Luther wanted to distinguish the value of Old and New Testaments by seeing the Old as 'Law' and the New as 'Gospel'. This gave him a neat tool with which to separate out the wheat of the pure gospel (which for him was found in Paul's New Testament letters) from the chaff of a superseded legalism (identified with the Old Testament and Jewish Christianity). This thinking has had a profound influence on biblical scholarship right up to our own day. But it is misguided in some fundamental ways:

This 'Good Shepherd' is from a painting by Christians in the catacombs of Rome. The idea of God as a shepherd is taken straight from the Old Testament.

● It ignores the fact that 'law' is not the basis of the Old Testament faith – nor for that matter is it entirely absent from the New Testament. In both, law is placed in the context of a covenant understanding in which God's love is the foundation principle.

● Luther quite wrongly identified Judaism with a moralistic legalism. This was quite unfair even to the Pharisaic view which the Christian Paul so clearly rejected. At this point, Luther allowed his own reaction to Roman Catholic Christianity to colour his view of the Old Testament faith.

Calvin recognized some of these deficiencies, and instead he emphasized the importance of the covenant theme in both Testaments. By a careful comparison of God's relationships with people in ancient Israel and the Christian church, he was able to claim that the two parts of the Christian Bible hang together as a kind of 'progressive

A Roman schoolmaster with his pupils. Paul writes in Galatians of the law as 'our tutor to bring us to Christ'.

In both Old and New Testaments the moral demands which stem from faith in God are carried right home to the daily life of ordinary people.

revelation' in which the ancient promises made to Israel in the Old Testament found their culmination in the ongoing life of the Christian church. This view is not without its own problems. But at least it does try to take the Old Testament faith seriously, and Calvin's position is still widely held today by many conservative Christians.

After the Reformation, the question of whether the Old Testament is a Christian book was effectively shelved until our own generation. The European Enlightenment, with its emphasis on understanding the Old Testament as a collection of ancient books in the context of its own times, directed scholarly endeavours elsewhere. But in the last 100 years or so, the theological question has again come to the fore. A significant impetus in this came from the Nazi movement in modern Germany. The anti-Jewish feelings that this created inevitably had repercussions in the German churches, and the presence of the Old Testament in the Christian Bible became a burning political issue as well as a subject for theological reflexion. A whole string of German theologians began to adopt the same kind of stance as Marcion. Yet despite the political pressures, many German Christian scholars made a positive assessment of the worth of the Old Testament. Some of the most creative work was done at this time by scholars such as Walter Eichrodt and Gerhard von Rad, as well as the Swiss theologian Karl Barth.

Nowadays, Christian people adopt various attitudes to the value of the Old Testament:

● Some would want to give the Old Testament an equal value and authority to the New Testament, on the grounds that every word of each is the direct utterance of God himself. But we need to exercise considerable caution before accepting this picture too easily. For there are whole sections of the teaching of Jesus himself where he makes it clear that his message involved either a rejection or a very radical revision of some fundamental aspects of Old Testament teaching.

● Others argue that the Old Testament is completely replaced by the New, and so can be discarded. Here

again we need to preserve the kind of careful balance we find in the teaching of Jesus himself. For he also described his ministry as in some sense a 'fulfilment' of the Old Testament. We can legitimately argue about what that means – but it must certainly involve the assumption that the Old Testament has something to say to Christians, and therefore has a legitimate place in a Christian Bible.

● Some people try to distinguish between various parts of the Old Testament. They will separate things such as laws about priests, sacrifices, and purity (which Christians no longer observe) from other parts such as the Ten Commandments and the moral teachings of the prophets (which are still considered relevant). Calvin made a similar division to this. But it is a good deal easier to make such distinctions than it is to justify them. By removing such apparently irrelevant elements, we are in fact displacing some of the most basic aspects of the Old Testament faith. In addition, it is precisely in such concepts as sacrifice that the New Testament itself most often finds some correlation between the Old Testament faith and Christian beliefs about Jesus.

● It is also common for Christians to speak of a 'progressive revelation' of God's will and character running through both Testaments. On this view, God's will is revealed in a number of stages, roughly corresponding with the capacity of people to understand. So some of the more 'difficult' parts of the Old Testament can be explained as appropriate to a primitive age, but subsequently replaced by other more sophisticated notions, culminating in Jesus' teaching about a God of love. But this is an unhelpful idea. It is based on an outmoded evolutionary idea of an inevitable moral progress in human affairs. And it also confuses statements about God as he really is with statements about how people think of him. In addition, it contains the dubious implication that modern people invariably know more about God's will, and are more obedient to it than were the patriarchs, prophets and other leading figures in the Old Testament story.

Making connections

There are obvious difficulties involved in interpreting the Old Testament within the Christian Bible. We need to recognize that the Old Testament is in many ways a strange and alien book to modern people – whether Christians or not. Whatever assessment we make of the Old Testament faith, it is not the same as Christian faith, and

in practice when Christians read it they often find the Old Testament hard to understand, because it belongs to a completely different world from their own faith experience. Much of this strangeness can be dispelled when once we have set the Old Testament faith in its proper historical and social context – and that is what we have tried to do here. We may not find things such as sacrifice any more appealing, but at least we can begin to appreciate their significance in the total context of Israel's faith. But that does not mean we can simply set the Old Testament on one side. For in practice it is impossible to articulate an adequate Christian faith without reference to the Old Testament.

At the most fundamental level, it is a simple fact that we will not get far in making sense out of the New Testament itself if we are ignorant of the Old. Jesus and his disciples were practising Jews. They were thoroughly immersed in Old Testament ways of thinking about God and the world. For them the Old Testament faith was a living and vital part of their total existence. Of course, in many respects they grew out of Judaism, as they found some things had to be discarded or developed in the light of the exciting newness of God's actions in Christ. But for all that they continued to think of their new Christian experience very much in terms of the faith with which they had been brought up.

The earliest Christian churches used the Old Testament in its Greek translation as their Bible – and the language of the New Testament itself has a good deal more in common with that than with the secular literature of Greek and Roman culture. Inevitably, that language influenced the way they articulated their understanding of Christianity. Indeed, Old Testament language still permeates Christian thinking today. Modern Western Christians who have never seen an animal sacrifice still sing in their churches of the 'one true, pure immortal sacrifice' of Jesus, and many of them continue to call a part of their church buildings an 'altar', even though no blood has ever been shed there! It may well be that we need to examine all this imagery and articulate its message in different concepts for modern people. But to do that successfully we need to understand it all first – otherwise we will be in constant danger of throwing out the fact that Christ died for our sins along with the language of sacrifice, altar and atonement. And the place where we can get a proper understanding of all these notions is certainly the Old Testament.

But the Old Testament gives us more than just a linguistic and cultural background to the thinking of the New Testament writers. It also contains important statements of truths about God and his relationships with people and the world that are as valid now as they ever were. If we take the chapter headings under which we have explored the Old Testament faith, we can readily see how the key concepts of each section form an indispensable theological found-ation for the Christian faith as that is presented in the pages of the New Testament. There is such a close interconnection between both Testaments at this point that it is no exaggeration to claim that the Christian faith itself would make imperfect sense if we were to remove the basic affirmations of thé Old Testament faith from the Christian Bible.

The living God

Nowhere is this more strikingly obvious than in the case of beliefs about God himself.

● There is the truth that there is only one God, and that he is both all-powerful and yet personally interested in the welfare of ordinary people. Nowadays, theologians often talk of these two aspects of God's character in terms of 'transcendence' and 'immanence'. We can be quite sure that this language would have meant little to the people of Old Testament times. Indeed, it is unlikely that these truths about God would be perceived with equal clarity by all sections of the people of Israel. But they were certainly implicit in the very earliest creedal confessions which exhort the people to worship only one God – even if it was several centuries later that God's sole control of the world and its affairs was systematically asserted by the great prophets.

● Bound up with the fact that God is one is the belief that God's demands on his people are primarily moral rather than religious

Exodus 15:11–18

Isaiah 40:12–31; 41:21–29; 44:1–20

A great image for God in the Bible is that of a shepherd.

services or ritual taboos. We have already seen that this was a new idea, for most ancient religions were more interested in sacrifices and ritual than in morality. Yet the whole Old Testament understanding of worship makes no sense at all if these two aspects are separated.

● Then there is the notion of God's grace – the fact that he gives undeserved gifts to people. The entire Old Testament story is given coherence by the knowledge that God had done great things for his people, and on that basis he could challenge them to loyalty and obedience. Every stage of the story shows God's active concern to work for the salvation of his people – and this 'covenant' principle is still basic to any Christian understanding of God and his ways. The Old Testament, just as much as the New Testament, depicts God working in love for the good of his people. And though the focus in the New Testament shifts from events such as the exodus or the exile to centre on Jesus, there is still a basic assumption that God is an active and loving God, whose workings can be seen by ordinary people in the course of their everyday lives.

● We have observed at a number of points that the Old Testament does not describe God 'metaphysically', by asking what he is made of, but 'functionally', by asking how he behaves. The New Testament shares this approach, when it says in effect: 'Look at Jesus: this is what God is like.'

God and the world

It is not too difficult to show that important aspects of God's character are common to both Testaments. But without the Old Testament, the Christian faith would also be seriously lacking a perspective on the way God relates to the natural world.

● In the world of the earliest Christians, it was commonplace to believe that the natural, physical world in which we live was intrinsically evil, and any sort of meaningful salvation would therefore need to involve an escape from this world to some other, more 'spiritual' and therefore more perfect world. This was part and parcel of the Greek outlook, and as the Christian church moved out from Palestine into the wider Roman Empire it was always a temptation for Christians to agree with it. Though there were fierce arguments on this very point, Christians never did accept the view that physical existence in this world is second best. But they were able to assert the basic goodness of life only because of the strong Old Testament conviction that informed their thinking. As a consequence, instead of seeing salvation in terms of escape from this world, the Christian writers of the New Testament declared that the world itself had its own part in God's plan of salvation: the coming of Jesus meant vitality and renewal for the very stuff out of which the world is made. Without this, modern Christians would have little to say on the major issues of the twentieth century, such as the nuclear arms race or the use of the world's resources. But in taking the physical world into their expectations of salvation, the New Testament writers were quite firmly grounded in the Old Testament faith that had gone before them.

Romans 8:18–25; Colossians 1:15–20; Revelation 21 — 22

● When the New Testament sets out to explain how Jesus Christ relates to people, it again does so on the basis of the Old Testament view of people and their relationship to God. It takes for granted the basic theological concepts that we have located in the creation stories, and sees human sin as a barrier between God and people that needs to be removed if fellowship is to be restored. This whole structure of thought is so crucial for Christian theology that without this Old Testament insight it is doubtful whether the apostolic faith could have developed in the way it did.

God and his people

New Testament ethics also owe a good deal to the Old Testament.

● The notion of 'natural law' as we have discussed it in relation to the Old Testament is a fundamental prerequisite of the Christian faith. Paul takes it up as a key element in his explanation of how the life, death and resurrection of Jesus applies to all men and women, whatever their social or racial origins.

Romans 1:18 — 2:16

● Equally central to the New Testament is the covenant framework within which much Old Testament morality operates. The coming of Jesus was viewed as a further great act of God comparable with the exodus, and calling for a similar response of obedience and commitment. But the whole pattern of the Christian ethic is also based on the fundamental Old Testament assertion that people should behave like God behaves. The only difference is that the divine pattern is made even more explicit because of the example of Jesus himself, which Christians are called on to follow.

Matthew 5:48

Philippians 2:5–11;
2 Corinthians 8:8–9

● Then there is also the whole question of a Christian social ethic, which depends so much on the Old Testament heritage. For a variety of reasons, the New Testament has very little to say about how God deals with nations. Without the Old Testament, the Christian faith would be considerably impoverished at this point. For in the Old Testament faith we have the foundations of a Christian philosophy of history. No doubt the Old Testament position requires modification here and there in the light of the teaching of Jesus himself. But it is no coincidence that when modern Christians make pronouncements on social and political affairs they so often depend on the insights of the prophets and lawgivers of ancient Israel as they do so.

Worshipping God

Here too, the New Testament faith owes more than we sometimes think to its Old Testament antecedents.

● The style of worship of the early church – and of many modern churches – has grown out of the patterns of praise and joyful celebration that we have seen in the pages of the Old Testament.

● Even more striking is the correlation between the understanding of what worship means in both Testaments. For the undergirding principle of both Old Testament and Christian worship is that although God is a holy God – in every sense of that word – he is also a forgiving God, and the reality of that forgiveness can be represented in the events of worship in the presence of God's people.

● We can hardly ignore the vast importance that the theme of sacrifice has come to assume in Christian thinking. The New Testament writers asserted that in Jesus' life, death and resurrection, all that was promised by the sacrificial worship of the Old Testament had been brought to fulfilment. It was impossible to speak of what Jesus could do in the lives of his people without some reference to the hopes and aspirations of the worshipper in ancient Israel. Indeed, the whole concept of sacrifice is so significant in the Christian tradition that at least one large section of the church thinks of it not only as a series of theological metaphors and images, but as a continuing symbolic part of the ongoing liturgy of the worshipping Christian community.

Looking to the future

No one will wish to dispute the reality of the various connections we have traced here between the Old Testament faith and its New Testament development. Indeed, much more could be said along these lines which would reinforce the general picture presented here. But is all this just wishful thinking from the Christian's point of view? After all, it is easy enough to look at the Old Testament with the benefit of hindsight and convince oneself that this or that element of Old Testament faith is somehow related to Christian thinking. Are we perhaps in danger of falling into the same kind of subjectivism as those more ancient expositors who looked at things such as Rahab's scarlet cord and saw in them a clear reference to the blood of Jesus on the cross?

We are certainly not in the same predicament as the medieval scholars, for we have restricted our discussion here to features in the Old Testament faith which were an integral part of its historical development, and which were clearly perceived by the Old Testament writers themselves. But we still need to explain how we can be so sure that the Christian interpretation we want to place on these facts is not an alien intrusion into the Old Testament's essential message.

In the final analysis, of course, it is only our Christian conviction that Jesus is God's final word that enables us to see both Old and New Testaments as parts of the same story. But we could certainly qualify that by observing the simple fact that the Old Testament writers did see their faith as incomplete in itself, and therefore requiring some future 'fulfilment'.

In many important respects, the Old Testament faith was anchored in the past. Some of its most distinctive insights emerged out of the great events of Israel's history. When men and women wanted to know what God was like, they turned for an answer to events such as the exodus or the exile, as explained by the prophets and others. But they never thought that God was locked up in the past. Quite the opposite, in fact. For one of the Old Testament's fundamental convictions is that God can be known by ordinary people in the everyday events of their present life. The prophets extended these beliefs to their logical conclusion, observing that if

God was the Lord of the past, and if he also made himself known in the present, then he must be Lord of the future too.

The Old Testament historians express this view right at the beginning of their long story. For when God makes a covenant with Abraham and his family, he does so in the following terms: 'I will bless those who bless you, but I will curse those who curse you. *And* Genesis 12:3 *through you I will bless all the nations.'*

There is some debate as to the precise meaning of that last phrase. But it is certain that this blessing of the nations was not a reality at the time the Old Testament was compiled: it was a future hope that had yet to be accomplished.

As the Old Testament story proceeds, this hope is expanded and combined with other themes until a coherent future expectation emerges. This forward look to the Old Testament faith is so strong that Gerhard von Rad has described the Old Testament as a whole as 'a book of ever increasing anticipation'. We may trace at least three fundamental strands in this.

● **A new covenant** Perhaps the most notable is the expectation of a 'new covenant', that would take up and fulfil all the broken promises of the original Sinai covenant, and at the same time herald the beginning of a new era of relationships between God and people. This hope first emerged about the time of the exile, when it was clear that the original covenant had been a failure because of the disobedience and disloyalty of the people. For all its God-given

Promise and fulfilment

Many Old Testament themes are forward-looking and a number of them are taken up and developed in the New. In this way the New Testament builds on the foundation of the Old. Three such themes are central:

COVENANT

God made covenant agreements (e.g. with Abraham and Moses), whereby 'I will be your God and you will be my people'. But repeatedly these covenants broke down. Jeremiah predicted 'a new covenant', based on moral renewal.

At the Last Supper Jesus spoke of the wine as 'God's new covenant, sealed with my blood'. Many of the promises based on the old covenant are therefore taken over into the new.

New Israel

MESSIAH

As the great days of Israel became a thing of the past, the Jews began to look for a coming new age, and a Messiah (or 'anointed one') who would restore Israel's greatness.

Jesus' followers came to see him as the man in whom these promises were fulfilled. The title 'Christ' is the Greek word for 'Messiah'. But Jesus was a different kind of Messiah to the one the Jews expected.

A New Heart

The Holy Spirit

KINGDOM

God promised King David that his kingdom would last for ever. Yet it ended with the fall of Jerusalem. So the hope of a Messiah became linked to a new kingdom.

Jesus often spoke of himself as bringing in 'the kingdom of God'. But this was not a political kingdom. The kingdom is every part of people's lives in which God's will is done.

potential, they had been unable to keep its terms. As a result, leading Old Testament thinkers began to see that a complete change was needed in the lives of God's people if ever they were to do God's will. This change would be based on forgiveness for what was past. But its most striking feature would be a radical transformation of the human will in such a way that God would empower his people actually to keep the covenant. 'The new covenant that I will make with the people of Israel will be this: I will put my law within them and write it *Jeremiah 31:33* on their hearts.' The key to success is found in the new initiative from God himself to enable people to do his will: 'I will give you a new heart and a new mind. I will take away your stubborn heart of *Ezekiel 36:26–27; 11:19–20* stone and give you an obedient heart. I will put my spirit in you ...'

● **A Messiah** The Hebrew word *Mashiach*, like its Greek equivalent *Christos*, means 'an anointed person'. In the ancient Middle East both kings and priests were anointed with oil. We have already noticed the important part played by the king in so much of Old Testament life, especially in the southern kingdom of Judah. As the representative of God to his people, he was often referred to as *Psalm 2:7* 'God's anointed', even as 'God's Son'. This close relationship between God and the king in Jerusalem was cemented in the *2 Samuel 7:1–17* covenant made with the royal family of David. Because of that, the king was in a very real sense the focus of the people's hopes as they looked for God's will to be done in their midst.

If Old Testament social relationships were to reflect the character of God himself, then it was through the king that this would be put *Psalm 72:1–19* into practical effect. At least, that was the theory. But the reality was often different, as one king after another showed himself to be quite unfit, both morally and spiritually, to lead his people in ways that would reflect God's standards. Not that this prevented the prophets and others from hoping that the next king would be better. But from about the time of Isaiah onwards they were to become increasingly disillusioned with David's family. Though the prophets greeted each new king with optimism, their hopes for the future came to be *Isaiah 9:6–7; 11:1–5; Micah 5:2–5;* expressed in more idealistic terms that show their expectations *Jeremiah 23:5–6; Psalm 89:1–4;* moving away from the actual kings in Jerusalem and towards an ideal *132:10–12* king whom God himself would send to lead his people. It was out of this frustration that the messianic hope eventually was born. By the end of the Old Testament period it was widely believed that God would once more intervene in history, and send a new king who would perfectly fulfil the hopes and aspirations of the ancient Old Testament faith.

● **A new world** The Old Testament also looks forward to a time of physical renewal for the world itself. It often links failure in the *Genesis 3:17–19; Amos 4:6–12* lives of people with corruption in the world of nature. So it is not surprising that future personal and social renewal should also include plans for a revitalized world. This, too, became an important *Isaiah 11:6–9; 25:6–9; 51:3; 62:1–5;* part of the Old Testament view of the future, and many passages *Amos 9:13–15; Micah 4:1–4;* depict the material world sharing in the rejuvenation of the human *Ezekiel 47:1–12* world.

Nowhere in the Bible is the believer thought to have arrived at moral perfection. Paul, in his letter to the Philippians, takes an image from the chariot races and writes of 'pressing on' to reach that goal.

The Old Testament faith is not a closed system, but a dynamic living faith that always expects God to do new things. This message is given its most comprehensive form by one of the later Old Testament prophets. As he sought to encourage the exiles, Isaiah of Babylon told them to direct their attention away from sentimental assessments of the past, and to look for God to do new things in their

Isaiah 43:18–19   midst. He knew they could trust God not only because of his past deeds on their behalf but also because he was 'the first, the last, the

Isaiah 44:6   only God; there is no other god but me'. He also identified God's action on behalf of his people with the work of a figure he called 'the servant of Yahweh'.

Isaiah 42:1–4; 49:1–6; 50:4–9;   It is customary in Old Testament studies to refer to four 'servant
52:13 — 53:12   songs' which describe the work of this person. One scholar has recently suggested that these 'songs' are not in fact such distinct literary entities as has generally been supposed. But there can be no doubt that 'the servant' had an important place in the prophet's message. For he is portrayed as one who fulfils in his own life and experience all those aspects of God's will that Israel as a nation had been unable to accomplish.

Jewish readers of the Old Testament never identified this figure with the Messiah. That was natural, for one of the distinctive features of the servant poems is that he was to be a *suffering* servant – and the Messiah was always thought of as an all-powerful conquering king. But it was this very feature of the servant's work that led the early Christians to see here an expectation that had been fulfilled in Jesus himself. For especially in the final servant passage, we find two themes that correlate very closely with the facts of Jesus'

Isaiah 53:4–9   own life: the servant, though innocent, suffers for the wrongdoings of other people; and following that, God will vindicate the servant in such a way that the great and powerful will be astonished while those

Isaiah 53:10–12   for whom he suffers will realize he has suffered in their place.

Writing of this aspect of the Old Testament's forward look, Professor G. W. Anderson has commented: 'in spite of all uncertainties of interpretation, the anticipation in the fourth song of the Passion of Christ is one of the miracles of Old Testament literature.' For Christians, it is perhaps the one theme that helps them to see the continuity between Old and New. At the same time they recognize that the two Testaments are distinctive in their own right.

Many efforts have been made to identify the consistency of the Christian Bible. Terms such as the covenant, or the idea of 'salvation history' have been suggested as the cement which binds together such apparently discordant literature into one coherent block. But perhaps the only real continuity in the midst of such diversity and discontinuity is God himself.

God constantly occupies the centre of the stage – searching for people, making new relationships with them, and motivated only by his own generous love. God himself is the unifying factor in the message of both Old and New. From beginning to end, he is engaged in the establishment of order out of the chaos which so easily engulfs the life of society and of the physical world, as well as the personal experience of individuals. For Christians, that process culminated in the life, death and resurrection of Jesus, and the gift of the Holy Spirit at Pentecost. It is in this sense that both Testaments bear witness to him: 'Christ is given to us only through the double witness of the choir of those who await and those who remember.'

Gerhard von Rad

Other books on the Old Testament

The books listed here are restricted to those which the general reader could comfortably cope with, though one or two are for more advanced study (these are marked with an asterisk *).

Chapter One. Introducing the Old Testament
Interpretation of the Old Testament

G.W. Anderson (ed.), *Tradition and Interpretation*, OUP, 1979. Essays by leading Old Testament scholars, summarizing the present opinions on various aspects of the Old Testament books.

R. Davidson & A.R.C. Leaney, *Biblical Criticism*, Penguin, 1970. An excellent short account of the nature of modern study of the Bible and its presuppositions (New Testament as well as Old).

J. Goldingay, *Approaches to Old Testament Interpretation*, IVP, 1981/Inter Varsity (USA), 1982. A readable account of the state of play among Old Testament experts on many aspects of the subject.

H.F. Hahn, *The Old Testament in Modern Research*, Fortress, 1966 (2nd ed.). A helpful account of the work of scholars up to 1966. Needs to be supplemented by more recent books, though still worth reading.

J.H. Hayes, *An Introduction to Old Testament Study*, Abingdon Press, 1979 SCM Press, 1982. Covers the same ground as *Tradition and Interpretation*, though in a slightly more readable form.

*D.A. Knight & G.M. Tucker, *The Hebrew Bible and its Modern Interpreters*, Fortress Press, 1985. Encyclopedic introduction to the history of Old Testament scholarship over a whole range of topics, though with most emphasis on historical and literary matters.

J. Rogerson (ed.), *Beginning Old Testament Study*, Westminster Press SPCK, 1983. A helpful introductory book, setting out clearly and simply the various ways in which we can read and understand the Old Testament.

Old Testament background in the ancient world

W. Beyerlin (ed.), *Near Eastern Religious Texts Relating to the Old Testament*, SCM Press/Westminster Press, 1978.

M. Noth, *The Old Testament World*, A. & C. Black/Fortress Press, 1966.

J.B. Pritchard, *Ancient Near Eastern Texts Relating to the Old Testament*, Princeton University Press, 1969 (3rd ed.). The standard collection of comparative texts from other cultures and nations.

D.W. Thomas (ed.), *Documents from Old Testament Times*, Nelson, 1958/Harper & Row, 1961. A handy smaller collection of historical and religious texts relating the Old Testament to its wider background.

Old Testament history

B.W. Anderson, *Understanding the Old Testament*, Prentice-Hall, 1975 (= *The Living World of the Old Testament*, Longmans, 1978).

J. Bright, *A History of Israel*, SCM Press/Westminster Press, 1981 (3rd ed.). The standard conservative treatment of its subject.

J.H. Hayes and J.M. Miller, *Israelite and Judean History*, SCM Press/Westminster Press, 1977. An invaluable survey of the present state of research and scholarly opinion on historical issues.

J.H. Hayes and J.M. Miller, *A History of Ancient Israel and Judah*, SCM Press/Westminster Press, 1986. Probably the best all-round Old Testament history.

D.F. Payne, *Kingdoms of the Lord*, Paternoster/Eerdmans, 1981. From Saul to the fall of Jerusalem.

G.W. Ramsey, *The Quest for the Historical Israel*, John Knox Press, 1981/SCM Press, 1982. An account of the early period, including the patriarchs, exodus and settlement of Canaan.

The social life of ancient Israel

E.W. Heaton, *Everyday Life in Old Testament Times*, Batsford, 1956/ Scribners, 1977.

R. de Vaux, *Ancient Israel: its life and institutions*, Darton, Longman and Todd/McGraw-Hill, 1961. An invaluable insight into the life and culture of ordinary people.

Literary studies of the Old Testament

F.F. Bruce, *The Books and the Parchments*, Pickering & Inglis/Revell, 1971 (4th ed.). Deals with the text of the Old Testament, including the question of the Septuagint, Apocrypha, etc.

*O. Eissfeldt, *The Old Testament: an Introduction*, Blackwell/Harper & Row, 1965. A detailed literary study of the Old Testament books.

*R.W. Klein, *Textual Criticism of the Old Testament*, Fortress Press, 1974. A good general introduction to its subject.

J.A. Soggin, *Introduction to the Old Testament*, SCM Press/Westminster Press, 1976. Deals with the Old Testament book by book.

The Old Testament and archaeology

H.T. Frank, *An Archaeological Companion to the Bible*, Abingdon Press, 1971/SCM Press, 1972.

K.M. Kenyon, *The Bible and Recent Archaeology*, British Museum/John Knox Press, 1978.

Old Testament theology

R.E. Clements, *Old Testament Theology*, Marshall Morgan & Scott, 1978/John Knox Press, 1980. An introductory study showing the difficulties of defining what is meant by 'Old Testament theology' together with an account of some of the important issues raised by it.

R. Davidson, *The Old Testament*, Hodder & Stoughton/Lippincott, 1964. A helpful introductory study of the various strands that go to make up the Old Testament faith.

*W. Eichrodt, *The Theology of the Old Testament*, 2 vols, SCM Press/ Westminster Press, 1961 and 1967. An encyclopedic exposition of the subject, trying to use the idea of 'covenant' as the central theme of the Old Testament.

*G. Fohrer, *History of Israelite Religion*, Abingdon Press, 1972/SPCK, 1973. A good historical account of the development of Israel's religious thinking and institutions.

*G. Hasel, *Old Testament Theology: basic issues in the current debate*, Eerdmans, 1975 (2nd ed.). A judicious appraisal of some key elements of contemporary discussion.

J.H. Hayes & F.C. Prussner, *Old Testament Theology – its history and development*, John Knox Press/SCM Press, 1985. A helpful and succinct account of the history of interpretation together with a brief introduction to some of the issues involved.

*G. von Rad, *Old Testament Theology*, 2 vols, Oliver & Boyd/Harper & Row, 1962 and 1965. One of the classic Old Testament theologies, trying to establish 'salvation history' as the centre of the Old Testament faith.

H.G. Reventlow, *Problems of Old Testament Theology in the Twentieth Century*, SCM Press/Fortress, 1985. A useful introduction to some of the issues that the scholars are discussing.

H.H. Rowley, *The Faith of Israel*, SCM Press, 1956/Westminster Press, 1957. A generally enlightening attempt to distil some elements of a 'systematic theology' from the Old Testament.

*W.H. Schmidt, *The Faith of the Old Testament*, Westminster Press/ Blackwell, 1983. Not quite an Old Testament theology, but more than a 'history of religion' – though it is set out historically.

*W. Zimmerli, *Old Testament Theology in Outline*, John Knox Press, 1978. A systematic and scholarly treatment of its subject.

Section One: The Old Testament Story
Chapter Two. The founding of the nation

J.J. Bimson, *Redating the Exodus and Conquest*, Almond Press Eisenbrauns, 1981, (2nd ed.). Argues for a fifteenth-century date of the exodus.

D.J. McCarthy, *Old Testament Covenant*, Blackwell/John Knox Press, 1972. A survey of opinions on the covenant idea in the Old Testament.

A.R. Millard & D.J. Wiseman (eds.), *Essays on the Patriarchal Narratives*, IVP, 1980. A series of conservative essays arguing for the essential historicity of the patriarchal narratives, and trying to answer some recent criticisms.

A more radical reappraisal of history in the patriarchal narratives.

* T.L. Thompson, *The Historicity of the Patriarchal Narratives*, de Gruyter, 1974. Independently reaches similar conclusions to Van Seters.

R. de Vaux, *The Early History of Israel*, volume 1, Darton, Longman & Todd/Westminster Press, 1978.

Chapter Three. A land flowing with milk and honey

P.C. Craigie, *Ugarit and the Old Testament*, Eerdmans, 1983. A readable and reliable account of the discoveries from Ras Shamra, and a balanced appraisal of their relevance for Old Testament study.

J. Garstang, *The Story of Jericho*, Hodder & Stoughton, 1940. The classic story of the early excavations at Jericho.

J.C.L. Gibson, *Canaanite Myths and Legends*, T. & T. Clark/Attic Press, 1978, (2nd ed.). The standard translation of the texts from ancient Ugarit.

*N.K. Gottwald, *The Tribes of Yahweh*, Orbis Books, 1979 SCM Press, 1980. The most thorough presentation of the idea that the 'conquest' was a form of cultural revolution.

B. Halpern, *The Emergence of Israel in Canaan*, Scholars Press, 1983. Comprehensive analysis of the issues involved in reconstructing the early history of Israel.

J.L. McKenzie, *The World of the Judges*, Geoffrey Chapman/Prentice-Hall, 1966.

* A.D.H. Mayes, *Israel in the Period of the Judges*, SCM Press/Allenson-Breckinridge, 1974.

Chapter Four. A king like the other nations

W. Brueggemann, *In Man we Trust*, John Knox Press, 1972. A helpful exposition of the wisdom movement in Israel.

J.L Crenshaw, *Old Testament Wisdom*, John Knox Press, 1981/SCM Press, 1982.

F.S. Frick, *The Formation of the State in Ancient Israel*, Almond Press Eisenbrauns, 1985. An interesting examination of some of the sociological issues involved.

R. Gordis, *The Book of God and Man*, University of Chicago Press, 1965. An exposition of the book of Job.

*J. Gray, *The Biblical Doctrine of the Reign of God*, T. & T. Clark/Attic Press, 1979. Deals extensively with the theme of God's kingship, mostly following the arguments of Mowinckel.

H. Gunkel, *The Psalms*, Fortress, 1967. The only work by Gunkel to have been translated into English.

* D.M. Gunn, *The Story of King David*, JSOT Press/Eisenbrauns, 1978. A new approach to the Succession Narrative.

J.H. Hayes, *Understanding the Psalms*, Judson Press, 1976. A readable introduction to the book of Psalms.

E.W. Heaton, *Solomon's New Men*, Thames & Hudson, 1974/Universe Press, 1975. An assessment of the social changes that came about after Solomon's time.

* A.R. Johnson, *Sacral Kingship in Ancient Israel*, University of Wales Press, 1967.

* A.R. Johnson, *The Cultic Prophet and Israel's Psalmody*, University of Wales Press, 1976.

D.F. Morgan, *Wisdom in the Old Testament Traditions*, John Knox/Blackwell, 1981. A helpful assessment of the contribution of the wisdom movement to the concerns of the Old Testament as a whole.

*S. Mowinckel, *The Psalms in Israel's Worship*, Blackwell/Abingdon Press, 1962.

G. von Rad, *Wisdom in Israel*, SCM Press, 1972 Abingdon Press, 1973.

N.H. Snaith, *The Jewish New Year Festival*, SPCK, 1947. Strongly critical of the arguments of Mowinckel, Gray, and others.

R.N. Whybray, *The Succession Narrative*, SCM Press/Allenson-Breckinridge, 1968. An account of the interpretation of the Succession Narrative, together with a reassessment of its significance.

Chapters Five and Six. The two kingdoms/Judah and Jerusalem

B.W. Anderson, *The Eighth Century Prophets*, Fortress, 1978/SPCK, 1979.

J. Blenkinsopp, *A History of Prophecy in Israel*, Westminster Press, 1983/SPCK, 1984. Detailed study of the subject.

* R.E. Clements, *Isaiah and the Deliverance of Jerusalem*, JSOT Press/Eisenbrauns, 1980.

E.W. Heaton, *The Old Testament Prophets*, Darton, Longman and Todd/John Knox Press, 1977 (2nd ed.).

K. Koch, *The Prophets*, 2 vols., SCM Press 1982/3/Fortress Press 1982 4. Chapters on each of the major prophets.

J. McKay, *Religion in Judah under the Assyrians*, SCM Press/ Allenson-Breckinridge, 1973.

H. Mowvley, *Guide to Old Testament Prophecy*, Lutterworth, 1979, also published as *Reading the Old Testament Prophets Today*, John Knox Press, 1979.

R.R. Wilson, *Prophecy & Society in Ancient Israel*, Fortress, 1980. Assesses the social role of the Old Testament prophets.

Chapter Seven. Dashed hopes and new horizons

P.R. Ackroyd, *Exile and Restoration*, SCM Press/Westminster, 1968. An excellent study of the exile and its immediate aftermath.

P.R. Ackroyd, *Israel under Babylon and Persia*, OUP, 1970.

D.J.A. Clines, *The Theme of the Pentateuch*, JSOT Press/Eisenbrauns, 1978. An effort to understand the Pentateuch as coherent literature, rather than as a collection of separate sources.

A.D.H. Mayes, *The Story of Israel between Settlement and Exile*, SCM Press, 1983. Study of the Deuteronomistic History – what it is, and how it relates to the rest of the Old Testament.

* M. Noth, *The Deuteronomistic History*, JSOT Press/Eisenbrauns, 1981.

* G. von Rad, *The Problem of the Hexateuch & Other Essays*, Oliver & Boyd/McGraw-Hill, 1966.

J. Wellhausen, *Prolegomena to the History of Israel*, A. & C. Black, 1885.

* H.G.M. Williamson, *Israel in the books of Chronicles*, CUP, 1977.

Chapter Eight. The challenge of a new age

F.F. Bruce, *Israel and the Nations*, Paternoster Press/Eerdmans, 1963. Covers the whole of the Old Testament story, but is particularly detailed on the period of the book of Daniel and the end of the Old Testament period.

R.J. Coggins, *Samaritans and Jews*, Blackwell/John Knox Press, 1975. An interesting reappraisal of relations between the two groups.

D.E. Gowan, *Bridge between the Testaments*, Pickwick Press, 1976. A helpful account of the historical and literary developments in the inter-testamental period of Israel's history.

M. Hengel, *Jews, Greeks & Barbarians*, SCM Press/Fortress, 1980. A readable

account of the Maccabean period by a noted scholar (to a certain extent, this parallels his more detailed work, *Judaism and Hellenism*, SCM Press, 1974/Fortress 1981.

D.S. Russell, *Daniel*, St. Andrew Press/Westminster Press, 1981. One of the best recent commentaries on this difficult book.

Section Two: The Old Testament Faith
Chapter Nine. The living God

D. Baly, *God and History in the Old Testament*, Harper and Row, 1976. Almost a comprehensive Old Testament theology, but with a particular concern to grasp what the Old Testament means by the term 'God'.

*R. C. Dentan, *The Knowledge of God in Ancient Israel*, Seabury Press, 1968.

*R. Davidson, *The Courage to Doubt*, SCM Press, 1983. A valuable and comprehensive study of the 'hiddenness' of God in the Old Testament.

R. Gordis, *The Book of God and Man*, University of Chicago Press, 1965. A comprehensive exposition of the book of Job.

*G. H. Parke-Taylor, *Yahweh: the Divine Name in the Bible*, Wilfrid Laurier University Press, 1975. An exhaustive but readable account.

N. H. Snaith, *The Distinctive Ideas of the Old Testament*, Epworth Press, 1944. Detailed study of a number of key themes used to describe God.

N. H. Snaith, *The Book of Job*, SCM Press, 1968. A helpful survey of the possible ways the book of Job can be interpreted.

C. Westermann, *What does the Old Testament say about God?* John Knox Press/SPCK, 1979. A first-rate book by an eminent German scholar.

Chapter Ten. God and the world

B. W. Anderson (ed.), *Creation in the Old Testament*, Fortress Press/SPCK, 1984. A collection of essays (some of them classics) on various aspects of the creation theme.

R. Davidson, *Genesis 1–11*, CUP, 1973 (The Cambridge Bible Commentaries). A straightforward and helpful exposition.

D. Kidner, *Genesis*, IVP, 1967/ Inter Varsity (USA); 1968 (The Tyndale Old Testament Commentaries). Tries to reconcile Genesis and science, linking the Genesis creation stories with evolutionary thinking.

F. R. McCurley, *Ancient Myths and Biblical Faith*, Fortress Press 1983. A brief account of the relationships between some biblical materials and comparative ancient literature.

H. McKeating, *Why bother with Adam and Eve?* Lutterworth Press, 1982. A readable and illuminating answer to the question, setting it in the broader context of belief.

* J. W. Rogerson, *Myth in Old Testament Interpretation*, De Gruyter, 1974. A comprehensive and helpful exploration of the whole concept of 'myth', as related to many themes in Old Testament thinking.

Chapter Eleven. God and his people

*A. Alt, *Essays on Old Testament History and Religion*, Blackwell, 1966 /Doubleday, 1967. Contains the essay on Old Testament laws referred to in our discussion.

J. Blenkinsopp, *Wisdom and Law in the Old Testament*, OUP, 1983. A valuable study of the relationship between these two strands of Old Testament morality.

J. L. Crenshaw, *Old Testament Wisdom*, John Knox Press, 1981/SCM Press, 1982. The most useful recent general introduction to the world of the wisdom teachers.

W. Harrelson, *The Ten Commandments and Human Rights*, Fortress Press 1980. Considers all the issues of interpretation and meaning raised by the Ten Commandments – historical, as well as theological and contemporary.

D. Patrick, *Old Testament Law*, John Knox Press, 1985/SCM Press, 1986. A useful introductory study of the various law books and the way they relate to one another.

* A. Phillips, *Ancient Israel's Criminal Law*, Blackwell, 1970. The study referred to in our discussion.

* J. W. Rogerson, *Anthropology and the Old Testament*, Blackwell, 1978. An interesting study of clan structures in ancient Israel, including useful discussions of questions relating to responsibility and corporate personality.

R. de Vaux, *Ancient Israel*, McGraw-Hill/Darton, Longman & Todd, 1965 (2nd ed.). A helpful discussion of the administration of justice, pages 143-77.

C.J.H. Wright, *Living as the People of God*, IVP, 1983 (=*An Eye for an Eye: the Place of Old Testament Ethics Today*, Inter Varsity (USA), 1983). The first new book on Old Testament ethics for many years. Especially good on social ethics.

Chapter Twelve. Worshipping God

*M.F.C. Bourdillon & M. Fortes, *Sacrifice*, Academic Press, 1980. An interesting and helpful study by both anthropologists and theologians. Technical in places – but well worth persevering with.

H. Ringgren, *Israelite Religion*, Fortress Press/SPCK, 1966. Good on worship, priesthood, and related matters, especially pages 151-219.

H. H. Rowley, *Worship in Ancient Israel*, Fortress Press/SPCK, 1967. A comprehensive and balanced study of the subject, dealing with it both historically and topically and covering the whole of the Old Testament period.

L. Sabourin, *The Psalms: their origin and meaning*, Alba House, 1974. One of the most comprehensive surveys of current thinking on the psalms and their place in worship.

R. de Vaux, *Ancient Israel*, especially pages 271-517.

Chapter Thirteen. The Old and the New

*D. L. Baker, *Two Testaments, One Bible*, IVP, 1976. An exhaustive survey of modern attempts to find a single theological unity between Old and New Testaments.

J. Barr, *Old and New in Interpretation*, SCM Press/Harper & Row, 1982 (2nd ed.). An incisive study of the issues involved, with many helpful insights.

*J. Becker, *Messianic Expectation in the Old Testament*, Fortress Press/T & T Clark, 1980. An account of selected aspects of the subject.

*R.T. Beckwith, *The Old Testament Canon of the New Testament Church*, SPCK, 1985/Eerdmans, 1986. A scholarly discussion of its subject.

J. Bright, *The Authority of the Old Testament*, Abingdon Press/SCM Press, 1967 (subsequently reprinted by Baker Book House). Essential reading on the problems of using the Old Testament in the Christian church. Faces all the most difficult questions head-on, and makes many helpful practical suggestions.

A. G. Hebert, *The Authority of the Old Testament*, Faber, 1947. An older examination of the subject, though still valuable for its historical and analytical approach.

* S. M. Mayo, *The Relevance of the Old Testament for the Christian Faith*, University Press of America, 1982.

D. G. Miller, *The Authority of the Bible*, Eerdmans, 1972. Contains a useful chapter on the place of the Old Testament in the Christian Bible.

*S. Mowinckel, *He That Cometh*, Abingdon Press/Blackwell, 1956. An encyclopedic study of the Messianic hope, from its beginnings through to New Testament times.

General Books

As well as the books listed above, there are many others covering the Old Testament writings. Commentaries can be especially useful, and the volumes in the following series will be found helpful and reliable. They are listed in order of increasing difficulty.

Old Testament Guides, JSOT Press/Eisenbrauns. A series of short books on specific sections of the Old Testament. Give helpful summaries of a wide variety of opinions, and indicate matters of particular importance in studying specific books.

The Cambridge Bible Commentary, CUP. A complete series covering the whole Old Testament in a straightforward way.

The Tyndale Old Testament Commentaries, IVP/Eerdmans. Written from a predominantly conservative perspective, making the findings of scholarship available to the ordinary Bible reader.

The New International Commentary on the Old Testament, Eerdmans. Volumes vary in complexity. Comments on the English text, though always relying on the insights of Hebrew scholars.

The New Century Bible, Marshall Morgan & Scott/Eerdmans. A good series, with detailed comments on the text.

The International Theological Commentary, Handsel Press/Eerdmans. An especially useful series, dealing with wider theological and cultural issues as well as detailed exegesis.

The Anchor Bible, Doubleday. An important scholarly series, though some volumes are eccentric and unrepresentative of the broad stream of opinion.

The Old Testament Library, SCM Press/Westminster Press. A mixture of commentaries and other major studies on Old Testament books. Often require knowledge of Hebrew.

Word Biblical Commentaries, Word Publishing. A major commentary series, based on the Hebrew text, though also giving some attention to theological and contemporary issues.

Hermeneia, Fortress Press. A scholarly and technical series of commentaries, based on the detailed study of the Hebrew texts.

SOURCES OF QUOTATIONS AND OTHER REFERENCES

Bible texts are always quoted from either the Revised Standard Version or the Good News Bible.

Chapter 2 Page 42   John Bright, *A History of Israel*, pages 91 and 94

       Page 44   John Van Seters, *Abraham in History and Tradition*, page 309

Chapter 5 Page 109   Albrecht Alt, *Essays on Old Testament History and Religion*, Blackwell, 1966/Doubleday, 1967, page 246

Chapter 6 Page 153   Hermann Gunkel, 'The secret experiences of the prophets', *Expositor* IX/1 (1924), page 428

Chapter 10 Page 242   John Calvin, *A Commentary on Genesis*, Banner of Truth, 1965, pages 79-80 (reprint of the Calvin Translation Society edition 1847)

       Page 252   D. Baly, *God and History in the Old Testament*, Harper & Row, 1976, page 123

Chapter 11 Page 283   E. Brunner, *The Divine Imperative*, Lutterworth Press, 1937/Westminster Press, 1979, page 86

Chapter 13 Page 332   G. von Rad, *Old Testament Theology*, volume 2, page 319

       Page 339   G. von Rad, in *Essays on Old Testament Hermeneutics* (ed. C. Westermann), John Knox Press, 1963, page 39

       Page 342   G.W. Anderson, *A Critical Introduction to the Old Testament*, Duckworth, 1959, page 118

The photographs in this book are reproduced by permission of the following photographers and organizations:

J.C. Allen: 214
Andes Press Agency: Carlos Reyes 227, 230–31
Ashmolean Museum: 303 (below)
Barnaby's Picture Library: 193
British Museum, reproduced by courtesy of the Trustees: 19, 31, 34, 53, 57, 66, 110, 120, 135, 137 (left and right), 141, 149, 169, 171, 189, 257, 260, 267, 277, 282, 310 (below), 311 (above left, right), 314
Cairo Museum: 61
Tony Cantale: 256 (top left)
Cephas Picture Library: Mick Rock 153, 228, 295
Green Lake Centre, Wisconsin: 325
Griffith Institute, Ashmolean Museum: 54
Haifa Maritime Museum: 60
Sonia Halliday Photographs: F.H.C. Birch 38/Pru Grice 22, 162/Sonia Halliday 33 (below), 42–43, 47, 52, 78, 122–23, 130, 132, 145, 154, 167, 239 (left), 251, 255, 256 (centre left), 264, 289, 326, 335/Anne Holt 131/Laura Lushington 43 (inset), 239 (right)/Barrie Searle 81, 104, 173, 197, 271, 308/Jane Taylor 33 (above), 39, 41, 49, 56, 58, 71, 113 (both), 115, 202, 203, 233, 283, 333/James Wellard 92–93, 177, 196
Ikyrkans Internationella Av-Tjanst: 266
Israel Government Tourist Office: 18, 85, 161
Israel Museum: 209 (right), 226, 303 (above right and left)
Jericho Exploration Fund: 181
Lion Publishing: David Alexander 21, 23, 24, 25, 75 (below), 76, 86, 91, 99, 101, 107, 112 (right), 114, 116, 128, 134, 146, 188, 195, 209 (left), 211, 212, 244, 247, 249, 262, 278, 306 (below), 307, 310 (above), 341/Paul Crooks 30/Jennie Karrach 256 (top right)/Jon Willcocks 127, 256 (centre right and below right), 329
Louvre Museum: 68, 74, 112 (left), 263, 302
Mansell Collection: 198, 210, 330–31, 331
Alan Millard: 75 (above)
Network Photographers: John Sturrock 265
Picturepoint: 323
Popperfoto: 207, 258, 275, 291
Jean-Luc Ray: 256 (below left)
Rex Features: 17, 64–65, 143, 144, 158
Staatliche Museen zu Berlin: 185
Tel Aviv University Institute of Archaeology: 316 (left)
Topham: 35, 216–17, 221, 259 (below), 285
Vorderasiatisches Museum, Berlin: 223
World Vision: 259 (above), 269, 311 (below left)
ZEFA (UK) Ltd: 252, 287, 316 (right), 319, 320

Index